California Firsts

California Firsts

By

ROCKWELL D. HUNT

President Emeritus of the Conference of California Historical Societies

INTRODUCTION

By

J. WILSON McKENNEY

Editor of CTA Journal

"The witness of past ages, the light of truth,
the life of memory, the guide of life and the
messenger of antiquity."—*Cicero on History*

210605

FEARON PUBLISHERS • SAN FRANCISCO

Library of Congress Catalog Card Number: 57-8463

PRINTED IN THE UNITED STATES OF AMERICA

RESPECTFULLY DEDICATED
TO THE
UNITED NATIONS
Whose Charter Was Drafted
IN
SAN FRANCISCO
1945
With a Hope That Springs Eternal

PREFACE

California is exceptionally rich in beginnings. To know about the first times—the genesis of things—is to be well on the way to the climax of the story. As the old maxim has it, "Well begun is half done." And the French have a saying, *"Ce n'est que la premier pas' qui coute."*

In studies of this kind the faithful chronicler joins hands with the inquisitive antiqarian in searching for those first events that set in motion chain reactions resulting in ever-widening circles of activity and influence. These in turn hold deep significance for the real historian and his vast audience. Knowledge of our local history affords a more complete entrance into our priceless heritage, and this is a principal asset among all our abounding resources. "Behold how great a matter a little fire kindleth."

No list of firsts, no matter how extensive, or painstakingly compiled, can possibly be absolutely complete: moreover, some beginnings remain obscured in the clouds of uncertainty. Again, it is not to be supposed that any considerable list is infallibly accurate or beyond the possibility of revision by further research. As Professor Herbert Bolton has said, "No one ever got there first," meaning, "The official discoverer always seems to induce a counter claimant. Every Christopher Columbus has his Leif Ericson."

The author will welcome any constructive criticism, as to factual data, serious omissions, or misleading statements, in anticipation of possible later printings.

This book is not intended to be a mere index or catalogue, or a chronology of California Firsts. It represents rather an attempt to give a readable account of significant or interesting firsts, while at the same time seeking accuracy as to factual data. The story itself is enhanced by giving some hint of the developments stemming from beginnings.

All the respective eras of California history — Spanish, Mexican, American — are included in the purview; but the preponderance is given to the American period, as is clearly demanded by a correct perspective of the whole.

It will be observed that in some instances selections of particular firsts have been made, rather than any attempt to include all items in the general category involved. For example, wheat is included but not all the different grains; pears, but not all fruits; iron and steel, but not all industries. The selections are intended to be typical, or of more than ordinary historical importance.

This volume should be an aid in filling a need in the schools of California, and a useful reference in the libraries of the state. It is certain that no two writers would select identical items of significant firsts. The list here presented is itself a first—in no sense definitive. It is hoped that it will serve to stimulate further study and research, prove helpful to writers in California history, and be of real interets to a wider circle of readers.

Some of the firsts selected may appear by themselves of little consequence, yet viewed in a larger perspective they may be seen to be of distinct importance, and—best of all—may be an easy and intimate approach to the great treasures of the fascinating history of the Golden State. And who, in this inquiring age, does not wish to know the first of everything?

ROCKWELL D. HUNT

CONTENTS

Contents

INTRODUCTION

This burgeoning commonwealth, California, changes daily. Its orchards melt before the subdivider's bulldozers, its institutions fade away and revive anew in response to the demands of a fluid society. In the affluence of the post-war years, we count our increasing numbers, list our achievements, and set our eyes toward an even brighter future, giving little heed to our short history and our humble beginnings.

Governor Knight identifies the basic strength of California as a vigorous blending of "Elsewherians" with the state's native sons and daughters. The people who stream into California from other states—at the rate of over 1,000 a day—bring strength, imagination, and daring. They bring a capacity for accomplishing the impossible because the Golden State is the Mecca of their dreams. They mingle with natives who have nurtured an intense sectional pride, a patriotism rivaled only by that of Texans. The resulting amalgam has created a series of "firsts" in contemporary achievement which has caused the world to accept "the Golden State" as a literal meaning.

Our growth in agricultural production, industrial output, and cultural contribution is like the growth of a great oak tree. The giant limbs spread wide, casting deep shade. Those men who pause therein may pause gratefully and marvel at the magnificent living creation—and be thankful that the tiny acorn survived.

The small beginnings, like acorns cast on fertile soil, have indeed grown into giant living things. Elsewherians and native Californians alike may find in this book a rich harvest of acorns, unearthed and identified by the Dean of California historians.

To boast a multiple of "firsts" is as characteristic of the typical Californian as is his capacity for taking a chance or his love of the out-of-doors. The newspapers printed the picture of the first man to drive across the newly opened Richmond-San Rafael bridge. Sports editors once extolled the physical prowess of the first swimmer to cross the choppy Wilmington-San Pedro channel. Who was the first man to scale Mt. Whitney? Such fame is ephemeral. None of this trivia will be found in Dr. Hunt's book, for he is a serious historian and educator of discerning judgment.

Writing this, his 17th book, in his 89th year, Rockwell D. Hunt brings a wealth of personal investigation and a long life of scholarship to the task of assembling more than 200 "firsts" which he regards as relatively significant in California history. Born at Sacramento in 1868, he personally observed many of the "firsts" which he has recorded in these pages. Careful study of countless sources—so numerous that a bibliography would be impractical—has provided him with the evidence necessary to complete this work.

Although vocabulary may limit use of this book as an elementary school text, it will no doubt prove a valuable reference for all teachers. It should be used extensively at high school level and should be a recommended volume for all California reference libraries. The recent Centennial Celebrations throughout the state and the marking and preserving of historical landmarks which resulted have whetted the interest of most residents. It should therefore be assumed that *California Firsts* will meet a demand for specific information of value to all Californians.

We will probably have a population of twenty million before 1975 and eighteen million will probably be living in less than twenty cities within the state. Our way of life will continue to change, as it has changed constantly since the beginning of the century. Will we hew out and destroy all the giant oaks? Or will we give some thought to the acorns from which they sprang?

J. WILSON McKENNEY

California Firsts

CHAPTER ONE

EXPLORATION AND DISCOVERY

"Whoever has wandered through the valleys and woods and over
the hills and mountains of his own state will be the one capable of
following a Herodotus in his wanderings over the globe."
—*Carl Ritter*

IN THE BEGINNING

A certain portion of the earth's crust, comprising approximately 156,800
square miles and known as California, has a pre-history of which no
man knoweth the age. We may simply say, "In the beginning"; but the
beginning is enveloped in the mists.

Geologic time cannot be measured in terms of the life-span of a man
—not even terms of the entire period of recorded history. Yet geology
is a definite conditioner of human history, an important handmaid to
the historian. A million years is incomprehensible to the historian; the
geologist takes his millions in stride.

Geologically, California is very old — no one knows for sure how old
within thousands of milleniums — but what of that! We must refer to
periods and eras, and not be concerned with years, or centuries. We go
back to the Pre-Cambrian age, and find that the oldest rocks of California consist of granites, with certain others, including metamorphic
and igneous rocks. But the human mind is incapable of comprehending
their antiquity — their extreme age may be anywhere from 700,000,000
to a billion years! True to the booster spirit of the Californian, one
geologist (Gilbert E. Bailey) has declared,

> The geologic history of the whole earth is completely shown in this state
> from "in the beginning" to the most recent formations; something that
> cannot be said of any equal area.

In the Preface to his *Adventures in Scenery*, Daniel E. Willard refers
to his appreciation of the geologic history of this western coast and how
it came to be what it is — "the most complex, the most varied, the most
stupendously interesting of all regions he has ever visited."

But our planet is never in a condition of complete rest—and California
is no exception. The changes that have taken place from age to age are
fantastic to the point of incredulity. In certain periods, the abundance

and variety of fossils, "medals of creation that mark the stony pages of the world's history," enrich our knowledge of the development of multitudinous forms of pre-human life.

J. Charles Miller says that the oldest known rocks are found in Tehama and Plumas Counties. In general, the Sierra Nevadas, and what were believed to be their predecessors, are credited with greatest antiquity, so great as to be awe-inspiring, bewildering. Try to compare the span of human history, be it 10,000 or 20,000 years, or even longer, then remember it is but as yesterday in the light of the awesome venerability of the rocks.

In early geologic ages, the physical appearance of California bore only slight resemblance to that of today. For example, we are told that the great valley was "a marine sea during the Eocene and up to the Middle Miocene, when the Coast Range was born." More recently was the glacier age: the last of the receding glaciers have not even yet wholly disappeared. How and to what extent the geologic changes have introduced and affected human life prior to the period of known history will be a subject to engage the geologist, the anthropologist, and the archæologist for years to come. To these men of science we willingly leave the problem. Only we cannot fail to recognize that the historian has need of the results achieved by all of them — they are among his foundation stones, upon which he must build; they afford him a vantage ground, which enables him to achieve a true perspective in telling the story of what man has done.

What then is the summation of the whole matter? First in California was "In the beginning," which it is given to no man to know or understand. Then came the vast æons of geologic ages, themselves of incomprehensible duration. Next emerges the period of human life, its own actual beginnings shrouded in the mists of time. After untold centuries, European enlightenment enters in the form of Spanish colonization. Finally, the Westward Movement of North American expansion — a mere speck in the history of the planet — brings us to our own day, thrice blest by our precious heritage.

FIRST CALIFORNIANS

The historian is unable to say when human beings first inhabited California. Even the anthropologists and archæologists can as yet give no definitive answer; but they are rather well agreed that all the prehistoric races of California and the western part of North America were of Asiatic origin, that the beginnings of this migration probably date back at least 10,000 years, perhaps much farther than that. Further studies, particularly of pre-history times and ancient peoples of Mexico and Central America, will doubtless yield additional data on the interesting question.

However, available information relating to the American Indians found in California by the first European explorers give us a fairly accurate and complete picture of the aborigines of the territory.

As a whole, they are believed to have been among the least developed of all the American Indians. It has been said that "they had the minds of children with the bodies and instincts of mature men and women — children who never grew up." They left no magnificent ruins like the pyramids and temples in Mexico. But many artifacts, such as arrowheads, beads, and stone mortars have been found; also the huge shell mounds in the San Francisco Bay region, and quantities of their shell money. All these have thrown light upon the character and culture of the original Californians.

No one can know how many Indians there were. Among the many estimates and guesses, we think the total population of what we know as California might have been between 130,000 and 150,000, which represents a greater density than the average for the United States as a whole.

There were more than twenty linguistic groups, based on similarities of language; there were several times that number of dialects and idioms. Sometimes one was unable to talk with a neighbor who lived only twenty miles away. While they had no written language, they were rich in legend and myth. The eagle and the coyote were regarded as sacred: they had solid respect for the grizzly bear.

The life of the Californian was exceedingly primitive and simple. The typical village, called *ranchería*, consisted of crudely constructed habitations, with a total population, on the average, of not more than 150 persons. The California Indians, often miscalled "Diggers," must be sharply distinguished from those of Arizona and New Mexico, and those of the Rocky Mountain region. They knew nothing of the "Happy Hunting Ground"— they were strangers to the "fierce joy of the Dakota hunter." Yet they had their own religious rites and ceremonies, usually associated with the *temescal* (sweat-house). It should be added that exceptions can be found to practically every generalization regarding the widely varying California Indians.

Their food included nearly everything in the animal and vegetable kingdoms, from venison to field mice, from acorns to wild flax seed: grasshoppers were a common article of diet. Clothing requirements were at a minimum. In warm weather the men and children commonly went naked; women wore short aprons made of roughly-woven grass or tules. Skins of animals were a protection against cold weather.

Young men usually purchased their wives; they could divorce them almost at pleasure — there was practically no such thing as woman's rights; authority of the men was supreme. But there was plenty of hard work for the women.

The fate of the California Indians was pathetic. One writer declares, "They have been more miserably corrupted and destroyed than any other tribes within the Union." But in more recent years there is a brighter side to the picture. Treatment of the Indians has greatly improved; today there are among them an increasing number of industrious and useful citizens.

FIRST EL DORADO

Contrary to popular belief, El Dorado, which is a contraction of *El Hombre Dorado*, was originally not a country, or place, at all — it was a person. As the words indicate, it was the Gilded Man, or the gold-covered one.

In the beautiful mythology of the Indians scattered over a wide range of territory from Alaska to Patagonia, El Dorado was the sun-god and culture hero — a kind of Indian Messiah. Professor Adolph Bandelier, famed American archæologist, has given us the story of the beginnings of the legend. He wrote, in his book, *The Gilded Man*:

> Lake Guatavita . . . became famous as the spot where the myth of the gilded man originated. When a new chieftain was chosen an imposing ceremonial was held. The men of the tribe, decorated with gold and emeralds, their heads adorned with feathers, walked in procession, shouting and blowing on horns, pipes, and conches. At the rear came the head men carrying the newly elected chieftain upon a litter hung with gold discs. His naked body was anointed with resinous gums and covered all over with gold dust, so that he resembled from sole to crown a brilliant piece of artfully shaped gold. This was *el dorado*. Arrived at the shore the gilded chieftain and his companion stepped upon a raft and proceeded on it to the middle of the lake. There the chief plunged into the water and washed off his golden covering, while assembled company threw in gold and jewels they had brought with them.

The Gilded Man myth, which really had a basis in fact, "flitting from one place to another," showed several variations: many attempts at discovery were made by English as well as by Spanish explorers. Charles F. Lummis concluded his account with this appraisal:

> No other myth or legend in either North or South America ever exer-

cised such a powerful influence on the course of geographical discovery; none ever called out such surpassing tenacity of purpose and self-sacrifice inherent in the Spanish character.

By the ignorant sailors who accompanied the early *conquistadores* the story of the sun god was easily twisted into something rich and golden — they had been promised untold riches. It was a fascinating myth. A remark of the great Hernando Cortez sheds considerable light upon the motives of the Spanish captains. He is said to have remarked to some natives of Mexico: "We Spaniards are troubled with a disease of the heart for which we find gold, and gold only, a specific remedy." It was this lure of gold that led many an intrepid navigator—and even the government itself—into enterprises filled with indescribable hardships, resulting in unknown graves for many, but lasting fame for the fortunate few.

The El Dorado myth had been strongly in evidence in northern South America centuries before the occupation of Alta California. Under the special circumstances which will rapidly come to mind, it must not be thought strange that the name should have been revived again and again, long after the Hispanic period, when newly discovered gold brought an avalanche of modern argonauts to California following Marshall's lucky find at Coloma.

The name took on new significance. It has become well perpetuated in the geography of the Minerva State. El Dorado County was one of the original twenty-seven counties of California, located at the very center of the mining activities during the feverish gold rush days. But the name also applies to a town, first known less romantically as Mud Springs; also it has been applied to creeks in Mariposa, Placer, and Santa Barbara Counties, and — not least of all — it is happily perpetuated in El Dorado National Forest. In our Western lore the "Gilded Man" will never be forgotten — the ancient myth is a unique part of the Californian's rich heritage.

MANILA GALLEON

It was more than two centuries after Miguel López de Legazpi was commissioned by Viceroy Luis de Velasco of New Spain to subdue the Philippine Islands that Spain actually occupied Alta California. Legazpi's commission was dated in 1564, only twenty-two years following Cabrillo's memorable discovery of Alta California.

Nevertheless the voyage of the first Manilla Galleon (as well as those that followed), was not without influence upon the course of California history.

The galleons have been described as "Huge, round-stemmed, clumsy vessels ... so overweighted in proportion to their draft of water that they could bear very little canvas, even with smooth seas and light wind." They were picturesque craft of mediæval style." For nearly three centuries, however, they represented the standard of maritime construction, "of an huge bignesse," "so high that they resembled great castles."

The main objective of the Manila Galleon was the discovery of "a safe and convenient route" from eastern Asia to New Spain; for the lucrative trading in the Philippines and other oriental points was greatly desired. Among the products chiefly desired were, from China, raw silk, velvets, gold and silver brocades, stuffs of many colors, ivory, musk, cushions, carpets and caparisons for horses, as well as fruit preserves and a variety of spices, nuts, caged birds, porcelain, and precious stones; from Japan came ornamental screens, wood caskets, cutlery, and wheaten flour; from Molucca, different kinds of spices, cotton cloths, jewels, fancy needlework, and lace; from Siam came rubies, sapphires, and rhinoceros horns.

But the voyage was a very long one, sometimes extending to more than 200 days, and it was fraught with much peril. Particularly to be dreaded was the California coastline around Cape Mendocino, with its severe winds and fogs, and the constant danger of scurvy.

However, reports from the Manila Galleons served to bring to the mind of King Philip II of Spain the desirability of surveying the entire region and of permanently occupying it at some time in the future. The dream, after many years, eventually came true.

The first of the many galleons, captained by Miguel Legazpi, was the *San Pedro,* a small vessel of 500 tons, which started from Acapulco November 24, 1564. It seems a wonder that she was able to weather the storms at all. The return trip was under Andrés de Urdaneta, who was an Augustinian friar but perhaps better known as Legazpi's pilot. The course proceeded far to the northward in the hope of gaining a favoring wind; it was followed by other navigators for a score of years. The voyage had consumed 129 days.

There was plenty of misfortune — and no end of confusion: it is recorded that Urdaneta's pilot, his master, and fourteen of the men died. The voyage, nevertheless, along with that of Francisco de Gali, some years later, was instrumental in pointing the need of discovering a route between Manila and Acapulco, on the coast of New Spain, and of locating a suitable station for refitting.

At best, the history of the Manila Galleon is a story of somber hue. The daring and downright courage displayed by the navigators was a striking illustration of the matchless dogged colonizing spirit of the Spanish pioneers of the sixteenth century. "That early Spanish spirit of *finding out*," Charles Lummis has declared, "was fairly super-human."

FIRST NEW ENGLAND

In the autumn of 1620 one hundred and two English Pilgrims, filling the little *Mayflower* almost to overflowing, sailed for North America. On the 22nd of December they landed at Plymouth Rock and set to work to found a colony. That was the beginning of New England. In 1643 a union was formed including Plymouth, Massachusetts Bay, Connecticut, and New Haven — known as the "New England Confederation."

But Judge John F. Davis calls attention to an earlier "New England" in North America. This was "Nova Albion," claimed by Francis Drake for his queen — *"the first New England on this continent"* — on the 17th of June, 1579, forty-one years before the *Mayflower* landed at Plymouth Rock. Drake's memorable voyage was made in the *Golden Hind*, and Drake himself was the first English captain to circumnavigate the globe.

Being highly favored in receiving personal assistance from Queen Elizabeth, Drake had spread his sails in 1577 for the voyage whose purpose was "to singe the Spaniard's beard" — in other words, to plunder Spanish vessels, especially richly-laden Manila Galleons he might overhaul in Pacific waters. Sailing down the eastern coast of South America and up the western, he took much booty from ship and port. As a single instance, he tells of a Spanish ship at Panama from which he seized, "besides fruit, sugar, meal, and other provisions, eighty pounds weight of gold, thirteen chests of silver coin, twenty-six tons of unrefined silver, and a quantity of jewels, plate, and precious stones."

With an immensely valuable cargo on the *Golden Hind*, Drake feared to return to England via the Straits of Magellan because of indignant Spanish captains who might be lying in wait, so he pointed his prow northward, hoping to discover the mysterious Northwest Passage, and thence proceed to the Atlantic.

Drake sailed on and on until he passed the present northern boundary of California, thus probably being the real discoverer of Oregon. Being beset with "nipping cold" and "thick mists and most stinking fogges," he gave up the search for the elusive passage and turned toward the south. Reaching "a convenient and fit harborough" — some thirty miles north of San Francisco, he came to anchor on the 17th of June, 1579, and remained in the vicinity until July 23. For many years it was believed he had entered the Golden Gate and discovered San Francisco Bay, but it is now generally agreed that no white man passed through the Golden Gate for many years after 1579.

Drake careened and cleaned his ship and proceeded to take possession of the country. The submissive Indians looked upon the whites as gods and acted in such manner that it was easy for Drake to believe that they conveyed to him complete sovereignty with the bestowal of "scepter, crowne, and dignity of the sayd countrie." He set up a monument, claiming title to "Nova Albion" for Queen Elizabeth. Religious services were conducted according to the ritual of the Church of England — the first Protestant services conducted in California. An inland journey revealed "a goodly country, and fruitful soyle, stored with many blessings fit for the use of man."

In the autumn of 1580 Drake sailed into old Plymouth Harbor, after almost three years, the *Golden Hind* having won the distinction of being the second ship to sail entirely around the world. The plans of Sir Francis and his queen for a colonial empire in America that should rival Spain's were rudely frustrated. New Albion fell victim to personal jealousies and political intrigues in Europe. Nevertheless the establishment of the first New England in far-away California proved fruitful in later history. "It is therefore fitting," says Charles E. Chapman, "not only in honor of the English navigator's great feat in itself, but also in testimony of the importance of his work as affecting the future of California, that a stone cross should have been raised to his memory on one of the hills of San Francisco overlooking the Golden Gate and San Francisco Bay."

DISCOVERY BY THE WHITE MAN

What Spaniard was the first to discover Alta California? A simple question, not so simply answered, it may be likened to another question — who first discovered gold in California? Gold was known to exist long before Marshall's discovery in 1848. The Indians had seen it for many generations; but for the aborigines it held no special significance.

Viceroy Antonio de Mendoza of New Spain energetically set to work to execute important projects for land and sea explorations, his two prime objectives being to discover the illusive "Strait of Anian" (Northwest Passage) and the acquisition of the fabulous riches of the "seven cities of Cibola," reported by Marcos de Niza. Accordingly Vásquez de Coronado was sent out on his memorable land expedition in the year 1540. Two years later Juan Rodríguez Cabrillo was sent north in command of two small ships on what proved to be the famous expedition by sea.

Shortly after Coronado's departure in 1540, Hernando de Alarcón was sent out on a corollary expedition to connect with him. It seems well established now that Alarcón's launches proceeded north to the head of the Gulf of California and on up the lower Colorado River for a distance of some fifteen leagues. This would bring them to the extreme southeastern corner of what is now California, near Yuma. Dr. Herbert E. Bolton concluded that Alarcón touched California at this point a year or more before Cabrillo's well-known discovery of San Diego Harbor, in 1542. No exact date for this earliest "discovery," has been given.

Even admitting the truth of the Alarcón story, did his "discovery" have any real significance, or was it like the pre-Columbian discoveries of America, or the pre-Marshallian discoveries of gold? Similarly, the question as to whether Cabeza de Vaca, in his weird travels of several years earlier still, actually did set foot on what is now California soil, may be dismissed as unimportant for present purposes.

On the 27th day of June, 1542, the expedition of Juan Rodríguez Cabrillo left Navidad on a momentous voyage.

> "On and on sailed the two little ships," wrote Mrs. Sanchez, "alone on the vast unknown sea, alone with their God in the wilderness of waters. At times they were beaten back by the north-west wind, jealously guarding its secret; at other times they were becalmed, and rocked idly for days on the waves, unable to make a northing."

It was only after three long and difficult months, on September 28, 1542, that Cabrillo and his men entered a "very good closed port, which they named San Miguel." Beautiful San Diego Bay had been discovered. This was Alta California.

The epoch-making expedition continued on its northward way, commanded by Bartolomé Ferrelo after the unfortunate death of brave Cabrillo on San Miguel Island, until the farthermost borders of California were reached and passed. This was a legitimate voyage of discovery and exploration which established Spain's right to the *bona-fide* discovery of California and the first full-length exploration of its 1,000-mile coast-line.

Cabrillo, worthy of the proud distinction, is therefore to be credited with the memorable event which was to unlock the door to the great treasure-house of the nations and lead to the actual occupation and settlement of the "Land of Heart's Desire."

THE "MAYFLOWER" OF THE WEST

From 1542 to 1769, more than two and a quarter centuries, it was a very long time indeed from the discovery of Alta California by Juan Rodríguez Cabrillo to the first actual occupation by Spanish forces under Gaspar de Portolá and Junípero Serra.

Even then Spain had to be spurred to action chiefly by a well-based fear that she might be forestalled by a rival power. She had good reason to fear England, whose hold on America was tightening, especially following 1763, still more to dread the approach of Russia, threatening from the north. It was the visitor-general to New Spain, José de Gálvez, who appeared in the nick of time to meet the challenge by organizing the memorable sea and land expedition from Lower California to San Diego, in what became the northern province.

Early in 1769 a tiny fleet of three ships was formed and equipped at the port of La Paz on the gulf side of Baja California. These vessels were the *San Carlos*, or *Toison de Oro* ("Golden Fleece") as flagship, the *San Antonio*, or *El Principe*, and the *San José*. At the same time, as a part of the same expedition, two overland forces were being made ready, under Portolá and Serra.

No wonder there was excitement at the port of La Paz, or that Gálvez himself showed unwonted animation as he superintended the equipping of the vessels and the loading of their cargoes. The manifest of the *San Antonio*, signed by Captain Vicente Vila, included church furniture, mission property, provisions for eight months to a year (water, meat, fish, bread, cheese, sugar, flour, etc.), five tons of wood, sixteen sacks of coal, a small herd of livestock, some hens, and other items—which included 125 pounds of garlic and another of 300 pounds of red pepper!

As to personnel there were the captain and his mate, the cosmographer (Miguel Costansó), 25 Catalonian soldiers, a surgeon, 4 cooks, 2 blacksmiths, and a crew of 23 sailors and 2 boys—a total of 62 persons.

After a stirring address by Gálvez and the blessing bestowed by Serra, the brave little ship, with her companions, set sail in March, 1769, for the northern land, about which so little was then known.

On the 11th of April the *San Antonio* arrived at San Diego; eighteen days later the *San Carlos* appeared, with all on board suffering from the scurvy. The first land force arrived May 14, the second on the first of July, completing the expedition to Alta California.

Accounts of the historic expeditions to Monterey, and the accidental discovery of San Francisco Bay need not be repeated here. But it remains to note that the *San Carlos* "again plays a decisive and dramatic part in

California history," when on the 5th of August, 1775, at the approach of evening dusk she sailed through the Golden Gate and into the waters of San Francisco Bay, the first vessel, so far as is known, to enter the wonderful harbor that had strangely eluded all previous navigators.

And thus it was the small Spanish ship *San Carlos*, flagship of the tiny squadron that sailed from La Paz early in 1769, came to be known in our history as the "*Mayflower*" of the West.

NATAL DAY OF ALTA CALIFORNIA

Theodore H. Hittell, recognized as one of the foremost historians of California, made the suggestion that the first day of July, 1769, "is, as appropriately perhaps as any other, to be considered the natal day of Alta California." That was the day on which the original pioneers of 1769 by land and sea "came together at San Diego and the day which they themselves celebrated with salvos and salutes."

To be sure, Cabrillo had discovered the fair land more than two and a quarter centuries prior to this date, and numerous other Spanish captains had during that long interval sailed up and down the Pacific the full length of California, but no actual progress had been made in the definite occupation and settlement of the territory. Francis Drake had explored New Albion and laid claim to an indefinite area north of San Francisco Bay, in the name of Good Queen Bess of England; but the famous buccaneer had effected no permanent settlement. From the standpoint of our own day the long period of comparative inactivity along the Pacific Coast is difficult to explain, and complex contemporary conditions in Europe must be understood to supply anything like an adequate interpretation.

Reports of threatening Russian activity looking toward establishing communications between eastern Siberia and the American Pacific Coast finally stirred Spain to aggressive action. José de Gálvez, the great *visitador-general* of New Spain, prepared to send an expedition north to put into effect the long-deferred plan of the Spaniards—the occupation and actual settlement of San Diego and Monterey.

To insure success the expedition was of four-fold character, two divisions proceeding by land and two by sea. All were to meet at the port of San Diego, then press northward to Monterey. The first settlers arrived at San Diego on the 11th of April on board the *San Antonio*, and the *San Carlos* sailed into port eighteen days later. The expedition as a whole, continues Hittell, "can hardly be said to have arrived until July 1; nor was it till then that Portolá, the governor and general-in-chief, and Junípero Serra, the master spirit of the conquest, came up."

The expeditions were thus reunited at San Diego; but the sad plight of those Argonauts of 1769 can be but faintly imagined when it is remembered that the voyage of the *San Carlos* had consumed 110 dreadful days. Nobody on board had escaped sickness and all but two of the crew of twenty-four had died of the scurvy. The *San José*, which had been sent out with a fifth expedition, was lost, with all on board. Of the total number composing the original expeditions, nearly 300, approximately one-half, reached their destination.

Out of such travail, after perils by land and sea, the first permanent settlement by whites was effected in Alta California. The manifest of the *San Carlos* shows that besides church furniture, vestments, and silver utensils, the cargo included many articles, oil, dates, wine, maize, figs, sugar, lard, salt, red pepper, flour, rice, beans, raisins, hams, cheese, chocolate, candles, a few live cattle, hens, and 1,000 *pesos* in money.

We may well accept the suggestion that July 1, 1769, be considered the "natal day of Alta California." For then it was that the first tangible evidences of civilization and of Christianity came to claim this "terrestrial paradise." An actual beginning had been made of the Spanish occupation, soon to be signalized by the establishment of the mission, the *presidio*, and the *pueblo*.

SONORA TO CALIFORNIA OVERLAND

Very early in the history of California Viceroy Antonio Bucareli of Mexico perceived that a land route from Sonora in Mexico to Monterey in Alta California would be of highest strategic value. He feared encroachment from Russia at the north, and was also aware of the power of England following the Seven Years' War.

Bucareli made a historic decision — an expedition should be undertaken to explore a route through Arizona into California. To head this great task he commissioned Juan Bautista de Anza, who was eager to undertake it. The viceroy could not have made a better selection.

Anza, who had followed a military career for many years, was a seasoned military officer, characterized personally as "exceedingly affable, liberal, well-beloved by the Indians, punctilious, . . . no improper habits of life." Closely associated with Anza was to be Padre Francisco Garcés, a leader of apostolic zeal and personal piety that has been compared to that of Serra himself. Garcés was also an explorer of experience and distinction, having already garnered much information tending to prove the practicality of the route proposed. Garcés believed Anza to be the right type to head the enterprise.

Anza's petition had been referred to Engineer Miguel Costansó for an opinion. The engineer's report — a highly important document — estimated the straight-line distance from Tubac to Monterey at 180 leagues, and declared the utility of such a route unquestionable. After painstaking consideration Bucareli wrote, in September, 1773, that he had accepted the petition. Preparations went forward energetically.

The exploring party consisted of 34 men, 140 horses, 65 head of cattle, and 35 mules. All being ready, the company left Tubac on the 8th day of January, 1774, headed for the recently established San Gabriel Mission.

Without the loss of a man the historic march was successfully completed. One can imagine how the arrival at San Gabriel on the 22nd of March was hailed by the *padres* and the joyous ringing of the church bells. Anza pressed on to Monterey. Thus the route from Mexican Sonora had been demonstrated to be practicable. The great objective of the expedition had been attained.

The first memorable trek was forerunner to a second, on a far grander scale. Anza was to lead thirty soldiers and their families over the route and continue north for the settlement of San Francisco. It was late October, 1775, when the start was made, and what a cavalcade it was! Two hundred and forty persons, including entire families, a drove of nearly 700 horses, with 255 head of cattle, and all manner of equipment. Here was one of the most dramatic and spectacular episodes in the entire drama of California's colorful history!

The 1500-mile journey was successfully completed. The San Francisco *Presidio* was founded on the 17th of September, 1776, and on October 9 Mission San Francisco de Asís was solemnly established. The total result was to give permanency to Alta California, insuring it against foreign seizure for years to come. In 1924 a bronze tablet marked Anza's route at San Carlos Pass, bearing this inscription:

> On March 16, 1774, Juan Bautista de Anza, Indian fighter, explorer, and colonizer, led through this pass (named by him San Carlos) the first white explorers to cross the mountains into California. The party traveled from Tubac, Arizona, to Monterey, California. On December 27, 1775, on a second expedition into California, Anza led through this pass the party of Spaniards from Sonora who became the founders of San Francisco.

The remarkable expedition is declared by Charles E. Chapman to be "second only to the discovery of gold in 1848 in its positive consequences upon California history." Herbert E. Bolton has rendered a real service in completing his monumental work—especially *An Outpost of Empire* —tracing in detail the long, intricate trail of the Anza party. Referring to the brilliant achievement, Hubert Howe Bancroft declared: "Neither

De Soto, nor La Salle, Pike, Long, nor Frémont encountered greater difficulties than he, nor did any of them attack them with so much wisdom or courage."

Although Juan Bautista Anza, ably assisted by Francisco Garcés, carried through to complete realization the great enterprise, the resourceful Viceroy María Bucareli, responsible head of New Spain and representative of the king, is the one to be given chief credit for saving Alta California for Spain.

FIRST ENGINEER

Fear of encroachment by the Russians from the north was probably the principal reason why Spain decided upon the actual occupation of Alta California, which, after long delay, was actually begun in the year 1769. When all the difficulties and local conditions are taken into consideration, it is easy to understand why this occupation proceeded so slowly and imperfectly. Undoubtedly the most potent factor in the movement was the establishment of the Franciscan missions, under Padre Junípero Serra. The first *presidios*, Monterey and San Diego, were not strong enough to withstand any serious attack from an aggressive foe.

When Diego de Borica succeeded José Arrillaga as governor of the province of Alta California in 1794, it did not take him long to perceive the pitiful weakness of the fortresses. The precarious situation was seen as a still more urgent problem by virtue of the visit of George Vancouver, distinguished British commissioner, who had been ordered "to explore the entire coast, to examine into the extent of Spanish possessions, and to seize all unclaimed territory." Vancouver's sharp eyes did not fail to note the weak defenses, and he was surprised at the slight attention paid to the health and comfort of both officials and common soldiers. The Spanish authorities agreed something must be done.

In accordance with the governor's request, the Viceroy of New Spain (Mexico), Branciforte, sent in 1796, a company of Catalonian volunteers under Colonel Pedro de Alberni. Attached to this company was Alberto de Córdoba, a qualified engineer, the first trained engineer to be assigned to Alta California.

Recognizing that the young engineer was a man of ability, the governor lost no time in making good use of his talents. Córdoba recommended a site at the northern end of Monterey Bay for the founding of a new *pueblo*, to be given the name Branciforte; he planned extensive and greatly needed repairs for Santa Barbara and San Diego; then he was recalled to build a battery overlooking San Francisco Bay, at Black Point (now Fort Mason), where eight gun pits were built.

The versatile "Engineer extraordinary" undertook still other tasks. "Scarcely an engineering enterprise was projected," we are told, "that Córdoba did not inspect, and where practicable, improve." Not least of these were the irrigation systems which were so imperatively necessary to the various establishments. There is little doubt that the mission fathers profited greatly by his counsel and advice. It would be hard to estimate the total value of the services of the talented young engineer to the progress of Spanish occupation and settlement.

Córdoba was ordered to return to New Spain in 1798. His departure, in October of that year, was a distinct loss to the province. We shall remember Alberto de Córdoba as one of the most useful and efficient individuals connected with the Spanish occupation of Alta California during the last decade of the eighteenth century.

A SHIP BUILT IN CALIFORNIA

Although the Indians had been making crude boats (or canoes) and rafts from time immemorial, we cannot call their primitive water craft ships. The first real ships to appear in our California waters—not very imposing in the light of today, it must be admitted—were those captained by the Spanish *conquistadores*, beginning with Juan Rodríguez Cabrillo, in 1542.

When was the first vessel we can call a ship acutally built in California? And by whom? These are interesting questions.

Among the first Americans to settle in California was Joseph Chapman, reputedly a native of New England, about whose early life little is known. He was one of the men attached to Hippolyte de Bouchard, called by some a patriot, by others a pirate. In one of the many forays of the Bouchard party at Monterey, Chapman separated himself from it and so was on his own. This was in 1818, when political conditions in Alta California were anything but stable.

Chapman, who was then about thirty years of age, ingratiated himself with the Spanish leaders, and after a brief period of imprisonment decided to remain in the country. In a little while he had become the most famous foreign resident of that period. In fact he became a general favorite; and it was not long until he married one of the daughters of the Ortega family, which stood high in the Spanish aristocracry. The Chapmans had a family of five children.

Chapman became "a typical handy man," and has been called a "jack of all trades." He did odd jobs at the missions, planted a vineyard at Los Angeles, built several grist mills, even served as a surgeon on occasion. Most important of all, he built a ship, or schooner, the first, it is claimed, to be built in California. This was soon after he parted company with Bouchard in 1818. The sixty-ton vessel, framed at San Gabriel Mission, was transported with some difficulty to San Pedro, where Chapman launched it successfully. This unusual event is but one of several reasons for preserving the name and memory of Joseph Chapman in the story of a rather confused period of California history.

It is well known that the history of pre-American California also included the peninsula to the south, Baja California. Accordingly mention may be made of the building of another ship at a much earlier date, many years, in fact, before the first actual occupation of Alta California by the Spaniards.

In establishing early missions in Baja California the Jesuit leaders were in great need of a seaworthy ship to transport supplies from the mainland and to explore the gulf. Father Juan Ugarte, successor to Salvatierra as head of the enterprise, felt the need keenly; but in that barren land "there were neither planks, sails, rigging, tar, or other necessaries for such work, no builder, shipwright, sawyer, or other naval artificers."

Father Ugarte was indefatigable, and boldly determined to build a ship himself, having learned of straight trees more than a hundred miles northwest of Loreto. With the aid of Indians and incredible toil, he felled trees and shaped them into planks. In four months time the planks were piled on the beach; and under the watchful eye of the heroic leader, amazing as it seems, a sturdy ship gradually took shape.

In September, 1719, Father Ugarte nailed a crude cross to the bowsprit and actually launched his ship on the waters of the Gulf of California. Most appropriately he christened her *El Triunfo de la Cruz* (The Triumph of the Cross). She was the first ship built in California, and was said to be superior to any vessel previously seen on that coast. She rendered good service long after the death of her builder, as an illustration of the versatility of those early missionaries. Theodore Hittell declared, "like the *Santa Maria* and the *Mayflower*, she ought to be remembered and glorified in the histories of civilization yet to be written."

A SHIP ENTERS THE GOLDEN GATE

History was made by the small Spanish vessel *San Carlos* in the latter part of the eighteenth century. She was not much of a ship, as we reckon ships today, just a packet-boat so hastily built that on reaching La Paz she had to be unloaded and careened for repairs.

In January of 1769 she was ready, and all on board, having confessed and taken communion, listened to the parting address of José de Gálvez, visitor-general of New Spain. Theirs was a glorious mission, said the Señor, "for they were going to plant the cross among the heathen," and they were charged in the name of God and the King "to obey their pastors and maintain peace and harmony among themselves."

Then the little ship put to sea, destined to have an important rôle in the beginnings of the Spanish occupation of Alta California, a rôle not unlike that of the *Mayflower* on the east coast, for on board the *San Carlos* and her companion ship, the *San Antonio*, were pioneers whose descendants constituted California's real aristocracy. The first actual settlement was made at San Diego.

As a part of the northward expansion Monterey was reached, where mission and *presidio* were founded. It was decided that a ship should be sent further north to explore the recently discovered bay of San Francisco from the Pacific and for this mission the *San Carlos*, whose second name, *Toison de Oro* ("Golden Fleece"), later seemed prophetic.

Because of sudden failure of mentality on the part of Captain Manrique, Captain Juan Manuel de Ayala had been transferred to the *San Carlos*, and thus "became the leading figure in one of the most important events in the maritime annals of California." Ayala was instructed "to thoroughly explore the shore of the [San Francisco] bay, to ascertain whether the narrow entrance was practicable for the passage of ships, whether it afforded a safe harbor, and whether there was any strait communicating with the old San Francisco [Francis Drake] Bay."

The *San Carlos* set sail at Monterey July 27, 1775. Nine days later, August 5, Captain Ayala and his men found themselves at the looked-for entrance. In the gathering dusk, without map or chart, the captain boldly decided to proceed.

With the utmost caution he sailed the little vessel a league inside the bay and only a quarter-mile from North Beach. At half-past ten that August evening anchor was dropped in twenty-two fathoms. The *Golden Fleece* had made history, for she was the first European vessel to enter the great bay through the narrow passage referred to by the Spaniards simply as the Mouth (*la boca*), later given by Frémont the felicitous name Golden Gate. What Cabrillo and Ferrelo had failed to discover, what Francis Drake had failed to enter, had at length opened wide to Captain Ayala and his historic ship, the *San Carlos*.

Discoveries and explorations that followed make fascinating reading. What we know as Angel Island was named Nuestra Señora de los Angeles; another island which the Spaniards called Los Alcatrases, came by some quirk later to be named Yerba Buena (Goat Island), while the name Alcatraz became transferred to its present location.

In his official report Canizares (co-pilot) described San Francisco Bay in considerable detail. Captain Ayala reported to the viceroy that it was one of "the best he had seen in those seas from Cape Horn up . . . not one port, but many with a single entrance."

The sojourn in the divisions of the bay extended over forty-four days. On account of a heavy, forbidding storm, great difficulties were encountered, and it was not until the 18th of September that the brave little ship safely passed outward through the Golden Gate on her speedy return to Monterey. She had completed an illustrious mission.

FOREIGN VISITORS

The first Spanish settlements in Alta California were less than two decades old when Comte de la Pérouse, a distinguished Frenchman, paid them a memorable visit. This was in September, 1786, during the early part of Padre Lasuén's administration as father-president of the Franciscan missions. By that time nine missions had been founded, the first being San Diego (July, 1769). There were *presidios* at San Diego, Santa Barbara, Monterey, and San Francisco, also *pueblos* at San José and Los Angeles.

Pérouse, engaged in making a round-the-world reconnaisance, proved to be a keen observer, as was clearly shown in his copious notes, published years later in four volumes under the title, *Voyage atour du Monde*. Much of his time was spent at Monterey, the provincial capital of California, and selected by Padre Junípero Serra as official headquarters of the missions.

The distinguished Frenchman was received most cordially, and in turn he manifested a spirit of friendship throughout the visit. Among other things he introduced the potato into California and presented the *padres* with different kinds of seeds for planting. He reached the conclusion, however, that the province would be developed slowly under Spanish rule, and he failed to discover real promise of any great wealth, though he did recognize certain possibilities in future trade in furs.

As to the missions, it cannot be said that he was favorably impressed. To him they appeared to be making very slow progress toward a realization of their professed aims—conversion of the Indians to Christianity and teaching them the ways of industrious, productive civilized society. He formed the impression that at the moment the Indian was baptized, "he relinquished every particle of liberty and subjected him-

self, body and soul, to a tyranny from which there was no escape."
Everything appeared to be prescribed for the neophytes.

Pérouse was the first eminent leader from a foreign land to visit the
settlements of Spanish California. To be sure, he had been preceded by
Captain James Cook, who sailed from Plymouth in July, 1776, but
Cook's voyage had rather slight contact with the northwest coast, and
practically none at all with California.

It was not long after Pérouse's visit that a distinguished English
navigator, George Vancouver, was sent out by the British government
on an extended exploring expedition, with orders to effect a settlement
of the complex Nootka Sound controversy and make careful observations along the entire coast, examining the extent and nature of the
Spanish possession.

In November, 1792, Vancouver entered the Golden Gate and anchored
at Yerba Buena Cove. His party was the first to penetrate any distance
into the interior. He was charmed by the beauty of Santa Clara Valley,
"the stately lords of the forest," "pleasing eminences and valleys," and
the opportunities for "neat habitations of an industrious people." He
enthusiastically declared that San Francisco Bay was "as fine a port as
the world affords." Vancouver made in all three visits to California. His
three-volume narrative, *A Voyage of Discovery*, published in 1798, is an
important source of history for the period.

EARLY AMERICAN SHIPS

The first American ship to sail the Pacific was *The Empress of China*,
Captain Lemuel Shaw. A cargo of tea and silk was taken on at Canton,
and it was this that paved the way for a profitable trade with China.
The report of Captain Shaw's adventure led to "the epoch-making
voyage of the *Columbia*," beginning in the last of September, 1787.

Commandant José Dario Argüello of the San Francisco presidio was
warned by Governor Pedro Fages that a vessel named *Columbia*, "which
is said to belong to General Washington," had entered the Pacific Ocean
with a consort, *Lady Washington*, bent on making discoveries and
inspecting reported Russian settlements. Argüello had orders to seize
these ships if they came to San Francisco.

It is in this document, written by Pedro Fages, Spanish governor of
Alta California, so far as known, that is to be found the earliest reference
to the United States. Subsequent to that time, however, there was
increasingly frequent mention of the United States in various Spanish
documents.

Just as "Hollywood" is used in various countries as the world capital of the motion picture, and so universally understood, so the term "Boston" was commonly used to denote the entire country on the Atlantic side of the North American continent. As an illustration, Chapman cites the case of an Indian baptized at Soledad in 1793 as the son of an Indian who had been killed by Captain Robert Gray of the ship *Lady Washington*, "belonging to the Congress of Boston."

With the beginning of the nineteenth century American ships, usually called "Boston ships," arrived at California ports quite frequently. Their smuggling activities, their extensive trade with the Franciscan *padres* and the Spanish *rancheros*, constitute a familiar chapter in early California history. The *Otter*, Captain Ebenezer Dorr, had been the first vessel from New England to anchor in a California port—that was at Monterey, October 29, 1796. Within a few years the novelty of the appearance of these ships was gone, but Californians continued to be fascinated by the Boston ships and their assorted cargoes throughout the remainder of the Spanish period.

Strangely enough, what may be called the first shipyard of California was constructed, not by Spaniards but by the Russians, at Fort Ross. It was not a very pretentious affair, and it was short-lived. Numerous small craft were built. In 1816 *Rourmiantzof*, a vessel of 160 tons, was begun; two years later she was completed, at a cost of more than 20,000 rubles, and in 1819 she was launched.

Another item of interest, but which pertains to the early American period, is that the first ship to be used in California as a "prison brig" was the bark *Strafford*, which had been brought from New York in 1849, and was moored in the Sacramento River opposite I Street in the rapidly growing city of Sacramento. This inglorious ship, which had cost $50,000, was finally sold at auction for a mere $3,750.

SEA-OTTER HUNTING

A castaway crew of Russian sailors first discovered the real haunts of the sea-otter. In the year 1741, more than a quarter of a century before Spain occupied San Diego, Vitus Bering and his crew were stranded on a barren island far up in the northern Pacific. They killed some of those strange animals for much-needed food, tough and strong meat though it was, and used their skins with the fur for rugs and garments. At first they had no idea of the real value of the rich, beautiful fur that kept them from freezing, in the bleak Arctic winter.

When the sailors returned to Siberia with a stock of the pelts they had no difficulty in selling them for $200 apiece. Such was the beginning of the vast lucrative trade in furs, for it rapidly became known that there were thousands of the sea-otter in those northern waters. Of all occupations of the Russians in northwestern America otter hunting became the most important.

Business of the Russian-American Fur Company, which dated from the year 1779, proved to be immensely profitable. As a writer has expressed it, "the otter herds of the north Pacific became no less important to Russia than were the gold mines of Mexico and Peru to Spain."

Meantime, Captain James, distinguished English navigator, coming from the Sandwich Islands, which he had discovered early in 1778, had picked up a few furs, which were readily sold at high prices in China; and this led to a rapidly expanding trade with the Pacific Coast.

The French also became interested, especially through the memorable expedition of La Pérouse, in 1785. The choice fur was indeed a luxury, highly esteemed by the Chinese mandarins, as well as a distinctive mark of rank and wealth by Russian noblemen, with their otter-skin caps. The fur trade became "the shortest road to fortune for the adventurers of that wild and lawless frontier."

It was found that the coastal waters of California swarmed with both the sea-otter and the fur seal. The hunting was pushed farther and farther south. The fur-bearers were found in great numbers in San Francisco Bay, and in the rivers and creeks flowing into it. In the heyday of their activity the Russians speared from 700 to 800 otters per week in the creeks and inlets. During one season, it is reported they secured 80,000 skins at the hunting station on the Farallone Islands. Nothing was thought of but immediate profits: there was ruthless, indiscriminate slaughter of the fur-bearing animals.

The early interest of Americans in sea-otter hunting is illustrated by the coming of the American ship *Otter*, which dropped anchor in Monterey Bay in October, 1796. Valuable furs were the main object of the captain, Ebenezer Dorr, first Yankee fur trader. Learning that the taking of otter had been made illegal under Spanish rule, he turned to the fur-smuggling trade.

Smuggling expedients of various sorts were resorted to. It was found easy, for example, "to devise excuses for remaining in port a few days, during which covert transactions could be effected." Probably at least a dozen ship captains attempted to smuggle furs from the vigilant Californians. Illicit bartering proved to be risky business.

The movements of the famous *Lelia Byrd* (Captain William Shaler), most interesting of all American-owned smuggling vessels, read like fantastic fiction. They proved the presence of the otter all up and down the coast of California, revealed the weakness of the Spanish control, and the lucrative business in furs by Yankee captains. It is reported that in one year, 1807, Americans sold $136,000 worth of furs. Although the day of the sea otter was really over by the year 1820, it was largely through it that American leaders acquired a knowledge of Pacific Coast resources, and impetus was given to the sentiment for annexation of California.

Fortunately, the sea-otter did not become entirely extinct. For many years it has been strongly protected by law. In 1938 about 100 of another species of the furry creatures were discovered near Rainbow Bridge on the San Simeon Highway, perfectly at home in the off-shore kelp beds. "The gentle, shiny-furred animal has become a legend on the Pacific Coast."

COMING OF THE RUSSIANS

The alleged danger from the Russians on the north was the motivating force that influenced José de Gálvez, *Visitador-General* of New Spain, in deciding to send out the famous expeditions of 1769, which resulted in the founding of San Diego and signalized the occupation of Alta California by Spain.

California was thought of not only as a field for missionary endeavor, or as an extension of the Spanish colonial dominion, but also, as we have seen, as a barrier to the possible encroachments of the Russians and the British power in North America. Russia, however, did not prove to be a serious menace.

During the early Spanish régime a number of foreign navigators visited California. Notable among these was the Frenchman La Pérouse, already referred to, who in September, 1786, brought information of Russian settlements in the north, causing the Spaniards to speed up their activities in that direction.

Most significant was the expedition of Nicolai Rezánof, who had reached Sitka in 1805 as plenipotentiary for the powerful Russian-American Fur Company, his purpose being to inspect the Russian colonies and institute needed reforms. Rezánof found the colonists at Sitka on the verge of actual starvation; the dreaded scurvy was rampant and had already taken heavy toll. So desperate was the situation that he decided to sail south in search of food supplies, and to establish a settlement at the mouth of the Columbia River. Being unable to make a landing there, because of the strong outgoing current, he decided in his extremity to proceed to the San Francisco *presidio*.

Notwithstanding the Spanish regulations against entering the Golden Gate, he resolved, "at the risk of two or three cannon balls, to run straight for the fort." He dropped anchor under the very guns of the *presidio*, where there was not even a row-boat to reach the ship.

What happened there — the friendly reception, the "battle of wits" with the Spanish *comandante*, the historic romance between the brilliant chamberlain and the charming Concepción — has been told and retold. Rezánof was a winner! He had been able to obtain food for the starving colonists. But there was still no Russian settlement in California.

The Russians looked with longing eye upon the fertility and resources of California. They had been alerted to the possibilities by Rezánof's famous expedition. But Spain claimed the territory they desired. After two unsuccessful attempts, another voyage to the south was undertaken by Ivan Ruskoff with full equipment, which resulted in the selection of a site for a fort, eighteen miles north of Bodega.

On a bold plateau a rectangular fort was built and mounted with ten cannon. The fort was surrounded by a strong palisade, with bastions at the four corners. Inside the stockade a spacious house was built and comfortably furnished. The little chapel in one corner was the first church built in California north of San Francisco. That was the beginning of Fort Ross, in the year 1812. Because there was no satisfactory anchorage at the fort, the Russian ships wintered and made repairs at Bodega, where storage warehouses were built.

September 10, 1812, was the gala day that the fort was completed and dedicated with elaborate festivities. The colony included a hundred Russians and eighty Aleut hunters, and developed rapidly. The vegetable gardens were successful, fruit trees produced apples, pears, cherries, and peaches; grape vines were brought up from distant Peru, roses and other flowers from San Francisco.

Limited trade relations were established with the Spaniards, although the Russians were never granted formal permission to settle in the country. Baránof knew that Arrillaga was in no position to enforce the viceroy's order to remove the Russian establishment. The Russians were in great need of grain and cattle, in which branches they had little success at the fort, and the Spaniards were in desperate need of trade.

The sea-otter was so vigorously hunted by the Russians that within a few years these prized animals had practically disappeared between Trinidad and San Francisco. The Russians carried on a good business with the Spaniards in supplying manufactured articles of leather, iron, and wood. Governor Solá served notice on them to leave the country, but this the Russians ignored, knowing he had no means of enforcing the order.

The Russian establishment was short-lived. The last of the Franciscan missions was founded at Sonoma in 1823, largely as a barrier against Russian expansion southward. But it was the advance of the aggressive Americans and the Monroe Doctrine that brought on the crisis. Uncle Sam's announcement that "We should consider any attempt on their part to extend their system to any portion of this hemisphere as dangerous to our peace and safety," led Russia to take steps to withdraw from California.

The decision to depart became known to Governor Alvarado and brought great rejoicing at Monterey, with the expectation that the entire Russian equipment would fall into the hands of the Californians—or of Gen. M. G. Vallejo, *comandante* at Sonoma. But not so! Captain John A. Sutter surprised everybody by purchasing all the movable property, including the cattle. Vallejo was deeply chagrined to learn that his chance of acquiring the property was ruined.

In 1841 the Russians sailed away, never to return. Whatever hopes had been entertained of obtaining a strong foothold in California were gone and gone forever.

FIRST AMERICAN OVERLAND

Early trappers and traders were the true forerunners of the great migration into the West and California. In the illustrious list of these "mountain men" the name of Jedediah Strong Smith shines with conspicuous splendor not only for what he did as an explorer but also for what he was as a man.

Jedediah, a native of Mohawk Valley, New York, was the oldest in a family of thirteen children. When he became a partner to William Ashley at the age of twenty, his career really began. He was an eager student of geography, with a passionate desire to explore new territory. His early expeditions took him through central Missouri, on into the Yellowstone, to the Columbia River, and the region of the Great Salt Lake.

He heard of California, with its mountains and great central valley. He resolved to see it. In the summer of 1826, as a partner in the firm of Sublette, Jackson and Smith, he set forth at the head of a band of fifteen men. Encountering serious difficulties and all kinds of hardships in crossing the great American Desert, Smith's spirit remained undaunted. In late autumn he led his party into California through Cajon Pass, near San Bernardino, and on the 27th of November camp was made near San Gabriel Mission, not far from Pueblo de Los Angeles. This was five months after leaving Salt Lake. Thus Jedediah Smith and his hardy band were the first Americans who actually entered our California overland from the East.

Smith's ever-memorable travels in California, from south to north, from east to west, have been recounted in much detail by H. C. Dale, J. G. Neihardt, and Robert G. Cleland; and Phil Townsend Hanna has pronounced the chronicle of the historic journey of this "Knight in Buckskin" "a tale as thrilling and as full of incident as Alexander's conquest of Persia or Marco Polo's invasion of the realm of Kublai Khan." He and his party proved to be the vanguard of the great American advance. Their revelations caused many eyes to be turned toward California. Smith had found the end of the long trail.

As to this "Knight in Buckskin" himself, it is sufficient to say he was a young man of good appearance, fine physique, and keen blue eyes; with personal courage that knew no bounds; of devout Christian character, well recognized by those who knew him, which was the reason why he was called "Bible-toter" by his contemporaries — he always carried his Bible with him.

On Lincoln's birthday in 1924, a huge granite boulder, brought from Cajon Pass, was unveiled with fitting ceremony at Carthay Center, Culver City, bearing this inscription:

DEDICATED TO JEDEDIAH STRONG SMITH
PATHFINDER OF THE SIERRAS

To Jedediah Strong Smith the state owes a great debt of gratitude. It is well that the Centennial of his entrance into California, in 1926, was fittingly celebrated in schools and communities throughout the state and that the memory of his deeds and short life are imperishably inscribed on our hearts. The anniversary was also appropriately commemorated by the Historical Society of Southern California.

AMERICANS ACROSS THE SIERRA NEVADAS

Joe Walker, a native Tennessean, was one of five brothers, every one a six-footer, every one a man of the wilderness. Washington Irving calls Joe "one of the bravest and most skillful of the mountain men." Meeting Captain Benjamin Bonneville when he was thirty-three years old, Joe's big opportunity came. He was commissioned to select a band of fifty men and set out to the West on what proved to be a highly adventurous career as a trapper and trader. The success he achieved brought a unique distinction to Joseph Reddeford Walker, "Knight of the Golden Horseshoe."

The life story of this mountain man has been told by Percy Booth in his book, *West Wind*. The Platte River was reached on June 2nd, 1833. To cross the stream it was necessary to dismantle the wagons. But the real start of his high adventure came July 24, when Joe led his men out of Green River Valley, headed for the great mountains of the Far West. Following the winding Humboldt River, the Humboldt Sink was reached during the first week of September. Then the party was directly confronted by the towering peaks of the Sierra Nevada Mountains.

Joe Walker's resources—they were many—were taxed to the utmost: his early training, frontier spirit, personal fearlessness and versatility were all needed—but they sufficed. Hunting for a mountain pass, he found a stream (Walker River) which flowed into a lake (Walker Lake). He pushed on, ever westward, reaching the watershed that divides the Merced and Tuolumne Rivers, both tributaries of the San Joaquin. The intense suffering of the men must be left to the imagination. Many of the horses had been slaughtered to feed the famishing men.

Approaching the rim of a great, astounding miracle of nature from surrounding heights, they were the first white men to look upon the marvels of the grand Yosemite. That inspiring sight had but slight appeal then to Walker's half-dead men. Later they looked with amazement at the majestic California Big Trees (*Sequoia gigantea*), and the glories of the Tuolumne Grove were revealed to them. The wide-spreading San Joaquin Valley lay spread out before them, oak trees appeared on all sides; and, best of all, wild game abounded and grizzly bear, elk, antelope, and deer were brought into camp by the happy hunters. California had been reached, in the late autumn of the year 1833. Joe Walker had been the first to lead a party directly across the heart of the Sierras, into the land of El Dorado.

The San Joaquin River was followed through the delta to Suisun Bay; finally the shores of the great Pacific were reached. Then Walker proceeded with his band to Monterey, where he found Governor José Figueroa both friendly and gracious, and he was able to obtain permission to winter in the territory, then under Mexican rule.

His discoveries proved memorable — the Yosemite Valley, the Big Trees, Owens Valley, Walker Pass. Yet, as stated by John W. Caughey, "the greatest historical significance attaches to the route to California, which he had pioneered by way of the Humboldt Valley and a central Sierra crossing." Succeeding generations of Californians will be proud to claim "Old Joe Walker" as taking high rank among hardy mountain men and trappers whose names grace the pages of our colorful history. They were the pathfinders of the West.

AMERICAN SETTLER

Who was the first American to settle in California? To this question many incorrect answers have been given.

The Boston fur ships brought Americans to the California coast years before the beginning of the nineteenth century. In this the *Empress of China* was the real pioneer, arriving as early as 1784, but we have no record of actual settlers coming on these early Boston vessels. It is reported that an American whose name was given as John Groem (Graham?) arrived September 13, 1791, with the Spanish command of Alejandro Malaspina: but the further report that he *was buried* on that very day cancels any claim that he became an American settler!

John Gilroy, having changed his true name (Cameron) in order to avoid arrest and deportation, arrived in 1814, was baptized in the Catholic faith, married a young *señorita*, built an adobe home on his league of land, where he lived for many years. But Gilroy was a Scotchman, and not an American. He did antedate the arrival of the first American settler by a slight margin, thus supporting the claim to being the first *foreigner* to settle permanently in the territory.

Jedediah Smith has the distinction of having been the first American to lead a party overland into California. He came not to settle, but to trap, and his arrival was years after the coming of the first American settler.

Our best records indicate that a young seaman of twenty-nine, named Thomas W. Doak, arrived at Monterey in March, 1816, on the ship *Albatross*, that he deserted from the vessel and became the first bona-fide American settler in the province of California. On being baptized on December 22 of that year, he took the name Felipe Santiago, and was thenceforth a devout Roman Catholic. In 1820, with vice-regal permission, he was married to María Lugarda, daughter of José Mariano Castro, the ceremony being performed in the Mission Church of San Juan Bautista.

Doak (Santiago) seems to have been a carpenter, with a reputation for good habits, but without claims to real distinction. Most of his days were spent in the vicinity of the Mission, a very "peaceful and pleasant spot." With the aid of two Indian neophytes he painted the mission altar and pulpit. Being more of a sailor than an artist, his job was rather poorly done. Because the standard of piety was higher than that of art, his devoted work was approved, apparently giving universal satisfaction. After an uneventful life, quite removed from the major activities of the time, he died about the year 1848, leaving four children and a good personal record.

Daniel Call, an American youth of seventeen, landed at Santa Barbara later in the year 1816. Little is known of him. As many as a dozen foreigners, including Joseph Chapman, an American, are known to have reached California before the end of 1818. And previous to the time of the American conquest in 1846, numerous young Americans had come to California to settle, most of them becoming adopted Mexican citizens and marrying into prominent Spanish families. Among the descendants of some of these mixed families are today many useful citizens in various parts of the state.

NON-SPANISH SETTLERS

First among the non-Spanish white persons to make permanent settlement in California was a native of Scotland, who had lived mostly in England, known in history as John Gilroy, though his real name was John Cameron. In 1814 this young man arrived on a British vessel, and he decided to remain — as a youth of twenty he had run away to sea, eager for a career "on the ocean wave." The King's orders regarding foreigners in California were very strict: it was because a kind-hearted woman nursed him back to health, and through the intercession of a sympathetic captain, that he was permitted to remain.

In 1818 he applied for naturalization as an adopted Spanish citizen under the name Juan Antonio María Gilroy, stating that he had joined the Catholic Church. Two years later he was given permission to settle and own land, and to marry. He was granted a league of land, and it is on this *sitio*, near the southern end of Santa Clara County, that the present town of Gilroy is located.

Other non-Spanish settlers of very early dates who were admitted to citizenship and permitted to marry *señoritas* of the country included William G. Dana, Julian Wilson, John Temple, William A. Richardson, José Bolcoff, and William E. P. Hartnell.

Soon after the arrival of Gilroy also came an Irishman, John Milligan, who assumed the name "Mulligan." His career in California, however, was inconspicuous: he died in 1834.

It was in 1816 that the first American to remain in California arrived, if we make exception of the somewhat mythical "John Groehm," a member of the company under Alejandro Malaspina, mentioned on a previous page.

An early settler of some note was Robert Livermore, a young Englishman, who had deserted from an English brig in 1822. He established himself on the *Positos Rancho*, in what we now know as Livermore Valley. There he died in 1858, leaving a good name and a typical large family.

During the second and third decades of the nineteenth century small bands of hunters and trappers were approaching California from the east and from the north. Most of these, however, did not come as settlers. Of chief importance among them was Jedediah Strong Smith, first American to enter California overland, in 1826 — but that is another story, already told. Those who remained became *hijos del pais*, that is, they married the *señoritas* of the Californians and became adopted sons of the soil. Prominent among them was Henry D. Fitch, who arrived in 1827, eloped with Josefa Carrillo, and had a career filled with romance and excitement. Others of the period included Captain John Wilson, Daniel Hill, and James Black.

That was a period of slow infiltration of foreigners into the turbulent final years of Spanish rule and the early part of the Mexican régime. Most of those who came from the outside world to settle were undistinguished as individuals, but together they were forerunners of a great movement that proved to be of deep significance.

OVERLAND EMIGRANT TRAIN

Other white people had entered Alta California before 1841. There were the Spaniards, beginning with the expeditions commanded by Gaspar de Portolá, as early as 1769; there were the early American trappers, beginning with Jedediah Smith, who came in 1826; also there were Americans who finally settled in California, including William Wolfskill, Abel Stearns, George Yount, and Henry Bee.

The first organized overland train of Americans to enter California from the east was the Bartleson-Bidwell Party of 1841. This company, with John Bartleson as captain and John Bidwell as secretary, broke camp at Independence, Missouri, on Wednesday, May 19, 1841, headed toward the great West. Some slight hint of the difficulties encountered and vicissitudes suffered may be gleaned from the simple fact that it was the 4th day of November when the party, after reorganization and many changes in personnel, finally reached the cabin of John Marsh, near the base of Mt. Diablo, in California.

Included in the personnel of this party were such well known pioneers as Josiah Belden, Benjamin Kelsey and family, Joseph Chiles, and M. C. Nye. It is our good fortune that young Bidwell kept a daily record of the memorable trek, having promised his friends he would keep a journal. This journal was printed in a small edition in 1842. A copy is one of the rarest treasures of the Bancroft Library in Berkeley. Bidwell's detailed account, written many years later, appears in *The Century Illustrated Magazine* for November, 1890, and later still in *Echoes of the Past*.

It is impossible to describe here in detail the route taken by this party in 1841. It may be mentioned, however, that the route has been quite clearly identified through to Humboldt Valley in western Nevada. A heart-breaking decision that had to be made was that all the wagons must be abandoned. The bringing of the first wagons through the mountains into California constitutes another story.

William G. Paden of Alameda spent months of time tracing the route, stating that "From Humboldt Creek to San Joaquin Valley the trail was practically unknown." Paden concluded that Bidwell "came through the mountains some twelve or fifteen miles north of Sonora Pass and at a slightly lower elevation." It would be impossible to trace in detail the actual course of the party, rendered desperate by constant perils and terrible hardships, down the unblazed slopes and through the devious canyons of the Sierran wilderness; but after many forced retreats and indescribable difficulties they finally emerged into the friendly San Joaquin Valley at a point near the present town of Oakdale, in Stanislaus County.

The story of John Bidwell in California, from the beginning in 1841 to the end of the century, has become a significant part of the fascinating history of the commonwealth. His distinguished activities in the fields of agriculture, of politics, of philanthropy, most of all as exemplar of unbounded hospitality and nobility of character, have earned for him the title, "Prince of California Pioneers."

FILIBUSTERS

Filibusterism in California history means something entirely different from the obstructionist tactics sometimes associated with the United States Senate. Nor can filibuster be confused with the early *empresario*, who contracted with the Mexican government to recruit and introduce a number of families into the territory as colonists. California filibusterism usually involved "lawless aggression in the form of military expeditions into foreign territory."

The objects of the first American filibusters was the freeing of Cuba and other islands of the West Indies, or parts of Central America, from European control. In California some of the gold seekers, failing to amass immediate wealth, eagerly listened to the voice of a filibustering leader, for there was promise of excitement, conquest, and personal fortune.

Not a few were led on by the conviction that some sort of Manifest Destiny was calling upon the United States to occupy new lands. Then there was also the desire on the part of some to acquire new areas for the spread of slavery and thus restore the political balance in Washington, which had been broken by the admission of California as a free state.

The first filibustering expedition out of California was led by Alex Bell. Not long after California's admission to statehood Bell conceived the idea of reinstating the deposed president of Ecuador. Accordingly he sailed first to Panama, in 1851, where he received reinforcements from Ecuadorian sympathizers; then he made bold to continue up the Guayiquil River, with the intention of proceeding against the capital city, Quito.

But Bell was found to be lacking in the qualities of real leadership and statesmanship and he had little understanding of the Latin-American character. Even before he reached the city the rival factions of the country, as so often happened under similar circumstances, had composed their differences and had effected a reconciliation, and there they stood united in a desire to rid their country of the intruding Americans!

The whole affair, therefore, turned into a fiasco, the upshot of which was that the frustrated filibuster was compelled to retreat to Panama. There the remnant of his party was stranded, it gradually dissolved, and finally ended ingloriously. Bell himself managed to straggle back to Los Angeles, and finally to San Francisco, where he died in 1859.

That was the first filibustering attempt by a Californian, but it was by no means the last, nor was it the greatest. There was Joseph C. Morehead, whose proposed expedition to Baja California proved abortive; followed by the more ambitious undertakings of three daring Frenchmen, Pindray, Sigondis, and Raousset-Boulbon, who thought they saw brilliant prospects in Mexico, and indeed they gained considerable headway, but finally came to grief; and William Walker, "gray-eyed man of destiny," whose bold exploits brought him immense popularity and whose grandiose plans promised for a time glittering success and world renown — but at the last he was found guilty by court-martial, and his meteoric career ended before a firing squad in September, 1860.

With the tragic end of Henry A. Crabb, last prominent filibuster, such expeditions into Latin-American territory ceased. With the coming of the Civil War, the chief motives for filibusterism had lost their appeal.

COAST SURVEY

Early navigation along the California coast had been seriously fettered from the beginning: it was fraught with much difficulty and constant peril. Even before the signing of the treaty of peace with Mexico, some preliminary attention had been given to the subject at Washington, in 1847; but this was not supported by any appropriation.

In the year of Marshall's gold discovery (1848) the U.S. War Department directed the appointment of a joint commission "to promptly explore the Pacific coast harbors and rivers for determining needful defences, depots, mail stations, and safeguards for navigation." The project was helped forward by William M. Gwin, who had been a delegate at the Monterey Constitutional Convention, and was one of California's first U.S. Senators.

Thus the first effective work was actually undertaken during 1849 and 1850; and from that time onward followed rapid surveys, often being occasion for significant discoveries.

Scientific surveys of the coast were of special importance in the days of the gold-seeking argonauts, not only because of rapidly increasing shipping interests but as an essential preliminary to the building of lighthouses and coast fortifications. Senator Gwin was instrumental in obtaining an appropriation of $250,000 for the making for a very extensive survey. The general result was so to advance the work as to accomplish in a single decade as much as had been done on the Atlantic coast in three decades.

The effective organization of the survey work along the Pacific dates from the arrival of George Davidson in June, 1850, and is chiefly to be attributed to his genius and indusrty. His first work kept him for months at a time on coastal promontories or mountain-top camps, far removed from the amenities of social life. The contributions of Dr. Davidson, "pioneer west coast scientist," have only recently been fully recognized and brought to public notice, by Oscar Lewis, in his volume published by the University of California Press in 1954.

Up to his time the details of geographic positions, harbors, bays, and rivers were virtually among the *incognita*. As Lewis points out,

> There were no lighthouses, no fog whistles, not a buoy on thirty-three hundred miles of coast, and hardly a line of sailing directions. Ships came upon our waters with school atlases for charts.

It is recalled that the Golden Gate was dreaded by the navigator, especially as darkness approached and a high fee was often paid a pilot to bring the vessel in.

The coast survey was all the more valuable because at that time the pyramiding mercantile and shipping business in and out of San Francisco was done on the double-quick. Davidson's fundamental idea, in harmony with the national plan, was the preparation and publication of "such charts of the coast of the United States, of the harbors, rivers, bays . . . as would insure the greatest safety to the commerce of the country."

The name of George Davidson adds luster to any list not only of notable California pioneers but also of distinguished builders of our entire west coast. His services continued for many years, as in the triangulation of California, the making of hydrographic surveys, as chief engineer in explorations of the Isthmus of Darien for location of a possible ship canal, as Honorary Professor of Geodesy and Astronomy and later Professor of Geography at the University of California, and in still other capacities as teacher, writer, and scientist extraordinary. He died on the second of December, 1911, in his eighty-seventh year.

DISCOVERY OF YOSEMITE

In any list of Seven Natural Wonders of California the unrivaled Yosemite must be awarded a commanding place. Yosemite is a world wonder which has been rediscovered countless times by every nature lover who views its marvels and discovers for himself its matchless beauty. Each subsequent visit brings fresh revelation.

When considering the discovery of Yosemite by white men, the entrance of Francisco Garcés into Tulare Valley in 1776, and the Moraga expedition of 1806, which explored the lower course of the Merced River, may be ignored, not denying their significance in other respects. The coming of Jedediah Smith, the heroic young American fur trader, in 1826, did have indirect results that were more relevant; but Smith cannot be accredited with the actual discovery of Yosemite.

It should be noted that discovery of Yosemite is not to be confused with the actual entrance into the Valley. This will be made clear as we proceed. The "first inkling of the existence of Yosemite Valley" resulted from a memorable expedition, made in 1833 by an experienced frontiersman, Joseph Reddeford Walker, who had been ordered by Captain Bonneville to visit California. Washington Irving described Walker as "About six feet high, strong built, dark complexioned, brave in spirit, though mild in manners." In his California party were fifty men, about 200 horses, food, ammunition, and trade goods amounting to a year's supply.

Walker's exact route cannot now be traced in detail. Having climbed the Sierra Nevada from the east, the party proceeded west, in general, between the Tuolumne and Merced rivers, into what is now the heart of Yosemite National Park, following along much of the Mono Trail.

"Camped at Yosemite November 13, 1833"—so reads the inscription on Walker's tombstone, in Martinez. But it is clear from the description of the route that the camp was not in the Valley, for, according to Zenas Leonard's narrative, ". . . on making several attempts we found it utterly impossible for a man to descend, to say nothing of our horses. We were then obliged to keep along the top of the dividing line between two of these chasms."

The evidence is convincing that Joe Walker was in truth the discoverer of Yosemite, from the rim, although he did not actually set foot on the floor of the Valley. Also, members of the Walker party were the first white men to observe California Big Trees (*Sequoia gigantea*), some of them measuring "from 16 to 18 fathoms round the trunk at the height of a man's head from the ground."

What of the claim, commonly advanced, that James D. Savage was the real discoverer of Yosemite? Dr. Lafayette Bunnell, one of Savage's intimate acquaintances, has presented full detail in his important book, *Discovery of the Yosemite.* . . .

> The date of our discovery and entrance into the Yosemite was about the 21st of March, 1851. We were afterward assured by Ten-ie-ya and others of his band, that this was the first visit ever made to this valley by white men.

We regret there is no space for a description of the Indian troubles and the more than strange circumstances leading up to the Savage expedition, with his Mariposa Battalion, nor for the fascinating, almost legendary character of Savage himself. But he has long been recognized as the first white man actually to enter Yosemite Valley, and through his discovery, or entrance, this marvel of nature became known to the world.

By 1873, we are told, 12,000 tourists had visited the Valley, some entering by way of Mariposa, others by Coulterville, still others by Big Oak Flat. The 17th day of June, 1874, was a gala day. The "first stages rolled down the grades to the Valley floor, heralding a new era for Yosemite." More rejoicing greeted the building of the Wawona Road in 1875. In 1900 the first chugging automobile made its strange appearance in the Valley.

The names of "Old Joe Walker" and devil-defying Jim Savage must forever stand out on the pages of our history. No others can be found like either of them, and there is no need to disparage the achievement of either. Walker beheld the promised land, in part, from above; however, he was not permitted to enter. Savage marched boldly into California's wonderland, and the hosts did follow after him. "But no temple made by hands," wrote Muir, "can compare with Yosemite."

CHAPTER TWO

TRANSPORTATION AND COMMUNICATION

"History begins with the stone ax and ends with the morning newspaper." "History like charity begins at home."
—*Herbert Baxter Adams*

THE MEXICAN *CARRETA*

The actual date when the clumsy two-wheeled cart was first invented is not known, but Charles Lummis said, "it runs back at least into the beginning of the seventeenth century," in Europe. It was introduced into Alta California very soon after the beginnings of the Spanish occupation in the latter part of the eighteenth century. As a common means of transportation during the Spanish-Mexican régimes it played such an important part in the life of the period as to merit a place among the significant firsts of California. The other means of transportation were the horse and the mule. All produce, as well as much human freight, was hauled in the ox-carts.

Here was a species of wheeled vehicle, probably the only one of the time, "which never had a nail or a scrap of iron about it." Two descriptions of the old *carreta*, each by a man who had ample opportunity to see it in actual use, will be sufficient to inform us of just how it looked. First, we have the description given by John Bidwell, pioneer of 1841, and a close observer.

At this time there was not in California any vehicle except a rude California cart; the wheels were without tires, and were made by felling an oak tree and hewing it down till it made a solid wheel nearly a foot thick on the rim and a little larger where the axle went through. The hole for the axle would be eight or nine inches in diameter, but a few years' use would increase it to a foot. To make the hole, an auger, gouge, or chisel was sometimes used, but the principal tool was an ax. A small tree required but little hewing and shaping to answer for an axle. These carts were always drawn by oxen, the yoke being lashed with rawhide to the horns. To lubricate the axles they used soap, . . . carrying along for the purpose a big pail of thick soapsuds which was constantly put in the box or hole; but you could usually tell when a California cart was coming half a mile away by the squeaking. I have seen families of the wealthiest people go long distances at the rate of thirty miles a day, visiting in one of these clumsy two-wheeled vehicles. They had a little framework around it made of round sticks, and a bullock hide was put in for a floor or bottom. Sometimes the better class would have a little calico for curtains and cover. There was no such thing as a spoked wheel in use then.

The other description is by Charles F. Lummis, well-known champion of the old Southwest. Minor differences in detail must be expected, because of locality, materials available, and facility in construction. Wrote Lummis:

> This was a rude ox-cart (too heavy for any other motive power). Its two wheels were made each of three pieces of cotton-wood logs on a wooden axle without tires; its body and tongue of stakes hewn from the same soft timber. . . . In the remoter parts of New Mexico, . . . I have heard them two miles away shrieking down the road—for there was no axle grease, and wooden wheels on wooden journals, down-grade, gave vent to a protest as far audible as any sound I know of. . . .

Other details are described by Arthur Woodward, including the tongue, about fifteen feet in length, extending along the bed of the cart, the uprights, six on each side, two or three inches thick and four to five feet high, and the ox-yoke, concerning which Woodward says: "It was lashed to the horns of the oxen, fitting against the head just behind the ears . . . the animal pulled with its head and neck instead of the shoulders."

For the *fiestas* the carts "were covered with a brilliant canopy." "Sometimes this was a gay silk bedspread," continues Rose Winterburn, "worked in beautiful flowers; a long fringe hung down the sides almost to the axle, protecting the girls and women from the bright rays of the sun. Or lace curtains, Chinese crêpe, or bright-colored *rebozas* were used as canopies, giving beauty to the otherwise rude carriages."

But even the tortoise-paced *carreta* could be speeded up, on occasion. The plodding oxen might even be goaded into a full gallop, "rattling over the rough roads, the dust flying in clouds," with a score of dogs trailing along. In the carts rode the *señoras* and the children—the gallant *caballero* was always far more at home on his favorite saddle horse.

It is a far cry from the creaking, springless *carreta* to the elegant dashing automobile and super-constellation airplane of today; but the clumsy ox-cart came first, even before the covered wagon of the American settler, and will always have its place in the many-sided, picturesque history of California.

EARLY BRIDGES

The first California bridge of which we know was an unpretentious affair. A double interest attaches to it since it left a permanent memorial —a town called Puente, located a dozen miles east of Los Angeles. *Puente* is Spanish for bridge. The Portolá expedition of 1769 camped at San José Creek, July 30. Crespi reported that it was necessary to construct a bridge of poles to cross the miry *arroyo*. The following January the return expedition camped at the same place. Portolá called the surrounding plain *Llano de la Puente*.

First of the bridges of which we have definite description was that constructed to carry *El Camino Real* (Royal Highway) over an aqueduct at Mission La Purisima Concepción, in the fertile valley of Rio Santa Inés, in Santa Barbara County. It was a tiny thing, only as wide as the trail itself and a foot and a half across, simple covering for a small culvert, we would call it today. This bridge was built of stone slabs, in the year 1813. It has been preserved at the site of the old mission, which has been transformed into beautiful La Purisima State Park.

In referring to the old Mission Archives, Bancroft gives this note:

> There are a few allusions to work on the roads and bridges, especially between San Francisco and Monterey where Sergeant Pico was commissioned to bridge the Pajaro in 1816. All the lumber used was hewn by hand, there being no saw-mill. At several places one millstone was turned upon another by the direct application of horsepower without mechanism.

Another early bridge antedating the gold discovery was Hinckley Bridge, built in 1844 at Yerba Buena (San Francisco). About ten feet long, across the neck of a small lagoon, which at the time extended to the present location of Montgomery and Kearny Streets, constructed of planks, it was intended for the convenience of pedestrians walking from the base of Telegraph Hill down toward Clark's Point.

A great many bridges, large and small, were constructed during the early mining days, but they were proverbially "flimsy and perilous affairs." It was nothing uncommon for the stage coach, at the approach to a bridge, to stop and let the passengers walk across, which they were glad to do when they saw the empty stage trembling and swaying as it made its cautious way across.

The first suspension bridge of California is located at Bidwell Bar, at one time a flourishing mining town and county seat of Butte County; it crosses the Middle Fork of the Feather River, a leading tributary of the Sacramento. Materials for this bridge were transported from New York around the Horn, in 1853; the structure was completed in 1856, and dedicated to the pioneers of California. At its end, just across the highway from the Mother Orange Tree, stands the historic stone toll house, for many years regarded as one of the distinctive historic land-marks of the state.

An interesting feature is seen in the numerous covered bridges in different parts of California. Three of these that have survived are of sufficient interest to merit special mention. They are: one, built in 1862, crossing the South Fork of the Yuba River at the little town of Bridge-port, in Nevada County—this is believed to be the longest covered span (225 feet) in the entire United States; another, also built in 1862, at O'Bryne's Ferry across the Stanislaus River, a tributary of the San Joaquin; and, probably most famous of all, the third, built in 1864, at the historic town of Knight's Ferry, across the Stanislaus, still seen each year by thousands of interested persons.

Napa County gained considerable fame for its dozens of stone bridges solidly built from native rock during the second half of the nineteenth century.

WAGONS IN CALIFORNIA

To begin with, what is a wagon? There have been a great many kinds of wheeled vehicles, even of those of animal-drawn types. Perhaps the word "carriage" is most generic in its application to numerous variations of vehicles, though types of wagons are also legion.

The invention of the wheel ranks high among the great inventions of the world. Wheels are of great antiquity, as is well illustrated by the monuments of ancient Assyria and Egypt. The chariot antedates the Christian era by many centuries.

Among the types of carriage of modern times there are the "Barouche," the "Brougham," the "Phaeton," the "Victoria," the "Coach," the "Buggy," and, still others, using the term carriage in a general sense.

By "wagon" we usually mean a vehicle of four wheels intended for the transport of goods and persons, and not primarily for pleasure. The wagon certainly had a significant rôle in the drama of our early California history.

As is well known, California was an outlying province of New Spain (Mexico) previous to the American conquest. This relationship lends added interest to the little-known fact that as far back as the middle of the sixteenth century a sort of clumsy four-wheeled covered wagon was invented for freight traffic on the new Zacetecas highway. Philip Powell informs us that, "From about 1552 on, trains of these heavy covered wagons became standard equipment in the northern transport system, adding that "some of these new *carros* were big enough to serve as portable block houses...." *Carros* were heavier than ox-drawn *carretas*, with which we are more familiar. There is a remote possibility that a very small number of these primitive wagons found their way into Alta California, but of this we have no authentic record.

It was to be almost three centuries before American wagons were brought into our California. Incidental mention may be made of the queer vehicle—a kind of cross between a wagon and a carriage—brought into California from Mexico by Governor Manuel Micheltorena, in 1842. This had shafts, we are told, but was drawn by two mounted *vaqueros*, whose *reatas* (in lieu of harness) were attached to the pommels of the saddles and made fast to the shafts. General John Bidwell has given us a word picture of the pompous Mexican governor riding in state in his unique "ambulance."

Among the first American wagons brought into California were those coming across the plains with the "Stevens Company," in 1844. However, on account of the deep snow they had to be left in the Sierras, some of them near Donner Lake, the others at the head of the Yuba River. Early next spring (1845) they were brought down into the Sacramento Valley by Moses Schallenberger, Elisha Stevens, and other pioneers. But they had entered the present borders of California in late autumn of 1844.

Even previous to this, however, it is recorded that the Chiles-Walker party of 1843 had brought wagons, rumbling along Walker River, Walker Lake, and Owens Lake, before they were compelled to abandon them. These are believed to be the first to be brought into California by overland home-seekers.

Peter Burnett, first governor of the new state, has told us about the first wagon train from Oregon. This consisted of some fifty wagons, drawn by oxen, and a party of about 150 men, Burnett himself being captain. This was in early September, 1848, the destination being the gold fields on the American River.

Before California became a full-fledged member of the American Union several routes had been well established. The lure of gold resulted in the Great Trek. Then came the Days of '49. Endless caravans of sturdy wagons, with innumerable gold hunters have become one of the great epics of American history.

CLIPPER SHIPS

The demand for more rapid delivery of tea to New York from far-distant China played a large part in bringing in the era of the Clipper

Ships, beginning in the year 1843. But the clipper did not appear in California for several years thereafter. It was the 28th day of July, 1849, when the *Memnon*, of 1,068 tons burden, Captain George Gordon, entered the Golden Gate, 120 days from New York. Built in 1848 for the China trade, she was the only "extreme clipper" to reach San Francisco in the year 1849.

This new type of ship was an answer to the demand for speed. The situation at the time regarding world commerce demanded positive improvement in the construction of sailing craft. The spectacular entrance of California into world affairs following the great gold discovery in 1848 had a marked influence. The clumsy old vessels that "took from six months to a year to elbow their way from New York to San Francisco" were clearly outmoded: there must be something swifter, as well as lighter, and easier to maneuver. The beautiful clipper was the answer.

Special features of the new queen of the seas were: concave water-lines, increased length in proportion to width, and long, tapering bow, extensive addition of canvas, with the aim of cutting down resistance, and increasing speed. As Theodore Hittell expresses it, canvas was "tacked on every conceivable quarter where it could draw a breath of wind." There were many auxiliary sails. Most distinguished among designers was Donald McKay of New York, who, as Professor William S. Ament has so aptly said, "produced a harmony of line, beauty of proportion, and stateliness of motion which no handiwork of man has ever surpassed."

What has been called the Golden Age of Sails dates from 1850 to 1860, and it was opened by the *Sea Witch*—New York to San Francisco, around Cape Horn, in 97 days. The largest of McKay's clippers was the *Sovereign of the Seas*, 258 feet long, of 2,421 tons register. But most famous of all was the *Flying Cloud*. Great was the rejoicing in San Francisco on the last day of August, 1851, when this paragon of beauty arrived, only 89 days from New York—a real achievement.

In his interesting book *Clipper Ship Men*, Alexander Laing declares: "The clippers were half poetry." Although comparatively few of the gold hunting argonauts came to California on the clippers, and despite the fact that the powerful steamship made its appearance in California as early as 1849, the clipper ship, like the pony express, played an important as well as decidedly picturesque part in the colorful history of the emerging state. Donald McKay will be remembered for possessing the genius to create a vessel so near to perfection "that the difference is not worth an argument."

STEAMBOAT

The first steamboat in California waters was a tiny steam launch, only thirty-seven feet long, with no other name at first than "Steamboat," soon named the *Sitka*, since in 1847 it was purchased from the Russians by William A. Leidesdorff. Built at Sitka by an American, intended for the pleasure of the Russian Fur Company officers, it became known as *Little Sitka*.

The diminutive vessel was brought down to Yerba Buena (San Francisco), lashed to the deck of the sailing vessel *Naslednik*, and was intended to expedite the collection of hides and furs at various points about the San Francisco Bay region.

Its parts having been re-assembled and the boat put into running order on Yerba Buena Island, "Captain" Leidesdorff invited several gentlemen to "take a ride on the first steamer that ever spumed the waters of San Francisco Harbor." A very satisfactory showing was made. Several other short trips followed.

Then came a more severe test. Quoting from the diary of George McKinstry, Jr.:

> One bright day we left with flood-tide for the great Sacramento. A full complement of passengers was aboard, including Judge Lansford W. Hastings and Mrs. Gregson and baby. The *Sitka* was a cranky pygmy of a craft and rolled badly every minute. It was the most uncomfortable journey I have ever made. We left San Francisco on November 28th and arrived at New Helvetia December 4th—six days and seven hours out.

An old-fashioned ox-team could have made far better time!

The *Little Sitka*, instead of proving an unmixed blessing, turned out to be a sizable problem, its brief and dubious career was cut short on the last day of February, 1848 (months previous to any opportunity to participate in the great gold rush) when the first "breathing vessel" on the bay was swamped while at anchor in San Francisco. To this inglorious end it may be added that the *Little Sitka* was afterward with much labor raised and hauled away by ox-team, and with its steam engine removed, there was born a kind of schooner yacht which was named *Rainbow*. This reborn vessel served for years thereafter "as a packet on the Sacramento River."

But the lamented *Little Sitka* is to be thought of as a forerunner in California of the great age of steam navigation.

Among the numerous steamboats that were soon plying that river, mention is made of the *Antelope*, which on the 3rd of March, 1855, made the quickest trip to that date from Sacramento to San Francisco —five hours and fifty-six minutes.

The steamship *California* from New York was the first to come all the way around Cape Horn; and it was the *Oregon* that brought the glad tidings of California's admission into the Union on October 18, 1850. The powerful steamship presents quite another story from that of the tiny steamboat from Alaska.

PIONEER STEAMSHIP

It seems particularly fitting that the first steamship to complete a voyage from New York to San Francisco should bear the name *California*. The event itself was one of no small significance; it meant that the best of sailing craft, even including the graceful clipper ships, must inevitably yield sovereignty of the seas to steam vessels.

The *California* was owned by the Pacific Mail Steamship Company, whose story goes back to 1847, when Congress granted a subsidy for semi-monthly mail service from New York to Panama. Later a speculator obtained a subsidy for the Pacific side, which was purchased by William H. Aspinwall. Under his bold leadership the Company was organized in April, 1848.

It was the 6th of October, 1847, when the *California*, 1,050 tons burden, left New York almost unnoticed, for the gold excitement had not yet become general in the east. Her sister steamship, the *Oregon*, cleared late in December, and the *Panama* the following January. All were small wooden side-wheelers, but sensational reports about gold had filled all accommodations for passengers on these sister ships, while "the *California* churned her way in serene unconsciousness around the Horn."

Meanwhile there was a rush to get to Panama from New York, for the purpose of making quick connection with the *California* across the Isthmus. Through tickets on the eastern ships were oversold by the reckless agents, but how were the passengers to get from the Isthmus to San Francisco? It is reported that by the end of January some 1,400 passengers headed for California had been put ashore at Chagres!

The pilgrim adventurers made their way across the Isthmus as best they could, there to be added to those already awaiting the arrival of the *California*. Imagine the mob confusion and riotous excitement when on the 30th of January the *California* appeared and cast anchor two miles out! Those who managed to get to the steamship found their berths occupied by Peruvians! Hundreds were compelled "to find room as best they could."

At length the overcrowded vessel weighed anchor, but the hapless Peruvians had been forced to occupy the hurricane deck, while 400 eager Argonauts had taken possession of the regular sleeping quarters!

On the last day of February, 1849, the *California* completed that memorable first voyage by steam from New York to San Francisco. The side-wheeler churned through the Golden Gate, passed near the Presidio, and, in the words of Professor Ament,

> ... to the shouts of masses of spectators clustered on Telegraph Hill and gathered in dense crowds at the principal landings, paddled in past the line of the five American ships of war. Every rag of bunting had been run up, and the yards were lined with sailors. As she passed each ship a broadside in her honor boomed from the opposite battery and cheers rang from the rigging. Then she nosed through the abandoned ships and came to anchor not far from Clark's Point.

That pioneer voyage was a momentous event not only in the history of California and of navigation, but also in the history of the United States. Particularly did it reflect the enterprise and dauntless spirit of William H. Aspinwall and his associates.

The gold rush by sea had begun in earnest. The San Francisco harbor master reported that during the year 1848, 15,597 passengers arrived by ship around the Horn, and 6,489 by the route across the Isthmus of Panama. In addition to these nearly 10,000 more, picked up at various Pacific ports, joined the army of gold seekers on the ships to San Francisco in

> The days of gold,
> The days of '49.

EXPRESS BUSINESS

The well organized and efficient American postal system and the ramifying express business are commonplace today, but it was not always thus in California. We can now scarcely imagine the difficulties encountered in getting letters from the folks back east to the gold hunters in the days of '49. Complaints were loud and often angry, but even the greatest exasperation seemed to avail nothing. At the single post office in San Francisco men sometimes stood in line for hours, even all night, only too often to be told at last by the clerk, "Nothing here for you."

In the early summer of '49, Alexander Todd had an idea: for a dollar apiece he agreed to register the names of miners, make the trip to San Francisco, collect the mail addressed to his registrants, and turn them over personally at the rate of an ounce of dust per letter. Almost imme-

diately Todd was doing a lucrative business. Before many weeks his
list included upwards of 2,000 names. Other features were added, as he
also agreed to carry the miners' gold dust with him and deposit it in a
San Francisco bank for his clients for a five per cent fee; also he carried
letters down from the mining camps to be mailed at the post office. In
short, Alexander Todd became a combined mail carrier and express
man, the first regular expressman, he claimed.

That was the beginning of Todd and Company's Express, which
operated until 1851. With headquarters in Stockton, its service was
improved and expanded, daily express was introduced between the
Mother Lode centers and San Francisco, and gradually connections with
other newly established companies were made.

Another express line, with some claim to priority and significance,
was that of Weld and Company, also organized in 1849. This early
company operated between San Francisco and Marysville, by way of
Benicia and Sacramento.

Late in 1849 the powerful Adams and Company Express also appeared
in California—several lesser pioneer companies were quickly absorbed
or overshadowed; but in the rapidly shifting scenes occasioned by the
hordes of incoming gold hunters numerous companies continued to
spring up—it is reported that more than 250 in all were operating by the
year 1860.

By 1852 the Adams Company had become state-wide and had introduced new features, making it superior to any competing company.
Early in that year, however, the new firm of Wells, Fargo and Company,
or "Wells Fargo Express," eastern in its organization, made its appearance in California, and soon came to be recognized as a worthy rival
of the Adams Company. The new company undertook a very wide
range of services, all in the avowed interest of the public, and business
expanded with phenomenal rapidity.

To narrate the interesting story of Wells Fargo's bid for leadership,
the thrilling race between the two powerful companies, the final failure
of Adams and Company on "Black Friday" (February 23, 1855), and
the emergence of Wells Fargo as the supreme express company—all this
would take us too far afield. And yet it is a story typical of the stirring
history of the beginnings of the state of California.

FIRST OVERLAND PACIFIC MAIL

Better transportation and communication was one of the most urgent
needs of California during the gold days and early statehood. The gold
hunters felt that they were practically out of the world, as letters from

home were exceedingly slow in arriving and were few and far between. Many a lonely argonaut was tempted to start back to "Ameriky"—the United States seemed almost like a distant planet!

A good many stage companies sprang up, usually with Sacramento as the center. But the first great stage line affording transcontinental service, one of the longest continuous runs anywhere, was the "Southern Overland Mail," operated by John Butterfield, "the new ruler of the stages." According to the terms of his contract, he was to equip, stock, and furnish personnel for a route of almost 2,800 miles, all to be ready within a twelve-month period. For such a task he had to invoke all his previous experience and his executive ability.

To avoid the snows of the Rocky Mountains the route far to the south was chosen, via El Paso, Yuma, and Los Angeles. At first the schedule was set at twenty-five days, later cut to twenty-three days. On the 15th of September, 1858, the coaches started simultaneously at St. Louis and San Francisco, a truly dramatic event. The company's equipment included 100 staunchly built Concord stages, 1,000 horses, 500 mules and 750 men—150 of them drivers. Regular fare was $100, gold; letter postage was ten cents per half-ounce. It was indeed a daring enterprise.

A great ovation awaited each stage at its destination. In San Francisco the event was graphically described by the *Bulletin*, which gives this account:

> At a quarter after four o'clock the coach turned from Market into Montgomery Street. The driver blew his horn and cracked his whip. . . . At the same time a shout was raised, that ran with the rapidity of an electric flash along Montgomery Street, which throughout its length was crowded by an excited populace. As the coach dashed along through the crowds, the hats of the spectators were whirled in the air and the hurrah was repeated from a thousand throats, responsive to which the driver, the lion of the occasion, doffed his weather-beaten old slouch, and in uncovered dignity, like the victor of an old Olympic race, guided his foaming steeds toward the Post Office.

Travel by the Butterfield Overland Mail was far from luxurious. On the long journey, which sometimes required two or three days beyond schedule, occasionally saving a day or two, the only regular stop-overs were to change horses. There were no facilities for sleeping on the coach, and arrangement for meals *en route* were totally inadequate. There was no lack of complaints from many of the passengers, although others, who had experienced rough Western life, "pronounced the ride a thrill and a pleasure."

Several different overland postal routes were established, some of them with slight consideration for their real merits. In a time of reckless adventure it was scarcely to be expected that all plans would be scientifically drafted or that modern-type blueprints be prepared.

The early stage driver earned a place of honor all his own in those early days. Among the leaders are remembered Hank Monk, Ben Holladay, and "Old Brady"; but all must yield the palm to Dave Berry, who, many years later, had the reputation of being the oldest stage driver in California, claiming the astounding record of "half a million miles on the box of a stage coach."

The stage business enjoyed its golden era from 1858 to the Civil War. In the meantime the Pony Express dramatically appears on the scene: this in turn is superseded by the electric telegraph, and at length the iron horse crosses the continent. It's all a thrilling story. The Californians must be served. No wonder elaborate plans were made for a great Centennial Celebration at San Diego and numerous points from St. Louis west to the Pacific.

PONY EXPRESS

The unprecedented influx of gold hunters, beginning early in 1849, greatly stimulated the demand for more speedy communication between California and the east. The ponderous ox-drawn "prairie schooner" was altogether too slow. The steamship from New York or Boston and the overland stage were still not fast enough.

B. F. Ficklin of the transportation firm of Russell, Majors, and Waddell, conceived the idea of a much more rapid transit service from the Missouri River to California. He talked it over with Senator William H. Gwin in Washington, who, in January, 1855, introduced in the Senate a bill proposing weekly letter express service between St. Louis and San Francisco. Little was done for several years, however, largely because Congress was preoccupied with the crucial questions of slavery and slavery extension. But to George Chorpenning must be accorded much credit for giving reality to the idea, because in 1858 he actually made the trip from Washington, D.C., to Sacramento in seventeen days, bringing President Buchanan's message to Congress.

In the winter of 1859-60 William H. Russell, making the acquaintance of Senator Gwin, became alert to the situation—he thought he saw a good business opening. His partners were skeptical about any prospect of financial profits, but Russell had virtually made a commitment for the firm, so, early in 1860 they formed a new corporation and entered upon a period of tremendous activity.

The corporation took over the old stage line and organized the Pony Express line, first between St. Joseph and Salt Lake City. Full announcement of the service by the Central Overland California and Pike's Peak Express Company was made in the St. Louis *Republic* and the New York *Herald* on March 26th, 1860. "To San Francisco in 8 days!" Within two months the first pony express was all set to start from San Francisco and St. Louis simultaneously.

Full equipment called for nearly 500 horses, 190 stations, and 80 carefully selected young riders, each riding an average of thirty to thirty-five miles. The entire route was almost 2,000 miles. Great preparations were made to celebrate the actual start of the unique experiment of the Pony Express. On the afternoon of April 3, 1860, the outgoing mail from San Francisco was put upon a river steamer for Sacramento, while at the same time the west-bound mail, neatly tucked in four small pouches, was placed in the *mochilla*, and the young rider spurred his pony toward the next station west.

Nine days and twenty-three hours were occupied by the first trip westward from St. Joseph to Sacramento, scarcely half the time required by the Butterfield stage! The arrival of the first incoming express was the occasion for one of the most enthusiastic demonstrations in California's early history. The event was thus described by Senator Cornelius Cole in his personal *Memoirs*:

> Those who were there to witness it will never forget the arrival of the first of these pony expressmen in Sacramento. It was an occasion of great rejoicing and everybody, big and little, old and young, turned out to see the fun. All business for the time was suspended; even the courts adjourned for the event. . . . The little rider upon his blooded charger, under whip and spur, came down upon them like a meteor, but made not the slightest halt to greet his many visitors. . . . The whole cavalcade, shouting and cheering, some waving banners and bareheaded, riding at the top of their speed, dashing down J Street, might have been taken . . . for a band of wild Comanches.

The Pony Express proved to be the forerunner of the railroad in transporting mail to California, and that the route was feasible, the mountains could be crossed. But, interesting and romantic as it was, it quickly and completely disappeared after the completion of the electric telegraph, for, as a writer said, "The pony was fast, but it could not compete with the lightning." Of all the long list of worthy pony riders "Buffalo Bill" (William Cody) gained the greatest renown, and along with it a rather legendary character.

CAMEL CORPS

As the gold rush reached its height, a magnet drawing hordes of adventurous people into California, over devious trails and primitive roads, as well as 'round the Horn and across the Isthmus, the urgent appeals, amounting to imperious demand, for better transportation and overland mail service became incessant. The various responses constitute picturesque chapters in our history.

While the steam railroad and the electric telegraph were still in a nebulous stage, Jefferson Davis was laying plans for what seemed a preposterous experiment of introducing camels as a help to military transportation and a protection against hostile Indians in the southwest. Even before that George H. Crossman, Dept. Quartermaster-General, had conceived the idea (as early as 1848) of using the camel. His subordinate, Major Henry Wayne, investigated, and the more he investigated the more enthusiastic he became.

After three attempts to obtain a Congressional appropriation were ridiculed out of court, Jefferson Davis, then War Secretary, was able to obtain an appropriation of $30,000, in the year 1854. Wayne was appointed to head an exedition to Egypt and the Levant to purchase camels. His experiences were indeed unique, to say the least. "News of my coming flew before me on the wind," he reported, "and every sore-backed and superannuated camel in Asia Minor was doctored up and hurried to the coast to be generously offered to the United States at a grievous sacrifice of ten times its value."

Finally thirty-four of the gangling animals arrived at Indianola, Texas, where, when they reached terra firma, "They reared, kicked, cried, broke their halters, tore up the picket lines, and engaged in other fantastic tricks such as pawing and biting each other."

The expedition, under Edward F. Beale, set out for Fort Defiance, New Mexico on the 25th of June, 1857. The camels were on their way to California. Beale expressed delight in the way he thought the strange creatures could stand up to the travel—he believed they were sure-footed and could go on continuously barefooted over the difficult stony trail. But it was found that their padded feet could not bear the small (*malpais*) surface stones.

From San Antonio to the Colorado River, a distance of more than 1,200 miles, the trip required four months. The expedition arrived at Cajon Pass in late November, 1857—"twenty-four dromedaries and camels, a few Arabs, mules, etc." Beale had decided to treat the town of Los Angeles to a surprise. Selecting "Hi Jolly" (Hadj Ali) to accompany him, his small party reached the *pueblo* on November 9, 1857, at mid-afternoon. The inhabitants, their *siestas* just completed, were suddenly astir, their horses stampeded, trying to escape those ungainly, hump-backed animals. After two days of real excitement in the usually sleepy *pueblo*, the drivers again set off, heading toward San Fernando Mission and Fort Tejon, terminus of the long road and home for the camels.

Fort Tejon, now a historic site on Highway 99, had been an army post for three years. It served as a protection to the Indian reservation, primarily to prevent the white settlers from molesting them or dispoiling them of their land. It was there that camels were kept for a few years.

Every important post from Texas to California had its quota of camels and there were grounds for hope of success for the experiment, but the dream about the "Ships of the Desert" ended in disillusion and failure. The camels did not live up to their reputation in the rugged terrain of the desert floor; and, what was worse, they were extremely unpopular both with their keepers and with the American horses and mules. "Neither teamster, nor vaquero, nor army man wanted anything to do with the 'misshapen beast'." Americans seemed totally unwilling to understand them. Then came the Civil War, which speedily dealt the Camel Corps its death blow.

So strange legends were created about the camel roaming the desert wastes of the southwest. Some dromedaries were actually released in southern Arizona. There was "a great red camel," or "an ancient white one," or "a shadowy misshapen form," as Harlan Fowler has written, "drifting through the desert like a ship with ragged sails." The first appearance in California of the Camel Corps came near being its last. But it added a weird chapter to our history of many colors and a strange bit of legendry to our southwestern folk-lore. On Highway 60, west of Wickenberg, Arizona, now stands a monument to "Hi Jolly."

STEAM RAILROAD

The famous Gold Rush to California quickly brought to focus one of the greatest problems of the West, that of better transportation and communication. There was no end of discussion and speculation among the gold hunters regarding the practicability of the steam railroad.

As early as 1852 a small group of pioneers, including William T. Sherman, later of Civil War fame, conceived the idea of a railroad that would tap the mining regions of the upper Mother Lode by linking them with Sacramento, and thus shipping on the river to San Francisco. Sam Brannan was said to be the first man to propose such a railway.

As the idea germinated a young engineer named Theodore Judah was employed to make surveys, in 1854, for a possible roadway.

The first project was to build north to Marysville, then known as Mountain City, with branches to Coloma, Nevada City, and Stockton, but financial difficulties and the problem of shipping rolling stock from New York around Cape Horn prevented such a consummation.

Actual ground-breaking for a road that was to connect Sacramento with Folsom (a town founded by the railroad itself), a distance of a little less than twenty-five miles to the northeast, took place early in 1855. On the 9th day of August of that year the first rail was laid. Soon a trial run was made over a portion of the road. The short road to Folsom was completed on Washington's Birthday, 1856. It was known as the Sacramento Valley Railroad, and was California's first bona-fide steam railroad.

The maiden trip over the new road was described by the *Sacramento Union*:

> The occasion was marked by the gathering of a large crowd of people at the depot, who gazed upon the iron horse, harnessed for the first time, with mingled feelings of surprise and admiration. The train, consisting of three platform cars and the engine, was densely crowded. It started from the levee at about half past six amid the cheers of the excursionists.

In honor of the president of the Company the pioneer locomotive was named "C. K. Garrison," but later the named was changed to "Pioneer," since it was the first to be operated in California. The first conductor was George T. Bromley. The passenger fare was set at $2 each way.

At the Folsom terminus stages and freight wagons met the trains, carrying passengers and freight to such mining towns as Yankee Jim's, Cook's Bar, Fiddletown, and Mormon Island. At Sacramento connections were made with steamboats and other vessels down the river to San Francisco.

Within a few years (in 1865) the "Big Four" of the Central Pacific (Stanford, Huntington, Crocker, Hopkins) acquired the Valley Road properties, but the pioneer road was not suitably located to be linked into the great transcontinental system.

A Centennial Celebration was staged in Sacramento on the 12th day of February, 1955, commemorating the ground-breaking for the pioneer railroad. A bronze plaque marks the site at Third and R Streets. Perhaps the road was a very small affair, but it was a true pioneer.

The story of the first transcontinental railroad, culminating in the driving of the golden spike at Promontory, Utah, is one of the most thrilling in all the annals of California, with both local and national importance. A telegraphic dispatch announced the consummation thus: "*The last rail is laid! The last spike is driven! The Pacific Railroad is completed!*"

The first railroad in Southern California resulted from the enterprise of Phineas Banning, who operated a stage and freighting line between Los Angeles and Wilmington. In the autumn of 1869 the first train made its run over the Los Angeles and San Pedro Railroad.

Meanwhile the Southern Pacific was incorporated (1865), and in April, 1877, Los Angeles was given its first transcontinental connection by the driving of the golden spike at Soledad. We have thus witnessed the beginnings of one of the great railway networks of America.

ELECTRIC TELEGRAPH

A prevision of the magnetic telegraph for California was caught as early as 1849, when Joseph W. Revere published *A Tour of Duty*. Said Revere:

> There is another suggestion I would make, at the risk of being deemed visionary, and that is, the extension of the *Magnetic Telegraph* with all convenient speed, from St. Louis to San Francisco. . . . As a means of communication . . . the value of this telegraph can hardly be appreciated. . . .

It was not, however, until September, 1853, that the first local electric telegraph in California was celebrated. The wire stretched from the lighthouse at Point Lobos to the western city limits of San Francisco, at Larkin Street, thence along Broadway to Stockton Street, along Stockton to Sacramento Street, and on to the Merchants' Exchange (between Montgomery and Sansome Streets). The system was constructed by Sweeny and Bough for the purpose of giving shipping information.

We read in the *Alta California* of September 12, 1851, "The telegraph of Messrs. Sweeny and Bough of the Merchants' Exchange, is now in successful operation. The clipper ship *Crescent*, which arrived yesterday, was the first vessel reported by it." But the formal celebration of the opening took place on the 22nd of September. We quote from an editorial in the *Alta* of the 23rd:

OPENING OF THE TELEGRAPH

> Yesterday the opening ceremonies of the first magnetic telegraph company established and put in operation in the State of California were performed at the marine telegraph station at Point Lobos, eight miles from San Francisco. A magnificent dinner was given by Messrs. Sweeny and Bough, the proprietors of the line, to which about 300 of our citizens sat down . . . after the dinner a meeting was organized at which T. H.

Selby, Esquire, was called to the chair. . . . The English, French, and Danish consuls were present. . . . During the festivities many messages were sent into town and answered. The party separated about 6 o'clock, in good spirits, and very much gratified with the opening ceremonies.

The first message from San José to San Francisco, recorded by the *Alta* of October 13, 1853 is rather prosaic in character:

> Messrs. J. H. Coghill & Co.
> Send by the Steamer *Guadaloupe* tomorrow ten half
> barrels of clear pork.
>   G. H. Bodfish

When communication between San Francisco and Marysville was completed and "the first message was sent over the whole district," on October 24th, the *Alta* two days later recognized this through communication as "an era in our history."

The first message to the interior was sent over the wires of the California State Telegraph Company on the 24th of October. The line was completed between San Francisco and Los Angeles on October 8, 1860, when Mayor Mellus of Los Angeles and H. F. Teschamacher, President of San Francisco Board of Supervisors, exchanged messages.

The day of days was October 24, 1861, when, the transcontinental line having been completed, this thrilling message was flashed to President Lincoln:

> To his Excellency, the President
> Washington,
> D.C.
>   I announce to you that the telegraph to California has this day been completed. May it be a bond of perpetuity between the States of the Atlantic and those of the Pacific.
>   (Signed) Horace W. Carpenter
>   President, Overland Telegraph Co.

In his official message to the President, Governor John G. Downey used these prophetic words:

> May the golden links of the Constitution ever unite us as one happy and free people.

An immediate result of the transcontinental operation of Morse's "scientific miracle of the age" was the final doom of the romantic Pony Express; but the total influence of the telegraph with all of its ramifications in California history is clearly incalculable.

TELEPHONE

On the 7th day of March, 1876, U.S. Patent number 174,465 was issued to Alexander Graham Bell, of Salem, Massachusetts. Bell's application was for an "improvement in telegraphy"; his patent, however, signalized the official birth of the telephone. Bell himself has been immortalized as "The Man Who Contracted Space."

Almost immediately this revolutionary new invention was brought to California and put to use, at first in a very limited way, to be sure. The first telephone, a short private line established in 1876, connected the Merchants' Exchange with Meigg's Wharf, in San Francisco. A second private line was established the following spring, connecting the office of Frederick Marriott, Sr., then publisher of the *San Francisco News Letter*, on Merchant Street with his residence on Jones Street.

In the summer of 1877 the first simple telephone switchboard, serving eighteen subscribers, was installed in the office of the Gold and Stock Telegraph Company, at 222 Sansome Street. In the following year this firm became known as the American Speaking Telephone Company.

It was only natural that before long a rival company was put into operation, known as the National Bell Telephone Company. But, generally speaking, the extension of the use of the telephone was slow during those first years, and was practically confined to the San Francisco area.

With the coming of the 1880's progress became more marked. It may be said that the year 1882 marks the real beginning of the wider use of telephony in California. It was in that year that George Chaffey, who had met Mr. Bell at the Centennial Exposition in 1876 and had been struck with the possibilities of his invention, installed a private line from the city of San Bernardino to the newly founded settlement of Etiwanda, later extending it to Ontario, located six miles to the west. This is claimed to be, for that time, the longest line in operation in the world, as well as the first long-distance telephone in California. San Francisco's long-distance service began in 1883, by connecting with the city of San José.

In 1894 a switchboard for the Chinese population in San Francisco was established by Loo Kim Shu. The original members numbered 100, but in the course of time they increased to thousands.

The famous demonstration of the transcontinental telephone took place in the historic year 1915, when Alexander Graham Bell dramatically greeted Thomas A. Watson of San Francisco with "Come here, Watson, I want you." Watson responded immediately.

From such beginnings has developed one of the modern wonders of the scientific world—a striking exemplification of the advancing age of automation. If they had not already become commonplace in our modern life, such phases as the international, mobile conversation, news dispatches, radio-telephone, submarine cable, and many others, would appear truly miraculous. California has become a world leader in the number of telephones in operation, as well as in the wide variety and technical intricacy of applications.

CABLE CAR

The world's first cable car rumbled up Clay Street to Nob Hill, San Francisco, on the first day of August, 1873. On the 21st of March, 1953, the inventor, a canny Scotchman named Andrew Smith Hallidie, was honored by the dedication of a bronze plaque in Portsmouth Plaza. After more than four-fifths of a century the cable car still rumbles amiably in San Francisco, though in itself now little more than a "cocky little relic of by-gone days," a bewitching footnote to California history.

But there's a story back of the cable car. It took its beginning from one of the many "crazy dreams" that have made the City by the Golden Gate unique among world metropolitan centers, a city of surprises, a city with a soul. The cable car went to the heart of the people and made a place for itself in their affections that is still so conspicuous in the folk-lore of the old-timer, and a true Mecca for myriads of pilgrim tourists.

Early in 1872 a number of San Franciscans, including Hallidie and Henry L. Davis, became interested in the problem of running a railroad from the business section of the city up Russian Hill. About that time a skilled civil engineer named William Eppelsheimer, well recommended by industrialist Irving Scott, was employed by Hallidie, then a manufacturer of wire rope, and set to work to devise some kind of cable road that could conquer the steepest streets. By capitalizing on the ingenuity of Eppelsheimer, Hallidie was able to solve the problem of applying the cable, thus making it effective in providing practical transportation on the steep grades of San Francisco hills. The fortunate result was the cable car for the flamboyant city of contrasting lights and shades.

The cable gained rapidly in popularity. Before the great disaster of 1906, "they were all over town," the grandest line of all running right down Market Street. But only a few lines survived the earthquake and fire, for in the meantime the electric car lines had been established, and most of the cable lines were converted to electricity.

In November, 1929, the "beloved Pacific Avenue line" was abandoned;

and when the two-block line on Fillmore Street was dropped in April, 1941, and several longer lines in 1955, it really looked as if San Francisco was destined to lose her cable cars altogether.

That was too much! For the past decade there has been an intermittent battle royal between the sentimental and the "practical" forces of San Francisco, in the Board of Supervisors, in the ballot box, and everywhere, and the end is not yet. Banners have been displayed announcing "WE LOVE OUR CABLES" and "LET'S KEEP OUR CABLES," impassioned speeches have been made by vociferous women leaders, sentimental letters have appeared in the newspapers. One enthusiast went so far as to declare, "San Francisco without cable cars would be like Washington without the Capitol."

If pure sentiment and sanctimonious utterances are not enough to insure the retention of at least a token cable car system, then comes the hard-headed corollary that the total abolishment of the cables would now result in a net financial loss to the city, for San Francisco is also commercially minded, and the claim that recent publicity of the cable car has alone brought millions of dollars to her coffers from the pockets of untold numbers of tourists is hard to refute.

The cable car came the better part of a century ago, and if it has since become an antique, it should still be retained, say the citizens, for San Francisco seems determined to cling to her title as "the city that knows how." Little did Andy Hallidie, the canny Scotchman, imagine when his first car rumbled up Clay Street back in 1873 that it would one day loose such an avalanche of emotion as to engulf the entire community! He could not have dreamed of the sentimental attachment for the product of his genius by the nostalgic citizens of the kaleidoscopic city four-fifths of a century later.

Two famous lines remain in operation today: California Street, topping Nob Hill; and Powell Street, from Market to Fisherman's Wharf, with its picturesque man-powered turntable sandwiched between streams of motor-powered vehicles.

BICYCLE

William K. Clarkson was granted a patent on bicycles June 26, 1819—but they were then called "improved curricles," and for many years they were known as velocipedes. Another name sometimes applied to the contraptions was "Swift Walkers."

Bicycles were slow in making their appearances in California. San Francisco was the state's chief metropolitan center, but the sandy, unpaved streets and the steep hills of the city offered little encouragement for their introduction there.

In the course of time, however, a shrewd Yankee promoter saw certain new possibilities in the old Mechanics' Pavilion. Without hesitation he imported a supply of seventy-five second-hand bicycles to be offered for hire to the brave and hardy men who wished to rent them. These had the immense front wheel of that day.

The first organization of a bicycle club in San Francisco dates its origin in 1879. It boasted among its charter members, Columbus Waterhouse and George C. Perkins—the Perkins who later became governor of California. The bicycles then, and for some years later, had the lofty front wheel and tiny rear wheel, both with iron tires. It was something of a feat to mount one of the "high horses" and venture forth for a spin around the block, or to the park.

The first Rover Safety, with wheels of equal size, arrived in Oakland in 1887. Several months later the "safety" was introduced in San Francisco, where at first it met the jeers of the public. Some called it "Mohrig's goat." For a time the veteran wheelmen persisted in pedalling their high-wheelers and refused to have anything to do with the "monstrosity" called a safety.

But in 1888 the first safety championship races in the state were held in the city of Stockton. Tires of solid rubber made their appearance. In the early 1890's the pneumatic tires came into use, and professional men were not long in recognizing the advantages to be derived from the use of the improved types of bicycles.

By the end of 1893, 4,000 persons were riding the safeties in San Francisco alone. The bicycle had come to be a recognized and significant part of the professional and sports life of California's metropolis, as well as throughout the state generally. But it was not long until it was quite overshadowed by the "horseless carriage"—the automobile was to bring about an unprecedented revolution in the field of transportation. The bicycle is now mostly for young children. At any large city school will be found hundreds of the "kids' bikes."

AUTOMOBILE

Professor Clyde King is authority for the statement, "The gas-driven machine has brought an era as distinctive and creative as that brought by steam." France claims the honor of producing the first real automobile, in the year 1891. By the opening of the twentieth century they had become well established in the United States.

Here was another golden opportunity for California and the Golden State was alert. This land of beauty, romance, open spaces, and long distances could not remain disobedient to such a heavenly call. But first, there must be roads, for "an automobile without roads was as useless as a pen without ink." Accordingly, the Highway Commission was created by act of the legislature and approved by Governor James N. Gillett, March 22, 1909, authorizing a state bond issue of $18,000,000. That marked the beginning of the biggest road-building job up to that date.

It was high time! For in 1898 the first automobile was chugging along the streets of Oakland, first automobile in Pacific Coast history. It had been built by W. L. Elliott. When his outlandish contraption came sputtering down the avenue, the surprised people didn't know what to do; they were filled with amazement when Elliott navigated his machine up Mt. Hamilton, a run of fifty-six miles, on the 13th of September, 1898—elapsed time, five and a half hours; gasoline used, five gallons. In *Days of a Man* — his great Autobiography — David Starr Jordan refers interestingly to his experience in the Elliott automobile, in these words:

> It ran well on level ground, but a test in hill climbing was of course necessary. [Bailey Millard had invited Jordan to accompany him for the *San Francisco Examiner* on the Mt. Hamilton trip.] The machine crept gingerly up the twenty-six miles of sharply winding road to the summit, and in coming down wore out all the crude brakes devised by the inventor. But the essential fact remained that a horseless vehicle built in California had successfully climbed 4,400 feet of mountain.

The first automobiles were no "mollycoddle affairs." They afforded no protection to riders from wind, sun, rain, dust, and flying objects by "such affectations as wind shield, top, or fenders."

It took time and experience before the automobile won its way to popular favor. Even Woodrow Wilson, then President of Princeton University, blamed it for "the spread of socialistic feeling," calling it "a picture of the arrogance of wealth, with all its independence and carelessness." But following the great San Francisco disaster of April 18, 1906, "the fledgling auto proved its worth," not only to California but to the nation.

Then it was that General Frederick Funston's Army regiment from the Presidio took to the automobiles, mobilizing a force to fight the swiftly spreading fire and extending the far-flung supply-lines to give aid to thousands fleeing for their lives to places of safety. "Motor cars, piloted by their goggled owners, jounced over the debris-littered cobbles with cargoes of dynamite and other emergency equipment." Said one contemporary account:

> Many a family was enabled to escape from a home that is now a heap

of fire-stained ruins, with enough of household belongings to make life tolerable in the genial climate of California. . . . The value of services rendered by automobiles to San Francisco in her day of destruction and terrible peril can hardly be overestimated.

No other wheeled vehicles could be requisitioned on that fateful day than the motor car—it was on that day that the automobile in California came of age. It was no longer a nuisance in San Francisco, it was a blessing and a godsend.

In a single generation the registration of American automobiles in the state leaped from none at all to millions. And California has become the motor car state *par excellence*. The United States has set the pace for motorizing the world. In California, with its vast system of paved highways, is to be witnessed daily moving exhibition of a remarkable spirit of progress in the innumerable motorcade — a phenomenon unmatched by any other industry in the history of the race.

STATE ROADS

With the official signing of a document dated February 28, 1896, the Lake Tahoe State Wagon Road, including the Placerville Road from the junction near Smith's Flat to the Nevada line, became the first state road of California.

Effective agitation immediately preceding had resulted in an act "to create a Bureau of Highways and prescribe its duties and powers"— approved by Governor James H. Budd, March 27, 1895. Members of the Bureau drove a team of horses hitched to a sturdily built "buckboard" into every county of the state and then made a report to the governor. The historic report recommended an extensive system of state highways, to include twenty-eight routes—all before the dawning of the automobile era. The map filed at that time corresponds to a remarkable degree with the main features of the automobile system of highways developed in the past half-century.

In the minutes of the first meeting of the newly created Bureau of Highways, held at Sacramento April 11, 1895, we read:

> This is to certify that at a meeting of the members of the Bureau of Highways, *viz*: Marsden Manson, Joseph Lees Maude and Richard C. Irvine; held in the office of the State Surveyor-General this 11th day of April 1895 at 11:30 a.m., under Section 7, Chapter CCIII, of the Act approved March 27, 1895 . . .

The first work actually done on the projected state road consisted in

the construction of an 80-foot stone arch over the South Fork at River-
ton, which, with its approaches, was completed in the year 1901.

During the next several years numerous primitive log bridges, brush
fills, and stretches of corduroy road were replaced by improved bridges
and culverts and safe roadbed. The present generation of Californians
has no conception of the execrable quality of most early roads.

In this connection many will be surprised at the conspicuous part
played by the bicycle in advancing the cause of good roads. In a bulletin
Mr. Irvine stated:

> The influence of the bicycle upon this agitation for improved highways
> cannot be overestimated . . . this agitation for better roads is due more
> directly to the efforts of the wheelmen than to any other one cause.
>
> Any machine which enables a man to travel with pleasure, without
> discomfort and practically without expense, forty miles a day, is evidently
> one which has come to stay and the number of wheelmen will surely reach
> extraordinary proportions in the years to come.

It was clearly perceived by far-seeing leaders that good roads in
California were to prove a boon to all classes of inhabitants—farmers,
merchants, professional people, and tourists. A new Department of
Highways superseded the Bureau in 1897. But it was not long after that
until the first scenes of an astounding new drama were being enacted—
the automobile was coming!

The California Highway Commission was created by an act approved
by Governor James N. Gillett, March 22, 1909, and ratified by the people,
"to have full authority over the construction of a great system of highways under an $18,000,000 state bond issue." The amazing era of modern
highways for the Golden State was thus proclaimed to the wide world.

But still greater things lie ahead. California's share in the current
Federal Highway Program, calling for the expenditure of many billions
of dollars, is alone more than two billion dollars, to be spread over a
period of thirteen years. In spite of all this, and still other plans now
contemplated, however, the highway system will still prove inadequate;
for the demanding population of the state is expected to be 20,000,000
by 1970, while the number of vehicles will be at least 12,000,000.

California has become the world's chief playground; tourism has
become a vast industry; millions have succumbed to the fascinations of
the country, the attractiveness of climatic conditions, the opportunities
for earning a good livelihood and the progressive spirit of the people.
For all this the unmatched highways of the state are justly regarded as
an indispensable factor.

MOTOR BUS

In 1913 there sprang up in Los Angeles and other centers a nickel "jitney" service, which, with amazing rapidity reached thousands of individually owned second-hand automobiles. These motor cars, Fords predominating, were touring models in all stages of decrepitude. They were now made to carry unbelievable loads of human freight, and at the rush hours they almost choked the city streets.

The jitneys were not long in extending their operation to interurban runs, and, as service expanded, the owners began to use higher types of used cars. Where the matter would end, nobody knew, for everybody seemed to be doing it — artisans driving to and from their jobs; venturesome youth saw a prospect of interesting work and quick profits; nondescript workers and many unemployed wished to try their hand at the sporadic business; speculators were quick to see the chance for combinations with consequent gains.

The jitney grew to such popularity it became a serious competitor of the street car. There seemed to be a certain exhilaration about crowding into an old automobile and for some time it had the novelty of a fad, as well as affording real economy. Its shortcomings were readily overlooked, but it proved to be undependable even as a fair-weather bus, as on stormy days the people were glad to resort to the neglected street car.

By 1916 there were many individual jitney lines on interurban runs such as San Francisco to San José, Sacramento to Stockton, Los Angeles to Santa Barbara and to San Diego, and San Diego to Imperial Valley points. With no close co-ordination, but with keen competition, combination was inevitable.

The result of economical and successful motor bus operation was to the detriment or ruin of the competing railroads. Therefore the street car companies, forced to analyze the situation, perceived that there were certain advantages in motor bus operation and that under some conditions bus lines could be more economically operated than street railways. Gradually the idea emerged that the ideal transportation system would include the motor bus operated in coordination with the street cars.

It is clear, therefore, that the established railways adopted motor bus service in order to keep unified control in their own hands and more adequately to fulfill the obligation placed upon them by the public to operate this unified transportation system in the interest of the general weal.

The squadrons of jitneys disappeared from the city streets as quickly as they had come. Los Angeles is believed to have passed the first ordinance in the United States to take care of the outlaw jitneys. Viewed as a phenomenon of transportation, the privately owned horde of motley jitney busses thronging the streets of our cities for a time, must be regarded as a passing phase of the fascinating story of transportation. By the statute of May 1, 1917, the state legislature placed the control of motor bus transportation definitely in the hands of the California Railroad Commission, and similar action followed in practically all of the states.

AVIATION

California has almost over-night become the aviator's paradise. The growth of aviation has been sudden, spectacular, and transforming. Of the almost inexhaustible list of "firsts" in this magical industry only a select few may be included here.

On the second day of July, 1869, according to Marion and Marvin Martin, writing for *Westways* magazine (April, 1935), "the first aircraft, invented by a Californian and built in California, was launched upon a successful flight—thirty-four years before the famed Wright brothers got off the ground. Frederick Marriott, editor and publisher of the *San Francisco News-Letter*, was the inventor and builder of the 'Avitor,' as the plane was called." The company had been incorporated August 31, 1866: the "Avitor" was granted a patent November 23, 1869. But Marriott's patented machine was destined to be premature, really ahead of his times.

In an article on "California's Forgotten Eagle" (*Westways*, December, 1941) Farnsworth Crowder calls attention to John Montgomery, "aviation's forgotten man," who, two decades before the Wright brothers made history at Kitty Hawk, literally "took to the air," in an attempt which was at least something for the record. Twelve miles south of San Diego a tall monument, in the form of a stainless steel wing anchored in a concrete base, bears this inscription:

> John J. Montgomery made man's first controlled winged flight from this hilltop, August, 1883. He opened for all mankind, "the great highway of the sky."

It is claimed that Montgomery's glider flew a distance of 600 feet from the take-off. A San Diego airport, named Montgomery Field, has been dedicated to the memory of this heroic pioneer. San Diego has been called the "Cradle of Western aviation."

On the campus of the University of Santa Clara stands a tall granite shaft bearing this inscription:

                         Erected
              By the Citizens of Santa Clara
                       In Honor of
                        Professor
                  JOHN J. MONTGOMERY
                   The Father of Aviation
                Who from this spot sent aloft
                      Apr. 29, 1905
              The First Heavier than Air Glider
                   In Controlled Flight
              And Maintained Equilibrium

America's first international Air Meet occurred at Dominguez Field, near Los Angeles, January 10-21, 1910. It was on this memorable occasion that Paulham established the world record for sustained flight, piloting his Bleriot monoplane from the Field of Santa Ana Ranch and back, in forty-five minutes.

Next came the first attempt to land an airplane on the deck of a ship, on the 18th of January, 1911, in San Francisco Bay. A special platform had been constructed on the stern of the warship *Pennsylvania,* with a score of ropes stretching across this "runway," their slack ends being weighed down with sandbags. The landing was indeed dramatic. "The feat that many had pronounced impossible," wrote Robert Clark (*Westways,* February, 1947), "had now been accomplished." And continuing, Clark said, "Thus was the beginning of what was to make in thirty short years the most radical change in naval warfare."

The 23rd of September of that same year the inaugural flight of the official United States air-mail dispatch took place with Earle Ovington as pilot. Twenty years later, the same pilot re-enacted the historic scene in a tri-motored transport, accompanied by former Postmaster-General Hitchcock and six other national dignitaries. A special consignment of cachet mail was carried on a 1,000-mile trip from United Airport at Burbank, California, to numerous points in Southern California and Nevada.

The first regular passenger plane service between the town of Wilmington and Santa Catalina was instituted July 4, 1919, by the Chaplin Air Line. This was claimed to be the first commercial venture of the kind on record. The plane "Seagull" took off at 5 o'clock on that Fourth of July morning.

Air mail had its beginning in 1918, the terminal points being New York and Washington, D.C. But so obvious were the quickly perceived advantages that only three years later letters were flown across the continent to California in thirty-three hours. The growth of air mail has been truly phenomenal. The air mail service, as well as the passenger service, is undergoing constant improvement. Amazing as it may seem, in 1955 eight of the fifteen largest passenger carriers of the nation were airlines.

It was not until the 15th of October, 1944, that daily air-freight service was inaugurated, by American Airlines. The first plane, crowded with war priority freight and surplus space filled with Hollywood fashions, shoes, and 5,000 pounds of spinach, took off from Burbank for eastern centers. For years Los Angeles has claimed the distinction of being the world capital of commercial aviation.

The great variety and magnitude of air service is now almost bewildering. It has come to be a vital part of modern American living. Many sub-topics may be mentioned, such as air-mail, airports, gliders, helicopters, bombers, parachutes, jet planes, and women aviators. "The fastest fifty years in history"—these words were employed to characterize the half-century ending in 1953, and no end is in sight.

PANAMA CANAL

From the time when Vasco Nuñez de Balboa marched to the edge of the mighty Pacific, in 1513, and thus made it known to the civilized world, the problem of connecting the Atlantic and the Pacific by a waterway engaged the attention of thoughtful men. The subject was to hold vast significance for the history of California.

No wonder that for generations diligent search was made for a natural waterway. The Spanish authorities earnestly desired to establish convenient communication with their early settlement at Panama. From the *Geographical and Historical Dictionary of the West Indies* these strange words are quoted:

> In the time of Philip II it was proposed to cut a canal through the Isthmus of Panama, for the passage of ships from one ocean to the other: and two Flemish engineers were sent to examine the place with that object. They, however, found the obstacles insuperable, and the Council of the Indies at the same time represented to the king the injuries which such a canal would occasion to the monarchy; in consequence of which his majesty directed that no one should in future attempt, or even propose, such undertaking, under pain of death.

But that was not the end of the matter. At the time it was not known that the narrowest part of the continent was there. However, nothing tangible came of the wishful thinking during the Spanish régime, and when Spain lost the American colonies after the revolutions ending in 1823, the subject of an inter-ocean canal was dropped for a while, although before California became an American state negotiations were begun several times with Central American nations "looking toward the construction of a canal." French companies also expressed definite interest.

In the same period a franchise was given Aspinwall, Stevens, and Chauncey, representing American interest, to construct a railroad across the Isthmus. The railroad was actually built between 1850 and 1855. The Panama Railroad brought much benefit, but need for a canal was still felt.

Details of the many attempts and activities looking toward the construction of an inter-continental canal cannot be recounted here. The barest outline of a few must suffice. The appointment of a Canal Commission in 1872 by President Grant is a single expression of our national interest.

In 1876 came a report favoring a Nicaragua Canal over the Panama location. For years the question "Nicaragua *versus* Panama" was discussed everywhere, and was a favorite topic of college debating societies and civic clubs.

The Colombian government in 1878 granted a concession to Ferdinand de Lesseps and associates, with the approval of the French government, which gave France "the exclusive right for ninety-nine years to build and operate a canal between the oceans," under specified conditions. There were heavy expenditures, but the French enterprise was never completed.

On the 3rd of March, 1899, the U.S. Congress empowered the President "to make full and complete investigation of the Isthmus of Panama, with a view to the construction of a canal." That was the act signalizing the great awakening, after decades of half-stagnation. Foremost among the causes, wrote Benjamin Ide Wheeler, "was the opening of relations with the Philippines," thus illustrating the importance to California of the Spanish-American War.

Without serious difficulty the French property was acquired by the United States, but the proposed treaty was finally rejected by the Colombian Congress. Then followed the secession of Panama, under unique circumstances, the setting up of a new nation, and the recognition by President Theodore Roosevelt of the *de facto* government in Panama. Through his "fast footwork" and dogged determination Roosevelt was instrumental in constructing the Canal, the chief engineer being George Washington Goethals. In his address before the Pacific Historical Congress, in July, 1915, Roosevelt concluded in these characteristic words:

There is not one action of the American government, in connection with foreign affairs, from the day when the Constitution was adopted down to the present time, so important as the action taken by this government in connection with the acquisition and building of the Panama Canal. . . . I know that in the course of that action, every step taken was a step not only demanded by the honor and the interest of my country, but one taken with scrupulous regard to the nicest laws of national morality, and fair and upright dealing.

The monumental achievement was commemorated in San Francisco by the Panama-Pacific International Exposition, formally opened by President Woodrow Wilson, February 20, 1915. California was freed from her isolation by the completion of the Canal, "not only man's greatest engineering achievement," declared by Charles C. Moore, President of the Exposition, "but the most helpful single accomplishment of its kind in the world's history." The forecast made by President Wheeler in 1915 has been more than realized: 1) the eastern and western coasts of the United States have been drawn closer together; 2) the west coast of North America has been made accessible to the world; 3) the states and peoples of South America have been drawn decisively nearer to us; 4) Japan and our Pacific Coast have been drawn more closely together into a common area of trade and intercourse. The closing words of Rudolph Taussig's address of 1915 admirably epitomize the rôle of the Canal:

> We can only hope that the same general benefit to mankind which has always resulted from bringing together the peoples of the world, will also prove true in this instance, where they have been brought closer together by the Panama Canal.

DEEP-WATER INLAND SEAPORT

The city of Stockton (first named Tuleburg by Captain Charles M. Weber), county seat of San Joaquin County, enjoys the distinction of being California's first deepwater inland seaport, and to the present time it is the only California city so favored. The great man-made Los Angeles Harbor is really a part of the Pacific Ocean as the sprawling city was extended to salt water by the annexation of the "shoe-string strip" to San Pedro, after the fight for a free harbor, led by Stephen M. White of the U.S. Senate and Harrison Gray Otis of the *Los Angeles Times*.

The arrival of the lumber schooner *Daisy Gray* on the second day of February, 1933, at the uncompleted dock of the Port of Stockton marked the beginning of a new era for that inland city, for she was the first ocean-going vessel to enter the newly made port. Four and a half years later the *Point Bonita* was the 1,000th ship to come in.

To be sure, some seaworthy light-draft vessels made their way to Stockton in the tortuous San Joaquin River in the Gold Rush days, when the young city was the entrepôt for the Southern Mines. That set people to dreaming of a day when there might really be a deep-water port. But realization required time and hard-headed planning.

Men refer to the "Roaring Twenties" as the period in which Stockton "began to grow up into a city." There were important developments, such as the building of the City Hall and the Civic Municipal Auditorium. Then civic pride and community spirit strongly manifested themselves in concrete form. The dreams of earlier days had begun to take the form of thoughtful planning. Leaders petitioned Congress for government aid; surveys of the river channels were made.

When the first local bond issue of $3,000,000 came to a vote, it was approved by twelve to one. The city's investment included funds for purchasing rights of way, building a belt-line railway and necessary wharves and transit sheds. A fifty-year lease, expiring December 31, 1983, between the Port District and the City of Stockton authorizes operation of the city-owned facilities. Federal grants of almost $3,000,000 require no repayment.

Special facilities include the grain terminal, cotton compress, and belt-line railway. The Bulk Terminal, built by private capital, with its giant pulleys and loaders, has often been in use almost twenty-four hours a day, loading iron ore for Japan and coal for Korea.

The story is a long one, with many milestones. One writer has said: "Stockton's port, talked of for more than fifty years and the subject of active planning since the turn of the century, that day [February 2, 1933] became a reality." The building of the Port brought a diversification of the economy of the city, not matched by any other metropolis of the state, added shipping to agriculture and industry. The thirty-foot channel has brought ships from all parts of the world, with added wealth and prestige to Stockton.

Port workers steadily increased in numbers until World War II, then employees rose from 173 in 1945, year by year, reaching more than 3,000 in 1952. At times 100 trucks unloaded at the port in a single day. While lumber and potatoes were the first cargoes shipped, bills of lading later listed a wide variety of commodities produced or manufactured in the area.

With good reason the twentieth anniversary of the Port was celebrated in 1953. Eight ocean-going vessels tied up at the docks to participate. Regular terminal facilities were in full operation for visitors. In tribute to the occasion *The Stockton Record* said:

> On its twentieth anniversary the Port is in the lustiest health of its history. Tonnage records are being broken; expansion is under way; shipments of great variety are being sent to and brought from all over the world. . . . Today the future is brighter than it was twenty years ago, for the few doubters of that time have been silenced by accomplishment. The good judgment of the past has been confirmed; the loadstone has been discovered.

CHAPTER THREE

MINING — MINERALS

"The roots of the present lie deep in the past, and nothing is dead
to the man who would learn how the present comes to be what it is."
—*Bishop Stubbs*

FIRST MINES

When reference is made to early California mining one almost auto-matically thinks of gold. Years before gold mining days, however, there were the important quicksilver mines of New Almaden, located in the present Santa Clara County, a little more than a dozen miles southerly from the *pueblo* of San José.

Before the coming of the first American pioneers, even before the Spanish occupation of the country, the presence of cinnabar was known to the Indians; they used the red mineral to decorate their faces and bodies. In 1824 two Spaniards, Antonio Suñol and Luis Chabolla, dis-covered the source of the red rock, but it remained for Captain Andres Castillero to identify it as cinnabar and to bring about the opening of California's first quicksilver mine in November, 1845.

The name Almaden is a compound, derived from the famous quick-silver mine in ancient Spain. The Arabic *"al"* (meaning "the") and the noun *"maden"* (mine) give us "the mine." The old Almaden of Spain, known far back to the days of Pliny, was doubtless the greatest of all quicksilver mines.

When some of the red ore was first exhibited to Castillero he pro-nounced it silver, with an alloy of gold. But after some experimenting, he was convinced that it contained quicksilver, for by means of an impromptu reduction process he had produced minute particles of mercury in globular form. On the 3rd of December, 1845, he made formal declaration before the *alcalde* of San José: "I have taken out, besides silver, with a *ley* (alloy) of gold, liquid quicksilver, in the presence of several by-standers, whom I may summon on the proper occasion." He was anxious to obtain juridical possession of the property.

Castillero employed an American from New York, William G. Chard, who was able to devise a better method, still very crude, of reducing the ore. He finally obtained six whaler's try-pots of large size. "Three of these pots were inverted over the other three, thus forming with each pair, a furnace. By building a fire around these," continues the graphic description by Frederic Hall, "and having so arranged them that the mercurial vapor was conducted to the water, he succeeded in reducing about 2,000 pounds of quicksilver."

The discovery was made known to the Mexican governor, Manuel Micheltorena, and, in 1846, Thomas O. Larkin, American Consul at Monterey, communicated relevant facts to the national government in Washington. The site of the mine was also visited by John C. Frémont.

During the first years of American statehood of California about 200 men were employed at New Almaden, which had become a considerable village. Each month saw the production of some 7,500 pounds of quicksilver. Meanwhile there began a long, difficult and disappointing litigation regarding title to the property, the Supreme Court finally deciding that "the claim was invalid."

It is sufficient to add here that during the century beginning with the statehood of California (1850-1950) the New Almaden quicksilver mines produced more than a million flasks of quicksilver, valued at upwards of $50,000,000. Other mines, besides New Almaden, included the New Indria (Fresno County) and the Redington (Napa County). It should be added that the active production of quicksilver in California has by no means ended.

GOLD BEFORE MARSHALL'S DISCOVERY

Of one thing we may be certain—there was gold in California long before there were Indians, even before the most venerable Sequoias had begun to sprout. It is equally clear that Indians had seen gold unknown centuries before the coming of the white man. But in all that we see no historical significance, as the aborigines had also seen plenty of granite, and obsidian, and quartz crystals, and they knew nothing of the value of gold to men of another race.

The presence of gold was known to individuals of the white race long before Marshall's discovery in 1848. Some of the stories, to be sure, lack full corroboration. For example, Robert Jameson's book on mineralogy, published in Edinburgh in 1816, tells of "a plain fourteen leagues in extent, with alluvial deposits, in which lumps of gold are dispersed"— that particular plain, however, was never identified. Another account relates how a man named Black, a trapper on the San Joaquin River, "discovered gold there in great abundance," in 1829. But Black and his companions, all but one Smith, fell victims to hostile Indians. Smith alone knew where the gold was, but, so runs the story, his secret died with him in Arkansas. Again, it is said that George Yount, pioneer of 1831, for whom the town of Yountville was named, had first-hand information that Smith had discovered gold, at least the tradition was handed down.

William Heath Davis, in his *Sixty Years in California*, states: "The existence of gold in the Sacramento Valley and vicinity was known to the *padres* long prior to what is commonly known as the gold discovery of 1848." Indians had brought particles to the *padres*, then they were cautioned not to tell where it could be found.

Guy Giffen tells of the finding of small quantities of gold at San Isidro, in San Diego County; also that "Jedediah Smith entertained visions of wealth in the golden grains he discovered at Mono Lake in 1827."

Considering all the stories relating to gold discovery prior to 1840, sifting the wheat from the chaff (or separating the gold from the alloy), there is little reason to doubt that the presence of some of the yellow metal was known to at least some individuals. Even so we find no definite historical significance attaching to any specific discovery during that early period.

It was not until Don Francisco López found some flakes of gold clinging to the roots of wild onions he had pulled, in Placeritas Canyon, on the 9th day of March, 1842, that "the historian and the business man sat up and took notice." The site of this discovery is six to eight miles west of the town of Newhall, in Los Angeles County. The authentic story has been told and retold. "The news of this discovery soon spread among the inhabitants from Santa Barbara to Los Angeles," narrates Col. J. J. Warner, "and in a few weeks hundreds of people were engaged in washing and winnowing the sands of these gold fields."

Twenty ounces of gold, forwarded by Alfred Robinson for Abel Stearns, went to the U.S. Mint. Don Manuel Castañares reported to his Mexican government (1844) that "mining promised to be one of the most profitable industries of the province." He reported that previous to December, 1843, the placers had produced 2,000 ounces of gold dust, most of which had been sent to the mint of the United States. But American Consul Thomas O. Larkin was also busy. He wrote Secretary Buchanan (May 4, 1846), "There is no doubt but that gold, quicksilver, lead, sulphur, and coal mines are to be found all over California, and it is equally doubtful whether, under their present omens, they will be worked."

No attempt was made by the Mexican government to enact a system of mining laws. In short, Mexico failed to capitalize on what might have been her golden opportunity.

Under the sponsorship of the Newhall Chamber of Commerce, the recovered brass plaque that had marked the site of the gold discovery was replaced July 13, 1941, firmly set in a stout stone monument under a spreading oak. It remains true, however, that the López discovery, admitting its authenticity and paying just tribute to the discoverer, failed to merit wide acclaim and bring the great California gold rush and the Days of '49, which came only after the thrilling discovery by James Marshall at Coloma in January, 1848. The epochal event and its vast consequences had been reserved for the United States of America.

MOMENTOUS EVENT

The discovery of gold by James Wilson Marshall on the South Fork of the American River has been pronounced the most momentous event in all California history. Its consequences were so far-reaching as to be incalculable. All previous gold discoveries proved premature, without significant results. But Marshall's lucky strike at Sutter's Mill "focused the eyes of the world on California."

There has been no little controversy as to the exact date and place of the Marshall discovery. Marshall himself published a letter in 1856 in which he stated, depending on his memory, that he had found gold at Coloma "about the 19th" of January, 1848. Even later than that, he maintained that he had found the gold on or about the 19th of January.

In this, however, the careful historian is convinced that Marshall was in error, memory was not wholly dependable. The personal diary of Henry Bigler, one of the laborers at the mill, must be given more weight. In his entry for Monday, January 24, 1848, Bigler wrote:

> This day some kind of mettle was found in the tail race that looks like goald, first discovered by James Martial, the Boss of the Mill.

Supporting evidence was found in a statement by James Brown, who was at the time living at the cabin. Bigler's entry seems to indicate that that he had actually seen the gold particles and that he was sufficiently impressed to write down what he did write in his diary.

Here is a part of the significant record found in Sutter's diary:

> January 28th, 1848. Marshall arrived in the evening, it was raining very heavy, but he told me that he came on important business, after we was alone in a private room he showed me the first specimens of gold, that he was not certain if it was gold or not, but he thought it might be; immediately I made the proof and found that it was gold, I told him even that most of all is 23 Carat Gold; he wished that I should come up with him immediately, but I told him that I have to give first my orders to the people in all my factories and shops.

Preliminary to the grandiose Celebration of the Centenary at Coloma, in 1948, there was a most minute re-examination of every bit of available evidence by such authorities as Aubrey Neasham, Robert Heizer, and Joseph R. Knowland. The date generally agreed upon as having the highest degree of authenticity is the 24th day of January, 1848. It may still be, nevertheless, that some individuals, here and there, will be inclined to agree with an opinion of John Bidwell, expressed many years ago, that the date can never be absolutely established within a few days.

The "First Nugget" has been the subject of endless speculation. A small lump (or "flake") of gold, preserved by Elizabeth Wimmer, wife of Peter L. Wimmer, has been exhibited for more than a century as the original nugget. This, it was claimed, was given to Mrs. Wimmer by Marshall himself, and for years worn by her "like a necklace in a little buckskin bag." The intrinsic value of the gold today would be approximately $14.00. Only in 1956 the "Wimmer Nugget" was acquired by the Bancroft Library, in Berkeley. However, there is no conclusive evidence that it is actually the first piece of gold picked up by Jim Marshall.

In the extensive preparation for the great Centennial Celebration, in 1948, buried sections of the original tailrace were unearthed, the exact place where Sutter's Mill stood was located, and numerous timbers and other relics associated with the mill were found. Scientific investigations resulted in giving us a complete and accurate picture of the mill, with form of construction and true dimensions fully revealed.

It had been the wish of Sutter and Marshall that the big find should be kept as a profound secret. For a few weeks not many outside the immediate circle had any accurate knowledge of the epoch-making event. But it was inevitable that the news would get out.

The first printed notice of the discovery appears in the *Californian*, the pioneer newspaper, of March 15, 1848. It reads, in part:

> GOLD MINES FOUND.—In the newly made raceway of the Saw Mill recently erected by Captain Sutter, on the American Fork, gold has been found in considerable quantities. One person brought thirty dollars worth to New Helvetia, gathered there in a short time. California, no doubt, is rich in mineral wealth, . . .

And the sensational news was broadcast by Sam Brannan, as he dramatically strode down the San Francisco streets shouting, "Gold! Gold! Gold from the American River!" as with one hand he swung his hat and in the other displayed a bottle of gold dust.

The torch that was lighted by Marshall's discovery has never been extinguished, and it resulted in a vast conflagration, world-wide in its sweep, transforming in its character, that made California the Golden, Minerva State of the American Union, the focus of all eyes.

SILVER

In comparison with gold, in California the discovery of silver was hardly a circumstance — there is no memorable specific date to celebrate; volumes of California history have been written in which the word silver does not even appear in the index.

Nevertheless silver plays a significant part in the financial history of the Golden State, though (because of the artificial boundary line) it happened to come chiefly from the Silver State, Nevada. To recall that the presence of vast quantities of the obstinate "blue-stuff" (silver sulphide) was a bothersome impediment to the avid gold hunters before its value was discovered is one more example of the irony of history.

There seems to be no doubt of some knowledge of the existence of silver in California from the early gold days. Bancroft refers to a silver mining company organized in Stockton as early as January, 1851, to operate a mine near Los Angeles. Even before that date silver had been discovered near Carson, then believed to be in California, and there were other reports of discoveries in different areas. But all such discoveries attracted little interest—gold required only "freeing from the rock, while silver was an ore that could only be extracted by laborious processes after the rock was crushed." Gold was the powerful magnet; the eyes of the adventurers were focused on gold.

Strangely enough the chief silver deposits were found east of the main Sierran crest, as the great gold fields were on the western slopes. Gold usually occurred in its virgin state, silver in different kinds of ore. Silver was found, as was gold, largely in the eastern part of the state, much of it south of Lake Tahoe, especially near Owen's Lake, but the great preponderance of argentiferous deposits was east of the state boundary, that is, in Nevada.

The saga of the fabulous Comstock Lode, with its extravagances and excitement amounting to downright hysteria, happened in Nevada, centering in the now legendary Virginia City. But they were Californians who trekked there, helter-skelter, Californians who almost overnight became millionaires by their frenzied speculations. The impact on California finance was sensational. "Such sudden and violent extremes," declares Cleland, "turned the San Francisco Stock Exchange, on which the shares, or 'feet,' of more than a hundred of the Nevada mines were listed, into an indescribable bedlam of speculation." Many a man was ruined in the maelstrom. But also there arose above the horizon names of others on the scroll of California history who would never otherwise have been heard of. Conspicuous among the leaders were the four "Silver Kings"—John W. Mckay, James G. Fair, James C. Flood, and William S. O'Brien.

Then there were others during those exciting years whose persistence and participation in affairs were such that their names and deeds must always find a place in California's financial history—William C. Ralston, William Sharon, Darius O. Mills, George Hearst, Adolph Sutro.

The California Rand, Incorporated, known as "The Big Silver," was not discovered until 1918. It became California's largest producer. The rather weird story of this comparatively recent enterprise has been recorded by Dwight L. Clarke, one of the directors.

In the beginnings of the Spanish occupation of Alta California the planning of José de Gálvez, Visitor-General, won for him a place in our history, though he never actually set foot in California; so the vast riches produced at the Comstock Lode may be claimed as an integral part of the history of the Golden State, even though the silver itself was dug in the sister state of Nevada.

QUARTZ MINING

The great mass of early argonauts of gold rush days were completely ignorant of the origin of the gold they found along the beds and bars of running streams. Some thought an ancient volcano had spewed up the gold and scattered it all about. They did their mining with picks and shovels, sometimes with butcher knives and long-handled spoons; of course the pan, the cradle, and the sluice (with variations) came into general use.

The tracing of the nuggets and the quartz pebbles shot with gold back to their origin in the extensive quartz veins was a later but a very important development. In the summer of 1849 some gold hunters in Frémont's Mariposa grant undertook to trace a line of gold-bearing rock fragments back to their real source. They were led up to the quartz vein which seemed clearly to be the source of the scattered fragments. The placer deposits had been eroded from this vein. Then it was, in the summer of '49, that those adventurous gold hunters undertook to obtain the yellow metal from the vein, the first crude beginnings of quartz mining in California.

But the Southern Mines were not destined to hold the lead in quartz mining. In the month of June, 1850, came the first definite indication that gold-bearing veins existed at Grass Valley in the north. About the same time veins containing imbedded gold were found on the Feather River, near Oroville. Still, there was no lively or general interest in the quartz. In October, however, announcement of George McKnight's sensational discovery of the Gold Hill lode created wild excitement. This, as H. P. Davis tells us, was "the very beginning of the quartz gold excitement," initiating the extensive hard-rock mining of Nevada County.

Four youthful miners from Massachusetts had made the find on their very first day at the diggings. The event was appropriately celebrated at a miners' meeting where the enthusiastic orator of the day proclaimed the "the fountain-head of all the gold in California had at last been found." The Gold Tunnel outcrop was found on Deer Creek some 500 yards below the present Pine Street bridge. It was operated for several years, and is said to have yielded more than half a million dollars.

A real beginning in quartz mining had been made. During the early 1850's it "boomed into public notice." But the most valuable veins and most extensive operations were to be found not within the strict borders of the famed Mother Lode, or in the Southern Mines, but in Nevada County, with chief centers at Nevada City and Grass Valley.

With the rapid development of quartz mining the entire mining industry took on a new character. With the decline of the more primitive methods used in placer mining, thousands of gold hunters, most of them with small if any accumulated capital, found themselves unemployed, so naturally they drifted back to San Francisco and other centers.

Quartz mining requires capital, experience, and heavy complicated machinery. The rock must be crushed and thoroughly pulverized. The old Mexican *arrastra* and the Chilean mill were of very low efficiency. The business required a high degree of risk taking, but the stakes for the few fortunate winners were high.

By 1858 there were more than 280 quartz mills in the state, with at least 2,600 stamps. But of all these it is stated that not more than fifty mills were in successful operation. In more recent years Nevada County has held its high place in the quartz mining industry of California and the nation. The Empire Mine at Grass Valley is said to have more than nine miles of tunnels and shafts, calling for tremendous investments in operating equipment.

HYDRAULIC MINING

Old "King Hazard" had a golden opportunity to proclaim his sway during the gold mining days of California, for it seemed that almost everything was the result of chance. Take hydraulic mining. Plenty of room for speculation and argument! No single event, like Marshall's discovery at Coloma on the morning of January 24, 1848, can be pointed to in telling the story of the beginnings of hydraulic mining as it was not really a full-fledged discovery at all by any one man on any specific day, but came about rather as a natural by-product of simpler mining methods then in vogue, with separate beginnings in different localities, involving different individuals. This may be made clear by brief reference to a few of the accounts.

One such account is related in the Nevada *Transcript* of March 3, 1879, in part in these words:

> E. E. Matteson, the first man who ever used the hydraulic hose for washing down banks to uncover the gold-bearing gravel channels, commenced mining on American Hill, near Nevada City, in March, 1853. During that month he proposed to his partners that, as he had once narrowly escaped being killed while digging under a bank with a pick, they try directing a stream of water from a hose against the dirt. At first they opposed the idea, urging that it would not pay to go to the trouble and expense of fitting up the necessary apparatus. He shortly convinced them that the experiment was worth trying, and as he anticipated, it proved a success.

Matteson, though often regarded as the father of hydraulicking, had been preceded by others. For example, a Frenchman named A. Chabot, in 1852 used a hose about forty feet long and turned the water on the dirt and gravel, sweeping it "into the sluice box, where the gold was separated from the debris in the usual manner."

According to still another account, Edward McAuley (Macaulay) came to Little York, Nevada County, in 1852. He is reported to have found a leaky flume in the spring of that year, and noted that "the water from the flume had washed away a gravel bank and exposed gold-bearing gravels." Perceiving the possibilities of such a process, he started a series of experiments leading to "the fabrication of a canvas hose and a nozzle made from a gun barrel."

Once again, here is a statement from F. A. Partridge of Weimar, as given in the Oakland *Tribune* (Knave):

> It has been my impression that the first hydraulic mine was at Hayden Hill, on the Forest Hill divide, and that it was done by a group of Chinese miners. They had been working in Canyon Creek, on the other side of the river, and had been operating by ground sluicing. After much trouble with the white miners in this district, they moved to Hayden Hill. Ground sluicing did not work there, because of the difficulty of getting the water

high enough, so they put in a head-gate in their ditch and carried the water under pressure in a hose to the foot of the gravel. This hose was made from sails from ships lying in "Frisco," and the nozzle was hand-carved from wood. They later sold out to a syndicate, . . .

The above illustrates how the method we call hydraulic mining had its beginnings; and suggests the approximate dates involved, as well as several of the personalities. It dates from the early 1850's, with crude beginnings, presumably at different localities, independent of each other.

Of course, when it comes to a question of origins, it will be remembered that all placer mining was conditioned on the availability of water. The pan, the cradle, and the long-tom and sluice, all required water for operation. But too much water, occasioned by heavy rainfall or freshet, also interrupted the routine of the digger.

Hydraulicking may be regarded as simply a development of the long-tom and the sluice method. In 1854 there were approximately 4,500 miles of ditches in California being used for delivering water for mining operations. Two of the more extensive ditches resulted in a consolidation of the "Deer Creek" and the "Coyote," each two and a half miles long, into the Coyote and Deer Creek Water Company, which was the first such company to be incorporated in the country, "another first to the credit of Nevada City."

The expansion of hydraulic mining was truly phenomenal. It called for hundreds of miles of mining ditches and numerous storage dams. Sometimes wooden flumes were used, where ditches were not deemed practical.

Nozzles used for the hose at first were an inch or less in diameter; later they varied from four to nine inches. An eight-inch nozzle could throw 185,000 cubic feet of water an hour, at a velocity of 150 feet per second. Entire mountains were destroyed, leaving gaping wounds and unsightly scars in the ruthless search for the yellow metal. Hydraulic mining proved disastrous to entire sections of country for hundreds of miles: billions of tons of detritus were washed into the Yuba, Bear, and American Rivers and their tributaries, filling the beds with boulders and "slickens," causing frequent floods and seriously impeding navigation. The bed of the Sacramento River was raised several feet. Inevitably, the courts were invoked. After long, bitterly-contested litigation the great hydraulic mines of the Sacramento-San Joaquin watersheds were ordered closed in the larger interest of agriculture and public welfare.

Still another chapter, dealing with a subject akin to hydraulic mining, tells of more recent large-scale dredging for gold, which assumed huge proportions in many different localities, a subject likewise revealing highly controversial but also highly important welfare considerations.

"BLACK GOLD"

Among all mineral products of California petroleum ("black gold") holds a unique place in the realm of business and wizardry.

Some use of petroleum, or asphaltum, dates back to antiquity. Sun-dried brick employed in construction of the ancient city of Ur of Chaldea were treated with asphaltum about 4,000 years B.C. California Indians made use of it for various purposes long before the first white adventurers came.

Don Gaspar de Portolá was the first white man to discover oil in California: according to report, this was August 3, 1769, only a few weeks after the first entrance into Alta California by the Spaniards.

It was not until August, 1859, that the first commercial well in the United States was drilled, near Titusville, in Pennsylvania. "Uncle Billy" Smith had thus helped Edwin Drake launch the petroleum industry. And one of its founders was Lyman Stewart, later a pioneer and leader in the Union Oil Company of California.

It was during the early development of oil production in Pennsylvania that the oil seepages and asphalt in the southwestern San Joaquin Valley began to attract special attention. Thomas Harvey ("Coal Oil Tommy") obtained oil from pits north of Coalinga, which he peddled to farmers as a lubricant. Frank Latta states: "Harvey was probably the first man to produce and market San Joaquin Valley petroleum." He came from Pennsylvania in 1862 and was attracted by the Joaquin seepages. The first oil company of the valley was organized in late 1863 or early 1864, contrary to popular belief that there was no such organization before 1878. The Mariposa *Gazette* of June 4, 1864, gives a cheering account of the activities of Messrs J. M. Ketton and T. Choiser, stating that most of the stock of the company was "held by citizens of this County."

There was early interest in Southern California also, as evidenced by the editor of the Wilmington *Journal*, who declared, March 17, 1866:

> There is no longer any doubt as to the possibility of finding petroleum in this vicinity . . . the fact that oil can be found has been established. . . . If present indications can be considered a criterion, it will not be many months before Los Angeles County becomes noted for its flowing oil springs as well as its fruitful vineyards.

Phineas Banning was made president of the Los Angeles Pioneer Oil Company June 13, 1865. The Company announced in an advertisement: "They are now prepared to furnish merchants and others with illuminating and lubricating oils."

The oil excitement spread like a prairie fire. "Oil properties" were exploited from Humboldt County all the way to San Diego. Professor Silliman assumed that "California will be found to have more oil in its soil than all the whales in the Pacific Ocean!"

Because of lack of scientific knowledge and the fact that most of the boom organizations were not bona-fide companies, the first feverish efforts were generally unsuccessful, the great development was to come later.

The drilling of a well in Pico Canyon, not far from Newhall, in 1875, led to the construction of California's first commercial oil refinery, in 1876.

Edward L. Doheny brought in the first producing oil well in Los Angeles proper on the fourth day of November, 1892. Two of Doheny's associates were Charles A. Canfield and Samuel Cannon. In a short time sixty-nine wells were pumping, most of them in residential Los Angeles.

Since the beginning of the present century the oil production has reached astronomical proportions, its values so amazing as to make all the California gold pale into relative insignificance. And the end is not even yet!

NAMES IN EARLY PLACERVILLE

When we think of the '49-er gold mining camps as composed solely of nondescript adventurers, gold diggers, and heavy drinking gamblers, we miss one of the most important phases of the history of that glamorous period. Many men who later won wide distinction in various fields had been among the hard-working inhabitants of one or another of the camps, or "diggin's."

Take Placerville, for example, whose nickname "Hangtown" was applied after the hanging of three robbers in the fall of 1849 by determined men who took the law into their own hands. Among the names associated with early Placerville we find those of Mark Hopkins, who conducted a grocery store; Philip D. Armour, who in addition to mining operations ran a butcher shop; Charles Weber, before he founded Tuleburg, later Stockton; and John M. Studebaker, who drove a thriving business in manufacturing wheelbarrows for the miners long before he became a noted manufacturer of wagons and other wheeled vehicles.

It is quite unnecessary to rehearse here the activities of such leaders. Mark Hopkins became one of the "Big Four" who constructed the Central Pacific Railroad. Philip Armour took up the business of hog raising, still later becoming the head of the largest pork-packing business in the world. Captain Charles Weber left his name permanently in the history of California as the founder of the city of Stockton, which became the trade center for the Southern Mines, and many decades later the only inland seaport of the state. These were men who had dwelt and delved in the mining town of Placerville.

In view of special developments of national importance, the name of Studebaker merits a special mention—too seldom is it mentioned in California history books. There were five Studebaker brothers—John, Henry, Clement, P. E., and Jacob. As early as the winter of 1852 they began the manufacture of wagons. Six years later John returned to South Bend, Indiana, bought out Henry's interest in the business there, and ultimately the other brothers were admitted into the firm, known as Studebaker Brothers' Manufacturing Company, which won the reputation of being the largest establishment for manufacturing vehicles in the world.

John Studebaker lived to see the inauguration of the automobile industry and to have a highly important part in its development. He died March 16, 1917. The Studebaker corporation has more recently given to the nation and the world its distinguished President, Paul G. Hoffman. As these lines are written, we note the "Studebaker Hawks" (Golden, Sky, Power, Flight) as products of the Studebaker-Packard Corporation.

The later activities of the other Placerville pioneers mentioned — Hopkins, Armour, Weber — are familiar to history. Early beginnings of numerous other notable careers likewise stemmed from the industrious mining camps of the days of '49. By no accounting did Placerville stand alone in this important regard. As a single but conspicuous example, J. Loewenberg, in his lecture on the occasion of the centennial of the birth of Josiah Royce (November 20, 1955), stated: "... the world is beholden to Grass Valley for having produced and reared a great man."

DREDGE MINING

As hydraulic mining followed the simpler early placer mining in California, so dredge mining largely took the place of hydraulic mining after the hydraulic had been generally discontinued.

The basic idea of dredging, however, was by no means new. It dates back at least to the great Gold Rush days. Louis Stellman tells of a first instance in these words:

> In 1849 a dredge was built in New York and sent around the Horn on a sailing vessel. But, alas! it sank in the Sacramento River, whose sands it was intended to mine, soon after its arrival and was never reclaimed.

Among the other numerous devices brought to California (most of them proved totally worthless when put to the actual test) one was described as—

> a dredging machine sent out by an enterprising New York company, which was intended to scoop up golden sands from the bottom of the Yuba River; but it was found in the first place that the river was not deep enough to float a machine of that character, and in the second place that the clay and gravel that contained the gold at the bottom of the river could not, on account of its toughness and tenacity and the rocks among which it was distributed, be dug up by any dredger.

One promising device was the "gold-boat," planned to "shovel up golden gravel with mechanical thoroughness and in such quantities that even low-grade material would be worth mining." The thought of gold was always alluring to persistent experimenters. In 1877 the Risdon Iron Works of San Francisco built the first dredger made in California, for use on the Yuba River.

In some of the California rivers "bucket excavators" were tried out in 1882; but these gave way to "chain-and-bucket models," bearing some resemblance to grain elevators. It was half a century from the time of the great gold discovery before the first really successful gold dredging, as we know it today, was actually done, in the vicinity of Oroville, in Butte County. In the year 1910 that single field had twenty-five dredgers in operation. In 1915 the gold yield rose to $3,172,476.

It is of interest to note that the dredgers of the "bucket-elevator type" were also developed in New Zealand and more recently in the Klondike gold fields. T. A. Rickard's description of a typical dredger is given:

> The barge is constructed at the bottom of a pit, excavated by the use of scrapers and horses, to a depth sufficiently below the expected water level to ensure flotation and afford room for movement. Then the machinery is placed in position on the barge. As water is admitted, the dredger floats, and when it starts to work it digs its own way, filling the pit behind as it advances in the course of digging.

But there was constant activity in improving the dredgers. Whereas, the early hulls made of wood could be constructed at $100,000 each, the huge behemoth coming later and constructed of steel cost approximately half a million. With the technical perfecting of the machinery, the operator was enabled to handle at a profit vast quantities of material with a surprisingly small gold content.

It remains only to refer to the stupendous volume of work done by the gold dredgers during more recent years, along many river courses, and to the opposition raised by protesting people because of the unsightly piles of tailings thrown up by the dredgers, mile after mile, ruining for decades great areas of fertile land and seriously impairing otherwise attractive landscapes. The operations of the giant "earth-shakers" have been prohibited in many localities: a last-stand of great machines was in remote Trinity County, which, because of its almost complete isolation, was unaffected by the Anti-Debris Act.

STEEL INDUSTRY

The presence of iron ore in different parts of California was known from a very early date; but the production of steel in significant quantities is a very recent industry. Feeble beginnings, however, may be seen in San Francisco in 1849, when Peter and James Donahue built a crude furnace and made the first iron castings in California. From these beginnings developed the Union Iron Works.

In 1868 Titus Cronise foresaw that the consumption of iron would become greatly increased. He wrote:

> . . . it is highly probable that the erection of smelting works, already projected by this company, will be consummated, and the business of manufacturing iron will be entered upon at an early day.

Even as late as 1915, Fletcher M. Hamilton, a mineralogist, wrote these words: "In the past the reduction of such ores has always depended upon a cheap supply of coking coal." But he did discern signs of a large industry for the future.

Reasons for the slow development are not far to seek. They are seen in the dearth of mobile capital, the comparatively small industrial population, the absence of an ample supply of available good coal and other needed raw materials, especially cotton. California had not yet become a true manufacturing state — indeed, there were but few factories except in San Francisco. Scrap and pig iron was mostly imported from Europe. But the time came when the chief source of supply was in Utah; and the extensive deposits in Southern California looked more promising.

Before World War II there were no blast furnaces on the Pacific Coast. "There was no completely integrated plant west of Colorado." It may be said that one of the compensations of the war in California was the meteoric rise of the steel industry.

Without doubt the individual to be credited above others with this development is that magical entrepreneur, Henry J. Kaiser. The expansion of the Kaiser plant now occupies a site of 1800 acres at Fontana, forty-five miles east of Los Angeles. The chief source of iron ore is the is the Eagle Mountain Mine, located 163 miles east of the plant. By the year 1951 the Kaiser Steel Corporation was producing upwards of one-third of California's entire output. The figures have become astronomical. For years previously the Pacific Coast had been completely dominated by two giant eastern companies—Columbia (a subsidiary of U.S. Steel) and Bethlehem.

Much of California's recent industrial growth must be attributed to this great expansion of the capacity for steel production, and the diversification of the facilities for its use. Within a single decade the capacity mounted from less than 875,000 tons to 3,000,000 tons annually. Related fabricating industries have correspondingly increased by leaps and bounds.

Whereas, during the major portion of our history there was either no steel production at all in California, or it was a mere potentiality, it has almost suddenly taken rank among the greatest industries of the state.

CEMENT PRODUCTION

As is now well known, the use of cement, or concrete, in building, in some form, dates from remote antiquity. It has been found in the ancient ruins of Babylon, Egypt, Greece, and Rome. The Romans especially used cement extensively in building roads, aqueducts, walls, and piers. It is very far from being a recent product.

But the increase in the quantity and variety of uses, with particular reference to California, during the present century is truly sensational, and is a matter of great historical significance.

Deposits of lime and limestone with varying degrees of purity are widely distributed over the state. Harris Newmark, in his *Sixty Years in Southern California*, tells this interesting experience for about the year 1880:

> The first cement pavement in the city [Los Angeles] was laid in Main Street by a man named Floyd. Having bought Temple Block, we were thinking of surrounding it with a wooden sidewalk. Floyd recommended cement, asking me, at the same time, to inspect a bit of pavement which he had just put down. I did so, and took his advice; and from this small beginning has developed the excellent system of paving now enjoyed by Los Angeles.

As early as 1868 there was at least one cement mill in the state, located in Benicia, the rock used being a clayey limestone, which was quite abundant in that vicinity, as well as at Martinez. "These works," Cronise tells us, "have capacity to make over 200 barrels of cement daily, more than enough to supply the wants of the entire coast." (!) The peculiar limestone employed in the process of burning and grinding was found on both sides of the Strait of Carquinez, connecting San Pablo and Suisun Bays.

What may be called the first modern cement mill in California was established in 1894. By the year 1915 there were seven different plants; and by 1928 the number had increased to twelve in the state, with a total capacity of approximately 50,000 barrels a day.

Some idea of the amazing expansion of the state's cement industry during the early twentieth century is gained from the report of a production of 52,000 barrels in 1900, almost 5,000,000 barrels in 1910, and 14,105,000 barrels in 1927.

Both in magnitude and in the value of the product the cement industry, which seemed but an infant only a single generation ago, has become one of the very greatest in California, running into hundreds of millions of dollars in value. This is not difficult to understand when one is reminded of some of the many uses to which it is put—huge dams for conservation and flood control, long aqueducts and piping, city building in great variety, state and local highways, sidewalks, and still others.

The string of motorized concrete mixers—the first appeared in San Francisco in 1927—speeding down the avenue *en route* to some new city subdivision, may serve as a daily reminder of the important rôle of cement in our modern everyday life.

CHAPTER FOUR

RELIGION

"Religion it is that containeth and holdeth together all human
society: this is the foundation, prop, and stay of all."
—Plutarch

FIRST PROTESTANT SERVICE

The first Protestant religious service ever conducted in California, in the
English language, was held more than forty years before the *Mayflower*
dropped anchor at Plymouth Rock—a rather astounding fact not only in
the chronology of California but likewise for all continental United
States. The service was conducted by Rev. Francis Fletcher, chaplain of
the famous Francis Drake expedition.

According to an inscription on the "Prayer Book Cross," surmounting
a height in Golden Gate Park, San Francisco, the service was held
"about St. John's Day, June 23, 1579," which would be about July 3 of
our present calendar. The exact spot on which the event took place will
probably never be known; but it was presumably near the coast, somewhere in Marin County. Tents had been set up and a barricade built.
It may be assumed as certain that the official Anglican Prayer Book
was used in the service.

Drake ordered the service to be performed before the Indians: he and
all his company joined in the prayers and the singing of psalms. The
aborigines, filled with curiosity and wonderment, reflected an attitude
which led the Englishmen to suppose themselves "taken for gods." Music
being a kind of universal language, it was the singing by the Englishmen that attracted the special attention of the Indians.

From the time of Cabrillo's discovery of California in 1542 until the
sensational appearance of Drake on the *Golden Hind*, the Pacific Ocean
might be described as a "Spanish lake": conditions were suddenly
changed, however, by the English freebooter. Spain was alarmed—and
with good reason. Drake's booty included literally tons of gold and
silver. But his was the first circumnavigation of the globe by Englishmen—he was the first commander to complete the circuit: his expedition takes rank among the dramatic events of world history. His avowed
purpose was to find the elusive Strait of Anian (Northwest Passage);

but in reality very little practical attention was given to serious searching for it.

For generations it was generally believed that Drake had entered the Golden Gate and had discovered the San Francisco Bay. Where he did actually anchor is a question that has aroused no end of discussion. Henry R. Wagner concluded that while he visited certain inlets to the north of Point Reyes, he did not actually enter what we call Drake's Bay at all.

Precisely where he did land is still clouded with some uncertainty. But his actual stop lasted thirty-six days. He ceremoniously took possession of the country roundabout in the name of his good Queen Bess, giving the name New England (*Nova Albion*) to the vast but undefined region. It was during this stop, some thirty to forty miles west of north of San Francisco that Chaplain Fletcher conducted that first Protestant religious service on California territory. In *The World Encompassed*, we have a picturesque account of the strange sacrificial acts of the Indians, who appeared to regard the Englishmen as gods, concluding in these words:

> This bloudie sacrifice (against our wils) being thus performed, our Generall with his companie in the presence of those strangers fell to prayers: and by signes in lifting up our eyes and hands to heaven, signified vnto them, that that God whom we did serue, and whom they ought to worship, was aboue. Beseeching God if it were his good pleasure to open by some meanes their blinded eyes; that they might in due time be called to the knowledge of him the true and everlasting God, and of Iesus Christ whom he hath sent, the salutation of the Gentiles.

FOUNDER OF FRANCISCAN MISSIONS

Among all the many and distinguished religious leaders of California from the beginning until now, Rev. Fr. Junípero Serra, O.F.M., unquestionably holds first place in our history. Striking confirmation is seen in the almost spontaneous selection of this "Apostle of California" as first choice for a place in National Statuary Hall in the Capitol at Washington, D.C. He it was who, at the head of his band of Franciscan missionaries, planted and established Christianity and civilization in Alta California.

Serra was a native of the island of Petra, in the Mediterranean Sea, 120 miles off the coast of Spain, on the 22nd of January, 1723. He received the habit of St. Francis at the early age of sixteen. An unusually diligent and gifted student, even before his ordination he became lector of philosophy at his monastery; later he received the degree of Doctor and was made Professor of Theology at the University of Palma. It was the missionary spirit, which with him became a holy passion, that led him to bid farewell to the community of Palma, and in company with Palóu, Crespi, and a score of other missionaries set sail for Vera Cruz on the 28th of August, 1749.

After nineteen years of arduous missionary labors in New Spain (Mexico), Serra was honored with the appointment as Father-President of a band of sixteen missionary *padres* and charged with the spiritual conquest of Alta California. As one can well imagine, he received this appointment with sacred joy—his great life work had come to him, and he was fifty-six years old!

The life and labors of Junípero Serra are too well known to require fresh recital. In humble gratitude and spiritual exaltation he entered upon his matchless career when, on that 16th day of July, 1769, he devoutly raised the cross of Santa Fé in solemn ceremony and dedicated the first of the chain of twenty-one Franciscan missions of Alta California—San Diego de Alcalá. Ultimately he had the intense satisfaction of seeing nine missions established in his own lifetime.

Death took the venerable *padre* August 28, 1784, at San Carlos de Monterey, his headquarters and dearly loved official residence. He had made his final arduous but loving pilgrimage along the trail we have come to know as El Camino Real, from San Diego to Monterey, bestowing comfort and sympathy upon the worshipful Indian neophytes here and there along the way. His prayer that he might breathe his last at his favorite mission had been granted. His death brought his loving disciple Francisco Palóu temporarily to the office of father-successor, pending the formal appointment of Fermin de Lasuén, his real successor, to that post.

To Junípero Serra religion was everything. Nowhere can one find in all our history a man more perfectly embodying the qualities of true humility, godly zeal, and complete consecration to a holy cause. Californians will never cease to pay reverent tribute to the first Father-President of the California Missions.

THE FIRST CALIFORNIA MISSION

Early California was a child of Spain. Of the three institutions employed by Spain in the colonization of California (*Presidio, Pueblo,* Mission) the Mission holds first place. The missionary was an agent of both church and state.

When Spain decided to extend her conquests to Alta California, and, following the expulsion of the Jesuits from Baja California in 1767, the spiritual conquest of the north was entrusted to the Franciscan order, with Padre Junípero Serra at the head of a band of missionaries as Father-President, as already noted.

Preparations were made with great care. There were four expeditions to New California—two by land, two by sea. The land expeditions were conducted by Gaspar de Portolá and Rivera y Moncada; the ships *San Antonio* and *San Carlos* were commanded by Juan Perez and Vincente Villa.

On the first day of July, 1769, the historic expedition was completed by the arrival of Serra and Portolá at San Diego. Theodore Hittell has suggested that date as the birthday of Alta California. On the first following Sabbath the arrival and preservation were celebrated with a solemn mass and booming cannon. Preparations went rapidly forward for the founding of the first mission.

The actual beginnings at San Diego form one of the most familiar narratives in all our history. After indescribable suffering from the dreadful scurvy and all manner of deprivations, the little missionary band made ready for the ceremony. Padre Junípero's exalted spirit rose triumphant, filled with zeal to begin the work of Christianizing the benighted Indians.

In a little, hastily-constructed shack made of poles and brushwood, with grass roof, to serve as chapel, the standard of the Holy Cross was raised on the sixteenth day of July, 1769, thus signalizing the actual beginning of the mission history and the permanent occupation of Alta California.

The task of converting the curious Indians to Christianity seemed at first disappointing. But at length a baby boy was brought to the mission for baptism. Padre Serra was overjoyed. Just as he was about to perform the ceremony, however, the infant was suddenly snatched away by the witnessing Indians, leaving the saddened missionary "with the shell containing the holy water in his hands."

The site that had been selected, "two gunshots from the shore," looking out upon that matchless harbor, from the present Old Town, proved to be unsatisfactory because of floods or drought and the lack of irrigation water. Therefore, some five years later the mission was moved six miles farther up the valley.

There stands today the fully restored church, with "Mater Dolorosa," largest of five bells, hanging in the tower. Before its altar lie buried five of the *padres*, including Luis Jayme, California's first martyr.

Into the tiles of the cross is fitted a great bronze plaque bearing this inscription:

HERE
Fray Junípero Serra
The Apostle of California and
Founder of its Civilization
First Reared the Cross, Began
The First Mission and
Founded the Old Town—
San Diego
July 16, 1769
In memory of Him and His Works.

A CHRISTIAN MARTYR

On the first guidepost of *El Camino Real* (The King's Highway), at Mission San Diego, appears this inscription:

Erected by Mr. and Mrs. A. S. C. Forbes
In Memory of Fray Luis Jayme, the First
Martyr of California.
Father Jayme was massacred by the Indians
November 4, 1775. The Bell was Blessed
"Jayme" by Reverend J. C. Mesny.

When the first California mission was moved from Old San Diego to its new location in 1773, Fathers Jayme and Fuster were reported to be very happy, we are told by Francisco Palóu, "seeing that they were gathering in abundance the spiritual fruits of the vine-yard of the Lord."

But their earnest zeal was not according to knowledge, as the tragic event soon proved. Not a single convert had been made in many of the near-by *rancherías*. Moreover, the food supply at the mission was not sufficient to support the neophytes, most of whom were in contact with the native pagans roundabout, who gave evidence of an aggressively hostile spirit. There were unmistakable evidences of trouble ahead, though unperceived at the time by the *padres*.

Matters came to a head when one or two neophytes made their escape and connived with their pagan friends in stirring up a general uprising and a rebellion against the missionaries. Encouraged by the medicine men, the revolt reached serious proportions. It was agreed that there was to be during the night a simultaneous attack upon both the mission and the San Diego *presidio*.

The Spaniards were taken unawares. They had neglected to keep any effective guard at either *presidio* or mission—both were extremely vulnerable in case of attack. With their weird yelling and mass advance, the natives had little difficulty in breaking into the mission church, where they stole such articles as they thought might be of value to them, then applied the torch to the place. It is easy to understand how in the wild confusion the fire-trap wooden buildings, covered with roofs of tule, quickly burst into flame. There had been no such happening as this in the early mission history! The situation was indeed desperate.

With Christian faith and courageous heart Father Jayme walked calmly into the midst of the frenzied rebels, appealing to them with *"Amad a Dios, hijos"* (Love God, children). But all to no avail. Instead of being pacified, the inflamed Indians seized the good *padre*, carried him away for some distance, rudely disrobed him, then murderously beat him to death with their clubs, horribly mutilating his body. The rebel attack also brought other bloodshed, as well as distressing loss of mission property.

When Father-President Junípero Serra learned of the violent death of Jayme, with spiritual exaltation he exclaimed: "Thanks be to God, the soil is at length watered: now surely will follow the reduction of the Diegueños." California had been given its first Christian martyr.

FIRST BISHOP

Secularization of the Franciscan Missions of California, long fore-shadowed, became the unequivocal policy of the Mexican government in the year 1833—a policy which sounded the death-knell to the mission system. A law enacted in April of the following year insisted that actual secularization should be effected within a four-months period. Governor José Figueroa, sympathetic though he was, had no choice but to try to execute the laws.

The office of father-president of the missions automatically came to an end. For ten of the twenty-one missions administrators were appointed in 1834, for six more the following year, and for the remaining five in 1836. Ecclesiastical jurisdictions of the missions were to be "changed into curacies and the missionaries to be replaced with curates." This made it desirable to constitute the two Californias into a separate bishopric.

As a result of such drastic action, and its demoralizing effect upon the unprepared Mission Indians, the province of California suffered "internal convulsions" for a series of years. The degrading methods employed in effectuating secularization, and the unspeakably debasing effects upon the neophytes constitute a sad chapter in our history.

Earnest but fruitless attempts were made to remedy the desperate situation. Political conditions following the administration of Governor Figueroa were little less than chaotic. Finally Governor Juan B. Alvarado appointed William E. P. Hartnell, an early English pioneer of good character, as *Visitador* of the disintegrating missions. Failing to obtain the support of certain administrators, he resigned, thus ending the final serious attempt at restoration of the depleted missions. The mission system was dead.

Then on the 22nd day of June, 1839, Francisco García Diego, the *padre* who had served as prefect of the Zacatecas priests, was invested with the authority of bishop, to preside over the diocese of Alta and Baja California—first bishop of California. Actual investiture had been foreshadowed by a decree of the Mexican Congress of September 19, 1836. News of the actual appointment was received with joy and fresh enthusiasm at Santa Barbara, where the bishop was to take up his residence.

To Bishop García was given authority to use the mission endowment known as the Pious Fund, for the establishment of a cathedral and a college for the training of priests. Then came another upheaval: the new Mexican administration refused to deliver the Pious Fund to the bishop. Adminstration of the Fund was transferred to a subordinate and the property ordered sold, "proceeds to be paid into the national treasury." The projects of the bishop were effectually blocked.

Most distressing were the vicissitudes of the Catholic Church in California during the decade preceding the acquisition by the United States. The belated plans of Micheltorena, newly-appointed but unwelcome governor, came to naught. The resulting confusion was exceeded only by that of the temporal rule—or misrule. Further attempts to restore the mangled mission system ended in tragic failure. Titles to each of the cordon of twenty-one, with the sole exception of Santa Barbara, passed into the hands of private individuals, under titles, however, later pronounced invalid, by the United States government.

Thus it was that the first bishop of California, denied the revenue from the Pious Fund, stripped of power to collect tithes, was utterly unable to carry forward the essential functions of his office. Bowed down with grief he found surcease only in an early death, following quickly after the demise of Padre Narciso Durán, last father-president of the Franciscan Missions of California.

PROTESTANT SERVICES IN AMERICAN CALIFORNIA

On the first day of October, 1846, a party of fifty-seven Americans, with a train of fifteen wagons, reached the Sacramento Valley overland from "the States." A month later they were at Santa Clara.

Among them were Adna A. Hecox and family. Hecox and his wife were Methodists, and while not an ordained minister, he had an "exhorter's licence," which carried with it the right to preach.

A malignant form of typhoid fever broke out among the *Americanos* at Santa Clara, resulting in an alarming number of deaths. Mr. Hecox was called upon to conduct the funeral services. At the obsequies of Silas Hitchcock's daughter he preached a sermon from the text, "Remember how short my time is." C. V. Anthony, in his *Fifty Years of Methodism*, asserts: "This was, without doubt, the first Protestant sermon ever preached within the present limits of the State of California." The exact date is not recorded, but it was approximately the first of January, 1847. Hecox moved to Santa Cruz in February.

We must, however, point out that Samuel Brannan, a Mormon elder at the head of a large party of men, women, and children, had embarked in the *Brooklyn* at New York, February 4, 1836, and after a long, difficult voyage of six months had reached Yerba Buena (San Francisco) on the last day of July. His hope at the time was to plant a Mormon colony in California.

Brannan, often referred to later as the "renegade Mormon," must be credited with having performed "the first non-Catholic wedding ceremony, preached the first sermon in the English language, advocated the first public school . . ." in California. His Saints were called to worship "with a small hand-bell conveniently hung in the plaza." This was months before the arrival of Hecox at Santa Clara. Thus for a time Sam Brannan was the only preacher in Yerba Buena.

Rev. William Roberts, an ordained preacher, arrived at Yerba Buena (San Francisco) on Saturday, the 24th of April, 1847, coming "around the Horn," having been selected as missionary superintendent of the work of the Methodist Episcopal Church for Oregon and California. On the following day, being Sunday, Roberts preached a sermon in the dining room of a hotel. That sermon, preached in an adobe hotel adjoining Portsmouth Square, was believed by many to be the first Protestant sermon ever preached in San Francisco: the congregation was made up from the few families who had settled there, with a sprinkling of sailors and soldiers.

Shortly after the appearance of Roberts came other missionaries representing various Protestant denominations. The first Episcopalian service was conducted by Rev. T. M. Leavenworth, May 2, 1847, also in the adobe hotel, San Francisco. Chaplain Joel Newton of the *Columbus* preached in Ross' new building, July 11—Newton was Congregationalist. By the end of 1847 there were at least three Protestant ministers residing in California, who were also engaged in secular activities.

A considerable number of Protestant preachers arrived during 1849. Mention of them is made on another page.

JESUITS "DESCEND ON CALIFORNIA"

The introduction of any complete story of the Jesuits in California begins with Father Eusebio Kino and his associates, who landed at La Paz, in Baja California, April 2, 1683. There followed a very difficult and laborious period of the founding of missions: by 1767 there were thirteen Jesuit missions in the peninsula, their chief headquarters being at Loreto.

Neither Kino nor any of his associates ever set foot on the soil of Alta California. Suddenly, on the first of March, 1767, came a royal decree from Spain, following the lead of Portugal, expelling the Jesuits from Spain and her American possessions. This was indeed a heavy blow. After a period of confusion, the Jesuit missions were placed under the control of the Dominican Order, while the project for Christianizing Upper California was assigned to the Franciscans.

The Jesuits—more accurately the Society of Jesus—took their origin in 1534, though not officially approved by Pope Paul III until 1540. The founder was Ignatius Loyola, who drafted the rules on the basis of a military organization. To become a member required long and rigorous training. They were characterized by missionary zeal and the desire to establish educational institutions. In certain respects they stood in sharp contrast to the much older order, the Franciscans.

It was a long time before the Jesuit "descent on California" (to employ Henry R. Wagner's phrase), came in the days of gold, in 1849—thereby enters an interesting and important chapter in the history of the Golden State. But the priests came, not from the old Spanish *padres*, not from the eastern seaboard, but from the virile neighbor to the north, the Oregon territory.

Beginning with Father Peter DeSmet, in 1840, a band of zealous Jesuits—never large in number—had been working to establish missions in the northwest. Two of these missionaries, Michael Accolti and John Nobili, who had reached Oregon in 1844, are of special importance to this account, as we shall see.

After Marshall's gold discovery in January, 1848, almost at once the Oregon territory began to suffer depopulation. The southward migration to the gold fields increased in volume and momentum, leaving sparse population and pitiful support for the Jesuit missionaries; while the demand for evangelization in Upper California was almost suddenly increased to a marked degree. Out of such a situation something was certain to happen.

Facing the facts as they were, though official permission was obtained only after delay and with much difficulty, it is sufficient to state that Accolti and Nobili set sail from the Columbia River for San Francisco, December 3, 1849. Five days later they entered the Golden Gate, and the following day they "made their way into the city which was to incorporate them and the Society they represented into the very fabric of its being."

Wrote Father John McGloin,

> The Accolti-Nobili hegira to El Dorado was always to be cherished in Jesuit annals as the first entrance of the Society into American California, although, in 1849, California was not yet a part of the Union.

The Jesuit Centennial was solemnly commemorated on Sunday, December 11, 1949, at St. Ignatius Church and the University of San Francisco. As a preliminary to the culmination of the festival occasion, on December 8, solemn mass was celebrated and the Reverend Zacheus J. Maher eloquently retold the story of the coming of members of the Jesuit Order into California. Thenceforth their numerous and varied activities, concerning which it is not necessary to report here, have become an integral part of the history of the commonwealth.

EARLY PROTESTANT LEADERS

Leaders of Protestantism, representing different denominations, manifested keen interest in California as a field for missionary endeavor, from the very early period of American occupation. That the pathological conditions occasioned by the gold rush needed the refinement of the Christian gospel few will be inclined to question. "The highest adventure of California," wrote Leon Loofbourow, "was by the Argonauts of the spirit."

In one sense the story of Methodism in California begins with Jedediah Smith, the "Bible toter," who entered California overland in 1826, sometimes referred to as "one of Protestantism's forgotten men." He certainly ranks as one of the most remarkable trail-breakers of our entire history.

In the autumn of 1846 William Roberts of New Jersey received the appointment as superintendent of the expanding work of the Methodists in the Oregon territory. His administration as Superintendent of the Oregon-California Mission Conference, continuing until the formation of the Annual Conference, in 1853, is noteworthy. But Roberts had been preceded, in 1846, by Adna Hecox, a licensed Methodist exhorter, Elihu Anthony and his family reached San José in October, 1847: shortly afterward he preached the first sermon and formed a Methodist "class."

Then came those mighty men of Methodism, William Taylor, Isaac Owen, and Martin C. Briggs.

The first Baptist missionary to California was Osgood C. Wheeler, a native of Wayne County, New York. He arrived on the last day of February, 1849. To him must go the distinction of founding the first Baptist Church in San Francisco. He was instrumental also in organizing the San Francisco Baptist Association, of which he was the first moderator.

But before the arrival of Wheeler, T. Dwight Hunt, pioneer New School Presbyterian minister, had already rendered conspicuous service in San Francisco, having arrived in late October, 1848. Conducting the first Protestant communion service (January, 1849) is attributed to him. He was appointed chaplain at large, and in that capacity he maintained a union religious service and performed other religious functions. In 1850 there were the "Three W's of the presbytery"—Sylvester Woodbridge, Albert Williams, and James Woods.

As a most worthy representative of the Congregational Church Samuel H. Willey, a Dartmouth College graduate, reached Monterey in February, 1849, commissioned by the Home Missionary Society. That autumn he was the Protestant chaplain of the state constitutional convention, serving also as chaplain at the *presidio* and for six months as teacher of a pioneer Monterey school. Doubtless one of the most capable of all the early Protestant leaders was Joseph A. Benton, who arrived in San Francisco, July 6, 1849. His first sermon was preached in Sacramento, where the Congregational Church was organized in September. He was once introduced by Horace Bushnell as "the father and mother of Congregationalism in California."

An Episcopal clergyman, T. M. Leavenworth, reached San Francisco April 18, 1847, as a chaplain in Stevenson's Regiment. He preached a sermon on the second of May, but little was accomplished at that time toward organizing a church of his denomination. In 1849, however, J. L. Ver Mehr and F. S. Mines arrived in California; and under the leadership of Ver Mehr a parish was formally organized April 28, 1850. For a number of years this influential rector devoted much time and effort to educational work in San Francisco. The Unitarians were first organized in 1850, their first church being dedicated in 1853.

In that epochal decade, 1846-56, there were also many other Protestant leaders of different denominations, most of them young men who were not disobedient to their vision, deeply imbued with "a spirit of high adventure in the realm of religion." As a group of men of integrity, personality, capacity for endurance, and devotion to the cause they held dear, they must be accorded a secure place in the list of California Firsts.

THANKSGIVING DAY

On numerous occasions thanksgiving mass was celebrated in the churches of the early California Missions—the little band had been spared after suffering attack by hostile Indians, the supply ship had arrived when starvation was imminent, or gratitude was expressed for a bounteous harvest. But obviously on none of these occasions was the traditional annual Thanksgiving Day of the American people observed.

It was not until 1849, the year when California's first state constitution was formed, that a governor's Thanksgiving Proclamation was formally issued. On the 24th day of October of that year, even before the newly-formed constitution was put into operation by popular vote, military Governor Bennet Riley on behalf of the people issued the following

Proclamation

In conformity with the custom of other states and territories, and in order that the people of California may make a general and public acknowledgment of their gratitude to the Supreme Ruler of the Universe for His kind and fostering care during the past year, and for the boundless blessings which we now enjoy, it is recommended that Thursday, the 29th day of November next, be set apart and kept as a day of thanksgiving and prayer.

Thus was instituted in California the custom that had become more or less general throughout the United States of setting aside the last Thursday of November as a special day of Thanksgiving. By that day the main agricultural labors of the year are completed, the elections have been held, "summer wanderers are gathered to their homes." The proclamation had been issued by General Riley; but before the actual day arrived, the first state election had been held, the constitution adopted, and Peter H. Burnett elected first governor of the new state of California.

Observance of Thanksgiving Day in California, however, was far from universal, especially in the southland, during the dark days of the Civil War. Many of the newspapers were not at all friendly to the idea of a popular holiday. However, in 1864 Governor Frederick K. Low, a loyal Unionist, issued a resounding proclamation, appointing Thursday, November 24, "as the day of thanksgiving and praise to Almighty God." The proclamation continues:

I do enjoin upon the people of this state that, upon that day thus set apart, they rest from all secular labor and assemble in their customary places of worship and, with devout hearts, acknowledge His exalted goodness, His loving kindness, and His tender mercies. [The proclamation continues at considerable length.] Let us thank Him for the great and signal victories that have attended the arms of the republic, both on land and sea, during the past year; . . . for the unity of purpose which is everywhere apparent, that must result in a complete triumph of liberty, humanity, and justice over treason, anarchy, and barbarism. And, above all, let us rejoice at the prospect of an honorable and lasting peace, based upon national unity and obedience to constitutional law.

What has usually been regarded as California's first Thanksgiving Day was that of November 30, 1850, some seven weeks after Admission Day (September 9). Peter H. Burnett was governor. After more than a century of statehood one particular episode of that Thanksgiving Day is worthy of special notice. Rev. Joseph A. Benton, brilliant pastor of First Congregational Church at Sacramento and one of the most prominent religious leaders in the state, gave a remarkable discourse on the very ambitious topic, "California as She Was, as She Is, and as She Is to Be." On that occasion he seemed inspired to utter prophecies that made him a true seer. If those who looked upon him then as merely a brilliant dreamer could but behold from the vantage of the present, they would know that he had a true vision of the unparalleled growth and development that would come to the Golden State. Here are some of his prophetic words:

A million of people cannot fail to thrive by cultivating this virgin soil, and in fifty years they will be here to make the demonstration; farm houses will dot thickly every valley; marshes will be redeemed from overflow, and wastes will bloom in beauty and yield harvests of joy. The state will not fal behind in arts and manufacturing, and in commerce. With hundreds of miles of navigable bays and rivers, with 700 miles of sea coast, with earth's broadest ocean at her feet, gemmed with a thousand sea isles, and laving the shore of a continent, California is to be the Queen of the Seas, and within the Golden Gate are to be the docks and depots of a steam and electro-magnetic marine, of which all the steam marine that now exists is but the minutest embryo. The iron horse that has drunk the waters of the Mississippi will fly over mountain and plain and river, and breathe defiance in yonder beetling cliffs and towering depths of snow, as he dashes forward through the tunneled depths beneath, and comes through our streets to slake his thirst at the Sacramento.

FIRST CAMP-MEETINGS

The introduction in America of the "general camp-meeting" as a form of religious evangelism, dates back to at least the beginning of the nineteenth century. In it different sects were combined, though at the first Presbyterians, followed by Methodists, were the most active. Later the camp-meeting was usually conducted along denominational lines. It was well adapted to sparsely settled regions, but of questionable value in densely settled communities.

Families came in their wagons, and made camp together, usually in a grove of trees along a stream. The interest was so intense that often 10,000 persons would be encamped together—sometimes more than double that number. The religious meetings were continued for several weeks. The camp-meeting became a really significant phenomenon in our national history.

In California it came into use almost immediately following the introduction of Protestantism. From Methodist "circuit" to camp-meeting was but a step—in California quite a natural one. The camp-meeting, as Owen C. Coy has said, was "always associated with frontier Methodism." There were no buildings to accommodate large audiences. With increasing population "basket meetings" were held: these naturally merged into camp-meetings, which increased rapidly in interest and importance.

In the spring of 1851 Dr. S. D. Simonds conducted such a meeting at Sonoma which he claimed was the first ever held in the state. In connection with the meeting Dr. C. V. Anthony tells of an event "worth relating." Simonds was warned that the settlers "liked whiskey and would drink it on all suitable occasions." The story continues as follows:

> The meeting began under the most favorable auspices. Gen. Vallejo, the proprietor of the valley, himself and family Roman Catholics, sent two beeves for use of the campers. On Friday, a man of foreign accent drove on the ground with pies, cakes, and small beer for sale. Simonds objected . . . but on his protesting that he had nothing else to sell, and agreeing to have family prayers . . . , he was permitted to proceed with his business. . . . At length it became apparent that there was a drunken man in the congregation. He was taken to the woods . . . and there confessed that he had obtained his whiskey of the huckster in question. The next morning the peddler was gone, but the spot his wagon had occupied was covered with smashed pies, cakes, and broken bottles, indicating that violence had attended his departure. Two weeks later Mr. Simonds learned that the boys had thrown a lasso over the fellow's outfit and dragged it well out of the camp. They then told him that the climate of Sonoma was not healthy for men like him, and that if he knew what was best for him, he would locate in some other region. He acted on the advice at once.

Priority claims have been made for several other meetings, but without complete authentication. One refers to a camp-meeting held in Napa Valley in the summer of 1851. A writer refers to a similar meeting as the first that was held, near Nevada City, in July, 1852, by ministers of the M. E. Church, South. Certain it is that the institution expanded rapidly during the early 1850's, and that different religious denominations employed it. In addition to Methodists and Presbyterians, there were Baptists, the United Brethren, and, later, the Seventh Day Adventists. Interesting details are given by O. P. Fitzgerald.

Physical arrangements were simple—rough boards or puncheons for seats, pulpit platform slightly elevated, the grounds strewn with a bed of straw. Torches, candles, and sometimes kerosene lamps furnished the light—"nothing was superfluous." Whole families attended, sometimes bringing the family cow for fresh milk—even coops of chickens were not rare.

The order of services was quite definite. After morning prayers came the 11 o'clock meeting; following the lunch the 3 o'clock meeting, then the great culminating service in the evening. Preaching was usually of the vigorous uncompromising fundamentalist type. There was the "mourners bench" and the unctuous ejaculations of "Amen!" "Glory to God!" "Hallelujah!" Sunday was the most important day. Hundreds were converted as a result of a season's labors.

The camp-meeting was also an occasion of considerable social significance, at a time when opportunities were few. Families got together, there were reunions of scattered friends, and, "In the balmy evenings the young men could furtively woo the maidens."

As large churches were built in the cities and populations became more dense with modern means of communication and entertainment, the camp-meeting declined. Even to this day, however, it has by no means been completely abandoned.

Y.M.C.A. AND Y.W.C.A.

The celebration of the 100th anniversary year of the Young Men's Christian Association in San Francisco took place at the Whitcomb Hotel, on the evening of March 21, 1953. The centennial banquet was part of the program of the 19th Annual Conference of the Council, representing the Christian Associations in seven western states and Hawaii.

The formal organization of the Y.M.C.A. in San Francisco is reported in Rev. Albert Williams' valuable book, *A Pioneer Pastorate*. Dr. Williams was a pioneer Presbyterian preacher at the time. In his book appears the following direct account:

It was my privilege to be one of the founders of the Young Men's Christian Association of San Francisco. This cause, ever since I heard in New York, in 1832, the strong advocacy of a Scotch lay-brother in its behalf, had retained an abiding interest in my mind. In view of the need of such an instrumentality, especially in San Francisco, I was prompt to give to the proposal of organization a special attention. The meeting with this object in view was held in the First Presbyterian Church, and the draft of a Constitution was made by myself. At that meeting, July 18, 1853, the Young Men's Christian Association of San Francisco was formally instituted.

In commemoration of the second anniversary of the founding of the Association a special celebration was held in First Congregational Church of San Francisco, August 6, 1855. After music by a trained choir and devotional exercises, Dr. A. W. Scott delivered an eloquent address appropriate to the occasion. Then the Association proceeded to elect officers for the ensuing year.

Unquestionably the most outstanding Y.M.C.A. leader of San Francisco was General Secretary Henry J. McCoy, who served many years as active head of the San Francisco Association. He was big-hearted, jovial, and completely devoted to the task of bringing blessing and benefit to young men of every rank and class.

The spread of the Young Men's Christian Association throughout the world has been phenomenal. Probably no man has been more influential in this historic movement than John R. Mott, who attained to the stature of world statesmanship. He it was who, in the 1880's came as a young man to California to organize the first student Y.M.C.A.'s in the colleges, and who served as student leader in the International Committee from 1888 for many years, also as chairman of the World's Committee and Student Volunteer Movement—not to mention other important connections.

Another name of first-rate importance in connection with the Christian work among young men in California and abroad, is that of Robert E. Speer. Conspicuous among his many activities are to be mentioned his distinguished work in the Army and Navy, his service as President of the Federal Council of Churches of Christ in America, and his authorship of dozens of books and pamphlets, focusing attention on the world-wide Christian missionary movement.

The Young Men's Christian Association, now more than a hundred years old in California, distinguished for its work of uplift both in peace and war, has been established in seventy countries and is at present in the midst of a vigorous program of still greater effort and effectiveness. Dr. Paul M. Limbert is general secretary of the World's Alliance,

centered at Geneva, Switzerland. The Y.M.C.A. Centennial was celebrated in Paris in 1955 in a manner commensurate with its historic
importance. Meanwhile the work of the Association, begun in 1853,
continues with vigor and effectiveness in California.

In 1878 the Young Women's Christian Association was organized in
San Francisco. Largely through the energy and devotion of one woman
a group of ten volunteers formed the nucleus of that large and influential
organization.

The original purpose was to assist young women in finding satisfactory
housing, employment, and religious instruction. So successful were their
endeavors that by mid-century in San Francisco alone a staff of nearly
100 workers were directing the varied program under a strong board
of directors. In the year 1953 the "Y" celebrated its seventy-fifth anniversary with a Diamond Jubilee Pageant, "The Wicked West and
Woman, or, A Chronicle of Good Works in the Port of the Pacific."
San Francisco is but one of the many cities in all parts of California
where this organization of young women has established itself.

SALVATION ARMY

One of the world's great religious organizations of recent origin is the
Salvation Army, still less than a century old. Its founder was William
Booth of London. First known as East London Revival Society, in 1878
it was given the name of Salvation Army, being organized on military
lines. "General" Booth remained its head during the remainder of his
life.

By the year 1890 it had spread to Continental Europe, North America,
Australia, and India. In the United States its beginnings date from 1880.
As was to be expected, the Salvation Army, a militant type of aggressive
evangelical body, was not long in making its way into California.

Major Alfred Wells and Captain Henry Stillwell were chosen by the
General to begin work on the Pacific Coast. Extracts from a letter
written by Major Wells to Lt.-Col. Merriweather (published in *The
War Cry*, July 18, 1953) give interesting details—the following is quoted:

> I landed alone in San Francisco, July 21, 1883, and started the first
> Salvation Army meeting the following evening, July 22, 1883, in a little
> hall, 815 Montgomery Street, seating some 80 or more. . . . A short time
> later saw us in a little larger building, 632 Commercial Street, which
> remained for years the No. 1 hall.
>
> The early days were full of intense interest as our crowds were quite
> cosmopolitan both outdoors and in, and the converts were from all
> quarters of the globe. . . .

The Salvation Army spirit had caught hold of some good loyal folks in Oakland and in San José, and it soon fell to my lot to divide Sundays between San Francisco and Oakland where we soon had a good work on foot.

After some fourteen months two young captains were sent out from London, who shortly became Mrs. Wells and Mrs. Stillwell. Major Wells' letter continues:

> Their arrival put new life into everything, and San Francisco soon boasted of a brass band of 12 pieces, . . . and the comrades who became bandsmen were at the head of a procession which stirred the city, roused the devil, and gave us a lasting ad, if such were needed.

As early as 1894 the now familiar red Christmas kettles appeared, the idea having originated in northern California during a period of extreme financial depression. Capt. Joseph McFee, while walking along the waterfront, spied a huge caldron suspended in a ship chandler's shop. The thought flashed into his mind, "Why not place a soup kettle in a centrally located spot so people could help feed the hungry sailors by dropping coins into the kettle?" Christmas kettles have been standard equipment for more than half a century.

While the Salvation Army has no formal creed and expresses no denominational preference, it is positively Christian, with great emphasis on practical service intended to win the individual to a better life. All races and creeds are its beneficiaries without distinction. Among its many special features are noted the Home League, bringing cheer to shut-ins; the Family Bureau, providing counselling, employment, medical care and other assistance; Prison Service, now an indispensable service in police courts, jails, and prisons, with special help to discharged men and women; Summer Camp, as operated at Redwood Glen, in the Santa Cruz Mountains, for the benefit of boys and girls, as well as mothers with their babies; and Men's Social Service, with its workshop program, aid to alcoholics, veterans, and handicapped men. The street meetings have continued as a familiar feature.

In March, 1951, the Salvation Army Canteen Kitchen was opened at the Ferry Building, San Francisco. It provides not only coffee and doughnuts to service men, but furnishes hotel and travel information, even arranges with San Francisco families for evenings and home-cooked meals. The contributions made in U.S. Army have earned for the Salvation Army the highest praise. As J. Edgar Hoover declared, "The work of the Salvation Army is a great investment in the future of America." It embodies the practical teachings and the spirit of the Founder of Christianity.

CALIFORNIA'S ARCHBISHOP

As Junípero Serra was the first father-president of the Franciscan Missions of California, so Joseph Sadoc Alemany, a member of the Dominican order of the Catholic church, was the first archbishop. Each of the distinguished leaders won a large place in the history of the Golden West.

Alemany was born at Vich, near Barcelona, in Spain, in the year 1814. Early in life he became a Dominican friar. He came to the United States in the late 1840's, his first tour of duty taking him to Kentucky, Tennessee, and Ohio. In October of 1850 he arrived at New York.

While visiting the Holy City of Rome he was selected by Pope Pius IX to be Bishop of Monterey, in far-away California. With humility he said of the Pope: "I shall never forgot his words of encouragement when I accepted the burden of the Episcopate." Then he quoted these words of the Holy Father:

> You are going to a wonderful land, where the government respects the rights of man, where the people are understanding, where God has revealed the treasures of His Infinite Bounty, where men are generous, and I am sure that the Church shall not be in want . . . Depart in peace.

Up to 1853 his jurisdiction as bishop included all Upper California and Mexican Lower California. But in that year Lower California was removed from his Diocese, and the Archdiocese of San Francisco was formed, extending from Monterey to the Oregon boundary. Then it was that Alemany became Archbishop—the first in California.

On the 18th of November, 1855, St. Mary's Cathedral was filled with worshippers at the solemn presentation of the Pallium to the Archbishop, direct from the Pope at Rome, as a token of spiritual jurisdiction over the Catholic churches of the Province. The Pallium was "an emblem of humility, charity, and innocence."

For the thirty-five years during which he was Archbishop of the San Francisco Archdiocese he played a commanding part in the religious history of the state. He was more than the trusted head of his Church in the California metropolis: he showed special solicitude for the Catholics in the mining districts, dedicating many churches, including those along "the gold dust trail of the Mother Lode." Many classes of the faithful were confirmed by him in his reverent, graceful manner.

On the 29th of July, 1875, an impressive celebration was held in honor and in recognition of the twenty-fifth anniversary of his transfer from Monterey to San Francisco. He modestly referred to himself as the "Little Bishop." In reality, he was, in the words of Father Henry L.

Walsh, "more than an ordinary servant of God. He led a life of exceptional austerity. . . . No one ever saw him in anger."

After the appointment of Patrick William Riordan as coadjutor, with the right of succession, Archbishop Alemany was permitted to resign. Returning to Spain, he died in 1888. In countless ways his greatness of soul had manifested itself.

The greatly loved Archbishop adapted himself to the strange conditions he found in California "with surprising success." In summing up his remarkable career in the Golden State, Father Walsh pays him this deserved tribute:

> In prayer to God, with little thought of his personal comfort, he spent himself day and night, in order to secure a sufficient number of missionaries to send to all the mining camps, so that no one of the faithful would be neglected; . . . For thirty-four years he kept up this strenuous mode of existence, never curtailing his vigilance, . . . until failing health compelled him to depart from the people of California, whom he loved with the affection of a devoted father.

CATHOLIC CARDINAL

With ecclesiastical pomp and traditional ceremony, in the Vatican City, Pope Pius XII, in secret consistory on the 12th day of January, 1953, named twenty-four new Cardinals, bringing the Sacred College to its full strength of seventy for the first time in almost two and a half centuries, with a total of four members from the United States. Among the twenty-four new Cardinals only one was from this country, but he was from California—and this was the first time that the American West was thus recognized and honored in the Catholic Church. He was James Francis McIntyre, Archbishop of Los Angeles, aged 66, now become James Francis Cardinal McIntyre.

Announcement of the selection had been published to the world on the 29th of November, 1952. The elaborate ceremonies at the Vatican, associated with the important event, occupied virtually the entire week beginning January 12, culminating with the bestowal of the tasseled red hats by the Pope in a public consistory that "blazed with the brilliance of medieval pageantry."

It is significant that on the historic occasion Cardinal McIntyre, referring to communism as "a godless religion," averred that the Sacred College is "a symbol of an overwhelming desire for peace on the part of the Holy Father and the Church." He deemed all movements for peace basically religious in nature, since "peace has its origin in love of neighbor, and that love springs from love of God."

The election of our first Cardinal to the Sacred College of the Roman Catholic Church, whose seventy members rank next to the Pope himself, is an outstanding event in the religious history of California. Instantly it brings to mind the appointment of Junípero Serra, humble Franciscan friar, to be Father-President of the California Missions, and the elevation of Joseph Sadoc Alemany to be Archbishop of San Francisco, first California Archbishop, when the state was young. How different the scene in California that greeted the eyes of Serra in 1769 from that which Alemany witnessed in the first decade of American statehood! And scarcely less is the transformation that has been wrought in the Golden State during the century from Alemany to McIntyre.

What are the traits and qualities of this eminent cleric that commended him to the Pope for elevation to the Sacred College of Cardinals? First, there was earnest toil and labor from early childhood; there was rigorous discipline and severe training, with all seriousness and maturity of purpose; special services to the young were constant and true; perhaps chief of all was his deep spiritual dedication as evidenced by his long and distinguished career of upward striving and resplendent achievement in both faith and works.

California salutes James Francis Cardinal McIntyre. The chronicler enters upon the long record another highly significant first, in the field of religion, in the stirring annals of the Empire State of the Pacific.

CHAPTER FIVE

AGRICULTURE AND HORTICULTURE

"The harvest gathered in the field of the Past is to be brought home for the use of the Present." —*Arnold of Rugby*

WHEAT

When was the first wheat actually grown in California? The precise date is a matter of some doubt—and of little consequence: but essential facts regarding the earliest production of this basic cereal are well established.

Along with many other seeds and plants wheat was introduced by the Franciscan missionaries, whose first mission was established at San Diego, in 1769. Back of Fr. Junípero Serra and his associates, however, stood José de Galvez, Visitor-General, who really planned the colonization of Alta California. On his order agricultural implements and an assortment of seeds, including wheat, were carried by the colonists.

The first handful of seed wheat, according to Herbert Bolton, had been sent by the Jesuit leader Francis Kino across to Arizona to a giant Yuma chieftain; but little historical significance need be attached to this. Guadalupe Vallejo related that "The fathers at San Diego Mission sowed grain on the bottom lands in the willows the first year and it was washed away; then they put it on the mesa above the mission and it died: the third year they found a good piece of land—it yielded 195 fold." Some allowance should perhaps be made on Vallejo's literal statement—he obviously did not possess adequate documentary evidence.

In the attempts that certainly were made at the different missions, and later in the *pueblos*, mistakes were made, and the actual production of wheat during those first years was small and precarious. It is safe to say that no significant amount was harvested before 1775. San Gabriel Mission (founded 1771) soon became known as "the mother of agriculture in California," as it later developed into one of the most prosperous of all the missions.

First methods of wheat growing were crude in the extreme.

"The plow was a crooked branch, with a toe of iron; the beam was a straight branch lashed at one end to the plow, and at the other to the yoke, which again was a straight stick lashed behind the horns of a yoke of oxen

106

by thongs of rawhide," . . . "Of course," continues the description given by
Horace Davis, "such a plow could only scratch the ground, . . . The seed
was sown broadcast, and brushed in with the branch of a tree drawn twice
over the ground."

The method used in summer reaping was equally crude. The mowing
was done by hand, the sheaves were thrown upon a floor of prepared
bare earth; then a band of mustangs was turned in and driven round
and round to trample out the wheat. Finally, the grain, separated from
the straw and dirt, was loaded onto the creaking *carreta* and hauled to
the granary.

For several years preceding 1822 the exports of wheat from California
averaged about 1,000 bushels annually, in addition to small amounts
going to Sitka via the Russian port at Bodega. But after secularization
of the missions, all agricultural activity languished for a time.

With the large influx of American settlers, 1845-1847, there was
definite revival and marked expansion of wheat growing. In his informative book, *What I Saw in California*, Edwin Bryant tells of the fields,
along the American and Cosumnes Rivers, on the Marsh Ranch, in
Livermore and Santa Clara Valleys, and in other localities.

Then came the great gold rush, when the wheat crops were left in
the fields to rot—everybody made for the mines. Agriculture was
abandoned in the eager search for gold. But farming was not long in
coming back to its own. In 1858 the first shipment of wheat went around
Cape Horn to New York; and 1860 witnessed the real beginning of
wheat export from the Golden State. The far-flung fields and vast
production of the two decades following constitute an epic in California's remarkable history.

CULTIVATED FRUITS

A Jesuit missionary, Father Juan de Ugarte, has been called the father
of agriculture in *Baja* (Lower) California. He was second only to
Father Juan María Salvatierra in the work of establishing the chain
of Jesuit Missions in the peninsula to the south of us, the mother mission
at Loreto dating from 1697. During the years immediately following,
seeds and plants of cultivated fruits and vegetables, as well as cattle and
horses, were brought over across the Gulf of California. It is of record
that "there was a small garden and a few fruit trees at Loreto in 1701."
This was more than two-thirds of a century before the occupation of
Alta (Upper) California.

Cultivated fruits and vegetables were introduced into Upper California
with the founding of the Franciscan Missions under Father Junípero

Serra, begun at San Diego in 1769. It is to José de Galvez, illustrious *Visitador-General* from Spain, that credit is chiefly due "for ordering the carrying of seeds of fruits, grains, vegetables, and flowers into the new territory." From the planting at the first Mission the same varieties were carried to the missions subsequently founded until the entire cordon of twenty-one establishments boasted each of its own beginnings in the horticultural arts.

When George Vancouver, distinguished English navigator, visited California in 1792, he found at Santa Clara a fine orchard, "with apple, peach, pear, apricot, and fig trees, all thrifty and promising." At San Buenaventura, continues Edward J. Wickson, he describes "apples, pears, plums, figs, oranges, grapes, peaches, and pomegranates." To this list should be added, for other missions, olives, lemons, limes, citrons, and in one or two instances, date palms and cherries. Later the orchards at Mission San Gabriel, near Los Angeles, were found to be quite extensive.

Few of the early Spanish settlers and *rancheros*, however, seemed inclined to develop horticulture, so promisingly undertaken by the padres at the missions. Nevertheless, we learn that at *Pueblo de San José* luxurious fruits were grown within a few years after founding, and that before the year 1805 "more fruit was grown than could be disposed of in its natural state." By 1830 General M. G. Vallejo had planted fruit trees on his well-cultivated ranch at Sonoma.

Notwithstanding the sad decline of the mission properties from 1834 onward, important exceptions are noted in the instance of some of the orchards. For example, fifteen to twenty acres of flourishing trees and vines were found at Mission San José by Edwin Bryant, in 1846. Meanwhile early American planters had begun to make their appearance, one of the first being George Yount (after whom Yountville was named), who planted vines in Napa Valley in 1838, and fruit trees later. William Wolfskill was a pioneer orange grower of Los Angeles. In 1854 he purchased an orange and lime nursery from Doctor Halsey; and in April, 1857, says Harris Newmark, "when there were not many more than a hundred orange trees bearing fruit in the whole county, Wolfskill planted several thousand and so established what was to be, for that time, the largest orange orchard in the United States."

Following the introduction of fruits by the padres came a second introduction by Russian settlers, at Fort Ross, in 1812. Apples, chiefly, were planted by the Russians, with some cherries. A few trees said to be still surviving are "very old and mossy, and are not very thrifty, but still bear some fruit every year."

Horticulture did not assume real commercial importance in California for many years. But when the possibilities of irrigation, applied to the productive soil, became actualities under the fructifying warmth of the golden sunshine, California became the world's cornucopia. Supremacy has been achieved not only in citrus production but also in olives, figs, walnuts, almonds, prunes, peaches, apricots—in short, California has come to lead all other states in the output of more than a score of important products of the soil.

IRRIGATION

Irrigation of the land is an expression of the spirit of conquest whereby the soil may be made to produce maximum crops per unit of water used. No state has more diversified products than California, nor has any gained more from the artificial application of water.

The beginnings of irrigation in California date from the first occupation by Spanish settlers. The practice began at the first mission (San Diego), founded in 1769. After crop failures the first two seasons at the Old Town site, another planting was made the third season, this time near the present location of the mission.

The first serious irrigation project was undertaken in 1776, after the present mission site had been selected. A large dam, built of stone, was 254 feet long, twelve feet thick, and fourteen feet in height. From this dam a twelve-mile aqueduct of stone and tile carried the water, in Mission Gorge, to the mission lands. It was a large project, not completed until 1781. There was of necessity some irrigation at all the mission establishments—each had its orchard and vegetable garden.

In the meantime California's first civil settlement (*Pueblo de San José*) was founded in 1777. After the fields had been planted an irrigating canal was constructed for the purpose of bringing water from the Guadalupe River to the fields. A similar canal or ditch (*azequia*) was constructed for the second *pueblo* (Los Angeles), founded in 1781. This *zanja* system (open ditches for irrigation) was a unique institution coming down from the Spanish founders of the *pueblos*. *Zanjas* were constructed for different missions, in some cases from five to eight miles in length; also reservoirs and aqueducts were constructed. La Purisima, for example, had three large reservoirs and cisterns of masonwork, besides other improvements, enabling the *padres* to cultivate large areas of land. Materials used included stone, cement, and some brick. The manual labor was done, in the main, by the Indians. Thus it becomes apparent that irrigation, in some form and to some degree, clearly antedated the American conquest. It has been called "a race heritage of the Spaniards."

Under the American régime the first really significant attempt at irrigation was made in 1853, in San Joaquin Valley. A ditch was run from Mill Creek, near Visalia, to bring water for gardens and grain fields. By 1864 irrigation had begun to assume a very important place. In 1865 E. S. Holden pointed out its special advantages, declaring, "Nothing is more needed than water to make our valleys put on gorgeous livery of perpetual spring." About the same time John Bidwell said that properly conducted and applied irrigation would awake the barren hills and plains "as if by magic into such fertility and fruitfulness as to astonish even Californians themselves." The San Joaquin and Kings River Canal was begun in 1871: within seven years it was seventy miles long.

Many problems had to be faced, including a persistent prejudice of many farmers against the general principle of irrigation, contending that their land could produce crops without artificial watering—there was something belittling about irrigating the soil! But seeing was believing—good beginnings had been made; the value of the system was clearly demonstrated. Thrifty farmers began to replace the vast fields of wheat in the Central Valley with alfalfa, fruits of many kinds, vineyards, melons, and vegetables. Private irrigation systems included the California Development Company, Fresno Consolidated Canals Company, Sacramento Valley Irrigation Company, and others. It was estimated that the total irrigable agricultural land of California amounted to 22,000,000 acres, and that by 1917 more than 3,000,000 acres were actually under irrigation.

Still later came the development and perfection of numerous Irrigation Districts, with vast areas, still expanding. These have brought almost unbelievable production as a result of the intensive cultivation of our spreading acres of reclaimed, irrigated California lands. Vast conservation projects even now in process will result in greatly increasing the already immense production of our soil.

Looking to the future, with its inevitable increase in population, the water supply and its conservation has come to be regarded as California's Number 1 problem. Its commanding significance is emphasized by the statesman-like words of the then Governor Earl Warren:

> It is the solemn duty of our generation to plan wisely for the best use for all purposes of every drop of water. Upon such planning will depend the happiness and welfare of millions of people, of this generation and of future generations. Controlled and put to use, it is mankind's greatest benefactor.

CATTLE INDUSTRY

Cattle raising was easily the leading industry of Spanish and Mexican California. There was not even a close second. And the "cattle on a thousand hills" and in the smiling valleys were chiefly valuable for their hides—tallow was the main by-product: while they provided the principal meat supply, that was purely secondary in quantity, without commercial importance.

The introduction of cattle coincides with the Spanish occupation itself. The Franciscan *padres* under Junípero Serra who came on the historic Portolá expedition of 1769, knowing they were coming to a fertile land, brought with them many kinds of seeds of grains and vegetables, a small supply of farming implements, and a band of 200 brood cattle from the Jesuit Missions of Baja California. The extraordinary increase of these cattle, feeding on the wide acres of native California grasses, resulted in the multiplied thousands of the mission period and a little later on the great ranges of the *rancheros*.

The cattle of Spanish California were quite different from those with which we, at the present time, are familiar; they showed no evidence of scientific breeding. In general, they may be described as comparatively small-bodied, long, thin-legged, with widespread, sharp horns — much lighter in weight than our modern Herefords, to which their resemblance was slight indeed. They might better be compared to the native deer, which sometimes herded with them, and they were almost as wild. They were nimble and fleet of foot, well able to roam and forage for themselves in the vast, unfenced areas.

At the climax of the mission period, just before actual secularization under the Mexican régime, there was quite surely a total of upwards of 400,000 cattle on the mission ranges. To these must be added something like 62,500 horses, 320,000 sheep, besides many mules, hogs, and goats.

In addition to the chief uses (hides and tallow) cattle were used, as already stated, extensively for food of the people, including the Mission Indians. The meat was tough, but nutritious and of good flavor. Again, large quantities of soap also were made at some of the missions. Milk and other dairy products were used only very slightly, partly, strange as it may seem now, because of the great difficulty experienced in milking the cows. The milking process required the combined efforts of at least three persons. Mrs. Sanchez has given us this interesting description: "One held the animal by the head, another kept tight hold of the *reata* with which its hind legs were tied, while a third milked with one hand, holding the receptacle in the other." This unusual procedure was looked on "with absorbed interests" by any transient guests and other persons who chanced to be at leisure.

No complete history of early California could be written without an account of the cattle industry and its high relative importance, the beginnings of which have here briefly been told.

SHEEP INDUSTRY

The introduction and early development of California's sheep industry lacks much of the dramatic and romantic character attaching to the more spectacular cattle industry. But from the standpoint of wealth production sheep ranked only second to cattle. The mild climate and wide ranges afforded almost uninterrupted growth. With native grass the only feed required, the sheep matured at the age of two years, thus insuring large natural increase.

Immediately following the founding of the Franciscan mission and the *presidio* at Monterey (June, 1770), Governor Portolá dispatched to José de Galvez and the viceroy of New Spain a soldier and a sailor boy with a report of activities. When they reached a point about a day's journey south of San Diego they met Captain Rivera y Moncada, who, with twenty soldiers, was proceeding northward to Alta California with a number of cattle and sheep. These, Theodore Hittell tells us, "may be called the original of all the herds and flocks of Alta California." Within fifty years the small flock brought by Moncada is said to have increased to a total of something like two million sheep.

As with the cattle the first sheep in California were pastured on the mission lands. The method of handling them was the same as had prevailed in the old country for centuries. Of course there were no fences for many years. Shearing time was by far the liveliest part of the prosaic life of the herder, generally a very lonely kind of occupation.

The primary purpose of the *padres* in sheep raising was not to produce mutton but rather to provide clothing for the almost naked Indians. In this, however, they met with indifferent success, since it proved easier in practice to obtain cloth for clothing (mostly cotton) usually from the Yankee trading vessels that arrived in California ports from time to time. The mission sheep were of inferior breeds, with short, coarse wool, and came to be chiefly valued for their hides and the tallow—little actual use was made of the wool.

At Mission San Gabriel the flocks are said to have increased to 40,000 sheep; and some writers claim that at San Luis Rey the number reached at one time 100,000. However, it now appears that such figures are greatly exaggerated: it seems more likely that neither the sheep nor the cattle exceeded 30,000 at any one time.

Secularization of the missions in the 1830's played havoc with the California sheep industry. In less than two decades "the great flocks had all but disappeared." In the gold rush days of the early American period many sheep were brought in from Arizona and Mexico. In a single year, so great was the sudden demand for mutton that 40,000 sheep reached the California gold fields, where they sold for $16.00 apiece. But the following year prices dropped to $9.00 to $12.00 apiece. William Wells Hollister, who went to Ohio, obtained 6,000 merinos and drove them to San Bernardino, is known as "father of the real sheep industry" in the state of California. He made a fortune, becoming the "worthy magnate of San Benito County," whose county seat is a perpetual memorial to his name.

In 1867 the California wool production amounted to about nine million pounds. But the expansion of the industry was so rapid that a total of twenty-three million pounds was reported for 1872. It was during the following year that the "No-fence Law" was enacted, declaring that "cattle and sheep should not be allowed to run loose without a herder to keep them from trespassing." Protection was likewise provided for the grain farmers, who had become a significant factor in the agricultural economy of the state. There was many a clash between the wheat grower and the sheep herder, and still more and still sharper clashes between the sheep men and the cattle men.

OLIVE CULTURE

The famous expedition of Gaspar de Portolá and Padre Junípero Serra in 1769 brought to Alta California cuttings and seeds of a considerable number of fruit trees that proved to be the beginnings of some of our most important horticultural products. Included in the list were the orange, fig, pomegranate, date, and olive, probably forwarded from San Blas, in Mexico.

But neither Portolá nor Serra is to be given chief credit. It was José de Galvez who provided the cuttings and seeds, and who sponsored the expedition, though he never set foot upon California soil. His interest, backed by his vision and enterprise, won for him a firm place in California's stately Hall of Fame.

Some of the olive trees, planted at the beginning of the Mission period, weathered the storms and seasons of well over a century of time. During that early period, and for many years afterward, practically the only known product of the olive was the oil, which was used extensively in connection with religious services. Not until the last decade of the Mexican régime were small olive groves planted by the *rancheros*—the oil became an article of common use in the household. In his book, *The Natural Wealth of California,* Cronise points out that the oil "is more wholesome than lard, cheaper than butter, and would probably bear export to India, where lard is not used, on account of peculiar views."

In 1849 T. K. Stewart, who had brought 200 pounds of vegetable seeds to California the previous year, planted olive and fig trees along the American River, near Sutter's Fort. Up to that time it had been generally believed that the olive would not flourish except in Southern California. And the time was still far away when the value of the olive itself as food came to be recognized. In all California there were probably not as many as 20,000 trees in 1870.

It was not until 1872 that any serious attempt was made to put the olive industry on a commercial basis. Three names most prominently connected with the beginnings were Frank E. Kimball of San Diego, Elwood Cooper of Santa Barbara, and E. E. Goodrich of San José. Still, for some time virtually the only product of recognized value was the oil.

Then came planting of large tracts in the San Joaquin and Sacramento Valleys to olives, as far north as Shasta County, dispelling the idea that olives could not succeed outside of Southern California. For more than a decade following 1885 the extensive plantings amounted "almost to infatuation"— the market could not absorb the vast product.

The olive itself came tardily into use as an article of food—the perfection of methods of pickling the ripe fruit, the result of long and expensive experimenting, marked a great advance in the industry. Indeed, the revival which came after 1910, when improved methods were introduced, brought a complete change in the character of the industry. Pickling came to absorb three-quarters of the entire crop. The magnitude of the industry is illustrated by the fact that in the year 1925 the production in California reached 19,000,000 pounds.

More than eighty varieties of olive trees have been planted in the state. In the entire country it is only in California and parts of Arizona that conditions are favorable for olive culture. A well-kept olive grove is highly regarded as a thing of beauty—the shapely trees, row upon row, with their rich foliage of silvery sheen, the age-long sacred tradition surrounding it, yield exceptional esthetic value quite apart from the purely commercial aspects.

THE PEAR

As is now well known, among all the many varieties of deciduous fruit trees the hardy pear holds the distinction of attaining the greatest age.

Of all cultivated fruit and nut trees it ranks second in longevity, the olive holding the number one position, with its power of living on and on for centuries.

The pear, along with numerous other fruit trees, was introduced into California shortly after the founding of the first Franciscan mission at San Diego in 1769. A feature of each mission establishment was its small orchard; and no orchard was complete without at least a few pear trees.

What gives to us of today special fascination for the pear is the fact that at some of the old mission sites may still be found venerable pear trees living today, trees dating from the mission period, which officially ended with secularization in the fourth decade of the nineteenth century. There is something sentimental, a feeling of almost reverence inspired by the sight of one of these patriarchal trees, as at San Juan Bautista— the aged tree having survived for well over a century and a half. It has taken on the rugged appearance of the oaks of the surrounding forest, yielding still each year a scanty crop of fruit.

In early American days, also, during the gold mining period, many pear trees were planted in the Mother Lode and other districts, and as far north as Shasta County. Not a few of these can still be seen in some of the typical ghost towns and in flourishing communities.

But neither the mission orchard nor that of the mining camp ever had real commercial significance. In this, however, they yielded to American enterprise to such extent that in the year 1860 more than 350,000 pear trees were growing in California. Orchards were to be found over a very wide range, in the valley as well as on the hillside.

Most conspicuous among the many varieties of pears produced in the state was, and still is, the Bartlett, which has been called "the pear of California." It soon became the favorite for shipping. The ancestry of the Bartlett pear, we are told, dates back to pre-Columbian days in Europe; but in California the growers have "glorified it beyond all its previous popularity as a commercial fruit."

For many years the pear production, aided by scientific care, and extensive irrigation in some localities, has been an important part of the almost incredible amount of fruit shipped out of California. By mid-twentieth century more than 40,000 acres were devoted to its cultivation. For the single year 1954 more than 400,000 tons of pears were produced, valued at upwards of $30,000,000.

Despite all this, however, the tough old pear trees of the early mission days that have survived the onslaughts of the seasons through a half-dozen generations, and the rugged specimens dating from early mining days—these worthy forerunners of our own time must be given a place all their own among the fascinating firsts of California.

CALIFORNIA DATES

Dates are among the oldest of all cultivated tree crops. Records show them to have been of importance in Mesopotamia as early as 3,000 years B.C. Yet scarcely more than a half-century ago practically all the dates eaten in California were imported from limited areas in the Old World.

Credit must go to the Franciscan missionaries for planting the first dates in California, along with olives, pears, and other fruits and vegetables. But it is now well known that the coastal climate is not conducive to their fruiting: therefore, the date palm remained essentially an ornamental tree.

As a commercial possibility not only in California but in the United States, date culture had its real beginnings in Coachella Valley, about 130 miles southeast of Los Angeles on the way to Imperial Valley, a little more than half a century ago. It is relatively a very new industry.

In the year 1890 a few young date palms were sent from the U.S. Department of Agriculture to Coachella Valley. As every date grower now knows, date seedlings do not produce true to their own kind — the fruit from most of the seedling trees is likely to prove commercially worthless. Also, it is the female tree that produces the fruit, and it is impossible to determine the sex of the seedling for a number of years. Therefore it is the off-shoots from the female parent trees that are principally sought, since the sex and variety of the off-shoots are the same as of the parent tree.

Experimentation proceeded slowly, partly because of prohibitive costs in both time and money. It was not until 1913 that a non-profit group sent a representative to Africa for the purpose of purchasing off-shoots at a more reasonable rate. This venture proved successful, and marks the real beginning of the date culture of Coachella Valley, which has become an industry now running into millions of dollars annually. When sugar moved into first place among rationed foods during the trying days of World War II, choice dates—"Candy that grows on trees"—acquired added significance among those craving for sweets. Coachella date growers were given a new incentive to produce maximum crops of the delicious fruit. About one-third of the total product was sold in packages direct to the consumers. Among the comparatively few successful varieties, the Deglet Noor has been easily the commercial leader: this date originally came from Algeria.

Because of the temperature and soil requirements, successful production of high-quality dates is found in strictly limited areas. Desert heat and abundant water supply are essential. Date culture involves meticulous attention to numerous details—is almost an exact science in itself, but a fascinating occupation for the producer. Each Christmas season, year after year, thousands of gift packages of choice dates and date products are sent from Southern California to all parts of the nation.

POTATOES

Contrary to a very general impression, the lowly potato was not introduced into California by the early mission fathers. Palóu, in his classic biography of Serra, tells of many kinds of seeds of garden vegetables and flowers brought by the first party to San Diego, in 1769; but the impressive list does not include the potato, although more recently potatoes have been declared to be "the greatest food crop grown in the world." It is well known that during the mission days onions and red peppers were produced in greatest profusion.

Strangely enough, it was a Frenchman who brought the potato to California. It happened in the early autumn of 1786. The French dignitary, first in a succession of distinguished visitors from foreign lands to call in Spanish-occupied Alta California, was the friendly Comte Jean de la Pérouse, who stopped at Monterey ten days, and whose keen observations were afterward published in Paris in four important volumes.

Pérouse had brought some potatoes, in good condition, from Chile. He it was who introduced them, causing them to be added to the already long list of vegetables produced at the Franciscan missions. This proved to be a great boon to the country, pronounced by the historian Theodore Hittell as "perhaps the most important service he did and one for which he must be considered a benefactor." The potato was not long in becoming one of the staple foods.

The great diversity of conditions as to soil and climate in vast areas of California have brought about enormous production of potatoes. Two districts that proved especially favorable are the Salinas and Lompoc Valleys. Later, large acreages of the Sacramento-San Joaquin delta lands were used, and still more recently many thousands of acres of newly-irrigated lands in southern San Joaquin Valley have been planted to potatoes, in Kern County alone the total of reclaimed land suitable for the production of this crop being more than 50,000 acres. As early as 1934 the production in the state as a whole exceeded nine and a half million bushels, valued at approximately $5,500,000.

Through skillful plant breeding by Luther Burbank and others who followed him, the quality of potatoes has been immeasureably improved, and the yield correspondingly increased. Some land best suited to the production of potatoes has produced more than 400 sacks, of about 120 pounds each, per acre of ground. This product, introduced into California one and two-thirds centuries ago by a distinguished Frenchman, has come to play a very important part in California's fabulous production of staple foodstuffs.

WINE INDUSTRY

Even before the beginning of the Spanish occupation of Upper California, in 1769, there were at least three vineyards in Baja (Lower) California, and grapes and wine had actually been produced there, at certain of the Jesuit missions.

This was in accordance with a very early law framed by Cortez himself, in 1524, demanding the introduction of vines into the country, the Spaniards being "required to graft shoots on the native vine stock which they have, or to replant it." Late in life General M. G. Vallejo, leading Spanish-Californian, wrote that his father, Don Ignacio Vallejo, told him that Padre Junípero Serra brought from Lower California the first vines and transplanted them at San Diego in 1769 or 1770. Thus it is clear that the culture of the grape vine in California dates from the very beginning of the Spanish occupation.

Within two generations there were vines at each Franciscan mission. At the time of secularization San Gabriel had the *Vina Madre*, with a maximum of more than 160,000 vines. Wine making was one of the conspicuous activities of the early Spanish colonists. Wine was produced for use as a beverage, for medicinal purposes, as an article of commerce, for frequent social occasions, and for religious purposes.

The first variety of grape produced was called the Los Angeles grape —it was of the Malaga variety, but had undergone considerable change during cultivation in Mexico. It is uncertain whether it was originally from the Malaga or the Alicante. Another variety was introduced north of San Francisco Bay about 1820, which came to be known as the Sonoma grape. But the term Mission Grape was generally applied to all during the mission period. Later was introduced the Zinfandel, a full-bearing red wine grape, which became the principal foundation of vines cultivated in dry districts.

The making of wine was begun even before the domestic vines came into bearing, the wild grapes being used; but wine is known to have been produced from domestic grapes sometime before 1795. And the production was not confined to the mission fathers. Governor Pedro

Fages planted vines at Monterey as early as 1783. The wine making proceeded with the development of the *presidios*, the *ranchos*, and the *pueblos*.

It was considerably later that wine became an article of commercial importance. A Frenchman, Jean Louis Vignes, who settled in Los Angeles in 1833, according to Irving McKee, established a formidable claim to the title of "first professional California wine grower." He was first to import European varieties of grapes and to foresee the destiny of the new industry. William Heath Davis regarded him as the pioneer in both wine making and orange cultivation.

William Wolfskill, Kentucky trapper and trader, beginning in 1836, showed great enterprise, which resulted in 1858 in a total of 55,000 bearing vines. In the north Agoston Haraszthy, a Hungarian refugee of noble blood, was acclaimed the father of viticulture of the Sonoma area. The name of his son Arpad Haraszthy is closely associated with the development of the industry.

By 1870 grape lands were paying from $100 up to $2,000 an acre—wine was selling at from 25 cents to $1.00 per gallon, and there were 25,000,000 grape vines in the state. Two decades later the number of vines had jumped to 120,000,000.

In the meantime, the raisin crop had so increased that it was soon to eclipse even the wine industry. The growth of the table and raisin grape industry during the past half century has been phenomenal. The "Sun-Maid" brand of raisin is known all over the world. Truly the grapevine has played an important rôle in the drama of California agriculture.

STATE AGRICULTURAL SOCIETY

The first agricultural association in California met at Sacramento, October 8, 1852, in the American Theater. C. T. Hutchinson was president; an address was delivered by Dr. J. F. Morse. A fair was held for a week or longer, which may be regarded as a forerunner of the first State Fair, held in San Francisco, in 1854.

Early in that year (1854) the State Agricultural Society was formed and was incorporated May 13 by special act of the legislature, its first president being F. W. Macondray of San Francisco. The chief objects of the Society were to conduct fairs and promote agriculture in the state. As an encouragement the act of incorporation appropriated $5,000 per annum for the first five years, to be used for premiums.

In 1863 the election of a "Board of Agriculture," to be entrusted with the affairs of the State Agricultural Society, was provided for by the legislature. Fairs were held under this arrangement until the adoption of the new state constitution of 1879, which cut off governmental assistance, unless the Board of Directors were appointed by authority of the state. Then the legislature empowered the governor to name the board members, and also divided the state into "agricultural districts," each district embracing several counties.

One of the most distinguished presidents of the State Agricultural Society was John Bidwell, owner of Rancho Chico and for a time California's foremost agriculturist. In his presidential addresses he urged the importance of good training in the arts and industries, and pleaded for the better cultivation of the soil and more adequate conservation of our natural resources. Some of his utterances have proved to be prophetic. In 1869 he said:

> I do not believe that real and permanent prosperity will dawn upon us until we become, to a considerable extent, a manufacturing as well as agricultural and mining State. . . . Do not misunderstand me that manufactures are the only desideratum. We want combination and cooperation of enterprise. Agriculture must be better and more varied, to embrace everything within the range of our unequalled and diversified soil and climate.

For many years Bidwell's prominence in the State Agricultural Society was outstanding. With him diversified farming might be called a magnificent obsession. He warned against exhaustion of the soil, favored rotation of crops and the rest to be gained by summer fallow. He showed unremitting, uncompromising hostility to private monopolies of every sort. And in his Annual Address of the year 1881 he revealed a rather startling global view. He declared:

> The bubble, isolation, has burst, and, lo, we stand face to face in competition with the world. We have discovered that we are no longer in a world by ourselves, but that we live on the same planet as other people, and that henceforth we must run the race of life in competition with all mankind.

More than one-fourth of all basic income in California was for years from agriculture. The strong State Department of Agriculture includes the State Board, with divisions of Administration, Plant Industry, Animal Husbandry, and Economics.

All in all, the State Agricultural Society has played a very significant part in California's history—its contribution to the ascendancy of the state in this important field has been a generous one. From the humble beginnings of a century ago the scope and magnitude of its activities have become truly impressive.

HONEY

Various species of wild bees have lived in the "honey-garden" we call California for a very long time; "probably ever since the main body of the present flora gained possession of the land, toward the close of the glacial period" — so thought John Muir. This gentle mountaineer-naturalist devoted the entire final chapter of his classic, *The Mountains of California,* to "The Bee Pastures."

"When California was wild," he wrote, "it was one sweet bee garden throughout its entire length, north and south, and all the way across from the snowy Sierra to the ocean." In his idyllic prose this master word painter continued:

> In this flowery wilderness the bees rove and revel, rejoicing in the bounty of the sun, clambering eagerly through bramble and hucklebloom, ringing the myrial bells of the manzanita, now humming aloft among polleny willows and firs, now down on the ashy ground among gilias and butter-cups, and anon plunging deep into snowy banks of cherry and buckthorn.

Many persons have thought that the first domestic honey bees were brought to California in March, 1853, by T. Shelton. He obtained twelve swarms, so the report goes, from a disgusted passenger at Aspinwall, on the Isthmus, landing one of them in safety in San Francisco. After the first season three swarms were thrown off in December, and two of these sold for $110 and $105 each.

But Mr. Bancroft points out that the first hive was brought in 1852, by W. A. Buckley of New York. Because of the drought Buckley's bees later suffered considerably in some areas, but they showed good increase along streams in San Diego County.

The "tall yarns" people used to tell about how "Wall" (W. W.) Kennedy, a Napa County '49-er from Indiana, "drove a swarm of bees" across the plains on his trek with the covered wagon, at a time when "most anything could happen," may be catalogued with a rich assort-ment of miners' tales of the good old days.

During the years 1855-56 a number of sizable importations of bees were made, and for a limited time honey found a ready market at $1.50 and $2.00 a pound. The first really successful importer of bees, John S. Harbison, became the leading apiarist of the state. In 1861 he published *The Beekeeper's Directory.* During the 1860's California had 30,000 bee-hives, most of them in San Diego, Los Angeles, Monterey, Santa Clara, San Joaquin, Sacramento, and Siskiyou Counties. But the bee-keepers suffered reverses, because the price of honey dropped to twenty-five cents a pound.

From such mixed beginnings grew the bee industry of California. For the year 1880 the total production of honey was placed at 574,000 pounds, with 14,600 pounds of wax. During the 1870's bee ranching "had become a type of bonanza farming in the foothills of Southern California. The rancher started out with a swarm of about 100 stands in October," as described by Carey McWilliams, "quickly increased to 400 stands, and shipped 40,000 pounds of the finest comb-honey in July."

Honey production has long since become a large-scale industry. More recently, Imperial Valley alone, reclaimed from desert by water, has produced more than 100 carloads annually. To improve marketing conditions the Consolidated Honey Producers of California has been organized. It is an industry that demands special skill; but with the application of scientific methods, there is room for further expansion.

In California the working season for bees is much longer than in the eastern states. In spite of the spoliation of nature, where once the bees were free to roam, the cultivated fields of alfalfa, the fragrant citrus groves and the vast stretches of white sage brush are available, assuring a supply of honey of excellent quality. When one considers the wild and cultivated flowers—fruit trees, grasses, grains, grapes, desert bloom— one must conclude that California is truly a land of honey, highly favored above other states.

FRENCH PRUNES

With each returning springtime expansive areas of lovely Santa Clara Valley are transformed into "a sea of blossoms, sixty miles long and twenty miles wide." This marvelous, mammoth garden, filling the "Valley of Heart's Delight," is dominated by the billions of pure white blooms of the millions of prune trees. Whence came these trees into California?

It is to Louis Pellier, a thrifty gold hunter from his distant France, that we are indebted not only for the French Prune but also, to a great extent, the beginnings of many fruit orchards and vegetable gardens of Santa Clara Valley. At the height of the gold rush fresh fruits and vegetables were at a tremendous premium, therefore brought fabulous prices. Hungry pioneers bought apples and pears at a dollar apiece: even at that the limited supply was of inferior quality.

Young Pellier was a keen observer. He quickly perceived that most of the fruit being snapped up by the miners came from the mission orchards around Santa Clara. Quoth he, "There is more gold in apples and pears than in the mines." The idea stuck. "One day," writes Frank

J. Taylor, "he threw down his pick and started for the valley, determined to turn to gardening. His search for the right kind of land took him eventually to San José," where there was already a small settlement of Frenchmen.

Next follows the beginning of Pellier's nursery, later widely known as "Pellier's Gardens," which was to "revolutionize Santa Clara Valley." Longing for fine trees like those of his native France, he bargained with his brother Pierre, in 1853, agreeing to finance his passage to the homeland if he would return with a supply of cuttings and seeds.

Three years later Pierre returned, with two travel-worn trunks filled with cuttings and seeds, the scions being stuck into potatoes, whose moisture would help keep them alive. That winter Louis Pellier diligently labored, grafting the improved scions on selected root stock, especially the wild plum. Fortunately some of the grafts lived, chief among them being the *Petit prune D'Agens*, from the old home place, near Bordeaux. It was not long till some of the young trees were sold to neighbors. In 1863 samples of the first California grown dried prunes were exhibited in the State Fair, in Sacramento. Chief credit for grafting goes to J. Q. A. Ballou and George W. Tarleton, who obtained scions from Pellier and helped "launch the California prune on its road to history." In 1866 the state had 650 acres of prune trees; by 1890, 90,000 acres. It is claimed that most of the myriads of trees of Santa Clara Valley sprang originally from Pellier's improved cuttings.

Nowhere else in the world are French prunes produced in such quantity. Beautiful Napa Valley may claim second place. And no longer are prunes simply the humble food of the plebeian—they have become an aristocrat among the fruits of earth.

Harvesting and processing of the annual prune crop have been standardized; the superior food values have been made known by attractive advertising of "Sunsweet" packages; actual marketing has become a highly developed industry through the cooperative California Prune and Apricot Growers Association, with headquarters in the city of San José.

During the month of March, for many years, neighbors and distant friends gathered on the flower-bedecked hill-slopes of Saratoga, nestling at the base of the Santa Cruz Mountains, to celebrate the widely-acclaimed Blossom Festival, where the air was redolent of the perfume rising from the swells and billows of a white sea of bloom from countless prune trees, gift of Louis Pellier, once a young argonaut from the plains of Bordeaux.

As for the "Valley of Heart's Delight" itself, the warm words of former President Herbert Hoover, spoken years ago, voice the sentiment of multitudes today:

> Having made my home in Santa Clara Valley for the last thirty-five years, and still having aspirations to return there as soon as I can escape from duties in other parts of the world, you may be confident that its beauties and its people are esteemed in my mind above all others.

STATE BOARD OF HORTICULTURE

The subject of horticulture in California is as old as the state itself—and older still, if we may employ the word informally. As we have seen, the Franciscan Mission fathers deserve credit for having introduced many kinds of fruit. In this is to be found the historical basis of today's horticulture.

Following the tragic secularization of the missions, the first orchards suffered swift deterioration—complete destruction in some instances. Even so, it must be admitted, at best the fruits had been of inferior quality when compared with our improved products resulting from modern plant breeding and scientific cultivation.

Early foreigners in California also planted fruit trees, the Russians at Fort Ross, for example. George Yount planted a small peach orchard in Napa Valley as early as 1838. In the early gold mining days some interest was shown in growing fruit in many areas for small home orchards, as in Placer and Sacramento counties. But viewed in larger aspects, only slight development in horticulture marked the decade of the 1850's.

It was not until 1883, during the administration of Governor George Stoneman, that the State Board of Horticulture was created. The creation of this Board signalized the beginning of scientific horticulture in California. Among its later activities of great value was the importation and dissemination of certain varieties of insects from Australia that are the natural enemies of most of the fruit-tree pests. These proved to be of inestimable benefit.

By legislative act of March 26, 1903, the State Commission of Horticulture was created, whose distinguished president, Elwood Cooper, "an enthusiastic fruit grower of Santa Barbara County, accomplished great and lasting good for the state." The development of California horticulture during the first half of the twentieth century has been remarkable, made possible largely by the organization and operation of a great system of irrigation districts, which capitalize on the vast snowfall in the Sierra Nevada Mountains, and the chain of cooperative associations that make available the markets of the world.

The Bureau of Fruit and Vegetable Standardization has as one of its important functions the fixing of standards "of quality and pack, also to marking requirements applying to thirty fruits, nuts, and vegetables" —provisions intended to prevent deception and mis-labeling of packages.

The transformation that has come to the wide-spreading San Joaquin Valley during the lifetime of many still living, from great unfenced wheat fields and vast desert areas into highly productive farms with well-kept orchards, vineyards, and fields of vegetables and cotton and rice, by the application of the fructifying power of water and intensive scientific cultivation of the soil—this may be regarded as a large-scale modern miracle. California has indeed become the world's copious fruit-basket.

SUGAR BEETS AND BEET SUGAR

The successful extraction of sugar from beets is a comparatively recent accomplishment. While the ancient Romans cultivated the vegetable to a limited extent, they did not know any practical method of sugar extraction. It was not until the middle of the eighteenth century that a German chemist of the University of Berlin made the important discovery; and it was not until the end of that century that a process of extracting applied on a large scale was invented. From that time on the sugar beet in Europe had an interesting, at times an exciting history.

It cannot be said that the sugar beet as a source of sugar came to California at the time of the Franciscans, along with olives, grapes, oranges, and pomegranates. The sugar beet industry in California was not really established until introduced by men who had studied the processes of making sugar in Europe—and then it was Americans and not Spaniards or Mexicans who successfully established it.

Meantime several varieties of beets along with turnips and other vegetables had come to be grown in abundance in California, both those for human consumption and those chiefly for cattle feed. John Hittell in his *Resources of California* reported:

> Our largest red beet (a mangel-wurzel) weighed 118 pounds—was five feet long, and a foot in diameter. It was three years old.

Hittell explained that instead of producing seed the second year the champion beet kept on growing, and continued for the third year!

The first successful beet sugar factory in California was built in Alvarado, Alameda County, in the year 1870. After many attempts and much experimentation, including four financial failures in nineteen years, E. H. Dyer had won success: he therefore became known as "the father of the American beet sugar industry." Dr. Harvey W. Wiley, Chief Chemist of the U.S. Department of Agriculture, 1874-1913, made scientific analyses, which were published and widely distributed.

The real development of this important industry in California dates from the year 1890. Two most important names of early sugar refiners are those of the Oxnard brothers—Henry T. and James G. In 1891 they erected a factory at Chino, California. To promote the industry favorable legislation was secured. In 1898 the American Beet Sugar Company was organized, and it took over the six Oxnard factories. Shortly thereafter the name of Claus Sprekels enters into the picture; the industry has become Big Business during the twentieth century, and at present it involves such huge production and vast amounts of capital as to be almost incredible.

The 200,000 tons of refined sugar produced in California in 1917 have mounted to many times that amount during the past few years. Lands and properties devoted to the cultivation of the sugar beet today represent capital amounting to many hundreds of millions of dollars. California's 1952 sugar beet crop, for example, was estimated at more than two and a quarter million tons. Nowhere in the world can this amazing story be duplicated.

SILK CULTURE

Authorities claim that the Chinese have reeled silk as long ago as 2640 B.C. They were Chinese who first brought silk cocoons into California, in the gold-rush days of 1849 or 1850. There was some interest in the question of silk culture almost from the beginning of our statehood.

In 1854 W. S. Letcher, an assemblyman from Santa Clara County, presented to the legislature a report for the committee on agriculture, which concluded by stating that "with encouragement and protection there was a future in California not only in all grains and fruits, but that, if wise care were bestowed on the subject, rice, cotton, tobacco, tea, coffee, and sugar might be embraced within the number." The report mentioned high-grade sheep and goats, and "mulberry trees affording food for the worms that might clothe the people in silks and satins."

Experiments in silk production were conducted near the present site of Riverside as early as 1867. The legislature offered a bonus of $250 "for growing and cultivating 5,000 or more mulberry trees of the age of two years, planted in suitable form and at proper distances for permanent silk culture"; also an appropriation of $300 for the production of each 100,000 cocoons "in good merchantable condition." The intention was to make silk production a fixed industry in California. In 1868 it was estimated there were some 4,000,000 mulberry trees in the state. So great was the foreign demand for eggs, however, that actual production of silk was seriously retarded.

Students of the subject claimed peculiar advantages in both climate and soil. In his *Natural Wealth in California* (1868), Titus F. Cronise said: "The extraordinary advantage of our climate have attracted the attention of silk men in Europe, and we are advised that the immigration of such persons in considerable numbers is probable." In his enthusiasm this author declared: "California destined to be one of the foremost manufacturers of silk fabrics for the consumption of the world." Why should Americans continue to import millions of pounds of raw silk from Japan?

But such outcome was not to be. In the following legislature the bonus provisions were canceled. Governor H. H. Haight strongly opposed the policy of "forcing capital out of one channel into another, either by protective duties or bounties."

In 1883 there was renewed activity in the production of silk. A state board of silk culture was established by the legislature. Certain interested women began to take a leading part: the Ladies Silk Culture Society of California was formed, and was incorporated in 1885. Mrs. Elsie Christine Hittell, talented wife of historian Theodore H. Hittell, was president. Many prominent men were made honorary members, including: Charles Crocker, George Davidson, Dr. Harvey Harkness, Professor Eugene Hilgard, D. O. Mills, Irving Scott, and Leland Stanford. In 1886 the Piedmont building was purchased—there were 6,000 trees across the bay from San Francisco. It began to look like a *cult* as well as a culture! People were exhorted to "Patronize Home Industry." More than 100 girls and women were employed at Piedmont alone.

But California was not destined to be a large producer of silk, the principal reason being that our skilled labor, at high wages, could not compete with the cheap labor of the Orient and southern Europe. Whatever hope of revival of the industry might have been entertained in recent years has been thoroughly shattered by the appearance of nylon, rayon, and other fabulous fabrics from strange derivatives — miracle products created overnight.

COTTON GROWING

Cotton was among the numerous plants introduced into Baja California by the Jesuit missionaries in the seventeenth century, long before the beginning of the Spanish occupation of Alta California. Some of the indigenous cotton plants of Mexico were brought by the Franciscan *padres* for propagation at their first missions, beginning with San Diego, although there is some uncertainty about the exact date of the first planting.

The earliest attempts at growing cotton in California, however, met with poor success, partly because of being located too near the ocean, partly because of climate and soil conditions. Numerous efforts were made, for cotton was a highly desirable product; but, generally speaking, all such efforts resulted in virtual failure, although to a very limited extent cotton was produced for a time at the auxiliary mission, Pala.

Even under the early American régime, the industry was quite slow to emerge. There was only feeble effort until as late as 1856, when the state offered premiums for successful cotton growing. An early indication of the awareness of its possible great future is seen in John Hittell's book, *Resources of California*, first published in 1863, in which he reported that some 2,000 acres were devoted to cotton growing; and in Hittell's book this prophetic statement appears: "When the water is supplied to the San Joaquin Valley, cotton will probably claim a large area as the most profitable crop."

In December, 1865, the first bale of California raised cotton was received at San Francisco from Fort Tejon, in Kern County; it may be added that the first bale of California made cotton cloth was manufactured that same month, at the Oakland Cotton Mill. But cotton growing was not yet ready to emerge as a successful industry.

After a diligent search by the United States Department of Agriculture for a variety of cotton suited for the soil and climate of California, the Acala of New Mexico was found to be satisfactory; and George Harrison, referred to as the "Papa" of the industry, himself a veteran cotton breeder, in 1934 offered a strain of the Acala to the growers of California. That may be regarded as the real beginning of the large-scale cotton industry in the state. As a protective measure, in 1949 that particular strain exclusively was permitted to be grown in the great cotton belt of California.

Mr. Hittell was right. Water had been brought to the southern portion of the San Joaquin Valley: cotton has become its most valuable crop on many thousands of acres. A faint idea of the vast magnitude to which the industry in California has attained in recent years may be gained from the fact that in 1951 the production reached 1,800,000 bales, being second only to Texas in the entire United States, with an estimated value of upwards of $300,000,000; and there was an average production of more than 600 pounds to the acre. Even under severe limitations as to acreage, cotton lint, in production value, incredible as it may seem, has reached first place among the more than fifty California field crops.

Many miles of irrigation canals now bring the indispensable water— for water is "the key that unlocks all this wealth." The cotton is irrigated from three to six times during the growing season.

Mechanical pickers are yearly multiplying in the land; more and more ginning mills appear, dotting southern San Joaquin Valley, which, until the coming of irrigation was semi-desert. Moreover, California produces cotton of distinctly superior quality. Ready markets are found in Belgium, Chile, Japan, Sweden, England, and other countries. The total amazing picture is another illustration of the superlative in the great empire state on the Pacific.

ORGANIZATION OF THE GRANGE

The National Grange, or the Patrons of Husbandry, enjoys the reputation of being the first agricultural society of national importance in the United States. It was organized in the nation's capital, December 4, 1867, with William Saunders of the Department of Agriculture as first Master, and Oliver H. Kelley of Boston as Secretary. The establishment of the Grange, founded as a secret society, is regarded as the first important cooperation of concrete character undertaken by American farmers.

California was not long in swinging into line. On the 10th of August, 1870, its first Subordinate Grange was organized at Pilot Hill, El Dorado County. The twenty-nine charter members were duly organized by General Deputy A. A. Bayley.

Many farmers' clubs were formed early in 1873 in different parts of the state. But the club system proved largely ineffective and was soon abandoned in favor of the recently organized secret order known as the Grange, or Patrons of Husbandry: by the end of that year most of the clubs had ceased to exist.

At a convention held at Napa July 15, 1873, at which twenty-eight subordinate granges were represented, N. W. Garretson of the National Grange brought about the organization of the State Grange. The first State Master was J. W. A. Wright. The strongly-phrased Declaration of Purposes, prepared by Wright, has continued to be a guiding star for later grange activities.

The first Annual Convention of the California State Grange was held in San José, beginning October 14, 1873. By that date the secretary reported a total of 104 subordinate granges, located in all sections of the state.

Almost immediately the State Grange exercised considerable political influence. Both political parties were sharply criticized for permitting excessive freight rates on the powerful railroad and for "the prodigal expenditures of public money." But it may be said that the Grangers, as a whole, were lacking in political cohesion and commanding leadership. Of their keen interest in politics in relation to their own welfare, and of their zeal and activity during the politically complex period of the later 1870's, there can be no doubt. Their influence in the formation and adoption of the California Constitution of 1879 was admittedly quite considerable: the same may be said regarding their opposition to the immigration of Chinese laborers—and later, the Japanese.

Among the specific aims and objects of the grange may be mentioned the following: 1) establish cooperative systems of trade, bringing producers and consumers more closely together; 2) arrange for the purchase of farm implements directly from the manufacturers; 3) obtain direct shipments, on more favorable terms, with storage at lower rates and lower interest; 4) gradual substitution of cash for credit system. The grange has a liberal medical aid and hospital service program, as well as fire insurance protection and the benefit of legal service to its members.

This organization is still strong in California. It consistently strives for a better life for the farmer, maintains its complete independence from governmental control, emphasizes social activities of high moral character, and seeks to make better and more useful citizens through the association and cooperative spirit of its members.

NAVEL ORANGES

The early mission *padres* introduced into California not only the orange but also the lemon, olive, pear, and other fruits, as well as the grape and other vines. Generations passed, however, before horticulture came to assume any considerable commercial importance.

At the head of California's vast horticultural interests in recent decades has stood the great citrus industry, including several varieties of oranges, lemons, and grapefruit. Among these products the ranking variety has been the Washington Navel orange. The romantic story of this "golden apple of California" is now regarded as a classic of the Far West.

For many years the real founder of this sensational industry has been almost totally ignored, while his second wife, Eliza Tibbets, has mistakenly been given chief credit in numerous books and magazine articles. It remained for Luther Calvin Tibbets' daughter, Mrs. Minnie Tibbets Mills, after exhaustive research extending through several years, to present the true and complete story of the beginning of the navel orange

in North America, with the authentic version of this significant development. Mrs. Mills' complete account was published in the *Quarterly* of
the Historical Society of Southern California, Volume XXV, Number 4
(December, 1943).

One day in the month of December, 1873, Luther Tibbets, one of the
early colonists of the new settlement of Riverside, in Southern California, received a package from a friend in Washington, D.C., containing some small orange trees. These trees had been introduced into the
United States by the Department of Agriculture from Bahia, Brazil.
But as early as 1869 a letter had been received from Bahia by Horace
Capron, Commissioner of Agriculture, mentioning "a seedless orange
of large size and fine flavor." After some correspondence a box arrived
in Washington containing twelve newly budded young trees. Those in
Tibbets' package were from the twelve. He could not then dream that
his prize would "revolutionize the horticultural methods of the day and
that it would bring more wealth to California than all the gold mined
in the state since 1848."

Tibbets took particular pains with the precious little trees. He banked
them for the winter; then in March "he carefully dug the holes and
prepared the soil for the reception of the three trees which he planted
twenty feet apart along the west end of his house. . . . Around each tree
he put a protective fence." In spite of all precautions, one of the original
three trees was "trampled by a cow and died." Extra care was taken
with the remaining two.

In the months that followed Mr. Tibbets suffered much tribulation
because of the trespassing on his property by neighbors' horses and litigation resulting therefrom—but that must not concern us here.

It was in March, 1874, that the two trees were planted in the ground;
but not until 1878 were they "allowed to bear fruit, then two oranges to
a tree." There were plenty of skeptics and pessimists around—most
growers "believed that the seedless fruit was but a short-lived curiosity."
But Luther Tibbets had faith; he used buds for propagation and
advertised the new variety far and wide.

The occasion for the tasting and decisions as to the merits of the four
carefully guarded ripened oranges came—it was a social event. Mrs.
Tibbets was "orange hostess." The guests "were wild with excitement
and enthusiasm." Into the struggling colony was injected new life.
Riverside would survive the severe depression and be put on the high
road to success.

> Visitors thronged to the Tibbets ranch to learn about the Washington
> Navel; money flowed in from the sale of budwood. A great new industry

had been started: its development has been sensational. "Seedless Orange Tibbets and his wife" visited Pasadena, Los Angeles, and Santa Barbara in their new buggy. Luther modestly gave Eliza more than generous credit, always referring to the phenomenal achievement as "ours," never simply "mine."

No doubt this gracious attitude of Mr. Tibbets toward his second wife helps to explain the long-standing conception, as well as to throw light upon the inscription on the monument that for many years has stood at the head of Old Magnolia Avenue in a little square surrounded by an iron railing, where the first Washington Navel tree bore its golden fruit year after year. Here is the text of the inscription:

> To Honor
> Mrs. Eliza Tibbets
> And to Continue Her Good Work
> In planting at Riverside in 1873
> THE FIRST WASHINGTON
> NAVEL ORANGE TREES
> In California
> Native to Bahia, Brazil
> Proved the Most Valuable
> Fruit Introduction Yet Made by
> The United States Department
> of Agriculture
> 1920

The Valencia orange (sometimes called "Summer orange") came into production some years later. The first commercial planting was in 1883, with R. H. Gilman, planter.

VALENCIA ORANGES

In the year 1880 R. H. Gilman planted California's first commercial grove of Valencia orange trees, in Orange County. This first grove consisted of four rows of trees, eighty-five trees to the row. In 1934 Mr. Gilman, then eighty-eight years of age, returned to Placentia to join in the celebration commemorating his historic planting fifty-four years before, under the auspices of Grace Parlor 242, Native Daughters of the Golden West.

It was the venerable Mr. Gilman's big moment. At the dedication program, February 1, 1934, there was the unveiling of a bronze marker implanted in a granite monument. Paul Armstrong, general manager of the influential California Fruit Exchange, was principal speaker. By that time the four rows of tiny trees planted in 1880 had been multiplied into literally millions of trees, covering 131,000 acres, and producing an annual crop of 34,000 car loads of the juicy "summer oranges."

Mr. Gilman had moved to the original site in the early 1870's to manage the properties of the Southern California Fruit Company. He experimented with seedling oranges, and later budded about five acres of other varieties into the Valencias, which, according to Dr. A. D. Shammel, had come from a nursery in England.

A half-century after the planting of the first grove the manager declared that he had harvested as much as twenty-five boxes of fruit from some of the individual trees in a single year. And now, along with the Washington Navels, the Valencias give distinction to California for the production of oranges both as to quantity and quality.

The two varieties admirably supplement each other as to the respective seasons for ripening and harvesting, also as to texture and flavor. The shipping season for the Washington Navels is November-December in northern and central California, December-June in the south; for the Valencias it is June to October. The Valencia stands next to the Navel in commercial importance. Other varieties, such as St. Michaels, Jaffa, Thompson's Improved Navels, and Ruby Red, as well as seedlings, hold places of purely secondary importance.

FARMING FOREST TREES

On Saturday, August 26, 1950, the world's first redwood tree farm was dedicated in Hammond Grove, near Eureka, California. Participating in the unique ceremony were Governor Earl Warren, W. S. Rosecrans, chairman of the State Board of Forestry, and George B. McLeod, president of the Hammond Lumber Company, in the presence of about 2,000 interested persons.

"The inauguration of the tree farm movement," declared Mr. Rosecrans, "is recognition of the fact that trees are a crop and that it pays to grow them. It marks the transition from exploiting and depleting our forest resources to reproducing and perpetuating them." Alert professional foresters had for years been preaching the doctrine of perpetual forest yield, and thus establishing and maintaining the industry on a permanent basis. It was in the state of Washington that the movement to provide a continuous supply of lumber through scientific farming was started. This was in 1941.

For the redwood farm, dedicated in 1950, the Redwood Association had laid down four rules, which require the owner to give assurance of his willingness to maintain the land in condition for the production of forest crops, to provide protection from fire and other hazards, to practice selective logging, and to provide information to government authorities regarding his farm when requested.

By virtue of selective logging the young redwood saplings make very rapid growth—a tree two feet in diameter doubles its volume in a period of twenty years. Seedlings and young trees will make sufficient growth to justify reharvest in forty-five years, yielding a profit. It is by the careful application of sound farming methods that the Redwood Association and the owners expect to perpetuate the forests while at the same time providing a continuous supply of valuable lumber. "We are here today," declared Governor Warren, now Chief Justice of the U.S. Supreme Court, in his dedicatory address, "acknowledging the fact that we are but stewards of California's God-given abundance, as we dedicate our oldest living resource into perpetuity."

But the redwood does not stand alone among trees as a basis for successful farming. Within the last few years the Douglas fir has taken the lead in providing a tree crop. Until recently this fir was commonly regarded as worthless, a mere "weed tree," but desirable uses have been found for it and the demand promises to be permanent. Owners of many thousands of acres in Humboldt County are discovering that the planned tree crop will provide a more satisfactory yield than can be anticipated from the expensive clearing of the land for other farm purposes. Professor Emanuel Fritz of the University of California College of Forestry urges, for example, that "a perpetually yielding forest should remain in the Humboldt as a firm and enduring asset and tax base for the region."

A most recent aspect of tree farming is seen in the production of young firs to meet the great demand for Christmas trees. In a number of localities it is possible for customers to drive to a tree farm, pick out and cut their own trees for the Yuletide season.

Tree farming in California is still in its earlier stages, although more than 100,000 acres of Douglas fir alone have already been certified for that purpose, and several times that area are now ready for certification. The tree farm is tax-paying privately owned land operated for permanent yield, under necessary regulations laid down by appropriate governmental agencies. The dedication of the first redwood tree farm was a significant event in contemporaneous history.

COOPERATIVE MARKETING

Before the end of the nineteenth century the growth of horticulture in California had become extraordinary. The population was increasing rapidly, the vast production of wheat was giving way to the development of fruit and vegetable industries, wide new areas of fertile land were being reclaimed by the application of irrigation water.

But this important shift also brought its problems. For example, the greatly expanded citrus industries experienced serious difficulty in marketing their rapidly increasing product at a profit. In the early 1890's the individual growers were largely at the mercy of commission merchants and the high freight rates of the railroads. It often happened that the larger the crop the more deeply involved they became.

A few prescient leaders had analyzed the problems involved and were keenly aware of the unfavorable prospects. One of these, William H. Mills, contributed to the *Californian Illustrated Magazine* for October, 1892, a thoughtful article on "Marketing California Fruits," from which the following lines are quoted:

> The whole subject opens a wide field for contemplation, when we consider the leading factors of the problem. First, we have an unlimited capacity for the production of fruit. Second, we have economic advantages in its production, . . . Between the price paid to the grower, and the price paid by the consumer, there is a vast margin. The commission alone on the sale of our fruit is 7 per cent, and that of itself constitutes a market selling fund, which should incite distributors to the highest activity. The present method of distribution is costly to the consumer, and all high cost to the consumer means a small reward to the producer. The higher the price paid by the consumer, the less the producer will get. High prices discourage consumption, and enforce the condition of our production.

Efforts were made to meet the situation, but real success was slow in coming. As early as 1892 a local organization was effected at Riverside, known as the Pachappa Orange Growers' Association. The next year there was the Growers' Association of Claremont. Still others were formed at Duarte, San Bernardino, San Antonio, and Orange. But it was found that real success demanded union, or a more complete pooling of interests for mutual benefits. The result was seen in the organization of the Southern California Fruit Exchange, which in 1905 was broadened into the California Fruit Growers' Exchange.

Thus was brought into being what has proved to be largest and most successful co-operating marketing association in the world. By 1915 6,500 grower members were provided the facilities for distributing and marketing their fruit. The three foundation stones of the Exchange are: (1) local associations of growers; (2) district exchanges; and (3) the central exchange, which handles the most of the state's orange, lemon, and grapefruit crop. It is conducted on a strictly co-operative, non-profit basis, rendering its invaluable service to thousands of growers on an actual cost basis.

In time, on the basis of experience the functions of the Exchange were increased. For example, a powerful sales organization of more than national scope was effected, latest scientific information was provided for members, and a great advertising department became very active, capitalizing especially on the trade name, now known everywhere, "Sunkist."

The influence of the powerful pioneer co-operative marketing association was widespread. The California Fruit Growers' Exchange became the forerunner of the many cooperatives now operating in the state. Mere mention of a few of these at this point will suffice.

The California Almond Growers' Exchange came into being largely because before 1910 the growers chafed under the treatment of the brokers. The Davis Almond Growers Association, organized in 1899, was the first of a number of local selling organizations. Others followed. But the competition among local exchanges proved disastrous; by two or three important steps the problem was solved by the organization of the state-wide, non-profit cooperative corporation.

Another leading cooperative is the Walnut Growers' Association, which with its local centers and excellent reputation for integrity and good management, has won the confidence of most of the state's walnut growers. Still another trade-mark—now well known in all parts of the world—is Sun-Maid Raisins.

The amazing growth of the California raisin and table grape industries since 1900 is almost beyond belief. Note, for example, the first quarter of the century, during which from a yield of 12,000 tons in 1900, the production of table grapes had risen to 366,000 tons in 1926. Figures for the production of raisins in recent years are so stupendous as to be staggering.

And the *sine qua non* for all this is seen in the high development of cooperative marketing of fruits and vegetables, now in operation in literally dozens of state-wide organizations—its total absence from the scene today is virtually unthinkable; it has constituted one of the most significant chapters in the recent history of California.

WALNUT PRODUCTION

The native California black walnut trees are found in abundance in the southern and central parts of the state, varying in size from a mere shrub to a great tree, influenced by soil and environment. The larger nuts found in central California have an excellent flavor, generally preferred to that of the eastern black walnut. They have been used extensively in the homes, especially in farming communities; and many avenues and public roads are bordered by rows of attractive walnut trees.

But on account of their hard shells and certain other characteristics, the native walnuts have never had much commercial value, and they are not a serious competitor with the better, cultivated nuts commonly referred to as English walnuts. However, the root of the California tree, because of its hardy quality, is very widely used as a stock for the commercial nuts by grafting or budding.

It is likely that the mission fathers brought and planted a limited number of nuts from Spain; but little importance is attached to this. American pioneers planted some English walnuts in central and southern California, for their home use. But for decades they were of no notable commercial significance. In fact, it was not until well in the present century that the walnut industry attained any considerable magnitude.

No single event marks the actual beginning of the walnut industry as it became commercially important. Production for profit was growing slowly during the two decades from 1870 to 1890. The local market absorbed the product, which was harvested by the individual growers. With the increasing magnitude during the two following decades more than a dozen local marketing associations appeared. But after struggling with chaotic conditions in the market, a big step was taken when the California Walnut Growers Association was organized, in 1912. From that time the rapidly expanding walnut industry, under the energetic leadership of C. C. Teague, president, and Carlyle Thorpe, general manager, was really on the march; for instead of facing bankruptcy under ruinous competitive selling, the "growers turned to industry-wide cooperation as a sensible solution."

Thus began the story of one of the best organized, most successfully operated of all the cooperative marketing associations to be found anywhere. To the skill, perseverance and devoted leadership of C. C. Teague, more than to any other single factor, goes the chief credit: he has become the patron saint of the industry. Of all in-shell walnuts packed by all California growers during 1943 the California Walnut growers handled 85 per cent.

Of the many practical benefits that have accrued to the members, and indirectly to all growers, may be noted, obtaining the professional services of leading food brokers, guaranteeing quality packs and thorough, impartial inspection, procuring reduced transcontinental freight rates, establishing a preference among consumers for the "Diamond Brand" (stamped on every nut), cooperation with the Government Experiment Station and Extension Service, insuring continuous research into all new problems, and the development and employment of the newest, most improved "equipment for the handling and processing of walnuts, in-shell or shelled, both for Central and Locals, at cost." Now more than 10,000 growers share the benefits of the organization.

By 1950 the area covered by the Association approximated 130,000 acres. In central and northern California the industry continues to increase rapidly, while in the south the acreage decreases, because of the encroachments of the sub-divider and special mechanical industries.

The entire walnut industry, now of huge proportions, has been brought under a uniform, equitable surplus control program ably administered by a board of nine representative members. It is the story of "an outstanding example of how an organized agricultural industry, with a little government aid, sailed a charted course through troubled waters," and is presently well equipped to weather whatever storms may come in the future. The present corporate name of the grower organization is "Diamond Walnut Growers, Incorporated." Because of its efficiency, and the quality of service rendered, this Association is rightly regarded as a model among the numerous cooperative marketing organizations of California.

CHAPTER SIX

EDUCATION

"No one, therefore, should be discouraged from studying history. Its greatest service is not so much to increase our knowledge as to stimulate thought and broaden our intellectual horizon, and for this purpose no study is its equal."   —*William P. Atkinson*

FIRST SCHOOLS

California's first state constitution, drafted in the autumn of 1849, made provision for a common school system, declaring, "The legislature shall encourage, by all suitable means, the promotion of intellectual, scientific, moral and agricultural improvement." Thus it is quite natural to conclude, as in the words of one writer, that "The California public school system was born at the Constitutional Convention, which met in Monterey in September, 1849."

But the actual establishment of the school system under the constitution did not come until 1851, when the second legislature took the necessary action. In the meantime, it should be noted, there were public schools in California prior to such establishment, operating even before the constitutional convention itself. And numerous private schools, of a sort, with rudiments of a public system, are found to have existed far back in the early Spanish period.

The first school of which we have record was opened in Pueblo de San José, in 1794. Governor Diego de Borica ordered the *alcalde* "to compel the colonists to send their children to the school." Here was the first attempt to institute a system of compulsory education. However, too much importance must not be claimed for this—the school was discontinued two years later. Likewise the first school in Monterey, opened in 1796, had an equally precarious existence. For the period 1794 to July, 1846, Bancroft lists a total of fifty-five schools, in a total of eleven different sites, including San José, San Francisco, Monterey, San Diego, Santa Barbara, and Los Angeles. These early schools were feeble, intermittent institutions. Teachers with any kind of qualifications were hard to find, and the pay was wholly inadequate. Leading families often sent their sons to Honolulu, or Valparaiso, or even to Paris, to be educated.

A notable event occurred in 1834, when William E. P. Hartnell, an

Englishman who had married a California señorita and had become an adopted Mexican citizen, established near Monterey a private school called *El Colegio de San José*. Its rather ambitious curriculum included the Three R's, also English, French, German, and Latin, as well as some philosophy, bookkeeping, and Christian doctrine. Governor José Figueroa was genuinely interested in promoting education: he strongly urged the founding of more and better schools. Not only did he encourage Hartnell in his project, but he went so far as to establish a normal school at San Gabriel, to be supported by taxes, to which the several *pueblos* were each to send two promising young men for teacher training.

However, it is generally conceded that the founding of schools and the education of children during the entire pre-American period was decidedly up-hill business. The character of the colonists as a whole, the disturbed political conditions and the spirit of apathy failed to produce a cultural climate that was at all propitious.

Instruction of the neophytes at the Franciscan missions was largely in religion, common crafts, and rudimentary domestic economy, with considerable emphasis on music. While the *padres* spent much time and effort in teaching the Indians, their activities can scarcely be regarded as having constituted schools in a true sense. Still, we would not withhold our word of praise from the zealous missionaries, nor from provincial governors like Borica, Figueroa, and even the unpopular Micheltorena, who in 1844 issued a proclamation ordering the re-establishment of the schools at San Diego, Los Angeles, Santa Barbara, Monterey, San José, San Francisco, and Sonoma.

FREE PUBLIC SCHOOLS

Precisely what do we mean when we say "school"? Will C. Wood, late state superintendent of public instruction, told of a ship-boy attached to one of the early hide-carrying vessels. When the ship was in port, this lad, too small to carry the hides, went out among the *ranchos* teaching the boys and girls to read and write. Was that a school? Some children were taught in their own homes, by their parents or by private tutors: does that constitute a school? When searching for the first schools in California one must keep in mind two things: first, the definition of school; second, tolerance toward others whose concepts may not be identical.

One report has it that the first American school was in Santa Clara as early as the autumn of 1844. A certain young woman who had just come to California, seeing youth grow up in ignorance, taught a few children the elements of an education, her sole equipment being one colored pencil—no slate or pencil for the children.

None of these, I think, can properly be called a school: a person can be a teacher, the child a learner, without a school. We mean by a school an establishment where instruction is systematically given by a teacher to pupils, or students. Two assertions may be made with full confidence: first, some rudimentary American schools did exist prior to Marshall's discovery of gold in 1848; second, in this early period religion and education were closely interrelated, as they had been in the east.

Credit goes to Mrs. Olive Mann Isbell, a teacher from Ohio, as teacher of the first American school in California. Mrs. Isbell and her husband Dr. Isbell, had migrated from Illinois in 1846. She settled at Santa Clara, where she was persuaded to instruct a little group of children. With almost no equipment, in a damp room of "the fast crumbling Santa Clara Mission," she taught from December, 1846 to March, 1847, when the family moved to Monterey. There she conducted a school for three months more. It was there that Walter Colton and Robert Semple, founders of California's first newspaper, first publicly agitated for general education.

On the authority of *The Annals of San Francisco*, we learn that William Marston, a Mormon, opened a private school in San Francisco in April, 1847—often mistakenly called the first in California. The building was a mere shanty, standing on the block between Broadway and Pacific Street. While Marston had fewer than thirty pupils and was woefully lacking in qualifications, he is often claimed as the first Yankee schoolmaster on the Pacific Coast. His school was discontinued after less than one year.

Commodore Stockton and Sam Brannan strongly urged the importance of schools, but it was not until February, 1848, that a board of trustees was elected for San Francisco, and a Yale graduate named Thomas Douglas was appointed teacher: his was the first school started by public action, but most of the teacher's salary came from subscriptions and tuition fees. It was a promising beginning; yet it ended in failure after a few weeks—gold on the American River had disrupted everything.

Several other schools were started during the early gold rush period, notably that by Rev. Samuel Willey in Colton Hall, Monterey, in March, 1849, and one by Rev. Albert Williams, in San Francisco later the same year. Both were a near approach to the free public school: neither quite met all requirements for such status.

It remained for a young Baptist layman, John Cotter Pelton of New

England, to advance to the actual establishment of the free public school in California. He conducted such a school in the small building erected by the first Baptist Church of California. Pelton had come to California for the express purpose, as he himself states, "to inaugurate the free public school system—the dream of my youth and the idol of my heart." On the 26th day of December, 1849, the Baptist Church "became the cradle of the Infant Public School." On the opening day only three children appeared; but within three months the number of pupils rose to 130. All honor to John C. Pelton, father of the free public school system of California! His is an honored name in our history.

SUPERINTENDENT OF PUBLIC INSTRUCTION

The first state constitution of California, adopted in November, 1849, made general provision for a system of free public education, with a Superintendent of Public Instruction at its head. Section 1 of Article IX reads as follows:

> The Legislature shall provide for the election, by the people, of a superintendent of public instruction, who shall hold his office for three years, and whose duties shall be prescribed by law, and who shall receive such compensation as the Legislature may direct.

That the delegates at the Monterey convention wished to encourage the education and general culture of the people there can be no doubt; as, note the very next section: "The Legislature shall encourage by all suitable means, the promotion of intellectual, scientific, moral, and agricultural improvement." Any school district neglecting to maintain and support a school for at least three months each year was threatened with the loss "of its proportion of the interest of the public fund during such neglect."

At the state election held October 7, 1850 (almost a fortnight before news of California's admission into the Union reached San Francisco), John Gage Marvin, a native of Pennsylvania, was elected first Superintendent of Public Instruction, running as an Independent and defeating four other candidates. He took office on the first of the following January, and served his full term of three years. But there was disappointing delay in the actual establishment of the public school system—the legislature failed to enact the needed statutes to give effect to the constitutional provisions.

Superintendent Marvin, in his report in January, 1852, complained that "Nearly three years have elapsed since the framers of the state constitution wisely provided for the establishment of common schools in California; yet, up to this time, no adequate provision has been made to carry out the intent and spirit of that instrument." The following year he reported that "A considerable number of pupils are taught in churches for want of suitable school houses. They are for the most part in charge of pastors of the same, from the choice of the parents of the children." Notwithstanding his broad training and many fine qualities, Marvin did not prove quite equal to the rather complex and difficult situation. With the people so absorbed in the mining industry and material development, the time was far from propitious for him.

It must be confessed that the state school system did not at first receive the popular support that was needed. Reasons for this condition are seen in inadequate financing, lack of available trained teachers, almost complete absence of suitable buildings, and great absorption of the people's interest in mining and personal gain.

However, Marvin did much to improve conditions and was able to create a favorable attitude toward the subject of public education, whose chief aim, he insisted, was the preparation for good citizenship. He championed professional standards for teachers, and consistently urged adequate financial support and good school-houses.

Largely because of his advocacy of public aid to church schools, he lost the political support of Protestant forces and failed to obtain the nomination for re-election by his own party—the Democratic. The nomination went to Paul K. Hubbs, who was duly elected Superintendent, June 21, 1853. Marvin died in Honolulu in December, 1857, still a comparatively young man.

There had been an attempt to repeal certain objectionable features of the law of 1853; but the entire proposal came to naught. Still, under the administration of Superintendent Hubbs the common school system of California regretfully lagged behind the commercial and industrial aspects of the dynamic young state. Not until John Swett, elected Superintendent September 3, 1862, took the reins did the public schools of the Golden State really come into their own. His wise and vigorous administration, inspired and sustained by his great devotion to the cause of popular education, won for John Swett the title "Architect of California's Public School System."

Likewise there was long delay in the establishment of a State University, though it also was foreshadowed in the constitution of 1849. It was not until the year 1868 that the University of California was formally established.

LIBRARIES

The library in California, as we moderns understand the term, belongs to the American period of our history. A few of the first families of the Arcadian days, to be sure, did have limited private collections of choice books; even before that there could be found at certain of the Franciscan missions numbers of volumes, chiefly on ecclesiastical subjects. But the first persons to arouse real interest in establishing circulating libraries were American pioneers, particularly early leaders in Christian endeavor.

Credit must go to Rev. Samuel H. Willey, one of the two chaplains of the constitutional convention of 1849, for establishing the first real library in California. Willey arrived at Monterey in February, 1849, as the representative of the American Home Missionary Society (Congregational). Without delay he set earnestly to work. Fortunately we have his own statement regarding the beginning of the library. I quote from his valuable book, *Thirty Years in California*:

> Before I got to be too busy otherwise, I proposed the plan of a library to the people [Monterey]. They entered into it heartily, and subscribed $1500 with which to buy books.
>
> I had a good supply of New York publishers' catalogues along with me, and so, with the assistance of others, I made out a very good choice of books. In due time they all came in good order, and so, on the present list of California public libraries, that in Monterey ranks as the one established first.

The beginnings of the State Library, located at Sacramento, are of historic interest. It was established by act of California's first state legislature, January 24, 1850, nine months before the state's admission into the Union. The nucleus of books consisted of a few hundred volumes, most of them law books for the use of state officials, donated chiefly by John C. Frémont.

During the first decade the Secretary of State was *ex officio* State Librarian; but in 1861 a separate office was established, and William Crapo Stratton was State Librarian until January 24, 1870. A board of trustees of five members was empowered to select the Librarian.

Up to 1899 the Library consisted of two parts—Law and General. During the first half of the twentieth century, development was very rapid, functions were greatly expanded. Of special interest to us is the excellent California Department, which contains a vast amount of valuable information, including invaluable newspaper files, unexcelled biographical materials, original data on early California settlers, authors, and musicians.

The Sutro Branch, in San Francisco, a rare collection of 90,000 volumes, was presented to the state by the heirs of Adolph Sutro. Much use is made of this, as well as the main Library at Sacramento, by serious research students and leading scholars in the field of California history.

Dating from the beginnings of statehood, the California State Library reflects much credit on the prescience of its founders in establishing this cultural feature in early pioneer times.

The Mercantile Library Association of San Francisco elected its first officers January 25, 1853. This was in response to the felt need for better library service when so many of the younger men were frequenting such places as the saloons and gambling houses.

In Southern California one of the first efforts toward the formation of a public library was made in 1859, by a group of prominent Los Angeles citizens. This project, however, was abandoned for lack of patronage. In December, 1872, another agitation resulted in the formation of the Los Angeles Library Association, which may be regarded as the forerunner of the institution of the public library of the area.

The free public library has long since come to be recognized as a leading cultural and ethical factor in every important center throughout the commonwealth.

CHARTERED COLLEGE

In the autumn of the year 1849 two young Methodist ministers of exceptional qualifications arrived in California, by different routes, at virtually the same time. These were Isaac Owen, who came overland, and William Taylor, who came 'round the Horn. They were to become two of the chief founders of the first college to be chartered by the new state of California.

It is likely that Owen had in mind the establishing of an institution of higher learning even before his arrival in California. As the event proved, his part in the actual founding was so conspicuous and so vital as to earn for him the distinction, Chief Founder of the College of the Pacific.

Three educational conferences were held leading up to the actual chartering of the College. First of these was in San José in January, 1851, at which the "founding of an institution of the grade of a university" was recommended. The second, in May, was held in San Francisco, where possible locations for the institution were discussed. The third, in late June, in Santa Clara, discussed the name of the school and decided upon Santa Clara as the site. The original name was California Wesleyan College, which, however, was soon changed to University of the Pacific.

The petition for a charter was drafted by Annis Merrill, prominent layman in the church and leading attorney. The charter was granted by the Supreme Court of the State on the 10th of July, 1851. The control of the institution was with the Methodist Episcopal Church. The foundation of the Santa Clara College (now University of Santa Clara) had been laid in March, 1851. This Catholic institution, however, was not formally chartered until April 28, 1855.

The actual opening of the University of the Pacific occurred, in its preparatory department, on Monday, May 3, 1852, with Edward Bannister as principal. In 1854 Bannister was relieved of his duties and Rev. Martin C. Briggs was elected president. The first regular college class to receive baccalaureate degrees, numbering five young men and five young women, graduated in the spring of 1858, under the presidency of Rev. A. S. Gibbons. Separate graduation exercises were held, since the Female Collegiate Institute and the Male Department were then virtually independent schools, although they had the same president and an identical board of trustees. With the exception of a single candidate in Santa Clara College in 1857, this was the first class to receive baccalaureate degrees in the state of California.

Largely through the insight and efforts of Greenberry Baker the University was moved from Santa Clara to College Park, San José, in 1871, and there it remained until 1924, when the move to its present location in the city of Stockton was effected. In the meantime, on the recommendation of President W. W. Guth, the name was changed from University of the Pacific to College of the Pacific in 1911, to conform more closely to the type and scope of work undertaken.

In 1951 the College of the Pacific celebrated the completion of its first century, under the slogan, "A Golden Century Crowns Pacific." Prominent among celebrants were President Robert E. Burns, who was inaugurated in 1947, and Chancellor Tully C. Knoles, who had served as president from 1919 to 1946. The first chartered college of California, still a church-related institution, is now well launched upon its second century, with its beautiful campus in the northwestern part of Stockton, facing Pacific Avenue.

OLDEST SCIENTIFIC BODY

The California Academy of Sciences commemorated its 100th anniversary on Sunday, the 19th of April, 1953, by an open-air program in the courtyard of the Academy, located in famous Golden Gate Park, San Francisco.

This firmly established and highly influential society claims to be the oldest scientific body of the entire West. The actual founding was accomplished when "seven men picked their way over the cobblestones of one of San Francisco's two newly paved streets to an office at what was then 129 Montgomery Street, to discuss the formation of 'a society for the promotion of science'." Its first name was The California Academy of Natural Sciences.

Other significant events in the young metropolis for the year 1853 include organization of the Mercantile Library Association, whose main objects were "to withdraw youths in particular from the haunts of dissipation, and to give to persons of every age and occupation the means of mental improvement, and a suitable place for passing their leisure hours"; and the third annual celebration of the vigilant Fire Department of the city with its many active members, a gala occasion for which "the whole city seemed to have turned out *en masse*"—an address was delivered by Frank Pixley.

One of the founders of the Academy of Sciences was Lewis Sloat, a nephew of Commodore John D. Sloat. Conspicuous in the list of donors to the Academy we note the names of Leland Stanford and Charles Crocker, who contributed to the establishment of the first museum, located at California and Du Pont Streets. In 1875 James Lick donated to the Academy land for a more adequate museum on Market Street between Fourth and Fifth, where the Emporium Department Store stands today.

During recent decades "the Academy has grown up with San Francisco." It is a far cry from the cabinet of miscellaneous specimens in a small office on Clay Street to the modern Museum in Golden Gate Park, including North American and African halls, Steinhart Aquarium and Hall of Sciences of today. But even that is not all.

In November, 1952, the new Alexander F. Morrison Planetarium was opened to the public. Plans were announced for a great Hall of Botany, to bear the name of Miss Alice Eastwood, distinguished former curator of the internationally famed collection of Western flora. The highly attractive and informative bi-monthly magazine *Pacific Discovery*, a Journal of Nature and Man in the Pacific World, now [1956] having completed eight volumes, is published by the Academy.

The California Academy of Sciences, having celebrated its first hundred years of constructive service, has made an auspicious beginning in its second century with the good wishes of the city by the Golden Gate and of the entire commonwealth of California. In the cultural life of the state it is an institution of which all the people may take just pride.

LITERARY SOCIETY

Four years before the first regular senior class graduated from the oldest chartered college in California with baccalaureate degrees, a group of serious-minded young men, interested in debate and oratory, constituted themselves into the Archanian Literary Society. Actual organization was effected on the first day of April, 1854, at the University of the Pacific, then located in Santa Clara. Archania thus claims to be the oldest organization of its kind not only in California but west of the Mississippi River. Its first president was J. C. Hamer, with Thomas H. Laine vice-president and John W. Owen secretary—all of whom graduated as members of the first class, in 1858.

The purpose of the Society, consisting of twenty-four charter members, is admirably expressed in the preamble to the constitution adopted:

> We, the undersigned students of the University of the Pacific, being desirous of mutually aiding each other in the acquirement of easy, graceful, and impressive manner of speaking, as well as skill in the use of language, and believing no other method so efficient for the accomplishment of these, our designs, as that used by Lyceums generally, have agreed to form ourselves into a body or Lyceum for the purpose herein mentioned, and to adopt the laws and rules following this preamble for government of the same.

The motto of the Society, adopted in 1859, was, *"Laureas Super Montem Scientiæ Carpe"* ("Seize the laurels of knowledge which are on the heights").

Meetings were held weekly during the academic year, the typical program including quotations, current events, essays, debate, and parliamentary drill. Aspects of the slavery question were hotly debated. Most of the members being of Southern extraction, feelings ran high and generally favored the South. Largely as a result of the intense feeling engendered, the minority faction (Northern) withdrew from the Society, and in 1858 the Rhizomian Society was organized as a strong rival to Archania. From that day to this the two societies have been rivals on the campus of Pacific. For many years each presented a special anniversary program as a feature of Commencement Week.

By the turn of the century the social features, which previously had been clearly subordinate to the literary and oratorical aspects of both societies, had come to hold primary significance. In keeping with the trend, Archania in 1925 adopted the Greek-letter name Alpha Lambda Sigma—changed the following year to Alpha Kappa Phi. Likewise Rhizomia, about the same time, took the name Rho Lambda Phi. Neither fraternity, however, has seen fit to drop its old original name.

Now the "Archites" and the "Rhizites" have their own attractive brick houses on Fraternity Circle, on the Stockton Campus.

It may be noted that meanwhile, as in restrospect seems only natural, the young ladies were not far behind the young men. In 1858 the Emendian Literary Society was formed by a group of students of the "Female Collegiate Institute." Emendia's weekly programs were of strictly literary character, under the adopted motto, *"Nulla Dies sine Linea"* ("No day without its lesson"). This Society, and its subsequently founded rival (Sopholectia), have more recently become Greek-letter sororities.

Literary and debating societies held an important place in the activities of virtually all the early institutions of higher learning. Similar organizations were often also to be found in college towns: the old tradition of Town *versus* Gown was thus perpetuated on a high level by debate, oratory, and other forms of literary programs. In the cultural development of the state the early literary and debating societies must be accorded an important place.

HIGH SCHOOLS

In his report to the Board of Education of November, 1852, Superintendent Thomas J. Nevins of San Francisco recommended the establishment of a high school. He stated: "There are in our schools at present an adequate number of pupils which may be sufficiently advanced by the first of January to constitute a girls' seminary department and a boys' academical department of a highly respectable character."

Up to that time popular sentiment had not been sufficiently strong to obtain the appropriation of public funds to support education beyond the elementary grades. In fact there were then but few public high schools anywhere in the United States.

On the 7th of January, 1853, the San Francisco Board of Education requested the Superintendent "to frame and present for the consideration of the Board a code of rules and regulations calculated to secure for the people the full benefits of the free common school system. . . ." The Superintendent was asked to outline a plan "for conducting the high school as two departments, one for the young men and one for the young women."

Results came quickly. The Superintendent reported to the City Council on the first of February, setting forth his plans and expressing the hope that within a few months he would be able to announce "that a high school and female seminary department were in operation." Each candidate for admission, according to his plans, must sustain a creditable examination in orthography, reading, writing, vocal music, arithmetic, geography. English, grammar, elocution, natural philosophy, use of globes, and history of the United States. The stated object of the proposed curriculum was "to fit young men for the practical duties and business of life or for admission into any of the best colleges or universities in the United States." The proposed course of study was to include a wide range of subjects.

There was further delay, occasioned largely by financial considerations and the general inertia to be overcome. The school board in 1854 expressed itself in favor of a high school for the ensuing year. In February, 1856, the Superintendent reported at least 150 pupils "far enough advanced for admittance to a high school," urging that "this most necessary school" be established. But not even yet was the sailing clear.

In July, 1856, definite steps were taken for the actual establishment of a high school; but such action was quickly rescinded on technical grounds of legality, and the "Union Grammar School," with certain courses appropriate to the high school, was ordered, though not without serious opposition; and, on the 25th of August, the new school was actually opened. This school from its beginning was referred to as a high school, indeed was a high school in everything but name, although it was not officially so designated for at least a year. An evening school was also started in the year 1856.

Finally, on the 8th of January, 1858, the name of the Union Grammar School was officially changed to the "San Francisco High School." Before the end of that year it had acquired a reputation, as reported by the Superintendent, "that commands the respect and favor of all our citizens." The first graduating class (December, 1859) consisted of twenty-two boys and thirteen girls. Such were the hesitant beginnings of California's boasted high school system, now numbering more than 400 districts and found in every part of the state.

NORMAL SCHOOLS

Largely through the interest and influence of Andrew J. Moulder, Superintendent of Public Instruction (1857-1863), California's first Normal School was established and opened in San Francisco, July 28, 1862. Previous to 1861 there was no apparent need for a normal school. Superintendent J. G. Marvin of San Francisco had reported, "The supply of competent teachers in California is more than equal to the demand."

But in 1861 the matter was brought before a State Educational

Institute, a special committee was appointed, and this committee reported a rapidly spreading movement for normal schools and the existence of a pressing need in California. A suggestion was made for an extremely modest appropriation of $5,000, which, it was stated, "would be sufficient to establish the school and put it into successful operation." For the project the actual initial appropriation by the state legislature was the tiny amount of $3,000!

When the Powell Street institution opened its doors to receive students — five young women and one young man were greeted by the principal, Ahvia Holmes. But before the end of the first term thirty-one students had registered, all but three of them being young women. The first graduating class (1862-63) consisted of four young women. John Swett gave the commencement address: he spoke seriously, yet in cheerful mood, to the graduates, sending them "on their mission with hope beaming brightly before them; a teacher's calling seemed the greatest on earth." The graduating class of 1863-64 numbered nineteen members, including one young man.

As State Superintendent Swett, who succeeded Moulder, reported in 1866: "The school is rapidly gaining ground, and its influence is beginning to be felt on the common schools of the State." But the cramped quarters soon became totally inadequate to meet the requirements of the rapidly growing school. After mature reflection the new principal W. T. Luckey, reached the conclusion that the school should be removed from the city of San Francisco, expressing a preference for San José as the most desirable location. Then O. P. Fitzgerald became state superintendent in December, 1867: with characteristic emphasis he declared: "San Francisco is not the place, for all experience proves that a school of this character cannot flourish in a great commercial city. . . . All things considered, San José is, in my judgment, the proper location for the State Normal School."

By legislative enactment San José was chosen. On the 14th of June, 1871, comfortable quarters were made available, and by July of the following year the new buildings were ready for use. The San José State Normal School had an illustrious career, to be finally superseded by San José State Teachers College.

In the meantime the Branch State Normal School at Los Angeles was opened in August, 1882, to become the Southern Branch of the University of California in 1919, and eventually the University of California at Los Angeles, coordinate with the institution at Berkeley. Another normal school was established in Chico, in 1889, later to become Chico State College. Similarly still other normal schools were established at San Diego, San Francisco, Santa Barbara, Fresno, and Arcata.

By act of legislature in 1921, all state normal schools were meta-morphosed into "teachers' colleges," then, finally, in 1935, into "state colleges." Meanwhile the School of Education of the University of Southern California had become one of the greatest teacher training institutions of the country. The development and expansion of teacher training institutions in the state in an attempt to meet the demands of our rapidly increasing population, including a number of private colleges and universities, constitutes a thrilling chapter in the history of American education.

KINDERGARTEN

The new gospel of Frederick Froebel, distinguished German educator, was not long in reaching California, even in days of slow transportation. Twenty-six years after the establishment of the first kindergarten in the Thuringian Forest—only eight years after the first in the United States —the first kindergarten of California was opened in San Francisco, in the fall of 1863. On September 10 of that year an advertisement appeared in two newspapers, reading, in part:

> Professor Charle Miel and Madame Miel respectfully announce that they have established a school for young children at their residence, No. 41 South Park, on the plan known as the Kindergarten. . . . References can be furnished as to the success of the school and its methods from patrons of M. and Madame Miel in New York City.

The opening of the San Francisco school was mentioned in the December (1863) *California Teacher*. An explanatory note added:

> As the name suggests, the school is designed specially for children from the age of three to six, who are gently led over the threshold of learning by the seductive charm of music, flowers, games, pictures, and curious objects.

A few months after this beginning in San Francisco Professor Miel announced the opening of a similar school in the town of Auburn; however, it apparently was short-lived, leaving no known traces. But the original school continued for several years, one of the very few at the time in the United States.

Pioneer kindergarten work was carried forward by Mrs. G. M. Blake, who opened a department in her school in Oakland, August, 1870, where children between the ages of four and seven were received. This proved to be the beginning of wider interest in the kindergarten method, which was strongly stimulated by Madame Weddigen, a "talented and earnest lady," who taught kindergarten in Mrs. Blake's Seminary. In his report for 1873-75 the State Superintendent of Public Instruction reported: "The opinion is gradually gaining ground that our common schools would be materially benefited, if not perfected, by the introduction of the kindergarten system."

Not yet had the gospel of Froebel been generally accepted as a part of the public school system, although Felix Adler, eminent leader of New York, was earnestly advocating it as "the alma mater of neglected childhood."

Late in 1876 a highly trained and devoted disciple of the German educator came to Los Angeles: this was Miss Emma Marwedel. In December she opened a kindergarten on Hill Street, with a training school for kindergarten teachers. Kate D. Smith, better known as Kate Douglas Wiggin, was one of Miss Marwedel's first trainees.

From that time on the movement developed rapidly. Miss Marwedel moved to Oakland, then to Berkeley, seat of the State University. Felix Adler gave a series of addresses which inspired the organization of the San Francisco Public Kindergarten Society. Other developments brought wider recognition and expansion of the work, greatly assisting in making it famous throughout the country.

It remains to mention three distinguished women who contributed generously to the cause of kindergarten in California: Madame Caroline Severance, "Mother of Women's Clubs," who had been instrumental in bringing Emma Marwedel to California; Mrs. Sarah B. Cooper, volunteer worker who enthusiastically hailed the new method as "the most beautiful thing I ever saw"; and Phoebe Apperson Hearst, generous supporter of the movement, of whose munificent contributions Mrs. Cooper said: "Your seven kindergartens are a beacon of light, guiding the little ones to the port of peace." Each member of this great trio of illustrious California women has won an enduring place in the Hall of Fame of the commonwealth.

JUNIOR COLLEGE

Contrary to a popular belief, the junior college movement was not born in California. As early as 1896 a private institution in Chicago, known as the Lewis Institute, took on the essential features of a junior college; and in Joilet, Illinois, there was established the first public junior college, in the year 1902.

It was in California, however, that the idea has had its most rapid growth and most extensive development. In 1907 the state legislature passed a law declaring that the properly constituted authorities "may prescribe post-graduate courses of study for the graduates of such high schools or other high schools, which courses of study shall approximate the studies prescribed in the first and second years of university courses." It is worthy of note that this was the first direct law in the United States providing specifically for the establishment of the junior college. Its effects were far-reaching.

First to take advantage of the law of 1907 was the city of Fresno, where under the guidance of Superintendent C. L. McLane the board of education acted to establish a junior college in the spring of 1910. Since there was then no public institution within 200 miles, other than the University of California, where students might continue beyond the high school courses, the Fresno board of education, with the cooperation and assistance of the University of California and Stanford University, took the necessary steps to make available the needed facilities. The demand had become so insistent that it was no longer to be denied.

A notable event in the development of the educational system was the founding of the Fullerton District Junior College, in 1913, the first junior college of California to be supported by a school district. Two main objectives were brought strongly into focus; the preparatory course, fitting students to enter the third (junior) year in a full college or university, and the "terminal" curriculum, intended by its vocational character to prepare for useful stations in life students who were not to proceed into higher education. These objectives have occasioned no end of discussion among educators and practical business men. On the 19th of April, 1953, Fullerton celebrated its 40th anniversary with a banquet sponsored by the Alumni Association.

One of the best examples of dual types of activities may be found in Chaffey Junior College of Ontario, in Southern California, whose fore-runner was Chaffey College of Agriculture, affiliated with the University of Southern California for a period of sixteen years. As an outgrowth from this came Chaffey Union High School in 1911, and finally Chaffey Junior College, whose vocational curriculum became strongly established.

Today (1956) California boasts sixty junior colleges, located in all parts of the state, with 70,000 full-time students. Junior college classes for adults enroll an additional 111,000, according to Henry T. Tyler, executive secretary of the California Junior College Association. In many communities the word "Junior" has been dropped from the names: thus we have "Pasadena College," "Stockton College," etc. This new institution has won an important place in the distinguished public school system of California.

VOCATIONAL EDUCATION

By vocational education we mean that specialized form of instruction which "seeks to prepare for a trade, profession, or work on a job." It tends to minimize the more theoretical, philosophical, and "academic" aspects of the curriculum and to emphasize more direct training for actual jobs and positions that enable the students to earn a livelihood. Great stress is placed on the development of special skills and appropriate techniques.

In a very informal but quite real sense, the beginnings of vocational education in California are to be found in the earliest years of the Spanish régime. One of the avowed purposes of Spanish colonization was to instruct the Indians in the arts of civilization. Teaching the fundamentals of agriculture and in the use of tools was one of the objectives of the early missionaries. A quotation of Zephryn Engelhardt, historian of the Franciscan Missions, is illuminating:

> Many of the *neophytes* were set to work at the various trades, such as the needs of the community demanded. Thus . . . we find them making bricks, tiles, and pottery, laying brick, doing carpenter work and mason work, making shoes, saddles, hats, clothes, candles, soap, tanning hides, melting tallow, shearing sheep, blacksmithing, etc. One of the chief occupations was the weaving of a kind of coarse cloth and blankets. . . . The women and girls would spin, sow, grind corn, and attend to household duties. . . .

It will be remembered that the California Indians were extremely primitive, and traditionally, quite indolent. It would be a grave mistake to assume that the *padres* were the well-equipped, skilled teachers like those of our day. Yet the regimentation and daily routine of the *neophytes* did bear some slight resemblance to certain modern trade schools, or training on the job. This is made clearer by a quotation from John Hittell:

> *Indian Work.* At sunrise all the people near the Mission were summoned to mass by the bell, and attendance was compulsory. After mass came breakfast, and then all the men and the unmarried women were required to work till 11 o'clock. A rest of three hours was allowed at noon, after which they worked till the afternoon mass, an hour before sunset. The chief occupations of the men were plowing, sowing, harrowing, threshing and hauling grain, herding the cattle, breaking horses, cutting and bringing wood for fuel, building houses, baking tiles, and weaving. There were a few carpenters, blacksmiths, tanners, and shoe-makers at every Mission, but they knew little of these trades, and had a scanty supply of bad tools.

The actual progress of the Indians in the arts and skills of civilized life was very slow. Too often they were the unwilling victims of exploitation, a condition greatly aggravated following the secularization of the missions, and especially during the exciting days of the gold rush.

For years there was virtually no development of vocational education in the new state—the concept had not taken hold of the peoples' minds. The Civil War period was not favorable for the building of educational institutions. Fresh impetus was afforded, however, by the Morrill Act of 1867; and the establishment of an agricultural, mining, and mechanical arts college became an important part of the newly-founded University of California.

Other examples of early vocational education, in special fields, are seen in the Lick School, in San Francisco, and the Cogswell Polytechnic School; and more recently the Frank Wiggins Trade School of Los Angeles. Business colleges, featuring bookkeeping and other commercial subjects, sprang up; and such subjects as mining, geology, and mineralogy were emphasized in schools of mining towns, as in Grass Valley.

It is apparent that vocational education did not really come into its own until the twentieth century. In 1914 Edwin R. Snyder became Commissioner of Vocational Education: under his administration and that of his successor, Nicholas Ricciardi, this important subject became well established.

California's present highly-developed department, partly supported by Federal funds, operates in five fields: agriculture, distributive occupations, home making, trades and industries, occupational information and guidance. Each of these has its Chief, and the five Chiefs, with the Director, constitute the Commission for Vocational Education in California.

EDUCATIONAL JOURNALS

When Harr Wagner, in 1895, was about to launch the *Western Journal of Education*, he asked President David Starr Jordan for a statement of the main purposes of an educational journal. Here is Jordan's reply:

> It should give the best of educational thought of the best men of the time. It should give the latest educational news concerning new movements, educational meetings, institutions, and representative men. . . . It should keep its readers acquainted with the best educational literature.

But Wagner's *Western Journal* was by no means the first educational journal of California. The very first attempt was in early pioneer times, and it did not fully incorporate all the functions described by Jordan.

The journal was called *The Bookseller*, which was originally intended as a trade journal.

Its first number, consisting of thirty-six pages, appeared in San Francisco in August, 1860, under the editorship of William H. Knight, who later became one of the leading assistants of Hubert Howe Bancroft in the preparation of his monumental work on the Pacific States in thirty-nine volumes. The noble purpose of *The Bookseller* is set forth in these words:

> As the pioneer teachers of California, we have our mission to work out; not to sit at the Golden Gate and receive a meager allowance of dollars and cents for the exhausting brain work of the school room, but by creative art to call into life a more rational and natural system of education. Let us be true to ourselves and our duties. While the miners with brawny arms are playing with the mountains like gods; while the farmers are making our valleys green with verdure and luxuriant grain; . . . it is our mission to deal with the more intangible yet mightier powers which underlie these visible facts, for our materials are thousands of brains, the batteries which shall generate all the electric forces which vitalize society.

But the times were apparently not ripe for such an educational enterprise—it continued publication for only a single year.

In the spring of 1863 plans were laid for the publication of *The California Teacher*, the initial number of which appeared in July of that year. One of its editors was John Swett, great champion of the common school. In a salutatory it stated:

> The time has come when the Pacific Coast may justly have a voice for the world. The thoughtful minds of the Atlantic States are turned to the setting sun with wonder and with hope. A new civilization is to arise here. A new and glorious part of a great nation is beginning to live and to grow with untold energy and power.

For ten years *The California Teacher* was the property of the State Teachers Association. In 1873 its control was transferred to the State Superintendent of Public Instruction. Three years later, because it lacked legislative support, it passed out of existence.

Among the numerous later and contemporaneous educational journals of California mention is here made of two. The *Western Journal of Education* was published in San Francisco by Harr Wagner, who continued for many years as editor. The *Sierra Educational News and Book Review* came into being in 1904, as a private venture of the Boynton and Esterly teacher's agency. The magazine was purchased by the newly incorporated California Teachers Association in January, 1909. Vaughn

MacCaughey was editor from 1923 to 1952, when he was succeeded by J. Wilson McKenney. In 1950 the name was changed to *CTA Journal*, which now proudly claims more than a half-century of publication. It is the vigorous official organ of the California Teachers Association, issuing nine numbers each year to its more than 85,000 members.

PARENT-TEACHERS ASSOCIATION

The organization of the National Congress of Mothers took place in the year 1897. Among its stated objects were:

> to promote conference among parents upon questions vital to the welfare of their children, to further develop the manifold interests of the home, . . . and to promote the formation of mothers' clubs and home-makers' clubs in all states and territories of the United States.

The general title was later changed to National Congress of Parents and Teachers. Parents were becoming "school-conscious, education-conscious." The feeling was growing that the gulf between parent and teacher stood in need of bridging, particularly in the interest of the children.

As early as the autumn of 1893 Mrs. Elizabeth Prior, a Los Angeles teacher who had just returned from a visit to her old home in Minnesota, organized child study circles at Hellman Street and Avenue 23. In 1898 Miss Mary F. Ledyard was brought to Los Angeles as supervisor of the new kindergarten department. She and Mrs. Prior found themselves deeply interested in a common cause, "the bringing together of the mothers of school children and their teachers in the schools."

The superintendent, James A. Foshay, was in hearty accord: thus many clubs were formed, and they functioned with increasing success. In March of 1900 Miss Ledyard was appointed by the National Congress as organizer for California. On May 8 of that year "The Los Angeles Federation of Mothers' Clubs" was organized. A fortnight later the constitution was adopted and officers duly elected, with Mrs. W. W. Murphy as first president. Cooperation of home and school had already reached a high state of development.

The organized movement, essentially a twentieth century trend, was soon extended to include grade teachers and mothers, then fathers, then mothers and teaching faculties in schools of all grades. In March, 1901, it included Pasadena and Long Beach; the following year Santa Ana fell into line. At the third Annual Meeting (November, 1902) the report showed forty-six circles in Los Angeles and fourteen in other towns, "all doing splendid work."

Meanwhile in northern California, largely under the influence of Earl

Barnes and Elmer E. Brown, a similar movement was progressing. The
formation of the San Francisco Congress of Mothers dates from 1907.
But for some time north and south functioned separately, resulting in
considerable confusion.

In 1912 Mrs. A. L. Hamilton of Pasadena took steps resulting in state-
wide organization, in the belief that it would be "for the best interests
. . . to alternate the state presidency between the northern and southern
parts of our State."

Thus it becomes apparent that the beginnings of the Parent Teachers'
Association in California were by no means like the formation of the
state itself, Minerva-like, but were a step-by-step development over a
period of a good many years, the great central goal, however, always
being "the advancement of child welfare in California."

In 1910 it was decided to divide the state into eight districts for extension work, each district to have its own vice-president. Modifications
came from time to time: the organization has continued to be highly
dynamic in character. In the words of Margaret H. Strong, "Any
activity which leads to the better adjustment of the child to the educational process is legitimate P.T.A. activity."

Support of the work of the California Congress of Parents and
Teachers came from Superintendents Foshay, Ernest C. Moore, and
Will C. Wood, and from members of the State Board of Education.
Mrs. Phoebe Hearst became a devoted patron. For many years the
movement has had the general endorsement of educational leaders,
though it would be inaccurate to state that 100 per cent of the schools
and school people are thoroughly convinced.

The program of the P.T.A. has taken on new features from time to
time; but its general policy is always to cooperate with the teachers,
never attempting actually to operate the schools. As to membership,
women have always greatly predominated, though men are by no means
barred, and "Fathers' Nights" and "Dads' Clubs" are growing in
number and influence.

Publications of the P.T.A. are numerous, including the official magazine *The California Parent-Teacher*, with its large circulation. Membership in California for 1954-55 exceeded 1,400,000, far larger than that
of any other state. A fitting motto for the organization is "Pull Together
Always." Another familiar slogan is "Teamwork Does It."

UNIVERSITY EXTENSION

We may ask Walter H. Page to be spokesman for statesman and
educators of our time, or any time, as, in referring to the ideals of

democratic government, he declares that under American democracy "every human being shall have his opportunity for his utmost development—his chance to become and to do the best that he can." The university itself, great as is its scope, important as is its function, cannot in itself afford this full opportunity to all the people. Its campus curriculum must be richly supplemented and projected to serve many who never reach the college halls, and to stimulate among the citizenry the spirit of "life-long learning."

University Extension, which may properly include various types of adult education, correspondence courses, and lectures, has become an important phase of the work of the university, in its widened scope. The word *Extension* was explained by Dr. R. G. Moulton to apply to more people, to life-long education, and to include all life interests. The general aim, as phrased by Leon J. Richardson, "is to cooperate with the citizens of the State who wish to study and learn as they might if they were at the University."

At the University of California President Horace Davis advocated extension work during his short term (1888-1890). Impetus was given to the thought when, in 1891, President William Rainey Harper of the University of Chicago startled the educational world by instituting a correspondence course in the study of Hebrew. Meantime the longer experience at Cambridge and Oxford in England attracted our attention.

The real pioneer of the movement in California was Charles Mills Gayley, one of the most renowned teachers and scholars of the Berkeley campus. He was a man of extraordinary breadth, with affiliations in several lands. In the spring of 1891 he read a paper on "University Extension, Its History in England and Possibilities in California." Only a few weeks later extension courses were announced in history, English, mathematics, and philosophy. Gayley himself was appointed Director, as well as lecturer on Shakespeare and other English topics. Other instructors included Thomas R. Bacon, George H. Howison, Irving Stringham, and, the following year, Joseph LeConte and Bernard Moses —all renowned teachers.

The movement was well launched, by leading scholars. Gayley continued as Director until 1902, when he was succeeded by Henry Morse Stephens, one of the most popular professors ever at Berkeley. A native of Scotland, he had studied at Oxford: after much experience in London, he came to Berkeley in 1902 at the invitation of Benjamin Ide Wheeler. He had large extension classes at various centers, his French Revolution course attracting most attention.

Stephens was succeeded by Ira W. Howerth as Director in 1912. In

1918 Leon J. Richardson became Director, continuing his activities, particularly in correspondence courses, down to the present time.

As was natural, other universities and colleges also developed extension and off-campus courses. Scarcely any center of population in the state is now without some direct or indirect contact with an institution of higher learning.

At the University of California, it should be noted, University Extension and Agriculture Extension have been entirely distinct organizations. There was extension work in Agriculture under Eugene W. Hilgard, beginning as early as 1875. In 1897 he was followed by Edward J. Wickson.

Closely allied to University Extension in important respects is the Department of Adult Education found in various institutions and school districts. As one example, the San José Department may be mentioned, under Director H. Price Webb. There are many ramifications of this work, one of the most fascinating being "The Adult Center Vagabonds; or Learning California History via Greyhound Bus."

Still another recent phase is suggested—educational travel. This has become a well-organized movement in the country; several institutions of learning in California now sponsor extended tours on which it is possible, under proper safeguards, to earn academic credits. In this field the College of the Pacific at Stockton is a pioneer, where the organization of plans began in 1927, under direction of Dr. G. A. Werner.

CALIFORNIA TEACHERS' ASSOCIATION

John Swett, California's fourth Superintendent of Public Instruction and one of the great educational leaders of his time, was instrumental in organizing 100 male teachers into the California Educational Society, May 4, 1863. This small nucleus was the beginning of the California Teachers Association, with its 86,000 members, the largest state teacher organization in the nation.

The infant society had two purposes: to publish an educational journal, *The California Teacher*, and to secure adequate funds for the maintenance of good public schools. The journal did not prosper. It was finally forced to suspend publication in its eighth year, and the society itself had a very precarious career.

The State Teachers Association, composed largely of San Francisco Bay Area teachers, was organized in 1875. In 1889 the Teachers Association of Southern California was organized at the State Normal School in Los Angeles. Three years later the San Joaquin Valley Teachers Association was born in the city of Fresno, later being renamed the

Central California Teachers Association. In the Sacramento area, the Northern California Teachers Association came into being, in 1897. Thus there were a number of independent, uncoordinated teacher organizations in California at the end of the nineteenth century.

The regional associations faced increasing difficulties in coordinating proposals and memorials to the state legislature, a condition leading to discussions early in the present century of the desirability of a unified state-wide organization. John Swett, veteran educator, was among those who recommended, at a meeting in Fresno in December, 1906, that all existing regional associations join in a single state body, to be known as the California Teachers Association.

On the 16th of January, 1907, CTA was duly incorporated, becoming in reality a federation of sections governed by a representative State Council of Education. Its membership grew rapidly from that date, including each of the numerous types of certificated personnel.

The original articles of incorporation state as the Association's purposes:

> To further the educational interests of the State of California, to give increasing efficiency to its school system, to secure and maintain for the office of teaching its true rank among the professions of the state, to furnish a practicable basis for unified action among those devoted to the cause of education in the state.

In this may be seen another indication of the growing spirit of unity in California, which has manifested itself in the educational, political, economic, and other phases of life.

The Association is well staffed, having seventy-four employees at present in its San Francisco headquarters building, on Sutter Street. Dr. Arthur F. Corey is executive secretary; J. Wilson McKenney is editor of the *Journal*, official publication of the Association, which reaches teachers in all parts of the state. Some idea of the multifarious work of the large federation is gained by the simple statement that staff and committee activity includes educational policies, financing public education, legislative, retirement, teacher education, youth activities, international relations, moral and spiritual values, salary schedules and trends, tenure, personnel standards, research, field service, public relations, publications, and special services.

CHAPTER SEVEN

GOVERNMENT — POLITICS

"The history of the world is none other than the progress of the
consciousness of Freedom."   —*Hegel*

FIRST PROVINCIAL GOVERNOR

In studying our early history Lower (Baja) California and Upper (Alta)
California are to be thought of as constituting for a time a single Spanish
province, commonly referred to as The Californias. The founding of
Mission San Diego in 1769 marks the beginning of the actual occupation
of Alta California by men of the white race.

The occupation was effected by virtue of the three-fold plan involving
religious forces (the mission), civic forces (the *pueblo*), and the military
factor (the *presidio*). The religious element, influential as it was,
definitely needed the military in acquiring and maintaining a foothold
in the progress of colonization.

When, in the year 1767 the decree came for the expulsion of all
Jesuits from the Spanish possessions, it fell to a military officer of noble
family and valuable experience to execute the harsh decree as it applied
to the Jesuit missions of Baja California. This gallant captain was
Gaspar de Portolá, who thus became military and civil governor of the
Californias in 1768. As the ruler assigned to the new province of Alta
California, he is more accurately to be regarded as military commander
rather than civil governor, down to July 9, 1770, when Felipe de Barri
became governor of the Californias, with official residence at Loreto, far
to the south, in Baja California.

Portolá's very brief career in California proved nevertheless to be
noteworthy. In our history, as one has written, "he must always be a
prominent figure." Despite the sickness and distress of many of his men,
and the unknown perils involved, with the spirit of a true soldier he was
determined upon the full performance of duty—he made ready to undertake the expedition to the north in search of Monterey Bay, which had
been so extravagantly described by Vizcaíno more than a century and
a half before. The gripping story of Portolá's March has been told and
retold. Failure to identify the famous port, "sheltered from all winds,"
was in reality a glorious success. Told in the words of Zoeth Eldredge:

As Columbus hoping to find an island had discovered a continent, and as Cortez seeking for a fabled California had found a real one, so these weary travelers . . . were to be rewarded by the discovery of a greater harbor [San Francisco] than was then known.

When the final crisis arose at San Diego, and a miserable death had claimed a number of the luckless soldiers, the pitiful remnant of Portolá's command seemed face to face with actual starvation, the courageous leader quietly took inventory of supplies on hand and resolved to stay as long as possible with Padre Junípero Serra, consecrated head of the Franciscan missionaries, of unconquerable spirit and sublime faith. But at the critical hour, far out in the harbor appeared the relief ship *San Antonio*. Food had come—California was saved.

Portolá never gained an adequate conception of the value of the province he was so instrumental in holding for Spain. He became so discouraged because of the apparent barrenness of the country through which he passed that he once remarked that "the Russians were welcome to such a desert."

Little is known of Portolá's later life. On the 9th of July, 1770, he sailed away on the *San Antonio*, "and California knew him no more." He was advanced in military rank, he served for a time as governor of Puebla, was finally ordered back to Spain, where he died in 1784.

In the history of California, as Nellie Sanchez has well said,

> . . . he must always be a prominent figure, as the first of her governors, the leader of the first party of settlers over the long trail from Velicatá, and the discoverer of San Francisco Bay. . . . He was a brave, capable, humane, and conscientious soldier, worthy in every respect of all the honor that California can give him.

FIRST *PRESIDIO*

Probably no one now living really knows how nearly our California came to being abandoned in 1769 and 1770, before Spain had gained firm foothold. And if the fair land had actually been abandoned, Professor Charles E. Chapman was not alone in surmising, "the Russians might be expected to extend their possessions to the southernmost extremity of the peninsula"—meaning Lower California. The military agency employed by the Spanish crown to protect the country from foreign and domestic foes was the *Presidio*.

José de Galvez, powerful Visitor-General of New Spain, set on foot one of the most far-reaching undertakings in all our early history. This included the establishment of two *presidios* at strategic points—one at San Diego, the other at Monterey. The *presidio* was a garrisoned fortress town, whose primary purpose was to protect the missions and guard against any foreign aggression. As a norm, each should have twenty-five soldiers, including a sergeant and two corporals. There were also the storekeeper, two carpenters, and two blacksmiths. Five soldiers with their corporal were assigned to each of the missions, for protection, chiefly against Indian attacks. Quite naturally there developed around each fortress a small town, or village.

California's first *presidio* was founded not at San Diego, but at Monterey. After appalling difficulties, the weary adventurers under Father Juan Crespi and Lieutenant Pedro Fages had re-discovered and identified Monterey Bay, "exactly as described by Sebastián Vizcaíno and Cabrera Bueno." On the third day of June, 1770, the ship *San Antonio* arrived, and "amidst the pealing of the bells and the firing of salvos of artillery a solemn mass was celebrated." Gaspar de Portolá, as governor, took formal possession in the name of King Carlos III of Spain, with all due ceremony. A messenger was dispatched to carry the news to far-off Mexico City, where it was received with salutes of artillery, the ringing of bells, thanksgiving mass, and general rejoicing.

Duflot de Mofras, a distinguished French voyager who visited California in 1841, gave us a graphic picture of the typical *presidio*. They surrounded it, he wrote, "with a ditch twelve feet wide and six feet deep. . . . The rampart, built of brick, was twelve to fifteen feet high and three inches in thickness; small bastians flanked the angles. Its armament consisted of eight bronze cannon; eight, twelve, and sixteen pounders."

Following the *presidios* at Monterey and San Diego came two others —San Francisco, founded in 1776, and Santa Barbara, founded in 1782. So each of the four districts into which Alta California was divided had its armed fortress. And around these have developed four of the most historic cities of our Golden State—San Diego, Santa Barbara, Monterey, and San Francisco.

FIRST *PUEBLO*

Beautiful Santa Clara Valley, sometimes denominated the "Paradise" of the Golden State, contains California's most ancient *pueblo*, as well as two of the old Franciscan missions and the famous New Almaden quicksilver mines. It had attracted attention as early as 1769, was seen by Father Crespi in 1772, and in 1774 was visited by Father Palóu and still others.

The *pueblo* was one of the three institutions employed by Spain in her efforts to colonize Alta California, the other two, as already noted, being the mission and the *presidio*. The *pueblo* was the planned civic settlement, or town. The settlers were called *pobladores*.

Under the general direction of Viceroy Bucareli of New Spain (Mexico), Don Felipe de Neve, who has been called by Chapman "greatest of the Spanish governors of Alta California," in an attempt to render the province self-supporting, resolved to establish two *pueblos*, San José and Los Angeles. Accordingly, on the 29th of November, 1777, a band of adventurers numbering in all sixty-six persons, including fourteen heads of families, under Lieutenant-Commandant José Moraga, laid the foundations of *El Pueblo de San José de Guadalupe*.

The first houses of the town were plastered palisades, with flat earthen roofs, constructed so as to face the *plaza*. Public buildings first being located, the remainder of the land was divided into small building lots for the use of the founders. To each family was allotted a *suerte*, or field, that might be irrigated by water from the Guadalupe River.

Regulations for colonization were based rather vaguely upon old Spanish laws. In June, 1779, Governor Neve promulgated a code of laws, the famous *Reglamento*, which set forth in detail the standardized plan for the California *pueblo*. As a sample provision we quote from Section 3 of Title 14:

> To each *poblador*, and to the community (*comon*) of the *Pueblo*, there shall be given, under conditions of repayment in horses and mules, fit to be given and received and in payment of the other large and small cattle, at the just prices which are to be fixed by tariff, and of the tools and implements at cost as it is ordained, two mares, two cows, and one calf, two sheep and two goats, all breeding animals, and one yoke of oxen or steers, one plow-share or point, one hoe, one *coa* [a kind of wooden spade, with a steel point], one axe, and one sickle, one woodknife, one musket, and one leather shield, two horses, and one cargo mule. . . .

It cannot be said that the first inhabitants of San José were very promising human material, for we read that in 1795 the population numbered 187 persons, "infamous for laziness and theft." For a decade or longer the population remained almost stationery. In 1805 the famous Alameda of trees uniting *Pueblo de San José* and Mission Santa Clara is said to have been planted. "As late as 1846," says Richman, "San José was described as 'a village of 600 to 800 inhabitants in a fine valley, of adobe buildings and very irregular streets, with thousands of ground squirrels burrowing in the *plaza*, and men and women of all classes engaged in gambling'." It should be added, however, that three years later the town was selected as the first State Capital of California, was incorporated as an American city in 1850, and has now become a beautiful metropolitan center of more than 100,000 people.

Los Angeles was the second California *pueblo*, founded under Governor Neve's plan, September 4, 1781. The elaborate celebration of its Sesquicentennial in 1931 was a gala occasion. The third civic community, called Branciforte, was founded near the present site of Santa Cruz, in 1779. It was to have military as well as civic importance; but it proved to be a failure almost from the beginning—in a little while it passed completely out of existence.

FIRST LAW-GIVER

During the entire period of the Spanish occupancy of Alta California (1769-1822) there was a total of ten governors of the province. Third on the list was Felipe de Neve (1775-1782), of whom the historian Theodore Hittell wrote: "He may be called the first legislator that California had and one of the very best."

What did De Neve do to earn the distinction of being our first law-giver? Undoubtedly his chief title to fame lies in his authorship of a code of laws for the Californians, known as the *Reglamento*. This was dated June 1, 1779, at the Royal *Presidio* of San Carlos de Monterey. It was not until October 24, 1781, that it received the formal approval of the King of Spain. The code was printed in 1784.

That the governor was acting under the authority of Viceroy Bucareli of New Spain need not detract from the credit due him—he was on the ground; he was the true author of the *Reglamento*. Bancroft declares: "It was certainly a mark of great confidence in his ability, and a still greater compliment was the adoption of his plan, without, so far as appears, a single modification." He had already established the first of California's *pueblos* and was soon to found the second. It is agreed that Bucareli was an able, far-seeing administrator. His directive of 1773, issued to De Neve, contained twenty-seven paragraphs, the last of the great documents from that viceroy to the governor of Alta California.

The extensive and detailed provisions of De Neve's *Reglamento* have been preserved in California Archives. Illustrative of the provisions a few extracts may be presented from Title the Fourteenth, relating to the political government and to methods of colonization. Section 1 declares the chief object to be "toward securing to his Majesty the dominion of the extensive country, which occupies a space of more than two hundred leagues," and to make this "useful to the State, by erecting *pueblos* of white people (*pueblos de gente razon*), who, being united, may encourage agriculture, planting, the breeding of cattle, and successively the other branches of industry, . . ."

Each *poblador* (settler) was to receive the equivalent of $120 and rations for the first two years, and specified amounts for the following three years. House lots and land areas were to be distributed in specified manner. To each settler, under conditions clearly set forth, was to be given, as mentioned above, a beginning of livestock and farming equipment.

The *pueblo* lands were to include house lots, common lands, sowing lands and pasture lands. To the community were to be given breeding animals, lands needed for municipal purposes and certain lots of land reserved for the benefit of the king. The plan of distribution was so devised as to adhere strictly to the principles of equality and justice. Each settler was to hold himself in readiness to defend the district and to proceed, in case of urgency, to any point to which the governor might order him. As a whole, the interesting plan of colonization included elements of paternalism, and of absolute monarchy, but withal a semblance of democracy.

Even before the promulgation of the famous *Reglamento* the *pueblo* of San José had been founded, in November, 1777. The other *pueblo* established under immediate orders of Governor de Neve was Los Angeles, in September, 1781. Viceroy Bucareli had foreseen that the early establishments in Alta California might in time become great cities; but neither he nor De Neve could possibly have visualized the cities of San José, Los Angeles, and San Francisco of today. The seed planted by California's first law-giver, pronounced the greatest of Spanish governors, has produced more than a hundred fold.

VIGILANCE COMMITTEE

The great San Francisco Committee of Vigilance of 1856 attracted national attention and is the best known among all the popular tribunals of California. But it had been preceded by the strong Committee of 1851, also in San Francisco, to which it was a logical successor. This in turn had followed by only two years the uprising against the "Hounds," or self-styled "Regulators," of the same city, which revealed some of the excesses and criminality associated with the rougher phases of the Days of '49—for the gold excitement had attracted to California, from many states and from foreign lands, a decidedly heterogeneous population.

We must go back still farther, however, to find the first California vigilance committee. This had no connection with the gold excitement

—it was in *Pueblo de Los Angeles*, in the spring of 1836. Its antecedents had to do with "a guilty love romance."

It appears that María del Rosaria Feliz, wife of Dominguez Feliz, had established illicit relations with the *major domo* of Los Feliz Rancho, Gervacio Alispaz. The husband became suspicious, but his faithless wife denied her guilt. When the lovers fled to San Gabriel, the husband followed and was slightly wounded by Alispaz's knife. By authority of the *alcalde* the woman was compelled to return to her husband's ranch, and a reconciliation was effected. But the reconciliation proved to be a sham.

Not long afterward, when husband and wife were returning from Los Angeles, Alispaz suddenly emerged from behind a tree, threw his *reata* over Feliz's head, pulling him backward from his horse. Then the guilty María dismounted, rushed to her strangling husband, and stabbed him. The *ranchero's* body was quickly buried in a ravine, and the guilty couple fancied that all evidence of the crime had been concealed.

However, through the barking of his faithful dog, Feliz's body was found, taken to the *pueblo* and buried from the mission chapel. Then events swiftly followed one another. After being haled before an extraordinary session of the court, the guilt of the couple appeared to be established; Alispaz was led away to jail, and María was "deposited" at a family residence for safekeeping.

Within a few days the outraged citizens held a meeting, April 7, 1836, at Juan Temple's house; a vigilance committee was formed with the title, *Junta Defensona de la Seguridad Publica* (United Defenders of Public Security.) Of this Victor Pruden (Prudhomme) was elected president and Manuel Argaza secretary. A military force of fifty citizens was quickly formed, and the demand was made that the prisoners be brought before the *junta*.

It remains only to relate that despite the refusal to deliver the prisoners, the key was taken from the jailer, Alispaz was taken to the plaza, where he made full confession, then died by the "fusilade" from a detail of twelve men. A similar fate awaited the guilty woman. It is reported that "She was placed in a chair near the dead body of her accomplice, and also died by the 'fusilade'."

Formal reports were sent to the *alcalde* of the *pueblo* in the name of "God and Liberty." This function having been performed, the first vigilance committee came to an end, in the spring of 1836, a full decade before the American Conquest and two decades before the great Committee of 1856.

UNITED STATES CONSUL

Up to the year 1844 the United States had no consular representative in the province of California, although several appointees had either resigned or failed to take office. Late in that year, however, an official document reached Thomas O. Larkin at Monterey announcing that he had been appointed Consul for California, and the appointment had been confirmed by the United States Senate.

Larkin was much flattered by this national recognition. Unlike many American settlers, he had consistently rejected all overtures to become an adopted Mexican citizen; he was without question the best qualified man in all California for the office of consul. Through intimate relations with John Parrott, consul at Mazatlan, and by his own keen observations, he understood how "business followed the flag" in outlying commercial ports. From the national standpoint, it had been deemed expedient, in view of American shipping and trading, also the bickerings and clashes with the Mexican authorities, to create this new diplomatic post. The choice of Larkin was mutually satisfactory.

One of the first acts of the new consul was to order from New York an elaborate official uniform, to be made to his order, with an ample supply of the "finest Navy buttons." His official outfit arrived ten months later! There were heavy epaulets, with dazzling gold braid, brass buttons galore, and two gold-headed canes added by his friend Alfredo Robinson, then in New York.

The scope of Larkin's official duties was of necessity wide and quite vaguely defined—California at that time extended eastward to the Rocky Mountain region, and the consul was charged with the welfare of American captains and seamen up and down the Pacific. The office may be compared to that of the first American *alcalde*, Walter Colton, a few years later, with its nebulous boundaries and diversity of functions. All kinds of trouble—governmental, commercial, marital—were referred to Larkin for settlement or adjustment. To an unfortunate seaman the consul was "*de facto* guardian, nurse, tailor, and undertaker." By his frequent reports and letters he rendered important service to his government, for he was able to deal intimately and promptly with the rapidly changing scenes.

While performing the numerous consular functions Larkin withdrew, at least nominally, from his merchandising business. It may be said that his two chief objectives were to make the wonderful resources of California known to the world, especially the United States, and to proceed in such a manner as ultimately to bring about the peaceful acquisition of the province by the American government. Distinct progress was made in the peaceful, friendly occupation by American settlers during those critical years when Mexico's hold upon California was known to be extremely feeble. Just what might have followed had not Frémont appeared must be left to conjecture.

A further honor, involving obligations of the utmost delicacy, came to Larkin in April, 1846, when he received his appointment as Confidential Agent for the American government. In the appointing letter from Washington, James Buchanan, Secretary of State, says:

> The confidence which he [the president] reposes in your patriotism and discretion is evidenced by conferring upon you this delicate and important trust. You will take care not to awaken the jealousy of the French and English agents there by assuming any other than your consular character.

The actual conquest of California proved to be an act in the War with Mexico. Nevertheless the career of Thomas O. Larkin won for him a place in California's Hall of Fame. As merchant, American consul, confidential agent, and sagacious friend and patriot, he was during several highly critical years the "most efficient instrument" in bringing about the acquisition of California by the United States.

AMERICAN *ALCALDE*

The settlers at the early *pueblos* of California in the Spanish régime were called *pobladores*. In matters of government they were under the jurisdiction of a kind of magistrate, or *alcalde*, who was subordinate only to the governor of the province. Thus the *alcalde* dates from the beginning of the *pueblo* system—the first *pueblo*, it will be remembered, was San José, founded in 1777.

Regarding the functions and duties of the *alcalde* we learn a good deal from certain instructions given by Diego de Borica, Governor of California (1794-1800). When he reprimanded a magistrate, charging him "with violations of his duty and with assisting crime instead of preventing or punishing it," he outlined the rightful functions of the *alcalde* with considerable clearness, demanding that they be performed "with the integrity of an honest man." Continuing, he said:

> you will present in your own person an example of well regulated demeanor and application to business. You will consent to no immoral practices, to no drunkenness, to no species of gaming that is prohibited by law. You will encourage and stimulate every *poblador*, who does not enjoy military exemption, to work his land and take proper care of his stock. You will permit no idleness. . . .

With the raising of the American flag by Commodore John Drake Sloat in 1846 came a change of rule in California, though technically the Mexican laws were continued in force for the time being. Commodore Stockton, Sloat's successor, appointed Walter Colton, a chaplain in the United States Navy, as *alcalde*, pending an election by the people. On being duly elected some two months later, he expressed deep appreciation for the honor—he was the first American *alcalde* in California.

> "It devolves upon me duties similar to those of mayor of one of our cities," he wrote, "without any of those judicial aids which he enjoys. It involves every breach of the peace, every case of crime, every business obligation, and every disputed land-title within a space of three hundred miles. From every other *alcalde's* court in this jurisdiction there is an appeal to this, and none from this to any higher tribunal. Such an absolute disposal of questions affecting property and personal liberty, never ought to be confided to one man. There is not a judge on any bench in England or the United States, whose power is so absolute as that of the *Alcalde* of Monterey."

Because of his integrity, humanity, good sense, and spirit of helpfulness, Colton was able to conduct his responsible office with dignity and substantial justice. The jurisdiction of his court was extremely wide. The *alcalde* was expected "to advise and admonish, to reprehend and punish, . . . indeed, to be a father to his people. To him they brought all their grievances of every sort, and if there was no law applicable, he made the law and applied it." Most common among the offenses were those associated with drinking and gambling.

In the summer of 1849, impaired in health, Colton left California for his old home; in January, 1851, he died and was given a funeral with naval honors. He deserved well of California and the nation.

The restored Colton Hall in the city of Monterey, constructed under his orders, is a fitting memorial to the man. On the 28th of November, 1955, a bronze plaque was affixed to the historic building bearing this tribute:

> Congregational minister, historian, author, and editor, who served as the first *Alcalde* of Monterey, from September 15, 1846, to October, 1848. On August 15, 1846, in partnership with Robert Semple, Colton established California's first newspaper, "The Californian"; he impanelled the first U.S. jury ever to be summoned in this State on September 4, 1846; and in 1847 was appointed judge of the U.S. Court of Admiralty.

TRIAL BY JURY

In his invaluable book *Three Years in California*, which is in reality a day-by-day record for the period 1846-1849, Walter Colton, first American *alcalde* in California, made this entry for Friday, September 4, 1846:

> I empaneled today the first jury ever summonded in California. The plaintiff and defendant are among the principal citizens of the country. The case was one involving property on the one side, and integrity of character on the other. . . . One-third of the jury were Mexicans, one-third Californians, and the other third Americans. . . . the plaintiff spoke in English, the defendant in French, the jury, save the Americans, Spanish, and the witnesses all the languages known to California. But through the silent attention which prevailed, the tact of Mr. Hartnell, who acted as interpreter, and the absence of young lawyers, we got along very well.

After an hour's deliberation, the jury reached a verdict, to which "both parties bowed without a word of dissent." The *alcalde's* entry for the day ends with these strong words of praise for the jury system, the opinion of twelve honest men: "If there is any thing on earth besides religion, for which I would die, it is the right of trial by jury."

The trial had been followed "with the utmost satisfaction and curiosity" by the inhabitants of Monterey. It should be added that in certain cases, early Mexican law authorized the right of a sort of jury trial, the jury consisting of three or five *buenos hombres*. This prerogative, however, was only rarely resorted to. To Walter Colton belongs the distinction of impanelling "the first jury ever to sit in California on a case tried according to American jury trial practice." Perhaps it did not wholly conform to American practice, since there were no lawyers present to assist! But what of that!

Among many other distinctions that came to Colton because of his conscious." The feeling was growing that the gulf between parent and Dr. Robert Semple, of the first newspaper (*Californian*), referred to on another page, the erection of historic Colton Hall in Monterey, in which the first Constitutional Convention was held in 1849, and his interesting and valuable books, especially his *Three Years in California*.

In summing up the traits of character of this first American *alcalde* of California, Henry T. Cheever in his *Memoirs* brings out four special points; Colton's benevolence and good humor, his superior skill in conversation, his ability to make and keep friends, and his unfailing tact and ready wit. "He thought, acted, and felt on a large scale."

STATE CONSTITUTION

The draft of the first constitution of the State of California was completed on the 13th day of October, 1849, under circumstances that were highly dramatic. The labors of the delegates at the convention held in Colton Hall, Monterey, had been brought to an end. It had been decided that California should seek admission into the American Union as a full-fledged state and not as an organized territory. How appropriate then is the epithet, the "Minerva State!"

The Monterey Convention had been called into being by proclamation of the *de-facto* governor, General Bennet Riley, setting aside the first day of August, 1849, for the election of delegates and the first of September for the actual meeting, in Colton Hall. There were in all forty-eight delegates, including seven Hispano-Californians, of whom General M. G. Vallejo was undoubtedly the most distinguished.

This convention consisted of a body of men perhaps younger than any other that met for a similar purpose, their ages ranging from twenty-five to fifty-three years, with an average of thirty-six. Dr. Robert Semple was elected president and J. Ross Browne was selected reporter. Browne's volume of *Debates* is the chief single source of information on the proceedings.

The delegates did their work well. When the moment arrived for the signing of the completed document, flags of the different head-quarters at Monterey and on all the ships in the harbor were unfurled, and the firing of the national salute of *thirty-one* guns proceeded at the *Presidio*—the thirty-first gun symbolizing the creation of the thirty-first state—California. Three lusty cheers were then given for the New State. The delegates repaired to General Riley's house, where Captain John A. Sutter expressed appreciation and gratitude for the aid and cooperation received, and Riley made simple but eloquent reply as he planned to step loyally aside in favor of California's new régime.

The convention ordered that 8,000 copies in English and 2,000 copies in Spanish of the constitution be printed and circulated; also, that copies be transmitted to Governor Riley and President Zachary Taylor.

The actual signing of the constitution in the upper room of Colton Hall, Monterey, was a dramatic, historic event. As the booming of the Presidio cannon resounded through the hall, the flags of the different headquarters and on board the shipping in port were unfurled. The description, as narrated in the *Alta California*, continues;

> As the firing of the national salute of *thirty-one* guns proceeded at the fort, and the signing of the constitution went on at the hall, the captain of an English bark then in port paid a most beautiful and befitting compliment to the occasion and the country, by hoisting at his main the American flag above those of every other nation, making, at the moment that the thirty-first gun was fired, a line of colors from the main truck to

the vessel's deck. And when, at last, that thirty-first gun came—the FIRST GUN FOR CALIFORNIA!—three as hearty and as patriotic cheers as ever broke from human lips were given by the Convention for the New State.

FIRST STATE ELECTION

Exactly one month after the day the first California Constitutional Convention had completed its labors, and under highly dramatic conditions had signed the constitution, the first California state election was held. It was Tuesday, November 13, 1849—and a dismal day it was, because the heavy rains brought swollen streams and muddy roads in every direction.

The election was held as planned, in good American fashion. Special interest was taken by the native Californians, who experienced a thrill as they cast their first free ballot. Despite the forbidding weather there was a total vote on the adoption of the constitution of 12,872, with a majority for adoption of fifteen to one. In Los Angeles the vote stood 315 to 17; in San Francisco, 2051 to 5.

Peter H. Burnett was elected governor by 6,783 votes, almost three times the number received by his nearest competitor. John McDougal was chosen lieutenant-governor; George W. Wright and Edward Gilbert were elected representatives to Congress.

The first legislature of the incipient state, comprising thirty-six members in its two chambers, met in San José Saturday, December 15, 1849. Five days later the two houses assembled for the purpose of electing two United States senators. John C. Frémont was elected on the first ballot, and William M. Gwin on the second.

Under date of March 12, 1850, the four men elected to Congress (Wright, Gilbert, Frémont, Gwin) issued a long Memorial addressed "To the Honorable the Senate and House of Representatives of the United States of America assembled," requesting "in the name of the people of California, the admission of the State of California into the American Union." Referring to the election of the preceding November, this Memorandum states as follows:

> The winter rains commenced several days before the 13th of November, and on that day one of the worst storms ever experienced raged throughout the whole country. The consequence was, notwithstanding the personal exertions of the friends of the different candidates for popular favor, that only about 15,000 votes were polled. . . . It is believed that there never was an election attended with less excitement. The sentiment in favor of the Constitution was nearly unanimous, and was entirely the result of the unbiased and deliberate opinions of those who were most interested in it.

No attempt was made to mislead or control public opinion in relation to the Constitution. No candidate sought success by either an ardent advocacy of its merits, or a broad denunciation of any of its provisions. . . . The truth is, that no political result in the history of any nation is more surely the honest expression of a public opinion founded in reason than the ratification afforded by the People of California to their Constitution.

Thus was the machinery of the thirty-first state put in motion. But since California was not formally admitted into the Union until September 9, 1850, the query arises, was it really a state when Governor Burnett was inaugurated and the legislature proceeded to make laws in San José? Waiving technicalities, we may declare, yes—to all practical intents and purposes, viewed from a local standpoint, California was a state in December, 1849, almost nine months before that memorable Admission Day. Its government was established in an orderly manner under our first constitution. All objections based on legalistic grounds yielded to the "obvious necessities of the case." Important fundamental legislation was enacted: the law-making body remained vigorously at work till final adjournment, April 22, 1850, still almost six months before knowledge of California's admission reached San Francisco. The patriotic activities of the interim were subsequently honored and validated by a grateful people.

STATE CAPITAL

The location for the capital of California was a subject of controversy long before admission into the Union in 1850. The rivalry between Monterey and Los Angeles had much to do with brief civil war between north and south, in 1836-37. But Mariano Chico, probably most hated of all Mexican governors of California, arbitrary and despotic, did not last long as governor. Juan B. Alvarado won official recognition, and Monterey remained the capital of the province—not without interruption—to the end of the Mexican régime.

It seemed quite logical that Monterey should be selected as the place for the constitutional convention of 1849. But when the delegates were completing their task, the question of permanent location of the capital for the new state evoked considerable interest.

Various proposals had been made in the convention, among places mentioned being San José, San Luis Obispo, and Benicia, one delegate even suggesting "some point east of the Sierra Nevada range of mountains, in the Great Basin, as near the central point defined in the Constitution as possible" (this was before the eastern boundary had been fixed). After considering numerous motions and amendments, San José was selected by a vote of 23 to 14. In his final remarks Delegate Joseph Aram said:

> I feel perfectly confident that San José will eventually be the capital; and I am willing to let the matter rest with the people, for I believe they will be nearly unanimous in favor of that point.

Here is the text of the report of the Committee on Miscellaneous Provisions, presented to the Convention on the 26th day of September, 1849:

> The first session of the Legislature shall be held in the Pueblo de San José, which place shall be hte permanent seat of government, until removed by law; *provided, however*, that two-thirds of all the members elected to each house of the Legislature shall concur in the passage of such a law.

The actual government of the new state was inaugurated on the 20th of December, 1849; but it was found that there was only one building in San José large enough to accommodate the legislature, and that was a half-finished hotel. By an arrangement hastily arrived at, this building, thereafter known as the first State House, became the property of the town. But while the crude building was being metamorphosed into a Capitol, the first Senate was obliged to meet at a private residence during almost half of the session. And besides, the winter of 1849-50 was unusually wet, with a total rainfall exceeding thirty-six inches. Naturally there were expressions of discontent and not a little grumbling. Nevertheless, much important legislation was enacted and the state government was well established at San José, first capital of the State of California.

Largely through the personal influence and generous spirit of General M. G. Vallejo, the people voted, October 7, 1850, to make the new town of Vallejo the State Capital. But at the appointed time the necessary accommodations were far from ready. The question of a permanent site as capital was debated all over again. When the legislature adjourned it agreed to meet for the next session at Sacramento. But even yet there was no abiding place—the city of Sacramento was flooded; the inconveniences were intolerable. In May, 1853, an act was passed "declaring Benicia the permanent seat of government in accordance with the provisions of the constitution."

However, the end was not yet. Sacramento made another and this time a successful bid for the capital. The town had become a populous incorporated city, one of the most progressive centers in the state, an important headquarters for trade and transportation. Her triumph was celebrated with sincere expressions of rejoicing. The restless capital of

California returned to the place where the seat of government has long since become firmly fixed—in spite of numerous attempts at removal, Sacramento remains today the capital of the "Empire State of the Pacific."

STATE GOVERNOR

The first state governor of California was elected almost ten months before California was admitted to the Union; and he resigned before his state had actually been in the Union four months. The election occurred November 13, 1849, when Peter H. Burnett received more than double the vote cast for his nearest opponent, Winfield S. Sherwood. Burnett, an Independent Democrat, was inaugurated December 20, 1849: he resigned January 8, 1851.

If his term was one of the shortest on record, Peter Burnett himself was one of the most colorful characters in California's long list of governors. He was something more than a typical pioneer. A native of Nashville, Tennessee, he had demonstrated his individuality at the age of nineteen by adding another 't' to his birthname (Burnet), believing that "the name would be more complete and emphatic when spelled Burnett." From his grandfather, Thomas Hardeman, he learned three maxims: "1) Pay your honest debts. 2) Never disgrace the family. 3) Help the honest and industrious kin."

The Burnet family, with its five sons and three daughters, experienced a very rigorous life, first in Tennessee, then in Missouri. In his fascinating book, *Recollections*—which fortunately he left for posterity—he refers to experiences in Howard County, Missouri, giving this picture of Home:

> We spent the first winter in a large camp with a dirt floor, boarded up on the sides with clapboards, and covered with the same, leaving a hole in the center of the roof for the escape of the smoke. All the family lived together in the same room, the whites on one side and the blacks on the other.

During the winter of 1842-43 a Congressional report on far-away Oregon fell into Burnett's hands. He learned that a new bill proposed to donate 640 acres of land to each immigrant, and sixty additional acres for each child. This meant that with his wife and their six children they would be entitled to 1600 acres! After years of hard living, burdened with heavy debts he was unable to pay, it is little wonder he determined to undertake the trek to Oregon. Then he set to work to organize a wagon party and was successful beyond anything he had any right to expect.

The trip to Oregon at that very early date, with its "ten thousand little vexations" that could not be foreseen, makes an intensely interesting story. Burnett kept "a concise diary of the trip as far as Walla Walla." As captain much of the way, he had to shoulder heavy responsibilities, finally resigning when serious trouble arose regarding the large herd of cattle. It was a large train of sixty wagons. A single glimpse of the morning starting hour is afforded in a word picture by Jesse Applegarth:

> It is on the stroke of seven; the rush to and fro, the cracking of whips, the loud command to oxen, and what seemed to be the inextricable confusion of the last ten minutes has ceased. Fortunately every one has been found and every teamster is at his post. The clear notes of a trumpet sound in the front; the pilot and his guards mount their horses. The leading divisions of the wagons move out of the encampment, and take up the line of march; the rest fall into their places with the precision of clock work . . . as the caravan draws its lazy length towards the distant El Dorado.

Peter Burnett quickly rose to a place of leadership among the early pioneers in Oregon. He was farmer, lawyer, legislator, and judge all combined. But with the first reports of gold excitement in California in 1848, his restless nature was again stirred to its depths—his urge to go was irresistible! "I saw my opportunity," he recorded, "and at once consulted with my wife. . . . She consented, and I came to California, and succeeded beyond my expectations."

No wagon had up to that time passed from Oregon into California. To Burnett goes the credit of organizing a wagon party and conducting it into the land of El Dorado, in the autumn of 1848—in this again is a thrilling story of pioneer days in California history!

Of such stuff was the man made who, after a residence of scarcely a single year, was made chief executive of the Minerva State not yet in the American Union. Peter H. Burnett was truly a man of action. How fitting that such a pioneer—the very embodiment of energy wisely directed, robust and dynamic, versatile to a degree—should be first to head the Empire State of the Pacific!

STATE LEGISLATURE

Pursuant to the first state election, held November 13, 1849, California's first state legislature met in San José, first state capital, on Thursday, December 20, 1849, when the state government was actually established by the inauguration of Peter H. Burnett as first governor. General Bennet Riley, as *de facto* military governor, bowed himself gracefully out of the picture, stating in his patriotic Proclamation:

> The principal object of all his wishes is now accomplished—the people have a government of their own choice, and one which, under the favor of divine Providence, will secure their own prosperity and happiness, and the permanent welfare of the new State.

The tasks that confronted the first legislature were of great significance to the new commonwealth. The fact that California had not yet been admitted into the Union of states brought a sense of added responsibility and of great delicacy to the members of the Senate and the Assembly. The actual event, however, indicates how well the legislature performed its function. In the opinion of the historian Theodore Hittell, "The legislation of the first session was not only the most important, but it was among the most judicious of all that has been done in the state." Referring to the sobriquet that came to be applied, "The legislature of a thousand drinks," Hittell states: "Whatever truth there may have been in the designation, it is certain that no legislature has ever sat in the state that did more work, more important work, or better work."

There was the necessity of drafting a complete code of laws for the new state, with their myriad of details. An entire series of acts had reference to the organization of counties and to county officers.

A very serious duty involved the choice of the system of law which should serve as the basis of the state's jurisprudence—which was better suited to promote the welfare of the people, the common law or the civil law? There was naturally much discussion, particularly among the lawyer members. It was not until April 12, 1850, that the much-amended report on the subject was finally passed and, the following day, approved by the governor.

Among the numerous statutes passed, some had a bearing upon business, some on social relations, some dealing with the legal interest rates, some with marital relations, especially those concerning property rights. The whole subject of taxation and a revenue system had to be dealt with. Still another series of laws dealt with the incorporation of cities and towns. One of the most important of all the legislature's functions was the election of two United States Senators. The selection of William M. Gwin and John C. Frémont is elsewhere reported.

During the eventful days of 1849 and 1850 the State of California was still in the making. The work was of far more than local significance. The contribution of the first legislature was generous and vital. Its acts were duly ratified after formal admission as the Thirty-first State.

UNITED STATES SENATORS

California's first United States Senators were John Charles Frémont and William McKendree Gwin. The history of the state could not be written without referring at some length to these two eminent leaders. Indeed their lives were so intimately intertwined with its history that any account of their activities and careers must necessarily embrace no inconsiderable part of the early history of the Golden State.

Captain Frémont, as is well known, was in reality the central figure of the American conquest of California. His relationship and his influence date from the time of his first western expedition, 1843-44. His activities have occasioned more controversy than those of any other Californian. By some writers he has been called famous; by others, infamous: he has been given the title "Pathfinder"; but some pronounce him tactless and unoriginal: he was court-martialed and found guilty of insubordination; later he won the Republican nomination for the United States presidency.

One of the most important acts of the first state legislature, meeting at San José in December, 1849, was the election of two United States Senators. Frémont was chosen for the short term. Accordingly he took up his residence in Washington, to labor with his associates from California, Edward Gilbert and George W. Wright, California's first members in the House of Representatives, for the admission of the new state into the Union.

William Gwin, a native of Tennessee, was a '49er who came to California not for the purpose of digging gold but expressly to enter the political arena. Even before coming he had set his sails for a seat in the Senate of the United States. He won the reputation of being the most able politician among all the forty-eight delegates of the constitutional convention at Monterey.

The desire of his heart was actually attained when, along with Frémont, he was elected to the national Senate. His was the full term. he has been described as a man of striking personality, "fully six feet two inches in stature, erect and stately, of herculean figure, perfect in its proportions, and with a carriage and bearing commensurate."

There can be no question that both Gwin and Frémont, along with Representatives Gilbert and Wright, exercised a strong influence toward the admission of California—finally consummated on the 9th day of September, 1850.

The actual political careers of the two Senators in Washington, and later, although of national interest, cannot be discussed here. Of Frémont it may be said, he was better fitted to the useful work of the topographical engineer than to that of either the general or the Senator. Gwin could never quite free himself from the taint of Broderick's damaging charge that he was "a wicked pro-slavery aristocrat." The end of neither life can be called a very happy one. Yet, despite all their weaknesses and shortcomings, both are remembered as among the most prominent leaders at a time of great local excitement and of national peril—their lives were memorable, their contributions unique.

STATE SUPREME COURT

Sections 1 and 2 of Article VI of California's first state constitution provide for a Supreme Court consisting of a Chief Justice and two Associate Justices. Section 3 reads as follows:

> The Justices of the Supreme Court shall be elected at the general election, by the qualified electors of the State, and shall hold their offices for the term of six years from the first day of January next after their election; provided that the Legislature shall, at its first meeting, elect a Chief Justice and two Associate Justices of the Supreme Court, by joint vote of both houses, and so classify them that one shall go out of office every two years. After the first election the senior Justice in commission shall be the Chief Justice.

In accordance with the above C. S. Hastings was duly elected Chief Justice December 20, 1849; Nathaniel Bennett and Henry A. Lyon were elected Associate Justices. Bennett was chosen for the six-year term (though he served but two years), Lyons for the four-year term, and Hastings for the two-year term.

Chief Justice Hastings was a native of Jefferson County, New York, born November 22, 1814. He studied law in Indiana and was admitted to the bar in 1836. He came to California in 1849, where he almost immediately rose to eminence. He was described as a "man of large stature, capable of great physical endurance, shrewd, energetic, alert in mind and body, simple in his tastes and habits, peculiarly adapted to the border, and was not to be found wanting in the ebb and flow of frontier life." He died February 18, 1893. He is gratefully remembered as founder of the Hastings College of Law.

Nathaniel Bennett was regarded as one of the ablest jurists and orators of California. He was born in Clinton, Oneida County, New York, June 27, 1818. Arriving at San Francisco the last day of June, 1849, he quickly became engaged in mining operations on the Tuolumne River. After three successful months he settled in San Francisco. Two leading addresses in his long career attest his unusual eloquence—his oration at the celebration of California's admission into the Union, delivered October 29, 1850, and that at the celebration of the completion of the Central Pacific Railroad, in May, 1869. He died in San Francisco, April 20, 1886.

The third member of the Supreme Court was Henry A. Lyons, who was elected by a bare majority. He it was who administered the oath of office to Governor John McDougal, following the resignation of Governor Peter Burnett, in 1851. Lyons resigned as Associate Justice on the last day of March, 1852.

In 1862 the number of justices on the Supreme Court was increased to five, and the term was extended to ten years. The new constitution of 1879 provided for a tribunal of seven justices, and the term of office was extended to twelve years. Sessions of the Court are held in Sacramento (the capital), San Francisco, and Los Angeles.

It is interesting to note that during the early years court transcriptions were written "in a fair and legible hand," and that the "penmanship approached the point of fine art." Later a change was made to the typewriter and linotype. Needless to say, the volume of work of the Supreme Court of California has increased almost infinitely; but its enviable record had its beginnings with the first formal session, in March, 1850, some five months before California's admission into the Union as the Minerva State. The only member of the Court to be elevated to the United States Supreme Court was Justice Stephen J. Field, who served from 1857 to 1863, resigning his state position when President Lincoln called him to the highest court in the Republic.

ORIGINAL COUNTIES

Previous to the acquisition of California by the United States it had no political organizations that might properly be called counties. Under the Spanish and Mexican régimes there were two grand prefectures; there was the prefect of the south residing at *Pueblo de Los Angeles,* and the prefect of the north, at Monterey. Later two additional prefectures were established (headquarters at Santa Barbara and San José): it is recorded that in 1829 *ayuntamientos* (councils) were held at all four centers. Beginning in 1831 there were five districts—San Diego,

Los Angeles, Santa Barbara, Monterey, and San Francisco. The settled portion of the territory constituted a comparatively narrow strip along the coast and near-by valleys—eastern and northern areas might almost be called *terra incognita.*

One of the first important duties of the first American legislature, acting under the newly adopted state constitution of 1849, was to divide the state into well-defined counties. Details were referred to a special senate committee headed by General M. G. Vallejo. The report of this committee was presented January 4, 1850. The original report recommended the boundaries of eighteen counties, as follows: San Diego, Los Angeles, Santa Barbara, San Luis Obispo, Monterey, San Francisco, San Jose, Mount Diablo, Sonoma, Benicia, Sacramento, Sutter, Butte, Frémont, San Joaquin, Oro, and Mariposa.

The first report brought much discussion and underwent numerous changes especially pertaining to the northern part of the state. Several name changes were proposed: Tuolumne for Oro, Solano for Benicia, Yolo for Frémont, Shasta for Reading, Contra Costa for Mount Diablo. Additional counties were also recommended: Coloma, Yuba, Colusi, Trinity, Marin, Mendocino.

Finally, on the 18th of February, 1850, the act creating the original counties and defining their boundaries, the fifteenth enactment of California's first legislature, was signed by Governor Peter H. Burnett. The twenty-seven counties thus created were: San Diego, Los Angeles, Santa Barbara, San Luis Obispo, Monterey, Branciforte, San Francisco, Santa Clara, Contra Costa, Marin, Sonoma, Solano, Yola, Napa, Mendocino, Sacramento, El Dorado, Sutter, Yuba, Butte, Colusi (later Colusa), Shasta, Trinity, Calaveras, San Joaquin, Tuolumne, and Mariposa. While the boundaries of some of the counties were rather indefinite, they represented the best that could then be done. By amendatory bills the name Branciforte was changed to Santa Cruz, and Yola to Yolo.

With two exceptions the county names were derived from the Spanish or Indian languages. The exceptions were Sutter (after John A. Sutter) and Butte, a French word meaning an isolated elevation—an upstanding feature of that area. General Vallejo, with whom John Bidwell was closely associated, is chiefly to be thanked for the euphonious Spanish and Indian names, such as Santa Cruz (Holy Cross), Contra Costa (Opposite Coast), Monterey (Royal Forest or Mountain), Mariposa (Butterfly), Sonoma (Valley of the Moon), Shasta (Indian Tribe), Mendocino (honoring Mendoza).

Other new counties were created by re-defining boundaries—Nevada, Placer, Trinity and Klamath being added in 1851. From time to time still others came into being by legislative enactment. Finally came the reclamation of Imperial Valley and the advent of Imperial County, by act of August 15, 1907. And so the original twenty-seven counties of California had been made into more than double that number, or fifty-eight in all, as they stand today.

CELEBRATION OF CALIFORNIA'S ADMISSION

News of California's admission into the Union reached San Francisco on the morning of October 18, 1850. Proudly the good ship *Oregon* steamed in through the Golden Gate, banners flying, official bearer of the best of good tidings to all the people, from Washington, the national Capital. On the ninth of September the California Bill had been approved by President Millard Fillmore.

Regular business in the bustling city of San Francisco stopped instantly. With exultant feelings everybody made haste to Portsmouth Square, there to give expression to pure joy—"*California is admitted!*" The *Alta California* reported:

> We have never seen so general and joyous excitement, nor anything comparable with it, . . . At once the American flag went up from every possible place in the city. . . . Unusual joy seems to prevail among all classes.

But that was not enough. The spontaneous enthusiasm and excitement stirred by the arrival of the *Oregon* must be followed by a formal celebration. This was set for the 29th of October, 1850, seven weeks after the actual Admission Day—but what did that matter! Never had there been such a celebration in San Francisco.

There was a great procession, in which marched men from the various nations then represented in San Francisco. The orator of the day was Honorable Nathaniel Bennett. In his eloquent address, after referring to the long delays and trying days before California's admission, he used this beautiful rhetorical expression:

> It was at such a time that the tidings of the event which we celebrate reached us, and the rebound of our feelings today is in proportion to the depth of our depression. If, when the tempest has gathered over the troubled waters, and the angry billows, lashed into fury, rave around the devoted bark, the winds are suddenly lulled, the waves hushed, and the warm sunshine again sleeps on the bosom of the tranquil sea, the thrill of delight which the hardy mariner feels is enhanced by the imminent danger from which he has just escaped.

Such was the first formal celebration of the admission of California. For more than a century each recurring Ninth of September has been celebrated as Admission Day: it has become a widely recognized holiday in the state, appropriately and devotedly commemorated by the California Pioneers, Native Sons of the Golden West, Native Daughters of the Golden West, and other patriotic citizens.

At the seventh anniversary (September 9, 1857), in addition to the great procession the Zetus Club sang the glories of the Golden State and the honored pioneers, to the air of "The Red, White and Blue." Here is a single stanza:

California, thou gem of the ocean!
The land of red gold and gay flowers;
The heroes now meet in communion
To brighten with joy the swift hours.
Thy banners in beauty are streaming,
Their stars the brave freeman's heart cheers,
Whilst Liberty's soft light is beaming
On the great band of bold Pioneers.

One other anniversary may be mentioned—the twenty-first, in 1871. Judge E. W. McKinstry was orator of the day. After describing the early society of gold rush days, he referred to California's admission in these words:

Then to the blue sky went the delighted and triumphant acclaim of this many-sided people; while thousands of grateful hearts were bowed in pious thankfulness that at last California was recognized as an equal and integral part of our glorious country. . . . We felt that we were no longer united to the great republic only by commercial relations, or even by a common love of freedom, common memories, and a common history; but that we were indissolubly connected with it by a political as well as personal tie.

California seems to have been a child of destiny. Her development since the first Admission Day, in 1850, has been one of the wonders of modern history. Again and again has she matched the classic symbolism of the brave men of '49—the Minerva State, sprung full-grown, in complete armor, from the brain of Jupiter! Her true function has been well expressed in the immortal words of Plato, in whose fine phrase the state is "Nature's gift to man to enable him to perfect himself in the good life."

INCORPORATED CITY

Sacramento, capital of the state for almost a full century, claims to be California's first incorporated city.

The name "Sacramento" (Holy Sacrament) was first given to the Feather River by Gabriel Moraga as early as 1808; but it was not long until it was applied to the lower Sacramento also (*Rio del Sacramento*). In 1841 the name was definitely established. Captain Sutter said he gave the name "Feather River" (*Rio de las Plumas*) to the Sacramento tributary because the Indians of that region used so many feathers for decorations and blankets.

Sutter's Fort (New Helvetia), founded in 1839, must not be thought of as identical with Sacramento. It was not until the autumn of 1848 that John A. Sutter, Jr., and Sam Brannan laid out the new town at the embarcadero, naming it after the river. The street plan was a very simple one—thirty-one numbered north-and-south streets, beginning at the river-front; and twenty-six east-and-west streets named for the letters of the alphabet, beginning at the north boundary.

With the early tide of immigrants induced by the gold excitement, the town grew at a very rapid rate—tents and canvas houses appeared overnight. In July of 1848, the war with Mexico having ended, there arose a movement for reorganizing the town government and placing it on an American basis. Up to this time whatever law and government existed is now seen to have been more nominal than realistic in character. Town councilmen were elected; J. A. Thomas and J. C. Zabriskie were chosen first and second magistrates.

After weeks of study and deliberation the Council submitted the draft of a City Charter; but because of the general apathy regarding public affairs among the better citizens and the active opposition of the gambling fraternity this charter was defeated in September.

The mortifying defeat stirred the Council, headed by A. M. Winn, to action. In early October there was another election, sponsored by the "Law and Order Party," which resulted in sustaining the charter by a decisive majority. After the adoption of certain amendments, Zabriskie and Benjamin Nickerson were appointed to present the document to the State legislature, at San José, urging its approval.

The bill for incorporation was introduced December 24, 1849. There was further controversy; Governor Peter Burnett exercised his right of veto. However, the legislature proceeded to override the veto, the amended bill to incorporate was passed March 13, 1850; and thus Sacramento became California's first incorporated city. It may be added that a new charter for Sacramento City was passed by the second legislature; this became law on the 26th of March, 1851, but without the support of Governor John McDougal.

In the meantime the city continued to increase rapidly in population; wooden buildings began to supersede the canvas structures, and brick also gradually came into use. Within a few years Sacramento won the spirited fight to become the capital city of the state, which distinction it still holds.

SQUATTERISM

Long before the admission of California, even before the time of the American conquest, there was more than a little of real "squatting" on land—indeed, the practice may justly be regarded as a common feature of the westward movement. Many an early pioneer in Missouri or in Arkansas was in reality a mere "squatter." He did not buy the land, but he found "a temporary shelter in a location where wood, water, and pasturage were abundant and where the hunting was still good." The squatter had little patience with governmental restrictions; as Frederick Jackson Turner said, "He rebelled against the conventional."

So it happens that numbers of the early American settlers in California were true squatters. They made homes sometimes within the poorly-defined boundaries of land-grants, sometimes in unclaimed localities. Near the end of the Mexican régime, and in anticipation of American rule, some were told that by a little judicious waiting the necessity for an official grant would be unnecessary. It was estimated by Lansford Hastings that in 1845 two hundred American farmers had settled north of San Francisco Bay, many of them in Napa Valley. It cannot be said that there was any specific event of historic significance to mark the beginning of squatterism in California.

A by-product of the gold rush of 1849 was the appearance of squatters a-plenty. Conditions were particularly favorable to squatterism. The spreading possessions of Captain John A. Sutter, for example, with his cattle and growing crops, proved too great a temptation to many an unlucky miner. American immigrants saw vast stretches of land unoccupied; and assuming it to be government property, it seemed quite natural to claim some of it as their own by the mere act of appropriation. Having hastily erected a make-shift shanty, it was an easy step to assert the claim of possession as nine points *plus*, in the law.

Legal technicalities and alleged titles were flouted, often with impunity. Who had a better right to the land, they protested, than "the hardy men who had faced the dangers of deserts and sierra?" Even Senator

Thomas H. Benton had defended trespassing by the pioneer, while at the same time denouncing the paternal government that was harassing to the squatter.

In and around the stirring city of Sacramento there were, very naturally, many squatters, and serious clashes arose between them and the legally constituted authorities. Conditions arose that rendered squatter riots inevitable. When two score of armed squatters made an attempt to regain possession of a certain lot, the mayor and his posse proved unable to suppress the riot — the mayor himself was dangerously wounded. Martial law was declared; troops were ordered up from Benicia, and 500 men were summonded for duty as an extraordinary police force. Peace and order were restored after a few hectic days. And all this occurred in August, 1850, before the admission of California into the Union.

Squatting about San Francisco also was much in evidence: it did not wholly cease until many land titles were settled in the courts of justice, often after long and vexatious litigation.

In the mining regions, as might have been expected, squatterism was widely practiced. When the restless prospector left his claim, eager for a "big strike" elsewhere, there was always a likelihood that before his return, several months later, his claim would be "jumped" by another, a prospect that was greatly increased if written notice of ownership or boundary stakes had been molested or removed.

Squatterism became a significant factor in local and state politics— it was by no means a one-sided issue. Not all squatters were either rascals or scoundrels. But the "professional squatter," who hired himself out for "the sole purpose of gaining possession of coveted land," was a real threat to law and order. The entire problem, of which the beginnings are here traced, must be studied in relation to the still larger question of land grants and land titles in early California, with due consideration of the traits of the pioneer settlers in their new surroundings.

STATE REPUBLICAN CONVENTION

On the national scene the first presidential nomination of the newly-formed Republican Party went to John C. Frémont, central figure in the American conquest of California. He received a large vote but was defeated by James Buchanan.

Earlier that same year (1856) the first California Republican State Convention was held in Sacramento, where on the 30th of April the temporary chariman, E. B. Crocker, called the delegates to order in the

Congregational Church. This in turn had been preceded by the first mass meeting of Republicans, held April 19—a meeting that had been broken up by the rowdyism and misconduct charged to partisan Americans and Democrats present.

At the state convention Nathaniel Bennett, eminent orator and prominent citizen of San Francisco, was made permanent chairman, and a half-dozen vice-presidents were elected. There was a total of 125 delegates, slightly more than half of them from San Francisco and Sacramento—only thirteen counties in all were represented.

Ten resolutions were adopted. Several of these had to do with phases of the slavery question. One favored "the prohibition of slavery in all the national territories"; another favored "preventing the increase of the political power of slavery" in the federal government; still another declared slavery to be "a sectional institution in which only 350,000 slave holders are directly interested, while *freedom* is a national principle, by which 26,000,000 of American freemen are secured in their rights." Thus the first California Republicans put themselves squarely on record as "opposed to the extension of slavery, and in favor of free institutions for our territories."

Another resolution favored "the speedy construction of a national railroad, by the most central and eligible route, from the Missouri River to the bay of San Francisco." The final resolution declared it to be "the duty of the people to select as candidates for office . . . only such men as are permanently located here," and whose moral character and business habits give assurance of sound economy and energetic law enforcement.

Twelve delegates were elected to attend the National Republican Convention, and a state committee was selected, including the following well-known leaders: E. B. Crocker, George Rowland, Cornelius Cole, Annis Merrill, and Charles Watrous. Opposition was offered to a resolution instructing the California delegation to vote for Frémont for president on the first ballot; the substitute finally adopted left "this matter entirely to the good sense and discretion of our delegates."

The year of the first State Republican Convention was characterized by one of the most intense struggles for social order ever witnessed in the United States. It was the year of the ever memorable San Francisco Vigilance Committee of 1856, a severe testing time for the entire commonwealth. Questions of slavery extension, of immigration, and better transportation were agitating the public. The new state was experiencing the growing pains of greatness. But California emerged from it all stronger than ever, following what proved to be a great moral renovation. It was a memorable year in Western history.

EARLY SENTIMENT FOR STATE DIVISION

A spirit of rivalry between north and south in California—amounting at times to open antagonism—has manifested itself from time to time in history, even ante-dating by many years the beginnings of American statehood. Still further back, the separation of Alta California and Baja California, as recommended by Governor Diego de Borica (1794-1800), may be mentioned, though having little bearing on the later controversy.

When one of the early Mexican governors, José María Echeandía, established the seat of government at San Diego, a spirit of rebellion was aroused on the part of the *arribanos* (uppers), and Agustin V. Zamarano led a revolt to make Monterey the capital. The result was a temporary division of California into two territories. Under Governor José Figueroa's administration (1833-35) the divided territory was reunited.

But the wound was far from healed. In 1835, José Antonio Carrillo, sometimes referred to as the "Machiavelli of California History," secured the passage of a decree by the Mexican Congress raising *Pueblo de Los Angeles* to the dignity of a city, declaring it to be the capital of the two Californias. More confusion followed—confusion confounded by the Alvarado Revolution of 1836.

San Diego joined forces with Los Angeles: the *arribanos* and the *abajenos* (uppers and lowers) were again arrayed against each other. Reviewing this mixed situation, J. M. Guinn wrote:

> For twenty years the internecine strife between the North and the South had existed. Three times had the territory been rent asunder by the warring factions. For ten years Los Angeles had struggled to become the capital. It had won, but the victory was dearly bought, and it was but half a victory at best. The archives remained at Monterey. The standing army of the territory, if it could be called an army, was stationed there, and there Castro, the military *comandante*, resided.

Coming now to the American period, the state division controversy has been from the beginning a matter of significance in the main current of California history. During the first decade of statehood the question of division in some form was brought up in nearly every session of the legislature. Among various proposals a bill was presented "to create three states out of the territory of California."

Governor John G. Downey (1860-62) in the year 1880 stated:

> From the morning of our existence as a commonwealth the southern

counties of this state have been uneasy and restless under the lash of unequal taxation and the unequal distribution of the benefits derivable therefrom.

Reasons for the early division may be summarized under five heads: 1) geographical extent, with dissimilar resources; 2) the early residents in the south knew little of American institutions; 3) landholders bore most of the expenses of government, without receiving proportionate compensation; 4) the more transient population of the north dominated the more static residents of the south; 5) people of the south were greatly discommoded because of the distance to the northern capital.

In the matter of state division 1859 was a memorable year. So near did Senator Andres Pico's resolution come to bringing actual division that, after adoption by both houses of the legislature, it remained only for Congress to ratify the state's action! Then came the national crisis and the Civil War—California had narrowly escaped division!

Since then the question has come up again and again. But the prevailing sentiment was for unity. With the astounding progress in transportation and communication, the industrialization of the state, and the redistribution of population, the old arguments for state division have at length lost their force—the long controversy between north and south has become a matter of history. California now considers herself one and indivisible.

NATIVE CALIFORNIAN GOVERNOR

California has had only one governor of Spanish blood since the American conquest in 1846. This was Romualdo Pacheco, a native of Santa Barbara, both of whose parents were of Spanish descent.

His father, bearing the same name, was a prominent figure in the Mexican period. He was an active officer in the Victoria party at the time of the insurrection that forced Governor Manuel Victoria out of the country. It was when José María Abila, with deadly lance at rest, charged on Victoria that Captain Pacheco dashed in between them to save his chief that he himself met death, in December, 1831. In the mêlée Abila himself was also slain.

The younger Pacheco was a babe less than two months old at the time of his father's tragic death. His early education was entrusted, in part, to private tutors, and was then continued at a school in Honolulu. His first pursuits were chiefly connected with the business of stock-raising, in which he became an expert. He excelled particularly in horsemanship, and in the use of the *reata* he had few superiors. We are informed that he "acquired a frame of great strength and agility."

More than once he assisted in capturing the powerful grizzy bear by means of his trusty mount and the skillful use of the lasso. He shunned intemperance and the vices common at that time, thus becoming "a fine specimen of physical vigor and one of the most promising of the native Californians of Spanish blood." For all this he is deserving of much credit.

At quite an early age Pacheco manifested deep interest in practical politics, which continued to attract him throughout most of his life. He was one of the relatively few men of Hispanic-Californian origin who served in a number of public offices, being a member of the state senate three different times and state treasurer for a single four-year term. In 1871 he was elected lieutenant-governor; and it was on the 27th day of February, 1875, that, on the resignation of Governor Newton Booth, a Republican, to become United States Senator, he succeeded to the governorship for the unexpired term, ending December 31 of that year.

As governor, Pacheco had little opportunity to distinguish himself. During most of his brief incumbency the legislature was not in session. There were no special events to bring him into sharp focus. Therefore he contented himself with endeavoring to maintain the affairs of the state in peace and prosperity.

It was while Pacheco was governor that the organization of the Native Sons of the Golden West was effected. In San Francisco there was a great patriotic parade on the Fourth of July: a week later the order of Native Sons became a reality, as recorded on another page.

Pacheco was succeeded as governor by William Irwin, a Democrat. But he did not relinquish his interest in politics. In 1877 he was elected to Congress over P. D. Wigginton by a single vote, taking his seat in December; but his opponent instituted a contest, as a result of which Wigginton won out and was given the seat in February. Again, in 1879, Pacheco was elected to Congress as a Republican, and was re-elected in 1880. As a legislator he had an honorable career, though it cannot be said that he won any great distinction in public life. He died in Oakland January 23, 1899. He may be regarded as a fitting symbol of the best California citizenship coming from the Spanish blood of the pre-American period.

NATIVE CALIFORNIAN U.S. SENATOR

To many of the older residents of Southern California the name Stephen Mallory White is almost a household word. It is not so well-known, however, that White was the first native Californian to represent California in the United States Senate. Having already attained national stature in the councils of the Democratic party, he was elected by the State Legislature to a seat in the upper house of Congress for the term March 4, 1893, to March 3, 1899. The election of Grover Cleveland to the presidency had brought him the coveted opportunity.

It is interesting to know that Stephen's father, William F. White (a native of Ireland), was a '49er, having arrived at San Francisco in January of that year. It was there that, four years later, the future senator was born, the actual birthplace being a humble cottage on Taylor Street. The family removed to Pajaro Valley and the young boy attended school in the town of Watsonville.

After his residence in Southern California, it is easy to be seen, he could present a valid claim as representative of the entire state—born in the northern metropolis, raised in the country-side, long a resident of Los Angeles, honored member of Ramona Parlor 109, Native Sons of the Golden West.

White enjoyed the advantages of a good education, graduating from Santa Clara College at the early age of eighteen; he was admitted to the bar of the State Supreme Court at Sacramento in 1874.

When he located in Los Angeles for the practice of law, that place was scarcely more than a village, but there were those who believed it had a future both culturally and industrially. It was not long before White had won a leading place among the attorneys of the southland. As a trial lawyer he was adept in strategy, masterful in debate, eloquent and convincing in addressing a jury.

In 1886 he was elected a member of the state senate: while at Sacramento, as president of the senate he served for a time as lieutenant-governor of the state. But even then he seemed destined to a higher political post. It was his distinguished service as United States Senator that gives him unmistakable claim to a worthy place in California's stately Hall of Fame.

Stephen M. White is known as the "Father of Los Angeles Harbor." No sooner had he taken his seat as Senator from California than he undertook the leadership in the memorable fight for a free harbor—a contest that continued for five difficult years. On the 9th day of May, 1896, Senator White spoke at length, leading the final debate that continued through five days. The amendment calling for the appointment of a special board of engineers was adopted, popular opinion had crystallized in favor of the San Pedro location—the battle was won. When "Our Steve," as his intimate friends called him, returned to his home, a special train was sent out to meet him. He came as a conquering hero—which, in actual truth, he was.

In the midst of life, while yet a comparatively young man, Senator White was taken by death, February 21, 1901. On the very day of his death Mayor Meredith P. Snyder of Los Angeles by proclamation made the suggestion of a suitable monument, which suggestion promptly became a reality. The leading paper of the city, while of the opposing political party, paid sincere tribute to California's "most distinguished son, her bravest, most high-souled public servant." Of him it said: "Good citizen, pure patriot, eloquent orator, learned lawyer, able statesman. . . . Not death itself can rob Los Angeles of the glorious record of her noble citizen. . . ."

Such was California's first native born United States Senator.

BEGINNINGS OF DIRECT LEGISLATION

The major instruments in direct legisaltion are the initiative, referendum, and recall. All these are now well established in California.

As early as 1895 Assemblyman Bledsoe introduced a constitutional amendment in the Legislature providing for the initiative and referendum; but it was to be sixteen long years before direct-legislation amendments were finally enacted and made a part of the state constitution, in 1911. This delay is explained by prevalent conditions vividly described by Franklin Hichborn, who, referring to the Southern Pacific Railroad, the liquor traffic, organized gambling, and segregated vice districts, had this to say:

> These various interests, constantly opposed by the reputable but unorganized citizenry of the State, were in politics to head off adverse legislation, and even adverse action in the courts. As time went on, these various interests united for political control. That control was known as "The Southern Pacific Machine." This machine organization dominated not only the state legislature, but the legislative bodies of practically every municipality and county in the State.

In the meantime, the first local initiative proposal in California of which we have record was made in the city of Alameda, in 1895, involving a special tax for a proposed new library. Signatures on the petition were duly obtained, but a mass meeting was necessary to compel the city trustees to carry out the peoples' mandate to place the measure on the official ballot.

During that year interested citizens organized the Direct Legislation League, of state-wide interest. Soon the leadership of this League went to Dr. John R. Haynes, well-known citizen of Los Angeles. His persistent and tireless efforts brought him the title "Father of Direct

Legislation in California." A strenuous campaign in civic education
was launched. Machinery was set up in Los Angeles "whereby on
petition of 15 per cent of the registered voters a city could initiate laws
and make changes in its charter." This amendment, adopted in Los
Angeles in 1902, and ratified by the Legislature in 1903, has been called
the first important victory in California in the fight for direct legislation.
It proved to be an entering wedge for the initiative and referendum
on a state-wide basis.

The cause enlisted the support of such conspicuous leaders as Rudolph
Spreckels, David Starr Jordan, and James D. Phelan. The Direct Legislation League obtained the endorsement of both major party candidates
—a clear indication that the measures had won great popularity.

The climax was reached with the historic political campaign of 1910,
resulting in the election to the governorship of Hiram Johnson, crusad-
ing reform candidate. He enthusiastically endorsed the passage of direct
legislation measures to restore to the people their control of the government. In 1912 by overwhelming vote the people of California ratified the
proposals for the initiative and referendum. The victory was due, in
large measure, to efforts of a small group of influential leaders, headed
by Dr. Haynes, and finally to the aggressive leadership of Governor
Hiram Johnson. Though differing in details in different localities, the
principles of direct legislation, like that of woman suffrage, have come
to be looked upon as matters of course, not only in California but widely
throughout the nation.

FIRST POLICEWOMAN

The police department of any American city had long been regarded as
"a man's world." But at length a Los Angeles woman successfully
stormed the fortress.

In the spring of 1910 a petition was presented to the Police Commission and the City Council requesting the passage of an ordinance
creating a legal position for a "woman police officer, who would be under
civil service with the same standing as her brother officers," an officer,
however, who should not simply duplicate the work of the men but
rather supplement their services, particularly in relation to women and
children.

After three months of vigilance and missionary endeavor, the desired
ordinance was passed on August 12th, and became effective one month
later (September 12, 1910). The first appointee was Alice Stebbins
Wells, who thus became the first regular policewoman not only of
California but also of the United States. It should be stated, however,

that Mrs. Marie Owen, the widow of a patrolman, is reported to have received an appointment to the Detroit Bureau of Police in 1893.

The "first feminine invasion of the police field" brought a flurry in the department and the city of Los Angeles. By some it was received with amusement; to others it brought ridicule; it was capitalized upon by the Pathé Weekly (forerunner of News-reels). But everybody got used to the innovation; and within five years the three matrons of the jail were also made policewomen, the second person to be appointed in Los Angeles being Mrs. Rachel Shatto, in 1912.

The appointment of Policewoman Wells was widely heralded throughout the country and in foreign lands. She was invited to speak before the General Federation of Women's Clubs in 1911, in San Francisco; other speaking engagements followed. Great curiosity was shown everywhere. In New Orleans a man over six feet tall begged her to arrest him—"I want to be arrested by a lady," he declared: but she made it clear that such an act was quite outside her jurisdiction.

So rapidly did the innovation spread that in 1915 Mrs. Wells organized the International Association of Policewomen, of which she served as president for five years. By 1916 policewomen had been appointed in at least twenty American states. In the following year the first class for training policewomen was given in the regular Summer Session of the University of Southern California, at Los Angeles.

Among the policewomen of today, special mention may be made of Mrs. Jack Sumner, of Los Angeles, an expert in judo and in marksmanship, who was recently named Policewoman of the Year for "outstanding service in the rehabilitation of women convicted of law violations."

Thus is illustrated in a special field the sensational advance in the scope of women's work, as a highly important phase of the twentieth century industrial and social revolution.

CALIFORNIA'S FIRST WOMAN JUDGE

In February, 1926, Georgia P. Bullock was elected judge of the Municipal Court of Los Angeles, the first woman judge of the state of California. She had already had judicial experience, as Referee of Women's Cases in the Police Court and Appraiser in the Probate Department Court of Los Angeles. In August, 1931, she was appointed Judge in the Superior Court of Los Angeles County; she has continued on the bench right down to March 1, 1956, the date she set for her retirement, after forty-three years in the legal profession, thirty-two of them on the bench.

Georgia Morgan was a native of Chicago. After attending public and private schools in Illinois, she married William W. Bullock in 1897. At the time of her retirement she had one daughter and five grandchildren. Mr. Bullock had been long deceased. After coming to California she entered the School of Law of the University of Southern California, from which in 1914 she graduated with the degree of LL.B., having already been admitted to the bar, in January, 1913. Flaming red-haired Georgia Bullock was frequently referred to as the "comely judge."

For her sincerity of purpose, her deep human interests, and her exceptional versatility she won for herself an enviable reputation throughout Southern California. Her voice was frequently heard at luncheon clubs on such subjects as juvenile delinquency and family relationships. By no means was her beneficent influence restricted to the court room. Her memberships and affiliations were unusually numerous and of high order. Insight into her character is afforded through her own words:

> The vantage point of the bench has given me the invaluable opportunity to meet my fellow human beings at critical moments in their lives, to dispense justice, tempered with mercy, and to abide by my conscience and my oath of office. . . . I have tried to grasp the spiritual, moral, and legal kernel of each case.

As the first woman to be elected to a superior court in California, Judge Georgia Bullock has rendered an exceptionally high grade of public service and has set an inspiring precedent for all who come after. Her splendid career has been one that may well be emulated by both women and men. Her high thinking is well illustrated by a remark she made in connection with her retirement:

> I want my fellow jurists, lawyers, close friends, and general public to know that I attribute to our Creator, not to myself, such gifts of intellect and temperament as I may have brought to the many-sided and exacting tasks that confront a jurist. I have done my best to have an understanding heart and to use whatever wisdom comes through me from the Creator.

The noteworthy career of Judge Bullock, considered in conjunction with such other careers as that of the first California Policewoman, that of the first Congresswoman, and that of the "Mother of Women's Clubs," adds significantly to the comparatively neglected aspect of the total California story—the public influence of woman in history.

UNITED STATES PRESIDENT

California cannot claim Herbert Hoover as a native son—he first saw the light of day in West Branch, Iowa. But through the period of his youth and early manhood he became so thoroughly Cailfornian that the mere accident of his birth elsewhere is not held against him by native sons. This indoctrination was rapid during his college days at Stanford University, where he graduated in 1895, an orphaned Quaker lad, at the age of twenty-one, having participated actively in student affairs. Thirty-three years later he was elected thirty-first President of the United States. California was signally honored.

One of the most fortunate events of the young engineer's life was his marriage to Lou Henry, also a native of Iowa, less than five years after his graduation. She was the first woman to graduate at Stanford with a major in geology. In addition to being a wonderful helpmeet to her illustrious husband and the noble mother of their two sons, she won distinction in her own right, as attested by the honorary degrees conferred by a number of institutions. The Lou Henry House at Stanford Campus is a fitting memorial to her.

Herbert Hoover's engineering activities (mines, railways, metalurgical works, etc.) took him to many lands, including Mexico, Canada, Australia, South Africa, India, Russia, China, and still others. Most fortunately for posterity he leaves his own extensive *Memoirs*, published by the Macmillan Company—there is no need of detailed recital here. Educational institutions at home and abroad have vied with each other in conferring honorary degrees upon him.

His conspicuous public service may be said to begin with his commission to represent the Panama-Pacific International Exposition (held in San Diego, 1915) during 1913-14. But overshadowing everything that preceded was his brilliant humanitarian service as United States Commissioner for Relief in Belgium during and immediately following the First World War.

Other assignments of great economic and social significance followed in rapid succession. In a letter to President Woodrow Wilson written in 1919 he said: "I feel the paramount issues are now . . . to secure a League of Nations that may be able to further correct the international wrongs . . . and deter the repetition of such wrongs in the future."

In March, 1921, he received the cabinet appointment of Secretary of Commerce at the hand of President Harding, which position he retained under President Coolidge. While his selection as standard bearer of the Republican Party in the presidential campaign of 1927 may appear natural and logical, it was not a result of long experience in partisan politics or political manipulation on his part. Hoover's life has been of a practical, business-like sort, always leavened by an all-pervading spirit of humanitarianism. He has clung tenaciously to his ideals, with the sincere belief in their realizable character.

California had already been represented by men of high renown at Washington in both houses of Congress; already she had contributed Stephen J. Field, appointed by Lincoln in 1863 as Associate Justice in the Supreme Court: later, a native Californian (Richard Nixon) was to become Vice-President; still later, another native (Earl Warren) has been honored by appointment as Chief Justice of the Supreme Court. In all this we have witnessed the rapidly increasing political importance in the nation and the world of California.

Herbert Hoover enjoys the high distinction of being not only first President from California, but the unique experience of having been the only living former president for many years, and living to enjoy the appellation "Our Elder Statesman" as he passed his four score years, beloved by his many friends, respected by the entire American people.

UNITED STATES VICE-PRESIDENT

Supernumerary, useless, a place of political banishment—such was the general characterization of our national vice-presidency down to our own time. Not so today! Instead of a non-entity, an officer with no need of an office, Vice-President Richard Nixon of California proved himself "one of the busiest, most useful, and most influential men in Washington," second most important man in the nation. Gone are the days when the vice-president sat alone and lonely, twirling his thumbs!

Nixon was one of the youngest men (age 39) ever to be elected to this position. By the election of this vigorous young leader another distinguished first was added to the long, impressive list for the Golden State.

Son of Francis Anthony and Hannah Milhous Nixon, Richard was born in Yorba Linda, California, January 9, 1913. While he was yet a young child the family moved to the town of Whittier, the home being located near East Whittier Friends Church, the church attended by the Nixons.

While in high school and Whittier College "Dick" excelled in American history, public speaking, and debate. After receiving his baccalaureate degree, second in his class, he studied law on a scholarship at Duke University, graduating there in 1937.

His law practice at Whittier was cut short by approaching World War II, in which he received a junior grade lieutenant's commission in the United States Navy. During his four-year service he rose to the rank of lieutenant-commander.

At the age of thirty-three Nixon was asked to stand as Republican candidate for Congress. With characteristic vigor he made the fight and won over New Deal Democrat Jerry Voorhis, representative who had been in office ten years. In 1948 he was re-elected: two years later, following his active part in the Alger Hiss case, he won again by a large majority—this time over popular Helen Gahagan Douglas, Hollywood actress and gifted politician, in the contest for a seat in the United States Senate.

Meantime Nixon had married Thelma Patricia Ryan, of his own age, in 1940, and their family circle was rounded out by their daughters Patricia and Julie. Resourceful Mrs. Nixon ("Pat") is indeed a true helpmeet to her energetic husband.

At the national Republican Convention in Chicago in July, 1952, Nixon was the unanimous choice for the vice-presidential nomination at a conference of thirty-five top supporters of General Eisenhower for the presidency. After the General indicated that the Californian was his own choice for running mate, the nomination came without opposition. Nixon was well on his way to what had so long been known rather facetiously as "the stepping-stone to oblivion."

Results of the November election are well known. But Richard Nixon, former U.S. Senator, was not long in proving to the world that a new kind of vice-president had come to Washington. His industriousness had found new avenues for helpful activities: his ready intellect had brought wisdom characteristic of leaders far beyond his years; his loyalty and devotion to American ideals had put confidence in the minds of millions of those who had been doubters. All these qualities admirably fitted the youthful Vice-President to be American ambassador of good will on his quite unprecedented tours of many lands, from the first year of his incumbency.

THE PUBLIC DEFENDER

Among the many things concerning which California ranks first is the office of Public Defender. Under a special enabling act of the State Legislature the county of Los Angeles adopted a new charter in January, 1914. This charter provided for the Office of Public Defender, which was the first such office in the United States: indeed, at the time when the charter was being drafted search was made for a precedent but none was found in any English-speaking jurisdiction, although Spain was found to have had something remotely similar four centuries ago.

The chief function of the office of Public Defender is the defense of persons charged with felony crimes. Any person appearing in the superior court, or at a preliminary hearing in any case triable in the superior, is entitled to the free services of the office if he has neither an attorney nor the means to employ one. This rests on the theory that it is the affirmative duty of the state "to do all that is useful to secure justice to every one," the crux of the situation being equality before the law. Hence the connotation of the term Public Defender is that of a "public official paid at public expense."

The first man to hold the office of Public Defender in California— or anywhere—was Walton J. Wood of Los Angeles, appointed under civil service regulations, who subsequently became a superior court judge, still later a justice of the District Court of Appeals. His deputies were Wallace T. Aggeler and Vermell Rapp.

By 1953 the office, with its forty years of experience, had become one of the largest, if not the largest, of its kind to be found anywhere. Ellery E. Cuff, Public Defender, in addition to his chief deputy, had a corps of fifteen deputies.

The functionary known as the Public Defender has become well established not only in Los Angeles County and California, but, with variation of details, in numerous other areas in the nation. In it we have a special agency charged with the duty of assisting in making actual, in our highly complex modern society, the honored maxim, "equal justice to all." Recent expressions given in a report by a group of San Francisco judges reveal the social value of the institution as they have found it in their respective jurisdictions. Superior Judge Eustace Cullinan, Jr., said: "The Public Defender's office has always given the people in my court and myself the very best of service. . . . I have nothing but praise for Gerald Kenny and his staff for the work they are doing." Superior Judge Twain Michelsen reported: "The functions of the office of Public Defender have always been properly and expertly administered during my incumbency in this court."

From this brief statement it may be seen that California scores another significant first, in the present instance in the realm of the administration of human justice.

CHIEF JUSTICE OF U.S. SUPREME COURT

With sincere pride California has seen one of her native sons elevated to the highest position in the judicial department of the United States government—Chief Justice of the Supreme Court.

In 1928 Herbert Hoover, a loyal Californian, though not a native, as already noted, was elected President; in 1952 Richard Nixon, a native Californian, was elected Vice-President; in 1953 Governor Earl Warren was appointed by President Dwight Eisenhower to the nation's highest judicial post.

Not a few other national leaders have come from California, who have represented every branch of the government—executive, legislative, and judicial. The contributions of the Golden State have indeed been generous and noteworthy.

The career of Earl Warren in his uninterrupted progress to eminence is of interest to all; in it has been exemplified an embodiment of what we call Americanism. His grandfather was a Norwegian carpenter who came to America in 1865. His father, who married a Swedish-born lady, came to California in the 1880's. Earl was born March 19, 1891, in Los Angeles, in a humble home on "dingy Turner Street." He began working very young, as newsboy, callboy, then freight handler, farm hand, and newspaper reporter.

As a high school student in Bakersfield his record was not particularly brilliant—he enjoyed playing in the school band and was good at baseball. At the University of California he was not one of the select inner group of brilliant students—he was just a healthy college kid who loved life, full of the vitality of youth. He worked along until his graduation from the law school, in 1914.

Warren became a junior lawyer in San Francisco and in Oakland, practicing for a short period, previous to his enlistment in the American Army, in 1917. At the time of his discharge, two years later, he was a first lieutenant.

His political career dates from his appointment as clerk of the Judiciary Committee of the State Assembly: from that time on he never engaged in private practice. After brief service as deputy city attorney for Oakland he became deputy district attorney for Alameda County, and in 1925 he was elevated to the office of district attorney, in which capacity he continued his work as public prosecutor for thirteen years, with a record so enviable as to earn for him the publicity claim as the "best District Attorney in the United States." Not one of the convictions he won as prosecutor was ever reversed by a higher tribunal.

In 1938 he was elected Attorney-General for the state; but soon his eye became fixed on the governorship. As nominee of both parties in 1942 he readily defeated the incumbent, Culbert Olson, who lacked the dramatic popular appeal in which Warren excelled. He experienced little difficulty in being reelected in 1946, again the nominee of both parties. Four years years he was vigorously opposed by James Roosevelt, Democratic nominee; but he won handily, thus becoming California's first three-term governor.

Earl Warren possesses a personality that it in itself a great asset. He is tall, robust, handsome, more than ordinarily congenial. His ideal family of wife, sons and daughters has likewise appealed to voters. His political philosophy is that of the progressive conservative, fully recognizing the changing order and facing the necessity of utilizing our best forces in meeting urgent world situations: since our world problems are new we must be prepared to "think anew and act anew."

On the last day of September, 1953, President Eisenhower named Governor Warren Chief Justice of the United States, describing him as "a man with a reputation for integrity, honesty, and middle-of-the-road politics," an appointment that had been widely anticipated. A few days later, with solemn traditional ceremony, he took the sacred oaths, and thus a native Californian became the fourteenth man in American history to occupy the nation's highest judicial position—the first from the commonwealth of California to win this pre-eminent position.

CHAPTER EIGHT

SOCIO-ECONOMIC

"We need to become more Pacific-minded. . . . The story of the
future is that East which is just westward of our West. It will be
an increasingly important fact in our lives, and perhaps the determining one in the lives of our children."

—Chester H. Rowell

LAND GRANTS

The pattern for living in early Hispanic California was set to a large
extent by the same force that has so effectively operated following our
American wars—this was "Land for veterans." To the soldier-*rancheros*
may be largely attributed the manner and style of California life in the
Arcadian age. Scarcely had the first mission and *presidio* been established when thought was given to the allotment of lands to private
individuals.

A soldier named Manuel Butron, who had married Margarita, an
Indian girl, was the first Spanish subject to obtain a parcel of land he
could call his. In 1775 he asked for a plot near Carmel Mission. Commandant Rivera and Father-President Junípero Serra approved, and
Butron was given actual possession, on the 27th of November, 1775, of
a 140-*vara* lot. This made Butron the pioneer land owner of California,
but it did not make him the first real *ranchero*. His claim was later
abandoned.

Not until 1784 was there an actual beginning of the true ranch movement. In that year several veterans obtained permission of the governor
(Pedro Fages) to pasture their cattle on land entirely outside *presidio*
and *pueblo* boundaries. Later that year Juan José Dominguez, an
experienced veteran of the Portolá expedition, drove his horses and
cattle from San Diego to a site near the present city of Long Beach.
He established what later was called Rancho San Pedro, extending
rather indefinitely over an area of many thousands of acres and including for a time the more than 30,000 acres of *Rancho Los Palos Verdes*.

Almost at the same time that Dominguez was establishing himself
on Rancho San Pedro another veteran, José María Verdugo, was
petitioning the governor for permission to pasture his cattle and horses

on a large triangular tract a few miles from Mission San Gabriel, comprising within its boundaries the sites of the present city of Glendale and part of Burbank. The petition was granted, and Verdugo was granted Rancho San Rafael with its more than 36,000 acres, the date of the grant being October 20, 1784.

Then quickly followed a grant to Manuel Pérez Nieto, three leagues from San Gabriel, "provided no harm is done to the Mission San Gabriel nor to the Pagan Indians of its environs in any manner whatsoever." This grant covered a vast but ill-defined area, later greatly reduced because of the insistence of the *Padres*.

Thus was inaugurated the system of Spanish and (later) Mexican land grants resulting in the establishment of the picturesque ranch life of the pre-American days of California history. The private ranches by 1790 numbered nineteen, most of them in Southern California. But it should be noted that Dominguez and the others did not receive grants directly from the King of Spain—theirs were provisional concessions, little more than permits for cattle-grazing from the governor of the province, who in turn served under the power of the viceroy of New Spain. Instead of being outright owners these pioneers had a sort of usufructuary titles of different grades.

The *ranchos* came to include much of the good valley land, near the coast, from San Francisco to the Los Angeles and Santa Ana River region. What we know as Arcadian California, as described by Nellie Van de Grift Sanchez, and the "Splendid Idle Forties" of Gertrude Atherton, came to full fruition not during the Spanish rule but during the Mexican régime, preceding the Bear Flag and the American conquest. The final settlement of many claims, under an act of Congress of March 3, 1851, involved long litigation, with unfortunate results to many of the Spanish-American families.

PIONEERS OF NEGRO ORIGIN

There were in California persons of negro blood long before the coming of the first Americans. The presence of a few negroes and mulattoes among the earliest Spanish settlers is of interest to the ethnologist and the antiquarian, but cannot be said to hold any considerable historical significance.

Less than a single decade after the coming of Portolá and Serra to San Diego in 1769, the first *pueblo* (San José) was founded, in 1777. Three years later the second (Los Angeles) was founded, and among its first *pobladores* (settlers) were two negro men and seven mulattoes. We have the names of Antonio Mesa, aged 38, and José Moreno, aged

22. Both had wives of negro blood. There were also listed nine children of either Indian-mulatto or Spanish-Indian-mulatto extraction. Of the very early settlers of Los Angeles nearly 50 per cent of the adult population were of negro origin, while 70 per cent of the children had negro ancestors. From the first settlements of the Spaniards even till now persons of negro blood have always been in California.

Toward the end of the Mexican régime we encounter a personality who made a positive impact upon his community and the provincial history of California. William Alexander Leidesdorff, eminent California pioneer of 1841, is not usually thought of as negro at all. But there was negro blood in his veins. He was a native of Virgin Islands, the son of a Danish sugar planter named William Leidesdorff, and a native woman of negro blood. Negro writers have been proud to claim him for their race.

As a youth he left his first home for New Orleans, to take up maritime trade. In this he prospered so greatly that he became a master of vessels plying between New York and New Orleans. Being of adventurous spirit, and yielding to the lure of the West and the Pacific, he purchased the *Julia Ann*, a 106-ton schooner, and in it he set sail for far-away San Francisco Bay.

It was in 1841, after a passage of severe buffeting, requiring months of time, that he reached his destination and brought his vessel to anchor in Yerba Buena Cove. His appearance at the sleepy little settlement that was to become dynamic San Francisco proved to be an event of real significance.

Leidesdorff threw himself into the upbuilding of the feeble community. He was the active instigator of several business ventures; he it was who launched the first steamboat — a tiny craft, to be sure — on San Francisco Bay. It came to be known as the *Sitka*. It had been built by an American in Alaska as a pleasure boat for the officers of the Russian Fur Company: but Leidesdorff purchased it, and in October, 1847, it was brought to San Francisco.

This daring pioneer is also credited with having built San Francisco's first hotel, named "City Hotel," located on the corner of Clay and Kearny Streets. He entered the political arena and became Vice-Consul to Mexico by appointment of Thomas O. Larkin, American Consul at Monterey.

Leidesdorff never married, but he entertained lavishly and held positions of honor in civic life. But his fascinating, many-sided career was brought to an early close by his death in 1848, a young man of thirty-eight. While there were negroes in California long before his time, and while his own lineage was mixed, it may be said that the more significant aspects of negro life and activities in California began with William Alexander Leidesdorff.

FIRST INHABITANTS OF LOS ANGELES

There is some basis for the claim that Los Angeles was the first legally ordained city of California, founded by Governor Felipe de Neve, September 4, 1781, since San José (November 29, 1777) was "rather in the nature of an informal, preliminary experiment."

The Indians found in the vicinity of Los Angeles, in the *ranchería* Yang-na, have been described as "small, squat in stature, of a dingy brown color." The men were entirely without clothes, the women wore little aprons of rabbit skin. Until the Spaniards appeared they had never seen a civilized man.

It is not historically accurate to feature the actual founding of the *pueblo* with elaborate pomp and ceremony. The actual beginnings were in reality quite informal: it was five years before the formal confirmation of the house-lots and fields of the settlers. But the informality was made up for by the heavenly name bestowed upon the humble settlement— *Pueblo de Nuestra Señora la Reina de Los Angeles* (City of Our Lady, the Queen of the Angels).

Now what about the Spanish settlers themselves, the first inhabitants of the *pueblo* that was destined to become the greatest of all the cities of the entire West. De Neve had great difficulty in enlisting the right kind of material to be the citizens of the new settlement.

Appeal had been made to the viceroy for agricultural people from Mexico, who should be healthy and strong, men of good character, men of industry who would set a good example to the Indians. Family life was to be encouraged. Allotments of land and livestock were to be liberal. Each settler would receive a plow-point, a spade, hoe, sickle, musket, and a tough leather shield. For the community there was to be an anvil, forge, crowbars, and needed tools.

For almost a year the captain was trying to find the desired number of settlers with the required qualifications. Results were far from encouraging. Rivera had to take what he could get: instead of the twenty-four families desired, there were only half that number.

The expedition set out from Mission San Gabriel on the fourth of September, 1781, the Governor with a detachment of soldiers leading the way, followed by the settlers — eleven men, eleven women and twenty-two children, a total of forty-four persons. For a description of the simple founding ceremony we quote Charles D. Willard:

The procession marched slowly and impressively around the plaza, followed, no doubt, by the wondering gaze of the Indians from Yang-na, . . . When the circuit was completed the priests asked a blessing on the new city that was about to come into existence. Then Governor Felipe de Neve delivered a formal speech to the settlers, . . . Prayers and a benediction from the padres concluded the ceremony, . . .

What sort of people were they who first made their homes in Los Angeles? Who were the heads of the first families? Willard presents the roster of 1781. First on the list comes Pablo Rodriguez, a twenty-five-year-old Indian, with Indian wife and one child; next is José Moreno, a mulatto, twenty-two years old, with mulatto wife; Antonio Villavicencio, a Spaniard aged thirty, with Indian wife and a single child; José de Lare, a Spaniard, aged fifty, with Indian wife and three children; Antonio Mesa, a negro of thirty-eight years, with mulatto wife and five children; and Basilio Rosas, a sixty-eight-year-old Indian, with mulatto wife and six children (these were three expelled families); next was Alejandro Rosas, an Indian only nineteen, with wife called "Coyote Indian"; then Antonio Navarro, a Spanish-Indian half-breed, with a mulatto wife and three children; last of all, Manual Camero, a mulatto, aged thirty, with his mulatto wife. Here is the summary: "Two Spaniards, one mestizo, two negroes, eight mulattoes, and nine Indians," with children of even greater racial mixture.

Only two Spaniards and two Indian children could claim regular racial ancestry. De Neve was fully aware that such a group would not immediately be capable of self-government. For a number of years the *pueblo* was under the guidance of a petty military officer.

Such was the unpromising beginning of what became the metropolis of the Southwest. It may be said that such a beginning enhances still more the marvelous achievement of more recent years. Harris Newmark reached Los Angeles in 1853, and because of his optimism was deemed a dreamer. When in 1915 he published his book, *Sixty Years in Southern California*, with prophetic vision he declared: "I believe that Los Angeles is destined to become, in not many years, a world-center, prominent in almost every field of human endeavor."

BEGINNINGS OF BANKING

In the days of the early gold rush the channels of finance, filled with swiftly-flowing, wildly-eddying currents, were dominated by trafficking in gold dust. This was "the one universally sought and universally valued commodity," wrote Ira Cross, "and was bought and sold, held for safe keeping, or exported." Conditions were far from favorable for formal banking. Like "Topsy," California banking simply grew. As John Archibald once aptly said, "San Francisco was still only a lump of civilization dumped down in the midst of a wild country."

Quite naturally San Francisco merchants often kept customers' deposits in their safes or strong boxes—and isn't that rudimentary banking? Then of course there were money lenders. So the firms that held deposits of coins and gold dust became buyers of dust and gold bars and lenders to customers, thus becoming the first real banking houses of California, the scope of whose activities rapidly broadened into various sorts of financial transactions.

Because of the unusual conditions obtaining and the lack of regularity and standardization, there is still some doubt as to the exact date and personnel of the first bona-fide California bank. The *Mercantile Trust Review of the Pacific* tells us that Robert A. Parker conducted a store in an adobe building on Dupont Street, San Francisco, as early as March, 1848, "and very possibly combined a little primitive banking with his other business."

Perhaps greater weight should be given to the claim that Dr. Stephen A. Wright's Miners' Bank, established presumably near the end of 1848, was really the first. It conducted a brokerage business; and it is said that Wright collected interest of from 8% to 15% a month on real estate loans! In November of that year Wright, with his partners John Thompson, Samuel Haight and J. C. Wadsworth, definitely organized, with a capital stock of $200,000. The Miners' Exchange and Savings Bank was an outgrowth several years later.

Another strong claimant to first honors was the firm of Naglee and Sinton, which opened banking quarters January 9, 1849, in the Parker House, San Francisco. On the withdrawal of Sinton the firm name became Naglee & Co. General Naglee's name is well remembered in San José, the place of his later residence.

There is no doubt that still other firms, as many as six, conducted at least limited banking operations in that historic year of 1849. Prominent among these was the establishment of Burgoyne & Co., established June 5. How a later run on the bank was stopped, as told by B. C. Wright, may throw a side-light on conditions in San Francisco in the days following the first gold rush. The bank was crowded with a mob demanding payment.

> Burgoyne & Co. had some real friends nearby, so word was sent to them to come over and assist in handling the situation. Soon one of them forced his way to the counter and threw down a bag of gold coins to be deposited. The crowd looked on with wonder. In a few moments another depositor

appeared with a bag of gold coins. A little later a third depositor came in and left a bag of coins. By this time the run had collapsed. The same bag of coins had been used and used over and over again, for as soon as received it was passed to a confederate at the back door and then brought in at the front door to be again deposited.

The San Francisco Accumulating Fund Association, incorporated June 22, 1854, may be regarded as "a mother of the family" of savings banks in California. Strictly speaking, however, The Savings and Loan Society, located on Washington Street, incorporated July 23, 1857, was the first real savings bank. Then came the Hibernia Savings and Loan Society, a good second, incorporated April 12, 1859.

The first banking institution in Southern California was organized in 1868 by Alvinza Hayward and John G. Downey, under the firm name of Hayward & Co., with capital stock of $100,000. But first in historical significance is the Farmers and Merchants National Bank of Los Angeles, which dates from the year 1871, and has maintained its distinctive identity for the better part of a century. Its succession of illustrious presidents includes John G. Downey, I. W. Hellman, Jackson A. Graves, and Victor H. Rossetti. Only recently it was merged into the Security-First National Bank. In 1875 there were two banks besides the Farmers and Merchants: the Los Angeles County Bank and the Temple and Workman Bank. At present two of the largest banking institutions of the world have headquarters in Los Angeles.

FIRST MONEY COINED

Among the Californians of the Spanish and Mexican periods actual money was very scarce. It was comparatively unknown as a common medium of exchange; but furs could readily be had, often taking the place of coined money. Even a bullock or a hide made a fair substitute when trading was little more than a refined form of barter.

As early immigrants from the United States and other nations appeared in increasing numbers, small quantities of money of different national mintage began to circulate. Then came the American conquest and the great gold discovery. Everything was measured in terms of the American dollar, or its equivalent in gold dust: but still actual money was scarce and people were flocking in, greatly increasing the need of a circulating medium.

In the early days, as pictured in the *Annals of San Francisco*, "the buyer would carelessly tumble out a heap of 'dust' in payment, while the seller would have his weights and scales ready for it, as a matter

of course. A little lump less or more to the quantity was of no consequence to either party." All sorts of transactions was conducted by the
use of the "ounce" or "pinch of dust."

In the meantime increasing quantities of coins from many countries
were being brought into California—England, France, Mexico, India,
Germany, and still other nations were represented — and approximate
values were bestowed upon their gold and silver coins, with slight
attention to intrinsic worth. But the demand for money far exceeded the
supply, especially since many of the better gold coins were hoarded by
importers. The money situation was rapidly becoming more complicated
—and more embarrassing.

As early as mid-summer of 1848 Col. Richard Mason, military governor, drew up plans for relief: these, however, proved to be illegal. The
clamor for coins grew louder and more insistent.

The first coins actually produced and circulated in California were
privately minted. In the *Alta California* of May 31, 1849, mention is
made of a "five-dollar gold coin struck off at Benicia City, though the
imprint is San Francisco." Two months later the ten dollar piece
appeared, also privately coined. So rapidly did things happen immediately following, we are informed, that "the closing months of 1849
saw a perfect avalanche of private gold." A number of big companies
coming from the east "brought machinery for coining." There were no
trustworthy precedents: instead of needed stability there was a chaos in
monetary affairs.

The underlying reason for private coinage was to relieve the acute
shortage of money. But the chief motive of those engaging in the business was private profit: this was reflected in the fact that the $5 and $10
pieces contained at least five per cent, and in some cases up to ten per
cent, less gold than their face value indicated, which was bound to bring
them into disfavor by merchants sooner or later.

One of the most interesting factors in the early California monetary
situation is the coinage of the $50 gold "slugs." Moffatt's Mint, near the
base of Mt. Ophir, in Mariposa County, was built of slate rock in 1850,
by John L. Moffatt, an experienced geologist, who had been appointed
in 1849 by President Taylor as U.S. Assayer for California. His first
issuance consisted in $50 slugs, "coined at his Mt. Ophir Mint, and were
legal tender, being issued under governmental authority." The *Daily
Alta California* of February 21, 1851, gives this description of Moffatt's
$50 "slugs":

> The new fifty dollar gold pieces, manufactured under the act of Con-
> gress appointing a United States assay office in California, and made under

the supervision of the United States Assayer, were issued by Moffatt and Co., yesterday. . . .

The coin is peculiar, containing upon one face an eagle in the center, around which are the words "United States of America." Just over the eagle is stamped "887 thous," signifying the fineness of the gold. At the bottom is stamped "50 dolls." The other face is ornamented with a kind of work technically called "engine turning," being a number of radii extending from the common center, in which is stamped, in small figures, "50"; around the edge is stamped the name of the United States assayer. We trust that all our readers may learn the character of this new coin by ocular demonstration.

Octagonal and circular slugs were later issued in considerable numbers. By the end of of the year 1851 more than a dozen assay offices issued private coins, most plentiful of which were the five and ten dollar pieces. There were also some twenty dollar pieces, which came to be called "double eagles," and a limited number of stamped ingots of gold, varying in value from forty to 150 dollars.

The San Francisco Mint was at long last assured by act of Congress July 3, 1852, though the building was not completed until the spring of 1854. Private coins continued to dominate as late as 1856. In all probability a total of more than five million dollars was thus issued in California.

IRON FOUNDRY

The first iron casting turned out on the Pacific Coast was made in San Francisco, in that stirring year, 1849. This was a "spring bearing" for the propellor *McKim*, constructed at a cost of fifty cents per pound. The small, crude furnace was the property of two brothers, James and Peter Donahue, and it proved to be the forerunner of the great Union Iron Works, for many years one of the leading industrial organizations of California.

In the original plant the furnace blast was produced by the use of two old-fashioned blacksmith bellows. In his fascinating book, *Lights and Shades of San Francisco*, published in 1876, B. E. Lloyd describes the early development of this pioneer industry, in part, in these words:

From this little "plant" the Donahue Brothers built up a very large business, enlarging and improving their establishment from time to time, and endeavoring to keep it in advance of similar works, which in course of time sprang up around them. In 1856 James Donahue sold his interest in the business to his brother Peter, who erected a large brick building on the site of the roofless workshop of 1849, and carried on the business in his own name.

In 1863 Mr. Donahue formed a copartnership with H. J. Booth and C. S. Higgins under the firm name of Donahue, Booth & Co. The business did not immediately prosper as expected; in 1865 the property was acquired by a new firm composed of Booth, G. W. Prescott, and Irving M. Scott, the firm name being H. J. Booth & Co. Out of this came the Union Iron Works.

Business increased rapidly, new machinery was purchased, the labor force was augmented, and within a decade it was probably "the most completely equipped foundry and machine shop on the coast."

The buildings, while not ornate, were well adapted for the respective purposes for which they were designed. Among the laborers promotion was based on merit alone; strict discipline was maintained throughout all departments.

Irving Murray Scott, a native of Maryland, became general superintendent of the firm in 1863. He it was who designed important machinery for the operation of the great Comstock mines and is credited with other significant inventions: in short, he became not only technical expert but chief entrepreneur for the Union Iron Works. To his able management was due, in large measure, the marked success of the establishment.

The famous battleship *Oregon* and other vessels were built for the U.S. Navy, which added to the prestige of this powerful corporation.

After important service as executive in the Mechanics' Institute, regent of the University of California, trustee of Stanford University, and in other capacities, Scott died in 1903. It was largely through his outstanding services that the Union Iron Works maintained virtual supremacy through many decades. Other foundries dating from an early period in California history included the Risdon Iron Works, and the Pacific Iron Works, which, dating from 1850, was the second oldest on the Pacific Coast.

CALIFORNIA MILLIONAIRE

Perhaps more than any other that could be mentioned Sam Brannan was the man of California "firsts." Even after discounting some of the extravagant claims made for him, the general appraisal made by George Hamlin Fitch remains essentially accurate—he was "one of the first men in the state who saw clearly its possibilities, and who gave without stint to develop its great resources."

Among the numerous "first" claims—which cannot here be critically examined—are that in his new home in Yerba Buena (San Francisco) he, a Mormon elder, preached the first non-Catholic sermon in California; he conducted the first non-Catholic wedding; he established the first newspaper in San Francisco, and was a member of the first City

Council; he was a defendant in San Francisco's first American-style jury trial; he built the first flour mill; he was an organizer of the Society of California Pioneers; he was a California "booster" from the start; he urged the building of the first school and was a member of the first legally elected board of education; he established, with two others, California's first chartered commercial bank; and he became California's first millionaire.

At the age of twenty-five Brannan came from New York to California "around the Horn," in charge of a party of Mormons (70 men, 68 women, 100 children), having been selected by Brigham Young, the basic purpose being to escape religious and social persecution. Keen was his disappointment when on the last day of July, 1846, he entered the Golden Gate and beheld the American flag—which he had hoped to escape—flying at San Francisco—Commodore Sloat had raised the Stars and Stripes three weeks earlier in Monterey.

He had hoped also to found the first newspaper in California, the *California Star*, but found, to his dismay, that Semple and Colton had beaten him with their paper, the *Californian*, whose first issue was dated August 15, 1846.

Sam Brannan's party almost doubled the population of little Yerba Buena; his extraordinary activity probably more than doubled the enterprise of the sleepy village. He seemed to interest himself in everything. He has been called "a fire-brand," "a very dynamo of enterprise."

Quickly surveying the unique situation and scanning the horizon after the gold discovery, he decided not to become a miner, but to open stores and sell provisions and goods of all kinds to the miners, and to acquire real estate on a large scale. When the city of Sacramento was laid out, he owned a quarter of its area. When rents in booming San Francisco were fabulously high, it was found that Sam Brannan owned a fifth of that young city, including the valuable Market Street property.

But he was also busy outside of San Francisco and Sacramento. He acquired property in numerous locations, including the vast estate of Abel Stearns in Los Angeles County (170,000 acres), and the famous Calistoga Hot Springs in upper Napa Valley. With characteristic enterprise he erected saw mills, quartz mills, and plants for smelting in the rich mining regions of the present Nevada County.

By 1855, so rapid and successful had been his business and bold developmental operations, he was reputed to be California's richest man —he became the state's first millionaire, as well as the first "Californian."

But the anti-climax is all the more pathetic because of the blinding speed in reaching the dizzy heights. He lost heavily in underwriting a land boom in Napa Valley; further losses resulted from his decision to float a Mexican bond issue at the disturbed time of Maximilian. His disappointment drove him to drink—and that was the prelude to the sad end of the man regarded by many as the most colorful of all the pioneers of early California, the man who, in the opinion of Hubert Howe Bancroft, "probably did more for San Francisco and for other places than was effected by the combined efforts of scores of others." More than any other person of his time he made the United States California conscious.

LABOR UNIONS

During the early California gold mining days there was a chronic scarcity of common day labor: most immigrants came to seek their fortune at the diggin's; a small number came to practice their professions, particularly that of the law. Among them all there were scarcely any regular wage earners; indeed, there were few jobs that could be called steady, and of course there was no generally accepted standard of wage rates or uniform wage scale.

Labor unions were organized among the bricklayers of San Francisco, however, as early as February, 1852. At practically the same time the printers organized in Sacramento; and two months later the San Francisco bakers organized labor unions. There had been a few strikes at even earlier dates. For example, the stevedores and longshoremen struck in May, 1851, for $6.00 per day—though apparently no formal union had been attempted at that time.

It may not be generally known, but there was serious unemployment in California in 1851-1852, as the first primitive methods of placer mining began to show marked decline. "One would scarcely believe it possible," wrote Ira Cross, "in the golden land where every ravine and hillside is full of treasure, that so many persons were to be found entirely out of employment."

But the depression quickly passed, confidence was restored in 1853. In the summer of that year many trade unions were organized: they were "especially rampant among the workingmen of San Francisco." Unions were to be found among carpenters, plasterers, painters, tinners, longshoremen, blacksmiths, and still other groups of workers.

The question of the "closed shop" gained some prominence in San Francisco as early as the 1860's. It is reported that the Journeymen Painters' Union obtained a closed-shop agreement in December, 1863. Before the end of that decade several strikes were called for the purpose of enforcing the closed-shop principle. Also, the "walking delegate," as the business agent was commonly called, appeared in the late 1860's. It became his duty "to go about the city and inspect each job in order to make sure that only union men of that craft were being employed."

The eight-hour labor day became an issue in 1865. It was closely tied in with the labor union movement. But the final achievement of this goal belongs in another story.

Much of the labor agitation of the 1870's was due to the presence in California of large and rapidly increasing numbers of Chinese laborers. Some 9,000 of them had been employed in the construction of the Central Pacific Railroad: many of them were now unemployed. The Chinese question was brought to a dramatic climax by the strange but powerful leadership of Denis Kearney, whose "sand-lot" oratory, coupled with the activities of the Workingmen's Party, headed by him, contributed significantly to the demand for a new state constitution, adopted in the year 1879, and ultimately to the total exclusion of Chinese labor.

The many-sided problem of organized labor has existed in some form in California almost from the beginning of statehood itself. In its varied aspects it has been a significant part of our total history.

EIGHT-HOUR LABOR DAY

In January, 1864, fifteen local labor unions, representing between 2,000 and 3,000 workers, formed an association known as the San Francisco Trades' Union. This organization was destined to have a comparatively short and decidedly up-and-down career.

The demand for a shorter labor day became a real issue in the year 1856, the ten-hour day having been legally established in 1853. During the closing months of the Trades' Union's short existence it took part "in a determined but unsuccessful demand for a state law establishing an eight-hour day." But internal dissension brought an end to the Union in the spring of 1866. It seemed to lack that "work-together" spirit, which is a prerequisite to the health of any central labor organization.

However, the question of an eight-hour day remained a leading popular issue until 1870, the most prominent and energetic agitator being Alexander M. Kenaday, a printer, who had served as president of the San Francisco Trades' Union.

Under Kenaday's aggressive leadership a petition said to have been twenty-two feet long, containing 11,000 signatures, was presented to the state legislature February 13, 1866, "asking that an eight-hour day be adopted." The issue aroused widespread interest; citizens held mass meetings in several California cities.

The bill passed the Assembly by a vote of 64 to 6. Meanwhile petty jealousy was doing its detrimental work, and internal dissensions increased. In the Senate there was rough sledding; the bill was amended to the effect that "it should not take effect until New York and Massachusetts should have adopted similar statutes." The amended bill, resulting from long conference discussion, was ultimately defeated by a vote of 19 to 18. All attempts at reviving the measure at that session were defeated.

Then the unions, having failed to obtain legislative action, undertook to reach the goal by other means. Several San Francisco trades, one after another, established the eight-hour day on their own initiative. In June, 1867, it was noted, "the fact exists that the eight-hour system is more in vogue in this city than in any other part of the world, although there are no laws to enforce it."

A new champion of the cause arose in General A. M. Winn, who wholeheartedly and unselfishly threw himself into the campaign. The carpenters introduced the shorter work-day after an impressive parade conducted in a very favorable manner. But unfortunately there was further bickering and a troublesome injection of partisan politics, all of which brought delay and otherwise impeded the progress of the workers.

In February, 1868, Gen. Winn announced the existence of fifty eight-hour leagues in the state, half of them in San Francisco alone. A new bill was introduced in the legislature of 1867-68. This time the strong lobby met only slight opposition. Along with the mechanics' lien the eight-hour bill readily passed the Assembly and the Senate and was duly signed by Governor Henry H. Haight.

A grandiose celebration was held in San Francisco, February 22, 1868, with torch-light procession participated in by the shipwrights, plasterers, bricklayers, stone masons, plumbers, ironworkers, and many others.

The two outstanding leaders in the movement were Kenaday and Winn. "These two leaders," said Dr. Cross, "gave freely of their time, energy, and funds and labored unceasingly for the betterment of the conditions of the workers." It was still many years before the eight-hour day was fully accepted and actually adopted in the country; but a beginning had been made, and the names of these pioneers will always be held in remembrance in California.

NATIVE SONS OF THE GOLDEN WEST

Albert Maver Winn, a native of Virginia and oldest of a family of eighteen children, arrived in San Francisco May 28, 1849, at the age of thirty-nine. He had already had extensive civic and military experience in Vicksburg, Mississippi, having risen to the rank of colonel in 1845. It is not surprising, therefore, that he interested himself immediately in the early affairs of Sacramento, and was selected mayor of the new city that autumn. In April, 1850, the state legislature recommended him for the rank of brigadier-general, and he was duly commissioned by Governor Peter H. Burnett.

General Winn was instrumental in effecting the organization of several civic societies, and he early became a champion of the labor movement. In his own words he tells of the inception of his idea that finally resulted in the founding of the Native Sons of the Golden West. Said he:

> For twenty years my mind has been running on some lasting style of monument to mark and perpetuate the discovery of gold. I could not think of anything that would not perish in the course of time. At last it came to my mind that an Order composed of native sons of the Pacific Coast would effect the object and be sustained by pride of parentage and place of nativity, while it would be an imperishable memento—an institution that would last through all time.

The first attempt by General Winn to effectuate the organization he had visualized, in 1869, was not successful. As Grand Marshall of San Francisco's Fourth of July parade, he invited all native-born California males over ten years of age to join in the parade; about 120 responded. But most of them were mere boys, who failed to impress their seniors. Moreover, it was felt that General Winn was a Southern sympathiser; for these reasons the attempt at organization proved premature.

In 1875, however, Winn, again a member of the Independence Day Committee, was able to bring about the successful participation in the parade of a more satisfactory native-born unit. Then followed speedy action. Within a week, the actual organization of the fraternal society, July 11, 1875, was achieved, with the adoption of constitution and by-laws. Here is the Preface to the first constitution:

> The Society of Native Sons of the Golden West was organized for the mutual benefit, mutual improvement, and social intercourse of its members; to perpetuate in the minds of all native Californians the Memories of one of the most wonderful epochs in the world's history, the Days of '49; to unite them in one harmonious body throughout the state by ties of friendship mutually beneficial to all.

The charter members, numbering twenty-one, voted to call themselves a "parlor," thus avoiding the conventional term lodge, or chapter. John A. Steinback was elected president. General Winn, the founder, and

George P. Anthony, who generously donated the use of his hall as a meeting place, were promptly elected honorary members, the only persons to enjoy that distinction.

At first membership was limited to white male persons born in California on or after July 7, 1846, the date on which Commodore Sloat raised the Stars and Stripes at Monterey. At a later time, however, especially to include leading representatives of the Mexican régime, like Romauldo Pacheco and Mariano G. Vallejo, the constitution was liberalized as to date of birth.

The great ideals for which the order stands include: "(1) belief in and respect for God; (2) love for any loyalty to American principles; (3) a willingness to tolerate the beliefs of others; (4) friendship; (5) charity."

In December, 1877, the order was expanded by the institution of a parlor in Oakland; then followed Number 3, in Sacramento. The first Grand Parlor, of state-wide scope and over-all authority, was organized November 29, 1878. From that time local parlors multiplied rapidly: within a decade they were to be found in scattered parts of the state, and ultimately they numbered into hundreds.

Among the many thousands of members of the Native Sons of the Golden West, a very brief list of some who have achieved eminence may be given: Theodore A. Bell, Eugene Biscailuz, Frank L. Coombs, A. P. Giannini, Benjamin Harrison, William Randolph Hearst, Hiram W. Johnson, Joseph R. Knowland, Richard M. Nixon, James D. Phelan, Charles H. Rieber, Earl Warren, and Stephen M. White.

The sister order, Native Daughters of the Golden West, followed the same general lines in organization and purposes, for women, as their brothers. Their activities closely parallel those of the Native Sons, with whom they fully co-operate. Today they have their own Grand Parlor, with local parlors functioning in all parts of California.

INDIAN RESERVATIONS

The nineteenth century history of the California Indians is far from a cheerful one. The way the so-called secularization of the Franciscan Missions was conducted and mis-handled by political authorities is a sad reflection on the picturesque Mexican régime.

But neither does what happened to the fragment of the Indian population during the early American period afford much reason for pride today: indeed, the story of the Indian during the second half of the century is a sordid one. He had no alternative but to submit to the white man's domination. Details are seldom stressed in local histories.

In 1847 General Stephen J. Kearny, military governor, named John A.

Sutter, M. G. Vallejo, and J. D. Hunter as adjuncts to the military, really first Indian agents under American authority. In 1849 Adam Johnston was made sub-agent, and was responsible to the newly created Department of the Interior. That same year Thomas Butler King, secret agent of the government to California, took a secondary interest in the Indian question. But in January, 1851, came the important step of the appointment of three commissioner agents, O. M. Wozencraft, G. W. Barbour, and Redick McKee.

Then it was that negotiations were entered into with numerous Indian tribes, on the general principle that "tribes whose lands had been taken over by the miners should be assigned tracts on the floor of the valley," and should be indemnified with useful supplies, such as beef and blankets. Edward F. Beale, newly appointed Superintendent, approved the eighteen treaties agreed to, but all these were rejected by the U.S. Senate. No recital of this melancholy chapter can be undertaken here.

A new program dated from the autumn of 1852, which called for a system of military posts, to provide for "the convenience and protection of the Indians." Each post was to have its resident agent, clothed with due authority. This system may be called the genesis of the Indian Reservations; the Indians must remain there, and were to receive instruction in civilized pursuits, including farming and simple trades, with a view to becoming self-supporting.

What is claimed as the first real reservation was set up, following serious mining troubles, and the intervention of U.S. troops, at the mouth of the Klamath River, "running up the river twenty miles and extending a mile on each side," and known as the Klamath Reservation.

The system, drafted chiefly by Beale and B. D. Wilson, became, as one historian expresses it, "the Kingpin of the United States' Indian Policy."

The swift disappearance of the California Indians was both pathetic and tragic. At the beginning of the American period their total population, reduced from almost double the number in their palmy days to perhaps 100,000, was decimated to such an extent that by the beginning of the twentieth century the remnant numbered less than 16,000. The principal reason given for the spectacular decline was the white man's greed for land.

Fortunately a brighter side to the picture was emerging. Under the Office of Indian Affairs, with headquarters in Chicago, more humane and enlightened management of the reservations, with their schools and other institutions, were in evidence. The reservations themselves were scrupulously guarded against unprincipled whites, and wise provision was made for the intellectual and physical welfare of the Indians. The sale of intoxicating liquor was strictly forbidden.

Ultimately the extensive reservation system was arranged under four agencies: the Mission, Sacramento, Hoopa Valley, and Colorado River (only partly in California).

The ultimate integration of the Indians into the American ciitzenry has of late made real progress. The Indian population has recently been increasing: more and more of them are becoming well-to-do, useful Americans.

CHINESE

Leading archæologists have contended that the North American continent, or at least its Pacific Slope, originally was peopled by Asiatic races. Some have gone so far as to assert that Mexico was quite surely inhabited by Chinese (or Mongolians) in prehistoric times. These people could have migrated to Alaska overland at that remote time, or they might have crossed the narrow straits in boats, or some might have been driven across the north Pacific further south by ocean storms.

If it can be definitely shown that the Chinese were indeed the progenitors of the American Indians, then it will follow that there were Chinese in California in the remote pre-history ages. In the meantime the interesting question is one for the archæologist and the ethnologist—perhaps also the antiquarian. The historian must be content to bide his time.

In the *Alta California* of San Francisco for May 10, 1852, we read:

> In February, 1848, the territory of California received its first Asiatic immigrants when the brig *Eagle* brought from Hong Kong two Chinese men and one Chinese woman. The men proceeded later to the gold diggings and the woman became a house servant in the family of Charles V. Gillespie.

Referring to the same event William Heath Davis, in his valuable book *Sixty Years in California* reports:

> The American brig *Eagle* arrived here [San Francisco] from Canton, China, on the 2nd of February, 1848, with two Chinamen and one Chinawoman, who were looked upon as curiosities by some of the inhabitants of the growing town of San Francisco, who had never seen people of that nationality before. During the winter of 1848 and 1849 it was observable that Chinamen were multiplying by immigration rapidly. . . . At the particular time there was no expression of alarm from the people of San Francisco that the Chinese would overrun the city of the bay and the State of California.

There is an obscure report of the arrival of a single Chinese immigrant in the year 1847, though details are lacking. In 1848 seven Chinese appeared in California, but they were merely in transit. The first bonafide Chinese immigrants appeared in San Francisco early in 1849: before the end of that year the number had reached 791. During 1850 the invasion leaped to over 4,000, and the following year to 12,000.

The first Chinese immigrants in California were treated with "distinguished consideration"—they were officially referred to in 1850 as "our Chinese fellow-citizens." Governor John McDougal (1851-52) complimented them as "one of the most worthy classes of our newly adopted citizens."

But all this was soon to change sharply. Governor John Bigler (1852-56) reflected this change in a special message calling upon the legislature to enact a statute prohibiting their further immigration. The feeling of antipathy toward the Chinese was greatly heightened by the knowledge of the rapidly increasing numbers entering the state. Before the end of 1850 the numbers exceeded 4,000. By 1854 the number of Cantonese exceeded 40,000.

The Chinese question is of such importance to California history as to justify mention of two other significant firsts. The first national Exclusion Act, suspending immigration of Chinese laborers for a period of ten years, became effective May 6, 1882. The first important Chinese-Western daily newspaper was the *Chung Sai Yat Po* of San Francisco, founded by Ng Poon Chew—its first issue is dated February 16, 1900. However, there was a little known newspaper, *The Golden Hills News*, in Chinese and English, published for a brief period in San Francisco in 1851. The Chinese question, with its many aspects, constitutes one of the most important race-relations problems of all California history.

JAPANESE

Japan's first official embassy to the United States, headed by Shimmi, reached San Francisco March 29, 1860. It marks the first time that a Japanese ambassador was accredited to any Western power. The transition of Japan during the few decades that followed from "an obscure, feudal power to a modern national state" is regarded as the most revolutionary factor in world political change in more than half a century.

Legend has it that numerous wrecks of Japanese vessels were long ago stranded on the American western coast, some of them generations before the beginning of the nineteenth century. Such stories are not of primary concern to the historian.

Previous to the epoch-making expedition of Commodore Perry to Japan in 1853 several attempts had been made to penetrate the "hermetically sealed Empire of Japan"; but there was no legalized emigration from the Oriental nation.

In March, 1851, several shipwrecked Japanese are reported to have reached San Francisco, where they were given a cordial reception—at a grand ball they were exhibited as curiosities. In 1858 the crew of a derelict Japanese junk were brought to San Francisco. Again the authorities were in a quandary as to what to do with them: the problem was solved when the Collector of the Port decided to send them home on the revenue cutter. During the following decade there were other cases of Japanese cast-offs being rescued and brought to California shores.

All this, however, while viewed as a forerunner of things to come, cannot rightly be called a part of the Japanese immigration. Official reports indicate that in one way or another 218 Japanese had come to the United States between 1861 and 1872.

The embassy from Japan that arrived in California in 1872, *en route* to Washington, was accorded a grand reception, a senate resolution "welcoming the minister and the embassy and expressing a hope that their coming might be the harbinger of a commercial intercourse that would add largely to the happiness of the people of both countries."

Not until 1891, however, did the number of Japanese immigrants of any one year exceed 1,000 in number; but ten years later the astonishing number of 12,626 was recorded. It was in that year that the first significant opposition to their immigration was voiced at a mass meeting in San Francisco; although Dr. C. C. O'Donnell, a well known agitator and politician, had raised the cry "Japs must go!" as early as 1886, when the total number in the state was scarcely more than 400.

The "Japanese Question" is an integral part in the history of California. Its long and complicated story is rendered more understandable by remembering that from the first it was colored by the facts and emotions regarding the Chinese question — the strong anti-Chinese attitude carried over to a large extent to the Japanese.

A series of articles in the San Francisco *Chronicle* in the early spring of 1905 brought the Japanese problem sharply before the people. The first Japanese exclusion meeting after the organization of the Asiatic Exclusion League was held May 7, 1905. Then, following the "separate school order" the question assumed national significance.

First of a series of state laws directed against the entrance of Japanese laborers was that of May 19, 1913, providing that "Aliens not eligible to citizenship may inherit or devise real estate only as prescribed by treaty," and limiting the leasing of agricultural lands to such aliens to a maximum of three years.

Three aspects of the California opposition to Japanese immigration were of special note—economic, political, and social. In the last analysis the crux of the situation was felt to be the threat of a race problem, prossibly even more difficult of solution than that of the American Negro. This deep feeling only the passing of time and the exigencies of World War II have been able to assuage.

HYDRO-ELECTRIC POWER

Though now known to relatively few Californians, George Chaffey, a native of Canada and long-time resident of Australia, was "one of the master irrigation engineers of Western America." Appearing upon the scene at a date much later than the gold days of '49, he was none-the-less a true pioneer in his special fields: moreover, because of his high service to the public, he merits the title of philanthropist.

In 1881 Chaffey purchased the Garcia Ranch, which was a portion of the Cucamonga, located east of Los Angeles. An early subdivision brought about the settlement of Etiwanda. In 1882 he purchased another portion of the ranch, whose subdivision became the occasion for the founding of the now flourishing city of Ontario. In that year he designed a small power plant in connection with the Etiwanda Irrigation System. By means of a crudely constructed dynamo there was put into operation what is claimed to be the first electric lighting system of the world.

It was George Chaffey who also established a primitive telephone line from Etiwanda to San Bernardino, which, at the time, was the longest telephone line in actual operation anywhere. The same pioneer is credited with laying out that superbly beautiful esplanade known as Euclid Avenue. No wonder that his biographer paid glowing tribute to this engineering wizard—"a man whose creative genius caused so many deserts to flower, whose foresight, strength and skill enriched so many communities." Elwood Mead recognized his sterling worth when he wrote:

> Mr. Chaffey was the first in Western America to combine hydro-electric development with irrigation. . . . He was the first to recognize fully the necessity for conservation of water supplies by lining his pipe lines to convey water under pressure; . . .

Chaffey deeded the waters of San Antonio Canyon to the newly-formed Ontario Company; but he was careful to reserve the right for making use of the water for the purpose of generating electrical power —"the first reservation of the kind known up to that period." Then the Ontario Power Company built a power house. But even before that the resourceful engineer had wired his own ranch house: it thus became the first house west of the Rockies "to be lighted with electricity developed by hydro-electric power."

All that was but a beginning. Transmission of power to Los Angeles followed, giving to that city its first electric lighting and power system. Not only so, but the City of the Angels was the first in America, if not in the world, to be "completely illuminated by electric lights." In the year 1882, F. H. Howland, then representing the Brush Electric Lighting Company, had made a canvass in the awakening city for the introduction of electric lights: by the end of August forty arc lights had been ordered by business firms and private individuals, the lights to be placed conspicuously atop towers 150 feet high. The proposition was promptly accepted by the Council — public opinion decreed it to be "the best advertisement that Los Angeles could have." It followed that on the last night of the year the city "was first lighted by electricity when Mayor Toberman touched the button and turned on the mysterious current."

Marvelous indeed has been the development of hydro-electric power since its beginnings with Chaffey and his associates, back in the early 1880's. In 1895 a great Electrical Carnival was held in Sacramento, where 30,000 visitors witnessed more than 400 arc lights (350 horsepower), all ablaze, honoring the auspicious event—actual demonstration for the first time there that electrical energy could be successfully transmitted over a long distance from the pioneer Folsom powerhouse to Sacramento. A decade later a writer remarked that Los Angeles, true to her booster spirit, was "the most electrically up-to-date city imaginable."

MOTION PICTURES

Early in the year 1906 George Van Guysling induced his brother A. H. Van Guysling to make a trip to New York City to familiarize himself with the business of making moving pictures at the office of The American Biograph and Mutuscope Company. On his return he associated himself with Otis M. Gove, a superior photographer, and together they opened in Los Angeles, March 6, 1906, the first place for the making of motion pictures. This was at 2623 West Pico Street.

The first picture actually made for exhibition was taken on June 10 of that year, at the Plummer Ranch, Santa Monica Boulevard and Vista

Street, in Colegrove (now in Hollywood). Among those present on that occasion, the Annual Field Day of the Vaquero Club, were Mayor Arthur Harper of Los Angeles, Dr. Fred Shurtleff, and Eugene R. Plummer.

But for the antecedents and background of the motion picture we must go much farther back. Leland Stanford's fondness for blooded horses is well known. As early as 1872 he conceived the idea of using photography to record the action of a trotting horse. He went to great expense in his attempt to get a photograph of his "Occident" in motion. Five years later E. J. Muybridge produced a picture of the horse "speeding with all four feet off the ground." Stanford was elated, not only because this proved him right in the contention that for a moment the trotting horse has all four feet off the ground, but also because Muybridge's success suggested the "possibility of photography as an effective means of studying animal locomotion."

A laboratory (studio) was erected; after a series of preliminary tests, twenty-four cameras were carefully placed at intervals of twelve inches. During 1878-79 Muybridge made a large collection of photographs of horses walking, running, and trotting, also including certain other animals in motion. Then the photographer devised a projecting apparatus, which he called the "zoopraxiscope," and was thus able to give an interesting exhibition at Stanford's home in the autumn of 1879.

Stanford determined to have a scientific analysis of the important results that followed this initial success. He therefore employed Dr. J. D. B. Stillman, an eminent scientist, for the purpose. Then followed Stillman's book, *The Horse in Motion*, published in 1882. With the details of the ensuing controversy, and the litigation brought on by Muybridge, claiming priority, we cannot here be concerned. Muybridge's first book, *Attitudes of Animals in Motion*, had been published in San Francisco in 1881. His subsequent publications included *Animals in Motion* (1899) and *The Human Figure in Motion* (1901), both published in London.

The striking fact is that the activities of Leland Stanford and his employees antedated by many years not only the actual making of the first motion picture in California, but even the first photographed pictures in motion produced by Thomas A. Edison and his helper in the laboratory, in the year 1889. When once firmly established the motion picture with phenomenally rapid development gave rise to one of California's chief industires. Since the first great boom of 1919-20 Hollywood has become a name that is known everywhere; Hollywood is today the recognized capital of the world's motion picture industry.

EARLY FRATERNAL ORGANIZATIONS

Benevolent and fraternal organizations, like various religious denominations, were well represented in California from early American statehood. Brief notes relating to two of the first to appear, together with mention of several of the others, will serve to suggest the place of this general subject in the total perspective.

Members of the Free and Accepted Order of Masons, an organization that reaches back into medieval history, made their appearance in California in very early times, though we do not have complete evidence to prove what individual among them reached California as the very first. There is no doubt, however, that a number of Free Masons, including ship captains, were really here years before the American conquest.

Captain John Meek, a native of Massachusetts, engaged in the Hawaiian trade: he was one of the organizers and a charter member of Le Progres Lodge No. 124—at the time of his death in 1875 he was the oldest member. Robert J. Elwell is credited with having been the first Mason actually to settle in California—he is reported to have arrived in 1824; became a naturalized Mexican citizen four years later.

No lodge was established during the Mexican régime, since it was well known that the Catholic Church looked with disfavor upon Masonry and other secret organizations. Nevertheless, some even of the Americans that embraced the Church expressed willingness to join the Order if given the opportunity.

The first known dispensation for a California lodge was issued to Robert F. Parker for San Francisco early in 1848; but for some unknown reason this lodge never eventuated. The first charter for a lodge was issued by the Grand Lodge, May 10, 1848, to Western Star Lodge No. 98, of Benton City, Tehama County. This came to be known as the Lassen Charter, named after Peter Lassen, an early pioneer. Other charters followed almost immediately. It was possible at that time for a Grand Lodge to issue "traveling charters," permitting those thus commissioned to form and maintain a lodge without specific location. When this was done a lodge number was taken in conformity with the members in the Grand Lodge granting the dispensation.

In the spring of 1850 the Grand Lodge was formed at Sacramento. In this the guiding spirit appears to have been Benjamin D. Hyam, who later became Grand Master for California. The first Grand Master was Jonathan Drake Stevenson. From this time on lodges were numbered in accordance with the granting of charters by the Grand Lodge of California.

As in the case of the Masons, members of the Independent Order of

Odd Fellows found their way to California at an early date. In the autumn of 1847 (the year when Yerba Buena took the name San Francisco) a number of Odd Fellows met informally at the Portsmouth House. They had regular meetings on Tuesdays, as is shown by the journals of 1848.

But it was not until the 9th of September, 1849, that Lodge No. 1 was formally instituted in San Francisco. While the members of Lodge No. 2 gathered at Sacramento in August of that year, the Lodge was legally instituted January 28, 1851. The California Grand Lodge was organized May 17, 1853, when the local lodges numbered eleven.

In Southern California the first Odd Fellows Lodge (No. 35) was instituted at Los Angeles, March 29, 1855, Gen. Ezra Brown being the leading spirit. The addition of new lodges in all parts of the state followed naturally.

It was only normal that in the course of time other fraternal and benevolent organizations made their appearance. A few of these may be mentioned: Knights of Pythias, first lodge formed March 25, 1869; Ancient Order of Hiberians, first, March 29, 1869; Independent Order of Red Men; Grand Army of the Republic; United Ancient Order of Druids; and still others. In 1876 there were more than 100 benevolent organizations in San Francisco alone. Their financial standing was indicated by the numerous asylums, hospitals, homes, and schools established and supported.

That the fraternal spirit extends beyond the grave is illustrated by the fact that to the south of Lone Mountain, near San Francisco, is the old Masonic Cemetery, and to the west the Odd Fellows Cemetery, with their many graves. In the *Lights and Shades of San Francisco*, published in 1876, we read:

> The bond of brotherhood that holds the living in such harmonious unity, is not broken by death, but is even more manifest to the world at the grave than in any of the ordinary circumstances of life.

WOMEN'S CLUBS

It would require something more than poetic license to refer to the Antinomian Party of early Massachusetts, founded by Anne Hutchinson in 1634, as a women's club in any modern sense.

More accurately, one of the first women's clubs in America was the New England Woman's Club, organized in Boston in February, 1868, by Madame Caroline Severance. Another, dating from about the same time, was the Sorosis, of New York City. The entire movement had its beginnings far less than one hundred years ago. And it was not until 1890 that the General Federation of Women's Clubs was formed.

Women's clubs have had a very interesting history in the state of California. To the Ebell of Oakland goes the honor of being the earliest pioneer club, dating its beginning on the 13th of December, 1876. In the Year-Book of 1896-97, and the following years, the founder is given as Adrian F. Ebell, and the Oakland club claims to be the first west of the Mississippi, the second oldest in the nation. The Oakland Ebell was incorporated in January, 1884, federated January, 1893, and became a member of the State Federation in February, 1900.

The organization was formed primarily for purposes of cultural development. The chief factor of early-day programs consisted of carefully written papers, or essays, prepared and read by members. As time went on special sections were formed. These included the drama group, the music group, the section on applied psychology, and a vivacious section on living issues.

Madame Caroline Severance, known as the "Mother of Women's Clubs," formed the Women's Club of Los Angeles April 13, 1878. It had twenty-four members at the beginning. This proved finally to be the forerunner of the Friday Morning Club, which dated its actual beginning from 1891, with Madame Severance herself as first president. The distinguished founder was the embodiment of the ideal of "plain living and high thinking," and her home on West Adams Boulevard, called "*El Nido*," became a center for intellectuals. The oft-quoted motto is:

> In essentials, Unity;
> In non-essentials, Liberty;
> In all things, Charity.

From the beginning strong positions were taken for equality of rights for women.

The Ebell of Los Angeles was organized in 1894, with "a serviceable and ornate home, within which for years broad courses of departmental study have been prosecuted with vigor."

In 1925 announcement was made of the construction of a new club house, "expected to surpass all the other homes for local club women." The elaborate group of buildings on Wilshire Boulevard are said to be the largest of all women's clubs: in membership also the Los Angeles Ebell has surpassed all others. A score of active departments present a wealth of programs that is almost bewildering in scope.

As a result of concentrated action, the California Federation of

Women's Clubs was organized in Los Angeles, in 1900. It may be added that a great impetus was given at the beginning of the vast movement by suffrage organizations, with such leaders as Elizabeth Cady, Lucretia Mott, and Susan B. Anthony. In California, however, the one foremost leader was Madame Caroline Maria Seymour Severance.

FEDERATION OF WOMEN'S CLUBS

When the theme of Women's Clubs in California is mentioned certain names are likely to come to mind spontaneously. These include Madame Caroline Severance, Mrs. J. W. Orr, Mrs. Clara B. Burdette, Mrs. Lovell White, and Mrs. Frank Gibson. To each of these there is some special distinction.

To Mrs. Orr goes the distinction of being a foremost pioneer in the organization and early life of the California Federation of Women's Clubs. She served as president of the California Club, pioneer civic club of women in San Francisco, and has held in succession the series of offices in the California Federation, which was organized in the year 1900, in the city of Los Angeles.

State federation is a natural corollary to national federation; it is quite rightly to be regarded as "an effective means of disseminating the plans, programme, and general recommendations of the executive body of the General Federation of Women's Clubs."

The national motto is "Unity in Diversity"; the motto of the California Federation is "Strength United Is Stronger." The program of the state federation is based upon general plans approved by the national body—every phase of activity in club life is covered. "Side by side with our educational and civic work," reported Mrs. Orr, "are carried on the literary, artistic, and musical studies, which first brought women together in clubs." Women's clubs, as Julia Ward Howe once said, "were a reserved force," which is finding its best expression through the federation of individual clubs.

Partisan action and partisan affiliation have been scrupulously forbidden from the beginning; no special interest may be advocated. In Mrs. Orr's own words,

> ... We are concerned with the betterment of social and industrial conditions, with the conservation of the child, with the preservation of our natural resources, with questions of public health and morals, and with the eternal warfare against war.

The pursuit of these major aims, it is held, "in no way reflects upon the integrity of the federation as a non-sectarian, non-political organization."

The California Federation has stimulated the organization of women's clubs in every section of the state; it has aided in the standardization of study and activity programs; it has given direction to civic work and cultural progress; it has initiated protective and remedial legislation as an effective instrument for human betterment; it has been consistently committed to the extension of woman suffrage and to the cause of the preservation and extension of equal human rights. The influence of women's clubs and of their federated endeavors, in California as elsewhere, constitutes one of the great imponderable forces in American life which no specialist or statistician can measure with precision, but which no statesman or historian can afford to ignore.

FISHING INDUSTRY

The food of the California Indians, both vegetable and animal, had been provided by Mother Nature—they did not cultivate the soil. In many areas fish of various kinds constituted an important part of the food supply—all the more so because of the ease with which they could be caught when compared with the difficulty of harvesting native seeds and hunting wild animals. The salmon in season was held in high esteem by the Indians, which also applies to the Americans from the beginning of their occupation.

Long before the American conquest the whaling industry along the Pacific coast had its beginnings. Captains of whaling vessels coming down from the far north with their catch found California "a most convenient port of call for the purpose of repairing their battered ships and taking on a supply of fresh provisions" for the long trip around the Horn. By 1855 about 500 vessels were thus employed, their chief rendezvous being at first the Sandwich Island, then San Francisco. As a single example, on April 1, 1855, it is reported, the whaling bark *R. Adams*, after an absence of six months, arrived at San Francisco with a cargo of 6,000 gallons of sperm oil and 1,500 gallons of black fish oil.

Arrivals belonging to the whaling fleet during the year 1867, according to Cronise, were twenty-two, "of which thirteen were from the Arctic Ocean, seven of these vessels belonging to the port of San Francisco." The season's product amounted to 13,149 barrels of oil and 186,000 pounds of bone. For generations whaling was an important as well as picturesque industry based in California.

The first adventuresome enterprise from San Francisco in the northern cod fisheries was undertaken in the year 1862: within four years the number of vessels employed had increased to eighteen. The cruise, however, was long and tedious, requiring anywhere from 95 to 193 days.

Like so many other California industries, the development of commercial fisheries has been almost unbelievable both as to magnitude and in variety and diversification. The vast product issues from about fifty varieties of fish and shellfish. For example, an unusual cargo was brought in by the schooner *W. A. Tarlton* in May, 1855, consisting of 580 terrapins from the Galapagos Islands, said to be the largest quantity ever brought in to that time. Fabulous amounts of sardines, tuna, and mackerel are processed.

It is a fascinating fish story. When in 1903 the great schools of sardines mysteriously failed to appear off-shore, the fish-canning industry of Southern California faced disaster. But one cannery ventured to experiment by putting up 700 cases of canned albacore. That proved to be the picturesque beginning of the gigantic tuna industry.

The demand for an economical protein-rich food at the time of the First World War found a perfect answer in canned tuna. The industry has grown and grown, until it requires eleven and a half million cases to satisfy the annual demand. Indeed, it has become America's largest fish-food enterprise. The tuna's meal-time uses are boundless: it was found to be ideal for snacks and sandwiches. More recently to the albacore have been added the yellowfin and the skipjack.

During the four-year period ending in 1946 four-fifths of the total national output of canned fish and shell-fish was the product of the Pacific area, and that included more than half of the product of the industry of the nation. In its fisheries California now leads the nation.

The fleets of commercial fishing boats range over a very extended field, in the western and southwestern Pacific, by no means confined to California waters. As one has said, "A lot of time and energy are expended every day to get the 'Aristocrat of the sea' from its home in the southwest Pacific to a can on the shelf of a grocery store in the Bay area."

Modern freezing equipment enables the fisherman to unload his cargo "ocean-fresh" at the cannery, where the exacting canning processes insure a product of highest grade. In California the processing is concentrated chiefly in the regions of San Francisco, Monterey, Los Angeles, and San Diego.

Referring to inland activities, there are a score of important hatcheries. Trout of several varieties are planted in the lakes and streams, located in different parts of the state, for the special pleasure of the nature sportsman. The State Fish and Game Commission sets the rules for fishing in California, and the rules are administered through the Department of Fish and Game.

SAN FRANCISCO'S BOHEMIAN CLUB

It is to be doubted whether anywhere in the world there exists a perfect counterpart of the Bohemian Club of San Francisco. Since its organization in March 1872, this most individualized club of the highly individualized city by the Golden Gate has been a special feature of the cultural life of the community.

Most of the original projectors were journalists, who seemed to sense the loss of many of the first brilliant galaxy of writers immediately following the early gold days. There were Daniel O'Connell of the *Evening Bulletin*, James F. Bowman of the *Daily Chronicle*, Joseph N. H. Irwin, a reporter on the *Evening Examiner*, Frederick Whymper, of the editorial department of *Alta California* as well as artist and mining engineer, and a few others.

The group held various meetings and issued invitations to selected prospects; but they experienced difficulty in finding illustrious persons to add to the membership; for, as Franklin Walker has pointed out, "surprisingly few of the writers of the golden fifties and silver sixties were left in the city." However, the charter members numbered eighteen men, with a strong tinge of journalism, including such names as A. G. Bierce, C. A. Wetmore, D. McCarthy, and Arpad Haraszthy. "If they were not all, individually, good financiers," Jerome A. Hart, himself later a member, remarked, "they were good fellows."

The beginnings of Bohemia in San Francisco were quite simple. The by-laws were far from severe, house rules were lenient, with few restrictions imposed. The price of the modest luncheon was twenty-five cents. It was eight years before a dinner service was begun. Informality was the general rule—visitors were numerous and were welcome.

The first article of the Club's constitution states:

> ...It is instituted for the association of gentlemen connected professionally with literature, art, music, and drama, and also those who, by reason of their love or appreciation of these objects, may be deemed eligible.

The Club quarters, on Sacramento Street, near Kearny, were quite unpretentious; later a more satisfactory location was found on Pine Street, near Kearny. Despite the informal nature of the rules, the election of members soon became a matter of very live interest: at times there were "carnivals of black-balling," the meeting more than once being thrown into an uproar.

As the programs developed, the terms "High Jinks" and "Low Jinks" came into general use. There was extempore speaking, carefully prepared recitations were presented by members; but almost from the beginning eminent musicians, actors, travelers, military leaders, members of royalty began to be invited. Then there were painters, sculptors, and cartoonists. Among the most notable speakers were D. M. Delmas and W. H. L. Barnes; among poets are mentioned Charles Warren Stoddard and George Sterling. There were Stephen Leach the actor, David W. Loring the musician, and a long list of others, both from the Club membership and distinguished visitors.

Bohemians were quite free to ignore precedent—they cared not how other men did things. Especially in their annual celebrations "they struck peculiar and striking notes of fun and entertainment that made an invitation eagerly sought after."

The Midsummer Jinks, with the setting of stately redwood trees in the forest, some sixty-five miles north of San Francisco, may be said to date from 1902, when the play "The Man in the Forest," was presented. The Annual Jinks have long since become "an elaborate and ambitious two-weeks toast to Nature, staged in a magnificent natural amphitheater in the redwoods," displaying "San Francisco's penchant for convivial communing with one another and for giving generous attention to the amenities of life."

The "High Jinks" might seem to imply "an effervescence of hilarity." On the contrary, as expressed by Ernest Peixotto, "It is a dignified proceeding, elaborately planned and most painstakingly carried out." One of the most beautiful of the Grove Plays was Will Irwin's "Hamadryads"; and George Sterling's "Triumph of Bohemia" possessed poetry of rare beauty. The theme has varied yearly, from Indian to Shakespeare, from Aztec to Gypsy. In all the world there is nothing quite like the Bohemian Club of San Francisco.

THE CAFETERIA

Here is a most popular institution—one that is very much at home in California and particularly in Southern California. To be still more specific, Los Angeles may with good reason claim to be the cafeteria capital of the world—perhaps the universe!

Long before the special type of eating place we are considering was even thought of, there was back in the 1850's in the southland the place called *cafetería*, with the Spanish accent. This, however, as Harris Newmark has pointed out in his *Sixty Years in Southern California*, was quite different: "It was rather a place for drinking than for eating." Nor did it bear any close resemblance to the more recent institution common in parts of Mexico, where a *cafetería* is "a small restaurant serving alcoholic drinks with plain meals."

The true prototype of the cafeteria, as we have come to know it, was opened in Chicago in 1895, on Adams Street between La Salle and Clark. It was operated by Ernest Kimball. But even a full decade before that crude beginnings might have been seen in the Exchange Buffet, for men only, established in New York in 1885. And in 1891 J. R. Thompson's Chicago restaurant, a semi-philanthropic enterprise, introduced the practice of offering a limited menu of hot foods with the self-service plan.

A true pioneer in the cafeteria movement in California was Miss H. S. Mosher of Michigan, who bravely opened her establishment on Hill Street, Los Angeles, in the month of May, 1905. Thus the real cafeteria in California is still scarcely more than half a century old. Miss Mosher's cash register (another modern invention) was a cigar box.

The underlying idea is to provide meals of wholesome food at lower cost by permitting the customer to serve himself. Service at the many restaurants previously operating was often limited to certain hours, with prices usually high for good clean food; and many patrons strongly disliked the common practice of tipping.

After Miss Mosher's initial experiment, others followed in the wake. Similar places were established in San Francisco; still more at other centers. In a comparatively short time there had sprung up thousands of cafeterias, many of them with splendid equipment, an atmosphere made attractive by music and other accessories, with marvelous variety of foods, not only in all parts of California and the United States, but even in a number of foreign lands. To the customer, as he moves along with his tray, is temptingly exposed a wide selection of many viands, most of them well cooked and hot. He is free to look, then indicate his choice, then carry his well-laden tray to the conveniently arranged table.

An excellent illustration of the development of the cafeteria is seen in the public school system and institutions of higher learning. Its growth has been so rapid as to bring expressions of amazement from many who for the first time find opportunity of learning the facts at first hand in a great school system like that of Los Angeles.

Richly furnished California cafeterias are specially attractive to multitudes of incoming tourists, particularly those of moderate means. To many of these newcomers it is still a novel experience when a group of easterners, or middle westerners have a meal together at one of the better establishments. And of late—it may be added—some of the better class restaurants and swanky clubs have adopted the practice of offering free choices from bountifully-laden tables of choice viands, known as the *Smörgäsbord*, a name which reveals its obvious Scandinavian origin.

CHAPTER NINE

LITERATURE AND ART

"If some of the conventional figures of military and political history occupy in my pages less than the space usually given them, it is because I have had to find a place for figures little heeded in common history — the figures of the missionary, the poet, the printer, the merchant, or the philosopher." —*John Richard Green*

FIRST BIOGRAPHY

Is it not peculiarly fitting that the earliest California biography should also be the best biography of the "Apostle of California," most renowned among all the great personalities of our entire history?

The most important aspect of the early settlement of Alta California by the Spanish in the latter part of the eighteenth century was in the religious factor, resulting in the establishment of the chain of Franciscan missions: at the head of the first band of missionaries was The Venerable Junípero Serra, Father-President; and it was his biography that was written by his beloved disciple and companion, Francisco Palóu, and published in Mexico in 1787, only three years after Serra's death.

This great book, truly a work of love and deep devotion, is titled *Relación Historica de la Vida y Apostolicos Tareas del Venerable Padre Fray Junípero Serra, y las Misiones . . . Escrita por el R. P. L. Fr. Francisco Palóu, Guardian Actual del Colegio Apostolica de S. Fernando de Mexico*; . . . The book was translated into English by The Very Reverend J. Adam, and published in San Francisco in 1884, under the title *Life of Ven. Padre Junípero Serra*. Another translation by C. Scott Williams, with an Introduction by George Wharton James, was published in Pasadena, in 1913.

Palóu's book is of first importance as a contemporary source of our California history. While the author clearly reveals his personal affection for Father Serra, the biography is full of valuable information not supplied by any other contemporary writer; and certainly no one could have had more intimate contact with his subject than Palóu, his almost constant companion and co-worker. No other work approaches it in its value as a contemporary history of the province of California down to the death of Serra, in 1784.

237

Fray Francisco Palóu, known as "The Loving Disciple," was elevated to the temporary presidency of the missions, to serve until Fermin de Lasuén received the formal appointment. It was at San Francisco, on the last day of February, 1785, that he dedicated his crowning work, the *Vida*. Its publication two years later at the College of San Fernando, Mexico, brought solace to his later burdened years. He had won distinction in his own name, as a Christian leader; he was most devout, always diligent and thorough as a student, zealous as a pioneer missionary, fair-minded and dependable as a historian. There was no one who could match the splendid contribution of the *Vida* and the earlier source book. Referring to the *Vida* Professor Charles E. Chapman has said; "it is considered, and must always remain, the most vitally important work on the early years of the Spanish occupation of California."

Others have told the thrilling story of the life and labors of Junípero Serra, who has been honored with a place in Statuary Hall, in Washington; but in the extensive body of early California literature the work that stands preëminent is the biography by Palóu, first biography of a Californian.

DESCRIPTION OF CALIFORNIA BY AMERICAN

The early Spanish authorities in California had good reason to fear the eager and adventurous foreign traders, including especially those from the United States. From several directions came threats to the dominion of Spain: there was England, following the memorable expedition of Francis Drake; the distinguished La Pérouse of France had paid a visit to Alta California; and increasing danger was seen from Russia, creeping down from the north. But most threatening of all was the lengthening shadow of the "Yankee Skipper."

The trade carried on was usually clandestine and illegal; but since it was so lucrative to the foreign visitors and so beneficial to the isolated Californians themselves, little was done of effective character to stop the unlawful traffic.

One of the early American ships to visit the coast of California was the *Lelia Byrd*, under command of William Shaler. This vessel, which was badly in need of repairs, anchored at San Diego, February 15, 1803, with the object of purchasing otter skins. Shaler ran into serious trouble with the *comandante* of the *presidio*; but he was able finally to effect his escape following the "bloodless battle of San Diego" (March 22). The brig sailed to China, purchased the cargo of another vessel, and had the temerity to return to the California coast.

After Shaler's visit American traders became more and more numerous. They had little difficulty in evading Spanish guards—often half-hearted in their own efforts to keep the traders away, because the people were more than willing to exchange otter and beaver skins for coveted articles on the Yankee ships, including necessities of life and various little luxuries, so eagerly coveted by the Spanish *señoras* and *señoritas*.

Captain Shaler's description of California, *Journal of a Voyage between China and the Northwestern Coast of America*, was first published in the year 1808. It contains a detailed and very interesting description of California, believed to be the first such published account by an American writer. Many of the advantages offered in California are pointed out, and the important document closes with a more than gentle hint of annexation to the United States as highly desirable and believed to be easy of accomplishment. Brief quotations will show why William Shaler has been called by at least one historian the "first American publicity agent for California," a stalwart forerunner of the doctrine of "Manifest Destiny":

> At great expense and considerable industry the Spaniards have removed every obstacle out of the way of an invading enemy; . . . in a word they have done everything that could be done to render California an object worthy the attention of the great maritime powers; they have placed it in a situation to want nothing but a good government to rise rapidly to wealth and importance. The conquest of this country would be absolutely nothing; it would fall without an effort to the most inconsiderable force; and the greatest efforts that the Spanish government would be capable of making towards its recovery would be from the shores of New Spain, opposite the peninsula, . . . In a word, it would be as easy to keep California in spite of the Spaniards, as it would be to wrest it from them in the first instance.

PIONEER NEWSPAPERS

Sam Brannan had decided on the publication of a newspaper in California even before he left New York. He embarked on the 4th of February, 1846, for the long and hazardous voyage to Yerba Buena by way of Cape Horn. It was the last day of July when he entered the Golden Gate. Within a fortnight he had a printing office, and, after considerable delay, the first issue of the *California Star* made its appearance on January 7, 1847.

But meantime, to the great discomfiture of Brannan, another California paper had already appeared: this was the *Californian*, published at Monterey by Walter Colton and Robert Semple, which made its bow to the public August 15, 1846, as California's first newspaper, a small weekly sheet. The old type used, as well as the press, had been brought from Mexico by Zamorano in 1834. The appearance of the *California Star* was mentioned in the *Californian* by Semple, who referred to it as "a small but very neat sheet . . . published and owned by S. Brannan, the leader of the Mormons, who was brought up by Joe Smith himself, and is consequently well qualified to unfold and impress the tenets of his sect." But this did not please Brannan, as is readily seen from the slurring note in the *Star* referring to the rival paper as "a dim, dirty little paper printed at Monterey, on the worn-out material of one of the California war presses. It is published and edited by Walter Colton and Robert Semple, the one a lying sycophant and the other an overgrown lickspittle."

Volume I, No. 1, (August 15, 1846) of the *Californian* is a feeble four-page paper, about 11¾ by 7½ inches, crudely printed on some yellowish cigarette paper that had been discovered and purchased, on the old Monterey press. It was printed one-half in English, one-half in Spanish. This little journal, however, has been fruitfully used by many writers in California history.

After precarious careers, the two papers—*Californian* of Monterey and *California Star* of Yerba Buena (San Francisco)—united to form the new paper, *Alta California*, under the vigorous editorship of Edward C. Kemble. In retrospect, in 1858, Mr. Kemble wrote:

> The *Alta California*, the Mother of newspapers, child of the union of the old Monterey pioneer and the San Francisco maiden press—its lineage extending back through half a dozen civil revolutions . . .—the *Alta*, as it is popularly known, began its career on the 4th of January, 1849.

For years the *Alta* was the leading newspaper of California. Today its files remain an invaluable source to the historian.

Other newspapers were started in considerable numbers, and within a few years they multiplied into the dozens. The first paper of Sacramento was the *Placer Times*, whose initial issue is dated April 28, 1849. Early in 1850 there came from the press the first tiny issue of the *Stockton Times and Tuolumne Intelligencer*. The *Sonora Herald*, established on July 4, 1850, enjoys the distinction of being the first of numerous newspapers published in the California mines.

Several early attempts were made to start a newspaper in southern California, beginning in the spring of 1850. Nothing tangible came out of the project for *The Southern Californian*. Then followed the effort of Theodore Foster, which resulted in *La Estrella de Los Angeles*, a small four-page paper, two pages printed in English, two in Spanish. The first issue of this paper, whose English name (*The Los Angeles Star*) quickly superseded the Spanish, appeared May 17, 1851.

The miners of the stirring new camp of Columbia, now a State Park, clamored for a "home town paper." Therefore the old Monterey press was hauled over the hills and set up. On the 25th of October, 1851, it was to print the first number of the *Columbia Star*, which proved to be extremely short-lived. Regarding its final chapter Mr. Kemble wrote: "As for the *Columbia Star*, it only blinked twice, and was then lost in the glare of the heathenish conflagration it had kindled."

BOOKS BY AMERICANS

Alfred Robinson's *Life in California* is usually regarded as the first book written by an American describing California. It was published in English in 1846 by Wiley and Putnam, New York. Robinson, with headquarters in Santa Barbara, represented the firm of Bryant and Sturgis, who in 1829 sent the first ship from Boston for direct trade with California.

The contents of the book, which has long since become a rare item of Californiana, may be further suggested "as comprising a description of the country and the Missionary establ' hments, with incidents, observations, etc. Illustrated with numerous engravings. . . . To which is annexed a historical account of the origin, customs, and traditions of the Indians of Alta California." A more accessible edition, with Appendix, was published in San Francisco, in 1891.

It should be stated that Robinson's descriptions would require thorough revision for present practical use—vast changes have taken place, as a part of our transforming history. Of much greater value today to the tourist or ordinary student are recent guide-books like those of Aubrey Drury, Hoover, and Rensch, and the *Guide to the Golden State*, compiled and written by the Federal Writers' Project of the W.P.A. But for the collector and the meticulous scholar, Robinson's *Life in California*, the original edition, will continue to be a highly-prized item of Californiana.

However, another book, written by another American, must not be overlooked. I am referring to *Two Years Before the Mast*, by Richard Henry Dana, published in Boston in 1840. Here we have "A Personal Narrative of Life at Sea," which, while not dealing exclusively with California, yet contains a great amount of interesting material touching the manner of life, customs, and activities of early Arcadian days. No single book concerning the period is more widely read today than *Two Years Before the Mast*, prominently listed among the "Zamorano Eighty," a narrative which has appeared in numerous editions and which has long been regarded a classic in its field.

Richard Henry Dana, "a young scion of a well-known New England family," shipped on the merchant vessel *Pilgrim* in 1834, as a common sailor, for the benefit of his health. Of his book he said:

> It is written out from a journal which I kept at the time, and from notes which I made of most of the events as they happened; and in it I have adhered closely to fact in every particular, and endeavored to give each thing its true character.

To the student of California, Dana's fascinating account is particularly valuable for its description and discussion of the fur trade, its side-lights on the condition of the Missions and the Indians, the instability of government, and the method of administering justice. Some of his words now appear almost prophetic, as, after enumerating the marvelous resources of fair California—long sea-coast with good harbors, fine forests, "waters filled with fish," countless cattle on the plains, superior climate, fertile soil—he writes: "In the hands of an enterprising people, what a country this might be! we are ready to say."

THREE PIANOS

There were no pianos in California until near the end of the Mexican period. That did not mean, however, that the people of Arcadian days had no love for music — quite the opposite! Nearly everything the typical Don did, Mrs. Sanchez tells us, "had to have its musical accompaniment, for, like all other Latins, the love of music was in his blood." The old love songs of the chivalrous young serenaders were not to be found in books, to be sure, were not even printed; but they "passed from mouth to mouth in the manner of folk-songs."

The old Californian had no opportunity to hear or learn the kinds of music we are accustomed to. But one might call them born musicians: they could sing their songs and play their guitars with skill and spirit. While their most popular instruments were the guitar or banjo and the violin, others were by no means unknown. For example, there was an orchestra at San Gabriel, composed of Indians, who played flutes, guitars, violins, drums, triangles, and cymbals. Some of the neophytes developed real skill: an Indian band furnished the music for General Vallejo's wedding.

During the later years of the Mexican régime there was a prominent merchant in Monterey, the provincial capital, named Don José Abrego.

An American trader named Stephen (Steven) Smith, who operated out of Baltimore, reached Monterey on his first trip in the year 1841. Being on very friendly terms with the merchant, he suggested to his friend Joe the idea of having a piano to furnish music for the dances, instead of using the guitar and violin all the time. Don José became interested, wanted to know how he could get one, and who would teach them to use it. The enterprising Smith said he could bring both the piano and a teacher out on his next trip. It was agreed!

When Smith reached Monterey on his next trip, in March, 1843, coming around the Horn, he had on board not one but three upright pianos—the only pianos in California! There was excitement among the élite of the staid town of Monterey. One piano was promptly purchased by Don Abrego; General Mariano Vallejo of Sonoma was happy to acquire another; and the third went to Eulogio Céllis of Los Angeles—the stated price of each being $600.

But the American captain also brought out a piano teacher, Professor Andrew Hoeppner, a German. When some time later the young Professor visited General Vallejo at his beautiful Sonoma home, incognito, and actually played the piano, there was real excitement in that home. "Before the evening was over," wrote Myrtle McKittrick, "a bargain had been struck between the two." The contract called for "giving lessons of music at least during five years, or more if it should be necessary, until the complete instruction of the children, both male and female." As compensation the General agreed to give a tract of land "to the extent of two leagues and half long by one quarter of a league wide. . . ." The signing of the contract was formally witnessed by Salvador Vallejo and three other persons. It is stated that the deal was closed months before the expiration date, and that the agreement in Spanish was recorded August 6, 1850. It is not difficult to imagine something of the personal pride and satisfaction experienced by the General, who was then well known as perhaps the wealthiest man in all California, with an unequalled collection of beautiful books, himself a culture-loving leader not to be outdone by any of his contemporaries. On one portion of Hoeppner's land the town of Glen Ellen, in the Valley of the Moon, was afterward established, not far from the celebrated home of Jack London.

According to E. D. Holden, there is no record of the piano sold to Don Céllis; "but both the Vellejo and the Abrego pianos have left their mark, the latter being in existence today [1934] in the possession of Don José's granddaughter." A sketch inscribed above the keyboard reads thus:

This is one of the first three pianos brought to California. Its history is as follows: In 1841 Captain Steven Smith arrived with his vessel in Monterey, and I engaged him to bring me a piano on his next trip to this country. In March, 1843, he returned to this city in a brigantine, he had three pianos on board, I bought this one for $600. He then sailed to San Francisco, where General Vallejo purchased another of the pianos. The third piano was afterwards sold to Captain Eulogio Céllis of Los Angeles.

It thus becomes obvious that the arrival of those three first pianos in Monterey on Captain Smith's ship in the early spring of 1843 was an event of some significance in the cultural life of early California.

CALIFORNIA MAGAZINES

If one may take certain liberties with the definition of "magazine," *The Golden Era* of San Francisco may be given the distinction of being California's first magazine. It was a new sort of venture—a small weekly paper carrying original poems and fiction, with occasional signed articles and the first dramatic department in the state. Franklin Walker has extravagantly pronounced it "the most important journal ever published on the Pacific slope." Its first issue is dated December 19, 1852.

The two young editors were J. Macdonough Foard and Rollin M. Daggett, aged twenty-one and nineteen, respectively. The venture flourished from the beginning. Within a month circulation rose to 2,000, 1,100 subscriptions coming from the northern mines alone. The editors made the claim it found its way "into every city, town, and mining district in the state." It was successful in identifying itself with the people of California in a remarkable manner. Among its contributors were Thomas Starr King, Charles W. Stoddard, Old Block (A. Delano), and "Dan de Quille" (William Wright). It outlived such magazines as *The Pioneer, Wide-West, Hesperian,* and even *Hutchings' Illustrated California Magazine.*

If a more meticulous definition of magazine is adopted, which would exclude certain publications perhaps better described as newspapers, then we may advance the claim of *The Pioneer* to priority. Thus Ella Sterling Mighels, in her valuable *Story of the Files,* pronounces *The Pioneer* to be "the earliest California magazine," a monthly journal beginning in 1854 and continuing regularly for twenty-four months.

In announcing his new venture the editor, Ferdinand C. Ewer, a young Harvard College graduate, said he hoped San Francisco had matured enough to support a monthly magazine carrying the work of those who were "desirous of distinguishing themselves in Poetry, Belles Lettres, and the more flowering paths of literature."

Ewer was able to attract articles of high quality, the contributors including such persons as Frank Soulé, John S. Hittell, John Swett with his poems, and "Dame Shirley," with her famous letters from the mines. Most striking of all articles was the editor's "The Eventful Nights of August 20th and 21st" — "being a peep into mystery of what befalls after death." This unusual piece attracted wide attention among spiritualists, who hastened to welcome Ewer to their belief; but the honest editor assured them that his mystery story was simply the product of his own brain—in other words, a grand hoax.

It may be remarked that the fine quality of *The Pioneer's* contents suggested a high intellectual level among the people of early San Francisco. But the magazine was unable to stem the tide of financial depression of the vigilante days: after a period of two years its career was ended.

Other early magazines of California included *Hutchings' Illustrated California Magazine*, founded in 1856 by J. M. Hutchings, of Yosemite fame, who also wrote "The Miner's Ten Commendments," and *Hesperian*, beginning in 1858, for most of its time a woman's magazine, founded by Mesdames Schulz and Day. At length, in 1868, *Overland Monthly*, under the editorship of Bret Harte, made its appearance. For many years the *Overland* maintained its place as the leading literary periodical of California, and indeed of the Pacific Coast.

ARCHIVES

By archives we mean original reports, documents or records relating to the history or development of any activity, family or other group, community or nation. The scope is extremely broad. The archives of an institution, as the Franciscan Missions of California, constitute invaluable source material for the research historian. Secondary material depends upon the sources for its validity. As Hubert Howe Bancroft pointed out, "The value of archive records is universally understood."

The original documents pertaining to the early history of Spain in America, even long before the entrance into Alta California in 1769, are still, for most part, to be found in Spain, chiefly in the cities of Madrid and Seville. From our standpoint, the most essential parts are housed in the General Archive of the Indies of Seville.

We are indebted to Professor Charles E. Chapman for his elaborate *Catalogue of Materials in the Archivo de Indias for the History of the Pacific Coast and the American Southwest*, published in 1919 by the University of California Press. In these documents are found much of the background of the history of our California. But no one collection, however extensive, is entirely complete in itself. Mexico City is the repository for the Central Archives, so important to the historian of Spanish California.

In making available to American scholars vast collections of documents pertaining to the Spanish and Mexican periods of our history Bancroft rendered a service not even approached by any other worker. While building his famous Library, through employed copyists he transferred to San Francisco thirteen collections, "the originals making about 350 bound volumes of from 300 to 1,000 documents each, besides an immense mass of unbound papers."

The original official papers had been turned over by the Mexican government at the time of the War with Mexico, and were deposited chiefly in the U.S. Surveyor's Office in San Francisco. These included "the originals, blotters, or certified copies of the orders, instructions, reports . . . correspondence" dealing with Spain, Mexico, and the United States, from the year 1768 down to 1850.

The archives of the Franciscan Missions consisted in "old leather-bound registers of baptisms, marriages, burials, and confirmations at each of the establishments. The most extensive collection was at Mission Santa Barbara. Of these Bancroft had extensive copies and compilations made for his growing library.

A further word must be said relative to the service of Hubert Howe Bancroft in preserving and making available thousands of documents and letters bearing on our early history. In approximately fifty collections appears a vast amount of information concerning the leading Spanish families of California, most extensive and valuable of all being his thirty-seven folio volumes of materials from Mariano G. Vallejo, "with not less than 20,000 original papers," of inestimable value.

Parallel to the Vallejo Papers are those of Thomas O. Larkin, in nine large volumes, currently being published by the Bancroft Library under the editorship of Director George P. Hammond. "This collection is beyond all comparison the best source of information on the history of 1845-6, which in fact could not be correctly written without these papers."

More recently, Owen C. Coy has provided a convenient reference in his *Guide to the County Archives of California* (1919). In general, it may be said that the archives of California, here and abroad, particularly pertaining to early Spanish beginnings, are among the most complete of those for all the states of the Union.

A PAINTER OF DISTINCTION

Referring to great California painters, the historian Theodore Hittell in 1897 declared that "few states can boast so bright a galaxy, commencing with the excellent, pioneer work of Charles Nahl and now flourishing in the brilliant, soul-fraught canvasses of William Keith, Thomas Hill, and others."

In any history of art in California, however, a few names would precede that of Nahl in time, though not in culture and artistic ability. Mention must be made of the fact that even in the pre-American period some of the work done by Indian neophytes at certain of the missions. The best of these undoubtedly reveal native talent and promise; but their artistic quality is not such as to concern us here.

In his comprehensive studies on "Art Beginnings on the Pacific," appearing in the first volume of *Overland Monthly* (1868), B. P. Avery has presented a wealth of information. The very first paintings belonging to the American period were not by local artists at all, but were brought in from outside for commercial purposes, hung in saloons and other places of resort. J. C. Duncan was "one of the earliest to introduce and encourage art in a liberal and critical spirit." Among the gold hunters were to be found some artists of merit, who came to dig gold but "remained to paint."

The art record of California may be said to have begun with the work of W. S. Jewett, notably his large oil painting done early in 1850. This is a landscape view from the crest of the Sierra Nevada Mountains, representing "an emigrant family who have just emerged from the wilderness and are catching their first delightful glimpse of the mountain slopes and valley of El Dorado." Jewett's most notable work was the full-length painting of John A. Sutter, which was acquired by the Legislature to hang in the State Capitol.

But because of his special training, his excellent ability, versatility, and his extensive product of artistic quality, Charles Nahl must be given first place among the early artists of California. He was a native of Cassel, Germany, a member of a family of distinguished painters and sculptors. He loved art for its own sake; he practiced his art in San Francisco for many years. He was at home "in portraiture, in still life, in *genre*, in fruit and flowers, and in object painting; equally facile and elaborate in sepia, in pencil, in crayon, in pen and ink, in water colors and oil; . . ." He stood above all his contemporaries in the delineation of the life and character of California. "Yet above all this," declared B. E. Lloyd, "there is a sublimity that does not fail to charm."

He was an artist of enormous industry. He produced many lithographs and etchings, and showed strong predilection for the classic; but, as Eugen Neuhaus has said, it is chiefly as the painter of the life in the California mines, "as lived by an adventurous, polyglot society of Americans, Indians, Mexicans, and Europeans" that Nahl will live in the annals of art.

Perhaps Nahl's best known painting is his "Sunday Morning in the Mines," which has long been a prize in the Crocker Art Gallery, located in Sacramento. This distinguished picture summarizes a segment of his own experiences in the Yuba placers in 1851. In the background appears a saloon, with its gambling brawl, men rushing off to a new "strike," a drunken youth flinging his "dust" away, a prospector in the cabin writing a letter home, and two others doing their weekly laundry. In the foreground is a "cradle," while one pioneer is reading from the Bible to two listeners. As an artistic composition, revealing the life and activities of the gold mining camp on a Sunday morning, Nahl's great painting is without an equal.

From Charles Nahl, the eminent pioneer painter, to William Keith, "Master of California Landscape," is but a step. Both have contributed richly to the culture of the Golden State.

PRINTING PRESS

In the year 1825 a young man named Augustin V. Zamorano arrived in California from Mexico to be secretary to Governor José María Echeandía. Zamorano wanted a printing press; but there was none in that part of the country. He arranged with a Boston sea captain, Thomas Shaw, for the purchase of the needed press and type.

The ship *Lagoda* arrived at Monterey in June, 1834. In its official invoice appears this item: "1 case, Printing Press, type and apparatus, complete."

The Zamorano Press is generally acknowledged to have been California's first. It was "a weather-beaten relic" even at that time, constructed on the old Ramage plan; and the "miserable assortment" of type seemed well-nigh hopeless. No attempt at actual use of the outfit was made for many months. Then an advertisement modestly announced service to the public, at specified rates, "and agreeing at more equitable prices with gentlemen who may wish to establish any periodical."

The most extensive, and probably most important among early products of this first press was said to be Governor José Figueroa's *Manifesto* of 1835, a volume of 184 pages. The following year the celebrated "Declaration of Independence" of Juan Bautista Alvarado was printed.

But, after all, was that the first printing press in California? Mary

Bowman, in her article, "The First Printer in California" (*Land of Sunshine*, Vol. III, pp. 30-31), tells of José de la Rosa, who came to California in 1834 with the *Compañia Cosmopolitano*, and declares:

> Included in their stores of goods and household effects, they brought a supply of type and a small printing press. Don José held a commission from President Santa Ana to do its governmental and ecclesiastical printing. He opened his office in Monterey and carried on the work alone, . . .

Mrs. Bowman reports that when she first met Don José, "he had passed the century mile-post, but time had dealt gently with him." He finally died in January, 1892, at the age of 102 years.

But in his elaborate study on Don Augustin V. Zamorano, George L. Harding states that there is no occasion to doubt that it was he who set up the first printing press in Alta California. However, as to the actual introduction of printing, this, says Harding, "is among the forgotten details of a period that seems more than a hundred years removed." Then he continues: "No one knows what was the first piece of printing done in California, or where, when, and by whom it was executed."

The story of the Zamorano Press is an intriguing one, all the more so because of certain elements of obscurity. It was taken to the headquarters of General Mariano G. Vallejo, at the "northern frontier" of Sonoma, where a small output of documents and pamphlets was issued. But not many years later it was returned to Monterey, where after some further slight use, the dilapidated outfit was "junked" in an old adobe.

Scenes shifted. Aggressive Yankees took over everything—among the Americans was Chaplain Walter Colton of the United States Navy, who was appointed *Alcalde* of Monterey by Commodore Stockton. This stately office demanded the use of a printing press for the "Proclamations" to be issued; and besides, Colton's keen mind saw an opportunity of producing the first newspaper in Alta California. To this end he associated with himself Dr. Robert Semple.

Diligent search revealed the old Zamorano press, "covered with dust and rust, its type all in 'pi,' and its ink-balls mice-eaten." By dint of hard work and the liberal use of oil, Messrs. Colton and Semple won the distinction of issuing, August 15, 1846, the first number of the *Californian*, California's first newspaper.

After being a silent witness to many a vicissitude occasioned by swiftly changing scenes, the old Ramage press was shipped to Sacramento, where, on April 28, 1849, the initial issue of the *Placer Times* appeared—Sacramento's first newspaper. But even that was not the end of the press brought to California by Zamorano. It had surely earned a place in a museum in San Francisco; but there was more work to do! The tent city of Stockton must have its fling: so, early in 1850, the *Stockton Times and Tuolumne City Intelligencer*—a portentous name!—saw the light of day; but not for long. Once more the old press was on the move, this time, as Carl Wheat expresses it, it was "loaded on a wagon and trundled off to the mines." The *Sonora Herald*, first newspaper of the southern mines, had its little day. Then to the proud boom city of Columbia, now a State Park, the over-worked relic was carted, and there the eager miners greeted the *Columbia Star*!

Sad in the extreme is the story that tells of the end of the old press. Because of financial reverses it was sold under execution; then on the night of November 13, 1851, it was taken out into the street, where ruffian vandals built a fire under it, and it was finally destroyed. Said E. C. Kemble, in his history of early California newspapers: "A greater outrage never desecrated the name of an American town, or disgraced American citizenship." A melancholy fate, indeed, for a relic that deserved a place alongside the old press of Benjamin Franklin in our national capital.

"POET LAUREATE OF THE '50'S"

Franklin Walker has given one of the chapters in his valuable book, *San Francisco's Literary Frontier*, the rather striking title "A Rash of Poetry." He tells of the verses of many "aspiring amateurs" of the 1850's, how they "Rhymed wistfully of seasons in New England, farms in Pennsylvania, and friends in Missouri." Favorite subjects were the homesickness of the pioneer, the ravishing view of the Golden Gate, and the majesty of the redwoods as a feature of the West.

If, as Ella Sterling Mighels sadly avers, "Poetry nearly always means glorified starvation for some one," her remark applies with double force to the unpropitious days of California literature in the 1850's. Then again, it would be unjust rigorously to apply the canons of modern literary criticism to the amateurish efforts of the youthful versifiers of the flush times. Still there was no lack of poets, even in those early years.

Among them, the names of three have come down to us probably the most well known—James Linen, John Rollin Ridge, and Edward A. Pollack. Of the three Pollack is given first place—all the more remarkable since he had enjoyed no formal schooling, yet gained a mastery of grammar and rhetoric and found reading his chief source of delight. Even at seventeen he had begun to write for the daily press in his home city, Philadelphia. He came to California in 1852, at the age of thirty.

After working at his trade of sign painting for some time, he began to study law, having become a regular contributor to the magazine *Pioneer Monthly* in 1854. He was duly admitted to practice law in the State Supreme Court. But he died on the 13th of December, 1856, which limited his literary career to a very brief period. He had won the high esteem of his contemporaries in San Francisco. A volume devoted to his verse, including a number of memorial poems by Frank Soulé and others, was published in 1876. He was called "Poet Laureate of the Fifties."

Among Pollack's poems 'The Falcon," "Olivia," and "The Chandos Picture" are said to be some of the best known; but his "Evening" (or "How the Clouds Come Through the Golden Gate") reveals him at his best. The first lines have been most frequently quoted, beginning—

> The air is chill, and the hour grows late,
> And the clouds come in through the Golden Gate, ...

And in the closing lines we find an outreach and graceful dignity that befit the true poet:

> For Heaven's kind, and everything,
> As well as a winter, has a SPRING.
> So, praise to God! Who brings the day
> That shines our regrets and fears away;
> For the blessed morn I can watch and wait,
> While the clouds come in through the Golden Gate.

Beginning with the "Flush Days of the Comstock" there was no dearth of writers, of both prose and poetry—"everything was in the high tide of a rushing and riotous régime." There were Joe Goodman and Rollin Daggett; then John Swett and May Wentworth, as well as still others. Miss Wentworth rendered a real service to early California literature in preparing a volume of verse, *Poetry of the Pacific*, which was published in 1866—in this is preserved, in compact form, the best of the California poetry of the early period. In her Preface she cautions the reader in these words:

> But it must be remembered that California is still an infant State — a Hercules in the cradle. The toiling goldseekers have had but little time or encouragement to cultivate *belles lettres*, and to the future we look to develop the rich mines of intellect as well as those of gold and silver.

Indeed, it was not long until our most illustrious writers, including poets, made their appearance—Bret Harte, Charles Warren Stoddard, Joaquin Miller, and then the "Loved Laurel-Crowned Poet of California," Ina Donna Coolbrith.

CHINESE NEWSPAPERS

Among the almost innumerable claims to distinction advanced by China one is that of publishing the first newspaper in the world. Tradition dates the *Peking Gazette* back to the tenth century of the Christian era.

The first Chinese to come to California had been attracted by that powerful magnet — gold. By the summer of 1852 there were close to 20,000 of them in the new state. The revulsion of feeling from referring to them as "our Chinese fellow-citizens" to the opprobrious "John Chinaman" had come to be almost universal, introducing a turbulent chapter in our state history.

In the early 1870's the appearance of a weekly newspaper, *The Oriental*, using Chinese characters, issued from a lithographic press, served to inform the Chinese population of the excitement their presence occasioned. For this paper, which attained a circulation of 700 copies, Fung Affoo was translator. The price was $5.00 a year. Historically it is regarded as of secondary importance.

In 1881, in the year preceding the enactment by Congress of the Chinese Exclusion Law, there arrived in California a youth of fifteen who had the courage to be different. This was Ng Poon Chew, of alert mind and active spirit. He had studied under a Taoist monk: in San Francisco, however, he became an active Christian, identifying himself with the Presbyterian Church.

As an unusually keen observer, eager to adopt American methods, he had the imagination to conceive of a Chinese newspaper in California. His friends laughed at the idea—who would be found to read a Chinese newspaper in San Francisco? But he was not to be discouraged. In 1898 the *Wah-Mei-Sun-Po* came out in Los Angeles as a weekly paper, with Ng Poon Chew as editor. But the weekly proved to be short-lived.

Two years later the *Chung-Mei-Yat-Po* made its appearance in San Francisco, as the first Chinese daily newspaper in America. Associated with Ng Poon Chew, managing editor, was Professor John Fryer, well-known authority on Chinese literature at the University of California. The only interruption in the continuous publication of this paper through many years was occasioned by the upheaval caused by the earthquake and fire of 1906.

Mr. Ng Poon Chew, eager to adopt Western methods in journalism, seized the occasion of a certain murder in San Francisco to convert his entire staff into "a corps of detection to work up" the case, thus jumping his paper in a single day to up-to-date journalism.

The wide-awake editor won considerable distinction and enviable popularity, at a time when the anti-Chinese feeling was still strong. He gained remarkable mastery of the English language, was called upon more and more frequently to address groups of Americans as well as Chinese. He was invited to give Chautauqua lectures and to speak at teachers' institutes, where he became a special favorite. He contributed richly toward a better understanding between Chinese and American, fully convinced that closer mutual acquaintance would bring increased good will.

To illustrate the scope of his activities, this editor-statesman was elected to membership in the American Academy of Political and Social Science, the Commonwealth Club of California, and other civic and religious organizations, even becoming a thirty-second degree Mason. Academic distinction was accorded him when the University of California conferred upon him the honorary degree of Doctor of Letters. The fine humor and wholesome spirit that delighted his audiences won for him the friendly title "Chinese Mark Twain."

By 1902 there were four Chinese daily newspapers in this country. But the first of these, *Chung-Mei-Yat-Po,* edited by Ng Poon Chew, is of greatest interest to us: its resourceful editor fairly won for himself a place in California's Hall of Fame never attained by any other of his countrymen.

It may be noted that in San Francisco and Los Angeles have at different times been published a number of newspapers in different languages. One of the earliest of these was the San Francisco *Journal,* in German, edited by Julius Froebel, which first appeared February 20, 1855.

FIRST POET LAUREATE

The only woman member of that coterie of distinguished California writers which included Francis Bret Harte, Charles Warren Stoddard, Mark Twain, and Joaquin Miller was Ina Donna Coolbrith (christened Josephine Smith). While not a native Californian, her love for the Golden State was surpassed by that of none other. Her kindly spirit, unfailing loyalty, and intellectual brilliance conspired to produce a personality that matched the charm and inspiration of her immortal poetry.

This "Sappho of the West" was given the unique distinction of being made "The Loved Laurel-Crowned Poet of California" by a resolution unanimously adopted by both houses of the legislature, on the 21st of April, 1915. (Edward Pollock has already been referred to as "the poet laureate of the fifties.") In this joint resolution Ina Coolbrith is cited as having "brought prominently to the attention of the world the glories and beauties of California forests and flowers, its climate, its scenery, its wealth and possibilities through the many brilliant poems, and she has contributed to the high standing of our literature, thereby winning the admiration and gratitude of all loyal Californians."

She had been a frequent contributor to the magazine *Overland Monthly* by invitation of its first editor, Bret Harte; other journals were happy to publish her musical verse. Her book *A Perfect Day and Other Poems* appeared as early as 1881; but the volume *Songs From The Golden Gate*, published in 1895, is probably her best-known book.

Ina Coolbrith, who in early life had experienced much sadness, lived to enjoy her title of Poet Laureate for almost thirteen years. She died in Berkeley, February 29, 1928. Later the title was bestowed on Henry Meade Bland, son of a pioneer Methodist preacher and teacher in the University of the Pacific and San José Normal School, who in turn was succeeded by John Steven McGroarty, well-known author of the Mission Play. After the lapse of a number of years, Gordon W. Norris, author of *Golden Empire*, was selected for the honor.

It was Ina Coolbrith, graceful lover of California, who set the high standard, as California's first Poet Laureate.

> She kept the sacred fires of romance burning;
> She was the vestal virgin of your shrines.

CHAPTER TEN

EXPOSITIONS — PAGEANTS

"History has its foreground; and it is principally in the arrangement of the perspective that one artist differs from another."
—*Macaulay*

FOURTH OF JULY CELEBRATION

In his important book, *Sixty Years in California*, William Heath Davis,
pioneer of 1831, refers to what appears to be the first elaborate celebration of the Fourth of July in the territory. This occurred at Yerba Buena,
later San Francisco. Much detail of the gala event is revealed in the
Scrapbook of Jacob P. Leese, who had arrived in California in 1833, and
lived mostly in Los Angeles until 1836. Then, moving to Yerba Buena,
he began construction on his house and store on the first of July,
Continuing the account:

> By the 'Glorious Fourth' the roof was placed in place—the sailors of
> the three vessels then lying in port had come to his aid—and the Stars and
> the Stripes were thrown to the breeze. Bunting and decorations were found
> aboard the *Don Quixote*, which also carried Leese's goods; an orchestra
> (a drum, a fife, a flute, a clarinet, a bugle and a violin) was assembled;
> and two 6-pounders from the Presidio supplied the necessary explosive
> din for a fitting celebration of the Fourth which ended on the Fifth.
> Besides the banqueting hall, there were erected a number of small tents
> in which to house his guests comfortably, for during the preparations
> Capt. [William A.] Richardson was kindly proceeding across the bay to
> Sonoma to invite all the principal families from that neighborhood as
> well as the chief residents of the country nearer by. Two events—each
> great in its way—were to be celebrated. First, the First Independence Day
> in California, and second, the arrival of Mr. Leese to the country, his
> welcome and house-warming. . . . The guests were happy as mortals could
> be and in short, all went merry as a marriage bell.

That Yankee captains who chanced to be cruising along the California coast remembered Independence Day there can be no doubt.
And that sometimes the Mexican authorities manifested a friendly
spirit seems equally clear. As perhaps a typical instance, W. H. Thomes,
in his book *On Land and Sea*, referring to the year 1843, the ship having

reached San Pedro from Santa Barbara on the 30th of June, reports, quite informally:

> The captain had been invited to spend the Fourth of July at the Pueblo. Mr. Foster procured him a horse, and we rowed him ashore on the afternoon of the third. He was got up in a gay style, but, for a wonder, did not wear his white beaver hat. . . . He told Mr. Prentice to celebrate the day in a becoming manner and to fire a salute of thirteen guns morning and evening, and to give the men plum duff, and half a bottle of Boston sherry for each person, except the boys. . . . The next morning we washed down the decks, and at 8 o'clock trimmed the ship with flags, fore and aft, and fired thirteen guns in good shape, . . .

Captain John A. Sutter has told us of an early celebration of the Fourth at New Helvetia (Sutter's Fort), soon after the American conquest, in the year 1848. "This was the first July 4th in the country under the American flag" wrote Sutter, "and all of us were in festive mood at such a happy circumstance." Governor Richard Mason and Captain William T. Sherman participated in the elaborate celebration. Excellent food was served, including delicacies which Sutter had recently purchased from a French vessel. "We also had sugar, fowl, game, beef, and many luxuries beyond the station of frontier existence" —so reported generous-hearted Sutter. One might readily guess the major theme of Philosopher Pickett, orator of the day.

But it now appears that Sutter was not entirely accurate in his statement, "This was the first July 4th in the country under the American flag." To be sure, the Treaty of Guadalupe Hidalgo, ending the war with Mexico, was not signed until early 1848; but the Capitulation of Cahuenga, which ended all opposition to American rule, is dated January 13, 1847 —this virtually completed the conquest. It was at Fort Moore in Los Angeles, named after Captain Benjamin D. Moore of the First United States Dragoons, that there was held an Independence Day celebration in the year 1847: this event, therefore, is claimed as the first Fourth of July celebration in California *under American rule.*

The building of Fort Moore was never entirely completed. It was located along the easterly line of what later become North Broadway at its intersection of Rock Street. Complete plans extended in a southerly direction, in front of the old High School grounds, for a distance of nearly 400 feet. Dedication of the uncompleted Fort took place at the celebration on Independence Day.

Because of the recent revolutionary physical changes in that section of metropolitan Los Angeles with the coming of the great automobile freeway system, the precise spot would now be virtually undiscoverable except for the historical marker placed to identify the site, one of the truly historic spots in Southern California.

FIRST THEATERS

The drama, in some of its many and varied forms, was very popular among early Californians. During the Mexican régime the *fiesta* and frequent celebrations were not lacking in the dramatic element. American pioneer settlers and gold hunters demanded entertainment, and plenty of it. As Lloyd wrote in his *Lights and Shades in San Francisco*, "the real life drama was a shifting panorama of tragedy, comedy, burlesque, and farce intermingled." The hardy '49-ers were only too glad to welcome entertainers, though the actual performance was sometimes of dubious quality.

There has been not a little controversy about the first theaters in California. This has been occasioned largely by confused meanings and uses of the term. When referring to the theater is it the physical structure, or building, that is meant? or the theatrical performance in a building erected for that specific purpose? or merely some kind of show that might be called a theater, irrespective of the physical setting? Obviously no single date or place could apply to all these meanings. The zeal for a favored location, expressed in a spirit of local patriotism, has also been a source of confusion. If there happens to be an established tradition in a town or community, the people there are loath to accept any contrary evidence, however authentic.

According to Bancroft; "The first public dramatic performances are claimed for the United States Garrison at Sonoma, in September, 1847, and for an amateur company, chiefly Californians, at San Francisco." Contemporary references to this company are found in *The Californian* (first newspaper) in October of that year, and later dates.

The building at the corner of Pacific and Scott Streets in Monterey is claimed as California's first theater: this was an adobe building erected in the year 1847, by Jack Swan, a pioneer of 1843, as a lodging home for sailors. Members of Stevenson's Regiment contracted with Swan to put on a play in the building. This play, titled "Putman, or the Lion Son of 1776," was presented in 1848, the first paid public performance, it is claimed, in California.

The adobe building fell into a state of disrepair: it was variously used as a drug store, curio shop, tea-room, "and other humdrum purposes." Not until 1937 was action taken to restore the theater, and the first performance in the refurnished building took place on June 3rd of that year. The reconstructed building is visited yearly by throngs of tourists as one of the many significant landmarks of historic Monterey, capital of the province before the American conquest.

But another city comes forward with its claim. Here is a statement by no less authority than Constance Rourke, in *Woman's Home Companion*, for May, 1928:

> And at Sacramento in October, 1849, the first complete theatrical performance in California was given in the new Eagle Theater, a small affair of canvas walls with a roof of sheet iron upon which the rain beat a smart tattoo. . . . The stifling interior of the theater boasted a dress circle and a parquet, the stage had a drop curtain.

The Eagle Theater opened October 18, 1849, with the "Bandit Chief" as its attraction. Reporting the opening night the *Placer Times* of October 20, 1849, says:

> The house opened to a full, and we may add, fashionable house, for the dress circle was graced by quite a number of fine looking, well costumed ladies, the sight of whom was very revivifying.

It may be of interest to add that at the "Eaglet," offspring of the Eagle, dedicated one hundred years later to the day, the California Historical Society held its meeting, Saturday, April 15, 1950.

To the old Eagle Theater, located on Front Street, erected at a cost of $80,000, goes the honor of being "the first structure erected expressly for theatrical purposes in California." Tickets sold at $3 and $5 in gold dust, valued at $12 an ounce. For a stage packing boxes were used; seats in the second tier were reached by means of step-ladder. The initial run was for a period of three weeks.

Illustrative of the fact that San Francisco quickly became the theatrical and musical center of the West, mention may be made of the successful appearance of a burlesque, "The Lady Killer of San Francisco" January 15, 1855, and of a new play, "The Daughter's View" (written by M. M. Noah); the following month Mozart's opera "Don Giovanni" was brought out with full cast March 8, and in April Mme. Anna Bishop, assisted by distinguished artists, gave a special rendition of Hadyn's celebrated oratorio, "The Creation."

In the backward *pueblo* of Los Angeles the first regular theatrical entertainment came in 1859. In the meantime the theater had become a prominent feature in all the mushroom towns in the north and in every important mining camp. San Francisco had become the great metropolitan center—lavish entertainment abounded there, often including artists and players of national renown.

THE CIRCUS

The Americans who came to California in the early mining days displayed an eagerness for musical and dramatic entertainment that seems quite surprising. Scarcely second to the theater and the musical troubadour was the circus performer. In short, the typical 49-er in California was entertainment-hungry.

In a big tent on Kearny Street, near Clay, San Francisco, was presented the first circus performance in California, on the 29th day of October, 1849. The show was advertised as Rowe's Olympic Circus. It was headed by Joseph Andrew Rowe, who as a young boy of ten had "started down the sawdust trail"—that was in 1829. After varied experiences in foreign lands, including parts of South America and the West Indies, he had reached San Francisco on the 12th of October, 1849.

Rowe was the founder of the Olympic Circus. The company included Mrs. Rowe, Master Rafael Lowe, William H. Foley, Signor and Signora Levero, Messrs. Stevens and Long, and Mr. Westcott was the ringmaster. Foley took the part of clown. There was fancy horse riding, and the Leveros specialized in rope dancing. The performance of Rowe's favorite horse, "Adonis," was such as to win immediate tribute from the *Alta California*. The prices of admission were, $3.00 to the pit, $5.00 to the boxes, and $55.00 for a private box. As we read in *Lights and Shades of San Francisco*, "day after day, and night after night [Rowe] entertained hundreds of eager spectators by feats of equestrianship and other performances ordinarily enacted in the circus ring."

From San Francisco the circus proceeded to Sacramento, and afterwards provided entertainment at other centers of population, meeting with a good degree of success. It is easy to imagine the delight such performances afforded the amusement-hungry miners of the gold days.

According to reports, Rowe's success was even greater in Australia, where the circus was said to be the first "to delight those antipodal residents." The fortunate founder returned to San Francisco at a later date with upwards of $100,000—a very large sum for those days—which made it possible for him to purchase the beautiful Rancho Santa Anita in Southern California.

Shortly following Rowe's Olympic Circus came the Foley Circus, which performed on Montgomery Street, near California Street. Then, in natural course, came others, though at rather remote intervals. What was known as "Circus Lot" was located on Jackson Street, at Montgomery. The appearance of the circus was infrequent because the transcontinental trip was long and difficult, and towns west of the Missouri were few and far between.

First to bring a circus across the plains, partly by railroad train, was John Wilson: his was a wagon show, without zoo. In Los Angeles the old Plaza and Stearn's Hall were leading places of amusement. It was in the Plaza that the Paris Exposition Circus performed in January, 1869.

With the completion of the Pacific Railroad, circuses came in greater numbers, the first with a real menagerie being Cole's, in 1878. After that, all of the popular circuses added California and the Pacific Coast to their circuits — there were Sells Brothers, Barnum, Bailey, Ringling, and still others.

STATE FAIR

The California State Fair, held annually, heads the impressive list of local expositions in the Golden State. For many years this has been the gala event of the capital city, Sacramento, beginning usually in late August and ending on or near Admission Day, September 9. It is managed and controlled by the California State Board of Agriculture, whose members are appointed by the governor.

Men who had been scouring the hills of the Mother Lode for yellow gold heard accounts of agricultural and horticultural wonders—reports trickled back home in letters to the folks. Knowledge that a marvelous destiny awaited California not only deflected the miners but brought new migrations to this land of superlatives. Tales of the well-nigh unbelievable fertility of soil—a pumpkin of 129 pounds, a watermelon crop worth $8,000 an acre! — were heard in the land: hundred per cent boosters may not have been very many, but they made themselves both numerous and vocal!

A group of progressive pioneers met one day in San Francisco in 1854, "to work for the State's development agriculturally, and to arrange for and conduct the first exposition of the State's products." Chief credit for starting the movement should be given to a thrifty Yankee '49er, Col. James L. LaFayette Warren, one of the far-seeing pioneers who perceived that California "can get more gold by tilling the soil than by mining it."

Then came the first California State Fair, held in San Francisco, in October, 1854. Agricultural products were displayed in a down-town hall, but the livestock exhibits were held at Mission Dolores. Exhibits were brought in from various districts on freight wagons drawn by mules and oxen. As reported in the *Alta California*,

> One hour spent in Musical Hall will afford more information concerning the vast agricultural resources of our beautiful State than could be acquired by traveling about for weeks from place to place. Flowers of every hue,

rare plants, mammoth vegetables, pictures, wax works, shells, minerals, agricultural implements, etc., displayed with much taste, form a beautiful picture.

The first Fair was pronounced a success. Immediately plans began to be formed for a second and larger one the next year, at Sacramento. For 1856 San José was selected as the site; in 1857 the Fair was held at Stockton and the following year at Marysville. The disadvantages of perpetual migrations were perceived, however, and in 1859 there was a return to Sacramento. After a spirited contest an amendment to the constitution of the Agricultural Society put an end to the discussion as to locality. The amendment states: "The society shall hold an annual fair at the city of Sacramento."

A contemplation of the numerous and diverse functions of the California State Fair awakens real admiration for the minds conceiving them and working with devotion for the advancement of the commonwealth. Charles W. Paine, for many years Secretary-Manager of the exposition, said in 1929:

We look upon the State Fair as a great show window for all California, and we regard it as an institution in which every resident of the State should take sincere pride and interest.

After six years of war-time shut-down the Fair reopened in 1947. Thus it becomes a permanent institution, greater and more impressive year after year, attracting hundreds of thousands of attendants. It provides an excellent medium for visualizing the unparalleled development of the State of California.

INTERNATIONAL EXPOSITION

The early fondness of Californians for holding fairs did not fully express itself in local county fairs, the larger State Fair, or even the National Orange Show—advertised as "California's greatest mid-winter event." There must be a great event of international significance.

When the colossal Columbian Exposition at Chicago was approaching its closing days in the autumn of 1893, certain fertile minds by the Golden Gate conceived the idea of holding in San Francisco a really big world's fair, which seemed entirely feasible if a large and hitherto unavailable collection of fine exhibits from all countries, already in the United States and assembled at Chicago, could be attracted to the Pacific Coast, thus furnishing the nucleus of an unprecedented exposition in California.

Back of the idea was the sober fact that San Francisco, like all parts of the country, had been suffering a grave business depression, even appeared to some to be on the verge of financial collapse. Prominent San Franciscans wanted to do something to divert the public mind from an imminent crisis. This thought was well expressed by Mike de Young, publisher of the *Chronicle*, who deemed it an imperative necessity that "something should be done to rescue the city of San Francisco from a commercial collapse." De Young's statement continued:

> I think it was a clear apprehension of the existing state of affairs that caused the suggestion to hold a Mid-Winter Exposition in San Francisco to be taken up and pushed with energy. . . . To all dissuading arguments the answer was promptly made that it could not injure California to make the attempt to hold an exposition, and that the fruits of success would be all the more appreciated because of the obstacles overcome.

On the last day of February, 1894, less than three months after the closing of the Columbian Exposition at Chicago, the California Mid-Winter Exposition was formally opened. San Francisco was host to an international fair second only to those of Paris and Chicago, an accomplishment that was brought about "without the gift of a single dollar from the nation, state, or municipality"—funds had been derived from voluntary subscriptions and contracts with concessionaires.

Thus was added another significant achievement to the many that marked the prodigious development of the rapidly growing State.

Prominent among exhibits were samples of the products of agricultural and horticultural industries. Mineral resources shown included not only the elaborate displays of gold, but also silver, copper, quicksilver, marble, onyx, and numerous others. Appropriately enough, there was a replica of Sutter's Fort and the cabin of James W. Marshall. The Fine Arts Building contained master paintings from France, Germany, Russia, Italy, Spain, and the United States. The many educational exhibits were noteworthy.

That the Mid-Winter Exposition was a success as a dignified form of advertising and promotion none will be disposed to deny. Moreover, it contributed generously to the upbuilding of a mutual understanding and spirit of unity within the state itself. The overall results are well expressed in the words of James D. Phelan:

> The Exposition argues for the taste and civility of a people who, until recently, were regarded in certain quarters as semi-barbarous, with Bret Harte as their best exponent. What Nature has done for California the Fair has done for her people. It has also exhibited to the world that God's bounty and man's enterprise were united on the Pacific Coast.

Other and subsequent international expositions in California, following the example of the Mid-Winter Fair, have done much to focus the world's attention upon the Golden State. These have included the Panama-Pacific International Exposition, officially opened February 20, 1915, when President Woodrow Wilson touched the key that closed a circuit at the wireless station at Arlington, Virginia; the Panama-California Exposition, which followed almost immediately and remained open during the year 1916, in Balboa Park, San Diego, transforming the Park into a place of rare charm and beauty; and more recently, the great Exposition on Treasure Island in 1939, which brought together a larger collection of famous masterpieces of painting than had ever been assembled in the Western Hemisphere.

INCEPTION OF THE MISSION PLAY

Of all the more recent lovers of the old California of the Mission Period and of the Arcadian Days of what Gertrude Atherton called "the Splendid Idle Forties," none showed greater affection or more complete dedication than John Steven McGroarty—he was possessed of a fervor that was truly evangelistic; his love for his subject was both passionate and esthetic.

And yet he was not born in California. He was a native of Pennsylvania. And he studied to be a lawyer, was admitted to the bar in 1894, and pracitced law two years. He came to California in 1901: almost immediately he began writing. Later he entered the field of practical politics, serving two terms in Congress (1935-39). But his was really the soul of a poet—his perennial subject was "California,"

> Where the hand of God hath flung it
> Down the middle of the world.

For many years McGroarty contributed regularly to the *Los Angeles Times*, especially the Sunday magazine section. Perhaps his most popular poem, "Just California," appeared in 1903; his volume *California—Its History and Romance* was published in 1911. One of his highest honors came to him in 1933 when, following the death of Henry Meade Bland, he was by vote of the state legislature made third Poet Laureate of California. Among his many other honors were the degrees of Litt.D. from the University of California (1925) and LL.D. from the University of Santa Clara (1927) and the presentation of his bronze bust to Los Angeles Museum, in October, 1934. His legions of friends knew him best as "Singing John, the Songster of the Green Verdugo Hills." His lovely home, nestling in the hills above Tujunga, was his castle.

Most brilliant and most effective of all his writing is the famous

"Mission Play," representing the first notable attempt to dramatize the story and achievements of the early California Missions under the devoted leadership of Junípero Serra. Fortunately we have his own account of the inception of the Play. Here it is:

> In the spring of the year 1911 I received a message from Frank Miller to spend a week-end at the Mission Inn to discuss with him a matter in which he was deeply interested. The following Sunday morning we walked together up the trails of Mt. Rubidoux to the great Cross on the summit erected in memory of Fray Junípero Serra, founder of civilization, Christianity, and the old Franciscan Missions in California. And there, that sunny morning, in the shadow of the Cross, Mr. Miller informed me of what was on his mind.
>
> He had lately returned from a trip to Europe where he had witnessed a performance of the Passion Play at Oberammergau, during which he was inspired with the idea of a Mission Play for California. Upon his arrival in New York he sought out his friend, Dr. Lyman Abbott, then editor of the *Forum*, and laid his idea before him. Dr. Abbott was enthusiastic over it and suggested that Dr. Henry Van Dyke, then professor of English literature at Princeton University, be chosen to write the play. Mr. Miller immediately contacted Dr. Van Dyke, who was equally enthusiastic, but who regretfully realized that he could not undertake the task for the reason, as he said, he would have to spend at least four years in California among the Old Missions, saturating himself with their romance and history. "You will have to find your man in California," Van Dyke told Mr. Miller who, after reaching home, went up to Stanford, at Palo Alto, to consult with his very close friend, Dr. David Starr Jordan.
>
> "Van Dyke is right," said Dr. Jordan. "You must get a Californian for the work." "But," said Mr. Miller, "who is he, and where am I to find him?" Whereupon Jordan replied, "You have him down there under your very nose. John McGroarty is the man for the job."
>
> So, that was how and why Frank Miller chose me to write the "Mission Play." He ensconced me and Mrs. McGroarty in the Mission Inn with all its vast facilities, comforts and hospitality at our disposal, and where, in due course of time, the manuscript of the Play was brought to a conclusion. . . . And so with his help and the help of others, a theater was erected for it under the shadow of the historic walls of Mission San Gabriel, in which the first performance was given on the evening of April 29, 1912.

The première was indeed a gala occasion. Since then the Play has been staged thousands of times and seen by several millions of delighted people.

The Mission Play is a "pageant-drama, sprung from the soil," the introduciton of Christian civilization to the western shores of North America. In it are graphically portrayed the glamor and romance of Old

Spain, the labor and self-sacrifice of the pioneer fathers, the garnering in of the rich harvest after the toil of the neophytes, and the beautiful singing and graceful dancing of the youth to the manner born. The specially constructed scenery helped to enhance the total effect of the unique pageant-drama.

With the renowned veteran Frederick Warde as Serra, ably assisted by Patia Power as Señora Josefa Yorba, and more than a hundred carefully selected players, the presentation was both a revelation and a sensation.

The first of three acts opens on the shores of San Diego Bay, in the historic year 1769. Between Act I and Act II there is an interlude of fifteen years. The locale of Act II is Carmel Mission, the loved residence of Father Serra—it is now 1784. The grandiose *Fiesta*, amidst the gaiety of youth and love and laughter, is full of brilliance and color—the pretty *señoritas*, the gallant *caballeros* and the richly gowned women, with Indians in full regalia: it is a scene never to be forgotten. Act II is at the ruins of San Juan Capistrano, 1847. All is sorrow and lamentation at the decline of the Missions and the ruthless seizures by the Mexican government. But, perhaps the *Americanos* will restore these broken walls.

The restoration of the old California Missions has gone forward with strong momentum since the death of McGroarty, August 7, 1944—each year they are visited by thousands. The present desire to see the presentation of the Mission Play revived and made traditional in our annals cannot occasion surprise—it is a part of the heritage of the Californian.

"CALIFORNIA'S OBERAMMERGAU"

Presented each year, at a series of evenings in Nature's own ideal theatre in the Hollywood Hills, is "The Pilgrimage Play," or the Life of the Christ, which has been called "perhaps the greatest demonstration of American ideals of good living that exists today."

This is a transcription of the World's Supreme Drama based upon the Four Gospels of the New Testament, as conceived and founded by Christine Wetherill Stevenson. To the gentle spirit of this devoted woman the heavenly vision unfolded itself until the matchless drama of Christ became an exalted reality. In it we see the greatest tragedy and behold the highest triumph of the human race. The Pilgrimage Play embraces the perfect ministry of Christ's life; it is produced in the exact words of the New Testament, and is free from any taint of sectarianism.

The first notable performance of "California's Oberammergau" was given on June 20, 1920. By now performances are numbered in the thousands. After a decade, presentations were for some years intermittent on account of war conditions. But long since it has become a great Southern California tradition, bringing spiritual exaltation through the highest forms of the theatrical arts. It speaks to old and young, consecrated saint and wayward sinner alike.

It is deemed an honor to be invited to have even a humble place in the large cast. To appear in the Christus rôle is indeed an exalted sacred privilege.

The Play is presented in a small natural amphitheater in El Camino Real Canyon off Cahuenga Pass, just outside the business center of Hollywood. The highest type of artistry has been invoked to perfect the setting. The finest, most effective modern lighting is employed with consummate skill, so that the effect of it all, with the bright stars overhead, is inexpressibly beautiful. Following the brief Prologue there are twelve episodes, closing with the touching Epilogue of Promise, with tender song and marvelous light—

> Lo, I am with you always
> Even unto the end of the world.

For its keynote the musical setting has the spirit of noble simplicity. "It does not obtrude upon the simplicity of the scenes in the wilderness"; it is subordinated to the drama, and it serves to symbolize the high spiritual concept of the Play. Year after year improvements in the wonderful setting and effective presentation have been introduced under the direction of The Pilgrimage Play Association and its Production Board: the central Story of Christ remains unchanged.

Christine Wetherill Stevenson has wrought a good work. She has added richly to the cultural and spiritual values of California. In "An Appreciation" Idah McGlone Gibson wrote:

> Among these everlasting hills a woman walked. Into her brain a vision stole—a vision of Love Divine. Straightway she went about her business of making others see.

GREATEST OUTDOOR PLAY

Helen Hunt Jackson's *Ramona* has been pronounced the "classic California romance of all time." The poignant story is "noble in conception and majestic in execution." It lends itself perfectly to dramatization and to pageantry; though it was four decades after its completion by the author before it was presented as a spectacular outdoor play by the twin cities of Hemet and San Jacinto. In this locale it was that "H.H." found some of her leading characters and many a stirring incident which cause her story to throb with human interest.

The script of the drama is the work of the late Garnet Holme, author of "Taquitz, the Desert Play." The inaugural of this gripping Indian melodrama, "Ramona Pageant," in the Ramona Bowl, near Hemet, in Southern California, where the natural stage is an entire mountainside, took place in the spring of the year 1923. Since that date the matchless drama has been witnessed by more than half a million persons, attracted from every quarter of the globe.

The presentation is always set in the early springtime, usually the last two week-ends of April and the first week-end of May, six performances in all, pridefully produced by the people of the two cities. The love idyll of beautiful Ramona and her Indian hero, Alessandro, has been reënacted by a cast of as many as 350 persons, the selection for the title rôle and that of the young captain of the sheep-shearers being drawn from the top ranks of the dramatic world. Because of interruptions occasioned by war the Silver Anniversary production occurred not in 1948 but in 1952.

Ramona Bowl, with a seating capacity of 6,000 persons, is picturesquely located in a canyon on the lower slopes of Mt. San Jacinto, in Riverside County, thirty-four miles from Riverside City. The paved automobile highway leads to within seventy-five yards of the amphitheater.

The approach of the quaint troubadours, strumming their guitars, brings back the scenes of Arcadian California of more than a century ago. The succeeding episodes connected with Camulos Rancho and the Exile, followed by the highly dramatic Epilogue with its grand finale, in the marvelous outdoor setting where the rugged mountainside serves as the stage—all this so vividly depicts the unforgettable scenes that the thrilled members of the great audience seem again "to see events of decades ago transpire before their very eyes."

Helen Hunt Jackson won literary immortality by presenting to the world her book *Ramona*, in 1884. After almost forty years the vivid drama inspired by the book and prepared by Garnet Holme, was given its première presentation—this was in the spring of 1923. Both book and pageant will live on and on as part of California's glorious heritage.

PASADENA ROSE TOURNAMENT

"Pasadena, the Crown City," "its streets blazoned with banners and decked with foliage"—such rhetorical phrasing is but a modest introduction to the reality of the Annual Rose Tournament, greatest of all the innumerable pageants of the fiesta-loving West. Each New Year's Day lovely Orange Grove Avenue, lined during past decades with palatial homes, and Colorado Street, main business artery of the city—usually a busy mart of trade with heavy lines of motor traffic—are transformed by some magical touch into incredible but actual wonderland. To this wonderland have come, even from the far corners of the land, hundreds of thousands of excited people—come to see and enjoy the marvel. It is the Tournament of Roses—among all California fiestas it stands unique and unapproachable.

The idea that germinated and finally developed into the famous Tournament dates back to 1888, when Charles F. Holder met with a group of ladies and gentlemen to organize the Valley Hunt Club, whose initial purpose was "to hunt jack-rabbits, foxes, and mountain lions with horses and hounds." Then inspiration came from witnessing the Carnival of Flowers at Nice, in France. For the actual founding of the tradition in Pasadena the individual who deserves chief credit was this same Dr. Holder, nature lover, sportsman, conservationist, author, and philanthropist.

A bright idea had been born and was taking definite, concrete form. At the beginning that was to produce a combination fête, fiesta, and tournament "to celebrate in poetic and beautiful manner the ripening of the orange," which took place about New Year's time in Pasadena. It was proposed as a fitting expression of nature's bounty in the San Gabriel Valley, in mid-winter. Some wished it called "Tournament of Oranges," but it was finally agreed to christen it "Tournament of Roses" —a name now known around the world.

A governing board for the non-profit organization was created, called "Tournament of Roses Association." In 1907 the first Queen was selected and invited to preside in state, with all her lovely attendants. For the royal entourage, each New Year, a particularly beautiful float is officially designated. As an indication of the magnitude of which the spectacle has attained, as early as 1925 more than half a million persons crowded the city to witness the "flower epic," a wonder parade of elaborately designed and faultlessly prepared floats, with their millions upon millions of fresh flowers, on New Year's Day. Nowhere else can such pageantry be witnessed.

Scarcely second to the gorgeous parade of flower-banked floats, running into hundreds, there has been during recent years the Annual Rose Bowl Football Game, a culminating contest staged in the afternoon, between the champion of the Pacific Coast Conference and a rival selected from among the best of eastern teams.

Great and wonderful is the Pasadena Tournament of Roses, witnessed and enjoyed by ever-enlarging throngs, each successive New Year's Day.

If this New Year a million and a half of people enjoy the *fiesta*, we may be sure there will be more next New Year. In one simple phrase the message of the superlative pageantry is, "The Southland is an invitation to health, happiness, and prosperity."

ROSE BOWL FOOTBALL GAME

The Annual Rose Bowl football game played at Pasadena each New Year's Day, now regarded as a classic, has become a major sports event of the nation. The Rose Bowl itself has become the grand-daddy—or grandmother, if you prefer—to a whole flock—or tribe—of "bowls" now scattered over the country of more recent birth—or christening. We now have the Sugar Bowl, the Potato Bowl, the Cotton Bowl, the Salad Bowl, and still other bowls—totalling at least a score—where football is also played on or near New Year's Day.

Back in the good old days of tall bicycles and horse-drawn carriages, the first of all New Year's football games at Pasadena, as a follow-up of the famous Tournament of Roses, was played in 1902—and what a game that was! It is an understatement to say that it was not a pronounced or unqualified success, as is clearly evidenced by the cold fact that no more games of the type—East *versus* West—were played until the year 1916.

The opposing teams in the 1902 game were Stanford University and the University of Michigan. The Stanford players, then known as the Cardinals, had won only three games during the season, had tied two and lost only to the University of California. Southern California was then years away from membership in anything like the Pacific Coast Conference. Representing the East was famous "Hurry-Up" Yost's "point-a-minute team" of Wolverines, which during the season had remained undefeated and had piled up a total of more than five miles gained!—all on the ground; for that was long before the day of the forward pass.

The second half of that game came near to being a literal slaughter—for Stanford. The record tells of one player "pressed into service despite a broken collarbone," of another who remained in the game fifteen minutes "with a broken leg and two broken ribs," and of a third casualty with a cracked collarbone. The final score—Michigan 49, Stanford 0. Obviously the time was not ripe for West *versus* East football.

But not everything was lost. James Wagner, then president of the Tournament of Roses, who had almost been run out of town for threatening to bankrupt Pasadena when required to give a $3,500 guarantee, came out on top financially—the great attendance of 50,000 had left a game profit of $4,000.

The four-horse chariot races that were put on as the afternoon attraction for a number of years proved to be no match in drawing power for intercollegiate football. The annual game was resumed, and was played at Tournament Park until 1923, when it was switched to the now world-famous Rose Bowl. The Bowl has been improved and enlarged several times, to its present capacity, but still is totally inadequate to meet the incredible demand for seats.

It must be said that, taking the series as a whole, the Pacific Coast Conference has given a fairly good account of itself against the selected eastern teams. It appears rather remarkable that up to the 1954 New Year's game the score-board showed a perfect balance between sections, of sixteen victories, sixteen defeats, and three tie games.

Of the western teams the Trojans of Southern California presented the best records—eight victories and two defeats. But the teams from the west for 1955 and 1956, Southern California and California at Los Angeles, respectively, suffered defeat. The popularity of the game remains undiminished: by television it is now witnessed each year by millions of "fans" from all over the nation—and beyond.

OLYMPIC GAMES

It had long been thought impossible to secure the great Olympic Games for California. But Los Angeles has the habit of deleting that word from her vocabulary and boldly announcing to the world, "It shall be done!"

Probably no man ever painted a more roseate picture or uttered more optimistic words of prophecy regarding the future of Los Angeles in population and material greatness than William May Garland. In the year 1921 Garland was a central figure at a luncheon attended by the four publishers of the leading Los Angeles newspapers. These were: Harry Chandler of the *Times*, Edward A. Dickson of the *Evening Express*, Max Ihmsen of the *Examiner*, and Guy B. Barham of the *Evening Herald*. Garland pointed out the sharp competition among nations for the Olympic Games, also stating that if the International Olympic Committee should decide in favor of the United States, there inevitably would be competition between such cities as New York, Philadelphia, Chicago, and others. Nevertheless, he boldly declared that Los Angeles was accustomed to doing things in a big way, and the Games could be brought to Southern California, provided the local newspapers would unite and pull together.

Garland's challenge was accepted by the publishers; a Citizen's Committee was constituted, the Community Development Association organized, and architect John Parkinson was engaged to submit a design for a great Sports Arena in Exposition Park.

Mr. Garland was selected as one of the two representatives from the United States on the International Olympic Committee. At the first opportunity a formal invitation was prepared and presented from Los Angeles to that body to hold the Tenth Olympiad in the City of the Angels. The ground-work had been well and skillfully laid; the invitation was accepted.

The huge Memorial Coliseum was constructed; the newspapers engaged in an intensive campaign of publicity, departmental directors and staff assistants were appointed, and Mr. Garland himself was indefatigable, visiting Europe repeatedly to confer with international officials.

July 30, 1932, was a proud day for the proud city of Los Angeles, for then it was that the Tenth Olympiad formally opened, every seat in the vast Coliseum being occupied, the entire arena beautifully bedecked with the flags of all the participating nations. From every standpoint the Olympiad was a pronounced success. The attendance exceeded that of any predecessor, twenty new Olympic or World athletic records were established, the world's athletes were admirably housed and cared for in the specially provided Olympic Village, and the Community Development Association was able, at the conclusion, to announce a handsome clear profit instead of a deficit.

It was one of the grandest exhibitions of pageantry ever witnessed in California. The closing day, August 14, 1932, was indeed spectacular. The array of the world's best young athletes stood in regimental order before the reviewing stand. After complimentary words from William May Garland and Count de Baillet-Latour, the impressive spectacle was feelingly brought into happy memory amidst the strains of "Aloha."

"SYMPHONY UNDER THE STARS"

It has been truthfully said that even from the earliest days of the Spanish régime Californians were fond of music. The guitars and the violins "furnished colorful romantic airs to gladden their hearts in the evening and on feast days." Many of the Indians were strongly attracted by the music, some of them developed real talent.

But it is a far cry from the simple rhythmic music of the gay *fandango* and the monotonous singing in the churches to the acme of perfection in the rendition of the world's choicest symphonies under the stars, in the beautiful amphitheater now known everywhere as the Hollywood Bowl.

Through the munificent generosity of William A. Clark, Jr., the Los Angeles Philharmonic Orchestra of 100 talented musicians was founded, in 1919. Almost immediately this group took rank as "a cohesive virtuoso musical body." Some of the nation's most famous soloists were brought to Los Angeles to enrich the programs offered by the orchestra in its numerous concerts. Distinguished conductors were engaged..

But in the year 1922 a unique feature was inaugurated that was both charming in itself and of high cultural quality. This was what has become internationally known as the summer festival of music in the great open-air amphitheater nestling in the Hollywood hills—"Symphony Under the Stars."

The beginnings of this captivating feature date from 1921, and to the genius and administrative ability of Mrs. Artie Mason Carter and the open-handed sponsorship of Allan C. Balch, Los Angeles, are we chiefly indebted for the successful launching of this inimitable enterprise in Western musical history.

The first guest conductor, for 1922, was Alfred Hertz. And now, year after year, each succeeding summer has brought to the music-loving public eight to ten weeks of "Symphony Under the Stars," presented magnificently by the Los Angeles Symphony Orchestra, under the batons of internationally distinguished conductors, with the participation of world renowned soloists. Here is a phenomenon that has no exact counterpart anywhere.

Many factors have contributed to make the Hollywood Bowl a spot of great distinction: certainly one of the greatest of these is the grand music festival of each successive summer. The seating capacity of the Bowl is about 22,000, and the natural amphitheater possesses remarkable acoustic properties. Located on Highland Avenue, south of Cahuenga Boulevard, it is within easy access to the people—and countless throngs have availed themselves of the matchless opportunity.

Two persons—among the many—must be given individual mention for their very special contributions toward the perpetuation and continued success of the festival; these are, Mrs. Leland Atherton Irish and Harvey S. Mudd, whose devotion to things artistic and cultural has known no bounds. But the musical history of Los Angeles can never be completely written without high tribute to L. E. Behymer, outstanding impressario. From his coming to Los Angeles stems the real history of music in the metropolis of the Southwest.

CHAPTER ELEVEN

MISCELLANEOUS

"The ideals of California are not found in geography, or in climate. They are found, as elsewhere, in the spirit."
—Ephraim D. Adams

OLDEST LIVING THINGS

The opinion is here advanced that the oldest living things not only in California but on the face of the earth are trees found in the Sierra Nevada Mountains. For a good many years the awe-inspiring California Big Trees (*Sequoia gigantea*), in the belief held by competent authorities, have been accorded the distinction. The Big Trees, found in a number of groves, are not to be confused with the taller, graceful redwoods (*Sequoia sempervirens*) of the California Coast Range, though both species are commonly known as "redwoods."

For the better part of a century people have been asking, which individual tree is the oldest living sequoia, and just how old is it? The answer still is, nobody knows to a certainty. There have been innumerable guesses by novices, and many painstaking estimates by experts. In 1896 David Starr Jordan too hastily made the statement: "It is safe to say that many of them have stood on earth at least 8,000 years." He would undoubtedly revise his estimate downward today.

John Muir once spent a day in clearing away the burnt surface of "a majestic old fire-scarred monument," and with the aid of his pocket lens "Counted a little over 4,000 rings, showing that this tree was in its prime about twenty-seven feet in diameter at the beginning of the Christian era." He wrote: "No description can give anything like an adequate idea of their singular majesty, much less their beauty." Following Muir's observations there has been a great deal of scientific investigation.

Not long ago James Clifford Shirley, ranger naturalist of Yosemite National Park, came out with the declaration: "The Sierra redwoods (*Sequoia gigantea*) as a class are no doubt the oldest living things in existence." Professor Willis Jepson determined (within limits of slight error) the age of one tree to be 3,226 years; and Frederic Douglas, after making a boring into the great "General Sherman" tree, expressed the

273

opinion that it is more than 3,500 years old. It was believed that the "General Sherman" and the "President," of Sequoia National Park, and the "Grizzly Giant" of Yosemite National Park, are the very oldest of all trees, each being in excess of 3,000 years. Which one of these is actually the most aged—nobody knows.

But what about the claims advanced for the "Bennett Juniper" (*Juniperus occidentalis*), discovered by Clarence K. Bennett in 1932, located some six miles by trail south of Sonora Pass Highway from Brightman's Flat, in the mountains of Tuolumne County? This venerable tree, about eighty-seven feet high, had a ground diameter of twenty-one feet six inches, its first limb being nearly six feet in diameter. It stands now in almost perfect condition. After long study Mr. Bennett has estimated its age at more than 6,000 years.

However, Dr. Waldo S. Glock, authority on tree rings, after estimating the age of the Bennett Juniper under three different methods, concluded that it is somewhere between 2,900 and 3,250 years old. He said: "It may well be that the age is distinctly more than 3,000 years; but until the entire stump is visible the exact age will not be known."

And now comes the claim that the unimpressive dwarf brisslecone pine (*Pinus aristata*), found near the town of Bishop in Inyo County, is oldest of all. Dr. Edmund Shulman, having made extensive studies of these trees, which he refers to as "Methuselah pines," believes three of them to be 4,000 years old. Further investigations are still under way. Isn't it all the more wonderful if California possesses *three* distinct varieties of the oldest living things!

Thus we find no definitive answer to the question, which individual tree, or even species, in California is actually the oldest. But until the juniper and the pine entered the contest it did seem safe to accept the statement of James Shirley, that the *Sequoia giganteas*, "as a class are no doubt the oldest living things in existence."

It may be added, briefly, that great age has been claimed for the Joshua tree (*Yucca brevifolia*). But only in the unrestrained imagination of the untrained tourist can the age of this remarkable "lily" be placed in the thousands of years. The giant cypress of Tule, in southern Mexico, has likewise been called "the oldest and largest tree in the world," its age placed by some as high as 6,000, or even 10,000 years. It is indeed a picturesque, marvelous tree: but Dr. Jepson expressed this opinion: "Liberals among scientists think it may be 2,000 or 2,500 years old. Honors for antiquity among trees therefore seem to remain with the Sequoias." Today we must content ourselves, with all due modesty, by concluding that if still older trees than any now known are discovered anywhere, they will probably be in California!

CHILD OF WHITE PARENTS

Much interest has been shown in the questions, who was the first child of white parents born in California? and, when and where did this event take place?

This question, and others of like character, may hold more significance for the antiquarian than the historian: nevertheless, a brief statement of the main points involved may be of sufficient interest to us to merit a place here.

Obviously, when we refer to a "white person" we must define our terms: but it may be sufficient for present purposes simply to state that it applies to a person with a white skin, or a member of the Caucasian race. In the present case, the "white person" really means non-Indian and non-Negro, which practically narrows down to Spanish.

Interested persons have done considerable research work trying to find a truthful answer to the main question: still, any findings will doubtless be subject to explanation or interpretation.

In Chapman's *California, The Spanish Period* these words appear: "Sergeant Francisco Soto, who thirty-seven years before [1776] had attained the distinction as the first child of the conquering race to be born at San Francisco." In the first volume of Eldredge's *History of California* the writer, referring to the old mission registers of baptism, has this to say:

> The first entry in the register is the baptism of Francisco José de los Dolores Soto, son of Ignacio and Barbara Soto, of the Anza party, the first white child born on the site of the present city of San Francisco, though not the first born in this state; that distinction should probably belong to the boy born on Christmas eve near the summit of the San Jacinto Mountains, to parents whose names were not mentioned either by Anza or by Font. José Soto was baptized August 10th. The second baptism was that of María Lorenza Sanchez, on August 25th.

However, Winifred Davidson of San Diego, after delving into the old mission records, reported, in 1941:

> Examination of the restored "First Book of Baptisms" at San Diego shows that the first white child of white parentage in what is now the State of California, may have been Joseph Francisco María de Ortega, the son of Lieutenant Don Francisco de Ortega, the discoverer of San Francisco Bay, and Doña María Antonia Victoria Carrillo, his wife. The

baptism of this child in February, 1775, is recorded in entry Number 431, which is signed by Father Vicente Fuster.

For some time historians had believed, apparently with good reason, that the distinction of being the first white child born in California belonged to Salvador Ygnacio Linares, born December 24, 1775. It was only after the discovery of the Ortega entry by members of the San Diego Historical Society that any question about the priority of the birth of the Linares baby, known as "California's Christmas Child," was raised.

In the light of the new evidence brought to light, Mrs. Davidson reached this conservative conclusion:

> Perhaps when time has cleared away all questions regarding him [Don Joseph Francisco María de Ortega] a fitting marker will perpetuate the fact that on what old San Diegans still call Presidio Hill was born, in February, 1775, the first white native son of the golden west.

Among many other "first births" in early California history may be noted the case of Jacob Leese, whose California wife gave birth to a daughter, named Rosalie, on the 15th of April, 1838, claimed to be the first child born in Yerba Buena.

But to Thomas O. Larkin and his wife Rachel goes the distinction of being the parents of the first children born in California "whose parents were both from the United States." Larkin had arrived at Monterey April 13, 1832.

FIRST LADY OF DISTINCTION

The fourth Spanish governor of the province of Alta California was Don Pedro Fages: he had been preceded by Portolá, de Barri, and de Neve—his own tenure extending from 1782 to 1791. Several years before his appointment to the governorship Don Pedro had married Doña Eulalia Callis, "a Catalan lady of quality"—that made her the *Señora Gobernadora.*

No lady of such distinction and importance had ever been in Alta California: and even now, when Don Pedro went to take up residence in Monterey Doña Eulalia, with young junior, Pedrita, remained behind. But Fages wished them to be with him; and after strong urging by husband and friends, she consented to go and join the governor at Monterey. The journey of the distinguished pair up from Mexico was an occasion of great rejoicing—grand receptions and ovations all the way from San Diego to Monterey. Troops, settlers, Indians—even the Mission Padres—hastened to do honor to the high-born Spanish lady—

the first of her quality to visit the northern settlements. Her arrival, which meant the beginning of social life, "marked an epoch in the history of the province."

But the bliss of the lady and her spouse was short-lived indeed. The conditions she found at the outpost of civilization were shocking to the sensibilities of Doña Eulalia. The uncouth, naked Indians, with their strange ways, were too much for her long training and feeling. But she endured her surroundings until the birth of a daughter (August 3, 1784); then real trouble began. She insisted on leaving.

When Don Pedro refused her leave to go, matters became rapidly worse. The irate *Señora Gobernadora* virtually banned her husband from her presence; at length she brought accusations of infidelity against him "in a torrent of words."

California's first lady of distinction turned out to be a real California firebrand. Pedro Fages was capable of ruling his people with at least a fair degree of success; but when it came to governing his wife in California he had no success at all! While he was away on a tour of duty he asked one of the good *padres* at Mission San Carlos to care for Doña Eulalia. She was forcibly taken to the mission; but her conduct there was far from that of the serene demeanor of the accustomed religious atmosphere under Franciscan *padres*. The sorely tried missionaries were driven by her continued violence to the point of threatening her even with stripes and handcuffs. Fortunately, they did not actually resort to these measures.

It may be recorded that after a quarrel of unprecedented bitterness and violence for a whole year the Don and his Doña were reconciled, in the autumn of 1785—something the governor had devoutly desired all along. Still Eulalia never did reach a condition of happy contentment in Monterey. Her heart was set on her husband's removal from office and their return to New Spain.

In the end she had her way—Fages finally asked to be relieved, and was succeeded in office by José Antonio Roméu, in the year 1791. One cannot help wondering how California's first lady of distinction would have conducted herself if she had been introduced into Alta California in the happy Arcadian Days of "Splendid Idle Forties" instead of into the crude, repulsive scenes of an earlier period that so deeply offended her finer sensibilities.

FIRST ELOPEMENT

Henry Delano Fitch was a dashing young American sea-captain. He has been described as "tall, blue-eyed, ruddy; a laughing and care-free, though shrewd Yankee." Señorita Josefa Carrillo, daughter of Don Joaquin Carrillo of San Diego, was an acknowledged favorite of southwestern society of that day—a real beauty of somewhat haughty bearing. She yielded to the spirited protestations of the bold master of the brig *María Ester*, who quite won her heart; her parents consented to the match, and kindly Friar Menéndez agreed to perform the marriage ceremony. It looked like for once there was nothing "to prevent the course of true love from running smooth."

It was in the year 1826 that Josefa (whose true name was María Antonia Natalia Elijia) first saw Henry Fitch. Fifty years later she confessed that her heart had been easily won "by the engaging manner and handsome person of the young mariner." The following year (1828) he announced his intention of becoming an adopted Mexican citizen: in 1829 he was baptized into Catholic faith under the name Enrique Domingo Fitch. All was in readiness for the wedding at the parental mansion.

The guests had assembled, excitingly awaiting the ceremony. Father Menéndez had actually begun the traditional service: then suddenly and dramatically the unexpected happened! An uncle of the bride, Domingo Carrillo, burst excitedly into the room, his right hand held forbiddingly high, shouting, "Stop! His Excellency Governor José María Echeandía forbids the unlawful marriage!"

Truth to tell, the Governor himself had been an unsuccessful suitor for Josefa's hand. But when the bridegroom urged the good friar to proceed with the ceremony with all haste, in fear he replied, "I dare not." Consequently, the wedding was not consummated. However, the priest was still disposed to be friendly: he confided to Enrique that there were other countries where the rules were not so stringent.

Then it was that gallant young Pio Pico, Josefa's cousin, came to the rescue by agreeing to assist in an elopement. "Late on the following night," records Nellie Van de Grift Sanchez, "the girl silently slipped out of the house and met her cousin, who awaited her on a swift horse. Swinging her to the saddle before him, he galloped to the spot where, by previous arrangement, the anxious lover had a boat waiting."

The rest of the story is quickly told. The good ship *Vulture*, riding at anchor off-shore, was soon reached: before morning the happy young couple were out on the broad Pacific, *en route* for Valparaiso. There, two months later, they were married by the curate. It was indeed a daring elopement, all the more memorable because elopements in those times were virtually unheard-of.

Don Enirque became one of California's great *rancheros*. His Rancho

Sotoyome contained eleven leagues of land, and was stocked with 14,000 head of cattle, 1,000 horses, and 10,000 sheep. He held various offices under the Mexican government, was engaged in the shipping business with Abel Stearns and associates. He died at San Diego at the early age of forty-nine, leaving eleven children. At the site of the town of Healdsburg, Sonoma County, is a picturesque peak named Fitch Mountain which perpetuates his memory.

CALIFORNIA BOOSTERS

Singing the praises of California is about as old as the history of California itself. Boosting and boasting—terms often quite synonymous—have been contemporary with each succeeding period since the discovery by Cabrillo, only a half-century after the grand event of Columbus. Cabrillo was delighted with the beautiful bay of San Diego and the land to the north was proclaimed a "goodly country."

A letter written by Sebastian Vizcaíno on the 23rd of May, 1603, led at least one writer to dub him the first booster of California. To his majesty the King of Spain Vizcaíno wrote about Monterey Bay:

> . . . it is all that can be desired for commodiousness and as a station for ships making the voyage to the Philippines; . . . This port is sheltered from all winds, while on the immediate coast there are pines from which masts of any desired length and size can be obtained . . . ; a great variety of game, such as rabbits, hares, partridges and other sorts and species, . . . and flying birds of all kinds, . . . This land has a genial climate, its waters are good and it is very fertile. . . . game such as deer, . . . bears, . . . and many other animals.

So optimistic and enthusiastic was Vizcaíno's description of "the famous harbor, sheltered from all winds," that it deceived Captain Portolá in his search for Monterey in 1769, and brought about the accidental discovery of San Francisco Bay!

Some of the distinguished foreign visitors to California during the Hispanic period might readily qualify as boosters in the light of their historic reports. Three of these are mentioned here.

In connection with the Nootka Sound controversy George Vancouver was sent out by England in 1792. In all he made three visits to California, which afforded excellent opportunity to observe conditions. His monumental report published in 1798, elaborates on the beauty, charm, and natural resources of the sections he inspected.

Captain William Shaler brought the American brig *Lelia Byrd* to anchor at San Diego February 15, 1803. He made two voyages to California, and published his narrative in 1808—"first known description of

California by an American writer." After describing in detail the natural resources of the country and revealing the weakness of the Spanish control, his report daringly continues:

> The conquest of this country would be absolutely nothing; for it would fall without an effort to the most inconsiderable force; . . . The Spaniards have few ships or seamen in this part of the world; the arsenal of San Blas would be their only resource on such an occasion, and that might be very easily destroyed. . . . In a word, it would be as easy to keep California in spite of the Spaniards, as it would be to wrest it from them in the first instance.

Little wonder that Cleland refers to William Shaler as "the first American publicity agent for California."

The French navigator Eugene Duflot de Mofras prepared a complete narrative of his explorations of the Oregon territory and the Californias during the years 1840, 1841, and 1842. His extensive report was published in 1844. Referring to the entertainment of the Spanish aristocracy, it appeared to him that "the young people were either riding on horseback or dancing all the time." But perhaps it would be deemed inaccurate to call these explorers avowed boosters.

Another Frenchman, however, might qualify as a real booster, or promoter. Regarding him we quote the words of John Bidwell:

> In November or December of 1840, . . . I came across a Frenchman named Roubideaux [Antoine Robidoux]) who said he had been to California. . . . His description of California was in the superlative degree favorable, so much so that I resolved if possible to see that wonderful land, and with others helped to get up a meeting at Weston and invited him to make a statement before it in regard to this wonderful country. Roubideaux described it as one of perpetual spring and boundless fertility, and laid stress on the countless thousands of wild horses and cattle. . . . He said that the Spanish authorities were most friendly, and that the people were the most hospitable on the globe; . . . His description of the country made it seem like a Paradise.

Bidwell himself, a pioneer of 1841, might fairly be accounted a promoter of more dignified type, from the time of his reference to Napa Valley, which he first visited in the spring of 1842, as "the nearest approach to an earthly paradise he had ever seen."

Still another, among many, must be cited for his real affection for pastoral California during the unique Arcadian days. This was Guadalupe Vallejo, who afterward wrote with much warmth and nostalgic sentiment of his home-land:

"It seems to me," he said, "that there never was a more peaceful and happy people on the face of the earth than the Spanish, Mexican, and Indian population of Alta California before the American conquest. . . . we often talk together of the days when a few hundred large ranches and mission tracts occupied the whole country from the Pacific to the San Joaquin. . . . we shall always be especially proud of the traditions and memories of the long pastoral age before 1840."

Included among early American propagandists are Thomas Farnham, Hall J. Kelley, and Lansford W. Hastings. Sam Brannan, of all Californians of that period, may justly be called self-appointed booster plenipotentiary. It would be impossible to name all the boosters belonging to the '49ers—they have been immortalized by Joaquin Miller. Every typical pioneer belonged to the Noble Order of California Boosters—with the exception of the luckless few like "Jeremiah Saddlebags," and even he long since became a rare classic in our early literature.

Climaxing the profession of the promoters, after the Chamber of Commerce had become a potent influence in California, was the superb performance of men like Frank Wiggins and William May Garland in Los Angeles, William C. Ralston and Mike De Young of San Francisco and James McClatchy of Sacramento.

OLD GLORY IN CALIFORNIA

When did the Stars and Stripes first float over California soil?

The confident reply from thousands is: "It was the seventh day of July, 1846, for on that morning Midshipman William P. Toler, under instructions from Commodore John Drake Sloat, raised the American flag over the Custom House at Monterey. The event signalized the American conquest of the province of Alta California."

But wait! Captain John C. Frémont antedated Sloat in raising our flag; for it was in the early spring of that year that he intrenched himself on Gabilan Peak on receiving Castro's peremptory order to leave the country. He hastily constructed a fort of logs. "While this was being built," he wrote in his *Memoirs*, "a tall sapling was prepared and on it, when all was ready, the American flag was raised amid cheers of the men." This episode occurred on the 5th of March, 1846, preceding the raising of the Bear Flag at Sonoma by several months.

Yet Frémont was not the first to raise the Stars and Stripes over California soil. In the autumn of 1842 Commodore Thomas Jones of the United States Navy was led to believe that Mexico had declared war on the United States; and rumor was afloat to the effect that California was about to be ceded to Great Britain for safe keeping. Therefore on the 19th of October, 1842, at the command of the Commodore, the Mexican flag was hauled down and the Stars and Stripes hoisted at the Monterey Custom House. Being convinced the next day that he had been mistaken, and that war did not actually exist, and that therefore the seizure of Monterey was premature, Jones ordered the flag to be pulled down, and with apologies restored the place to the Mexicans, then retired with such grace as the circumstances permitted.

Wrong again! At the historic house built by Jacob Leese in Yerba Buena (San Francisco) there was an enthusiastic celebration of the Fourth of July, 1836, described on another page. On that gala day an American flag was unfurled to the breeze—a full decade before Sloat's appearance at Monterey.

Once again! In 1829 Captain James Arthur visited California on the *Brookline*. Arthur's party went ashore to cure some hides—it was a lonesome time for the men. The idea occurred to them to prepare and raise a flag for the purpose of attracting attention of one of the vessels that occasionally sailed near the offing. The flag was made out of men's shirts, which furnished the colors—red, white, and blue. Captain Arthur afterwards wrote: "These men raised our national ensign, not in bravado, nor for war and conquest, but as honest men to show that they were American citizens and wanted company." And in his fascinating book *On Land and Sea*, which bears some resemblance to Dana's *Two Years Before the Mast*, William H. Thomes wrote:

> It is not generally known, but, nevertheless, it is a fact, that Captain James P. Arthur hoisted the first American flag that ever was seen on the shores of California. This was done at San Diego, in 1829, over the hide house of which they had charge. He made the flag out of blue and red flannel shirts, and showed it one day when an English frigate dropped anchor at the port, to the astonishment of the natives of Great Britain, who had no idea of seeing our national ensign in such an out-of-the-way place.

Who will come forward with a still earlier date? The impromptu act of Captain Arthur proved to be prophetic as well as picturesque and patriotic. It was like a finger pointing the way to Manifest Destiny.

NATURALIZED MEXICAN CITIZENS

In the nature of the case, California could not be expected to remain in a state of complete isolation. As more and more young men of adventurous spirit became acquainted with its attractions through reports of navigators and by actual visits, some were inevitably led to wish to settle in the country and try their own fortunes. Early foreigners included not only Americans, but also men from England, Scotland, Ireland, and Russia, although the Americans were strongly in the majority.

But the laws of Spain—later, of Mexico—were distinctly adverse to the permanent residence of these early foreigners, especially since most of them were not of the Catholic faith. Nevertheless, previous to the year 1830 there were to be found in California close to 500 foreigners, most of them young men, with varying status as to citizenship. By 1846 the number had more than doubled.

The story of the beginnings of this segment of population, with their adoption into Mexican citizenship, is an interesting one, though often slighted by historians. As early as 1814, a young Englishman, John Gilroy, whose real name was Cameron, arrived in California. Before being permitted to settle, he was baptised a Catholic, as Juan Antonio María Gilroy. In 1819 he received formal permission to marry: two years later, at San Juan Bautista, he married María Clara, daughter of Ignacio Ortega. Bancroft refers to him as "an honest, good-natured old sailor-ranchero, well-liked by everybody, much too fond of his grog and cards, careless and improvident." His name is perpetuated in the town of Gilroy, near the southern end of Santa Clara Valley.

Only four years after the arrival of Gilroy, Joseph Chapman appeared with the Bouchard expedition, but decided to remain in California. He was baptised in 1822 at San Buenaventura, and in the same year he was married at Santa Inés into the Ortega family. He became a general favorite and was a man of unusual versatility.

After another four-year period William Hartnell, another young Englishman, arrived. In 1824 he was baptised at San Carlos: the following year he was married to María Teresa de la Guerra. His naturalization was completed in 1830.

Others, whose names are familiar in California history, came. William G. Dana lost no time in falling in love with Josefa Carrillo, young daughter of Don Carlos; but was impatient at having to wait for baptism and naturalization. However, following his baptism in 1827 he was married to Doña Josefa the same year, though his formal naturalization was not completed till 1835. There were Alfred Robinson and Abel Stearns, arriving in 1829. Each year brought some addition to the immigrant roll. Most of them were unattached young men of dynamic quality and adventurous spirit; a majority of them were from the United States; and most of them sought wives from the aristocratic Spanish families of the soil.

It is not difficult to understand why they were attracted to the young *señoritas*, "who with their flashing black eyes, luxuriant tresses, and radiant complexions, were beautiful; all were vivacious, warm-hearted, industrious, and domestic in their habits." Nor is it strange that the hearts of the dark-eyed damsels were easily won by their ardent lovers; for, as Mrs. Sanchez has admitted, "the blue-eyed, fair-haired strangers were heroes of romance to them, and many of them vowed never to marry any but a man with the admired *ojos azules.*" The only objection came from young men of Spanish blood, who were jealous of their more energetic rivals.

During the first years of the Mexican régime political conditions in California were very unsettled. Such laws as there were could not be well administered — naturalization of foreigners followed no clearly defined formula. A naturalization law was passed by the Mexican Congress, however, in 1828, during the governorship of José M. Echeandía. It required all candidates

> to become Roman Catholics, to prove two years continuous residence in the country, to have a useful trade or occupation, to show good character, to renounce allegiance to all other nations, to swear to support the constitution and the laws of the republic. . . .

Following the governor's circular announcement a number of candidates were presented, including William Dana, John Temple, John Gilroy, William Richardson, and (the following year) William Hartnell. Numerous others, most of them Americans, were naturalized during subsequent years. A notable exception is seen, however, in Thomas O. Larkin, who refused to become a Catholic and who married an American woman.

That the vow to become a Catholic was often, though not always, taken lightly, and with mental reservation, is well known—the large land grants were eagerly desired. Also, at the time of the American conquest there arose the anomalous situation in which adopted Mexican citizens spontaneously supported the American cause, thus clearly revealing their deeper loyalty.

CHILDREN OF AMERICAN PARENTS

It was an American wedding; but also *"Al Modo Español!"*

Tom Larkin had arrived at Monterey, California, in April, 1832— alone. He had decided to remain true to his New England tradition and personal convictions, and, unlike many of his countrymen, he formed no matrimonial alliance with a Spanish *señorita.* But on board the *Newcastle* he had learned that Mrs. Rachel Holmes, who was *en route* to her husband in Honolulu, had become a widow. After brief correspondence, marriage had been agreed upon—Tom and Rachel.

Since neither had renounced the Protestant faith, and California was Catholic territory, the marriage ceremony was performed in 1833 at sea, under American auspices, by U.S. Consul Jones of Honolulu. The wedded couple disembarked at Santa Barbara, where a memorable celebration (*la gran fiesta de bodas*) awaited them. *La señora Yanqui* was to live among the Californians. The first night's entertainment did not end till the break of dawn. Then for several days there was feasting and games and dancing. Therein lies the claim that Rachel Holmes Larkin was the first American woman to reside in California.

The first child in the Larkin family was Thomas Oliver Larkin, Junior, born April 13, 1834—the first child of American parents born in California.

In 1840 the family included also two other sons and a daughter. In later years there were three more children. In order that they might enjoy the benefits of education and parental tradition, they were sent away, as they grew up, to other lands of preferred culture. Thomas, Junior, went to the Sandwich Islands, where he remained as a student several years.

Another interesting first is seen in the arrival of the wife and infant daughter of Benjamin Kelsey, reported as "first American woman and child to reach California by the overland route direct from the States." The Kelseys were members of the Bartleson-Bidwell party, of 1841. The name Kelsey in our California geography fittingly perpetuates the names of three pioneer brothers—Benjamin, Samuel, and Andrew Kelsey.

It may be noted that Mrs. Mary Young Walker, wife of Joel P. Walker, arrived overland in California some twenty days before the arrival; but Mrs. Walker came by way of Oregon.

Still another item relevant to this story may be mentioned. One of the important immigrant parties of early days was that known as the Murphy Party, of 1844. Shortly after their arrival at New Helvetia (Sutter's Fort), Mrs. Martin Murphy, Junior, gave birth to a daughter, to whom they gave the name Elizabeth. She is said to have been, according to Hittell, "the first child of American overland immigrants born in California."

DWELLING HOUSE IN SAN FRANCISCO

Captain William Antonio Richardson, a native of England, arrived at the *Presidio* of San Francisco in August, 1822, and a few months later decided to settle in California. In the course of time he married beautiful Señorita María Antonia, eldest daughter of *Comandante* Ygnacio Martinez. In 1835 he erected a rude building—really nothing more than a rough shanty—on the beach of Yerba Buena.

It has been repeatedly asserted that the building constructed by Jacob P. Leese in 1836 was the first house in San Francisco. Let us see.

William Heath Davis, whose personal knowledge of Richardson dated back to July, 1838, informs us that his tent—

> was the first habitation ever erected in Yerba Buena. At the time, Richardson's only neighbors were bears, coyotes, and wolves. The nearest people lived either at the *Presidio* or at Mission Dolores. The family lived under that tent about three months, after which Richardson constructed a small wooden house, and later a large one of adobe on what is now Dupont (Grant Avenue) near the corner of Clay Street.

But when was the first house actually built?

On Christmas Day, 1835, the ship *Alert*, made historically important by the presence on board of young Richard Henry Dana, lay at anchor in Yerba Buena Cove. It was six months prior to this that Richardson had erected his tent dwelling. At the instance of Governor Figueroa he had laid out the one street of the proposed village, where he put up his first home. With his wife and their little daughter Mariana he became the first inhabitant of the metropolitan city-to-be. In *Two Years Before the Mast* Dana makes specific reference to the Richardson domicile:

> Behind this point is the little harbor, or bight, called Yerba Buena, in which trading vessels anchor, and, near it, the Mission of Dolores. There was no other habitation on this side of the bay, except a shanty of rough boards put up by a man named Richardson, who was doing a little trading between the vessels and the Indians.

In the autumn of that year (1835) Richardson had rebuilt his first home to withstand the rains of winter; and—we may add—this was well, for Dana describes the downpour which greeted the *Alert* and compelled the crew to hang out rain-soaked hides all over the rigging of the ship for drying.

For the purpose of establishing the facts regarding the first house in Yerba Buena, a special committee of three was appointed by the California Historical Society in 1932: the report of this committee appears in the *Quarterly* of the Society, revealing the following conclusions:

1. That William A. Richardson was the founder of and first settler in Yerba Buena.
2. That William A. Richardson built the first dwelling or habitation in Yerba Buena, June, 1835.
3. That the Leese structure was put up July 3, 1836, a year after Richardson's.

4. That the wording of the inscription on a plaque recently placed upon a building at the southwest corner of Grant Avenue and Clay Street is both inaccurate and misleading. . . . This committee further suggests that Rosalie Leese, born April 15, 1838, should be referred to as the first child born in Yerba Buena, and not the "first white child born in San Francisco."

In January, 1847, Yerba Buena became San Francisco, "so that *presidio*, msision, and town might come under the same appellation."

If by extension San Francisco is made to include Mission Dolores from the beginning, then we must look still farther. Laura Bride Powers has reminded us that San Francisco celebrated her 150th birthday in 1936, and she asks, "What do you think the Spanish colonists who came with Anza in 1776 lived in if not in houses?" Thus it may be contended that the first buildings in San Francisco were those put up around Mission San Francisco de Asis (Dolores) in June, 1776. Still, in a very proper sense the houses built by Richardson and Leese may be considered the beginnings of the city of San Francisco.

WHITE WOMAN OVERLAND

Californians should hold the name of Nancy Kelsey in grateful and everlasting remembrance. She was the first white woman, an American, to make the long trek, overland, across the Sierra Nevada Mountains into California. This heroic exploit came long before the days of '49, before the American conquest, even before the first appearance of Frémont in the province. The fact that Mrs. Mary Walker, wife of Joel Walker, arrived in California nearly three weeks earlier need not detract from the distinction of Mrs. Kelsey, for Mrs. Walker had come by way of Oregon.

Nancy Kelsey, wife of Benjamin Kelsey, with their six-months-old baby girl, was a member of the famous Bartleson-Bidwell party of 1841, therefore one of these persons who constituted "The First Emigrant Train to California." The story of that journey, as told by John Bidwell, secretary of the party, occupying almost six months of time, packed with adventure and hardship and thrilling interest, has long since become a Western classic.

No one of the entire band endured the perils and the inexpressible privations with greater fortitude than was displayed by Nancy Kelsey. Joseph B. Chiles, a leading member, subsequently paid her this tribute:

She bore the fatigue of the journey with so much heroism, patience, and kindness that there still exists a warmth in every heart for the mother and her child, that were always forming silvery linings for every dark cloud that assailed them.

Not only did Mrs. Kelsey complete the memorable journey with her husband, but she participated with him in the historic events of California's passing from Mexican to American rule, "and followed him through all the vicissitudes of life, during good fortune and bad, until he passed away in Los Angeles in 1888." She survived her husband by eight years.

Highly appropriate was it that the Native Daughters of the Golden West should dedicate a monument to this heroic pioneer and mother—

In honor of

1823   1896

NANCY KELSEY

First white woman to cross
The Plains to California

Dedicated by
Miocene Parlor No. 228
Native Daughters of the Golden West
Nov. 21, 1937

Historians have too long neglected the virtuous California pioneer woman and mother. They were in reality a vital factor in the upbuilding of the Golden West. Many there were whose names are totally unknown to writers. Here and there we still happily have the records of such women as: Sarah Royce, mother of Josiah Royce; Virginia Reed Murphy, brave young girl of the Donner party; Mrs. J. W. Brier, only woman of the Jayhawker party; Jane Stanford, later the good angel to Stanford University; and Nancy Kelsey, first American woman to come overland direct to California. These, and all such as these, we gratefully salute!

In the famous party of 1841 were three Kelsey brothers—Benjamin, Andrew, and Samuel. The town of Kelseyville, in Lake County, and Kelsey Creek were named in honor of Andrew, first settler of that area. Benjamin and Samuel opened gold diggings in the present El Dorado County in 1848; these were first known as Kelsey's Diggings, then later the name Kelsey was given.

BRICK BUILDINGS

There has always been a lively interest in the subject of first houses or dwelling places of all kinds. It is also a subject that has occasioned no end of controversy.

The log house, which has figured so conspicuously throughout American history, was by no means unknown in California. It appears that

George Yount, the first American who settled in beautiful Napa Valley, after whom the town of Yountville was named, built the first log cabin—at least the first built by an American—in the year 1836. It has been described as being eighteen feet square below, with an upper story twenty-two feet square, provided with port holes in the walls for defence against the Indians.

Kiln brick had been used as building material in North America from the early seventeenth century. But in Spanish California the sun-dried adobe brick was the most common of all building materials for homes as well as for public places and at the Franciscan missions. So widely was the adobe brick used that a brief description may be in order. Following the usual method, a few sample bricks were made from the soil of the locality: if these were found to warp too much in the drying process, sandy soil was added to the "mix" until the drying would be uniform and smooth. The mud was mixed with finely chopped straw, or a vegetable substitute. Rectangular wooden molds were used, the regulation size being approximately 4 by 11 by 22 inches. Naturally, quality varied according to available ingredients at the different localities.

The burnt tile was extensively used for roofing during the later mission period: actual buildings constructed of kiln-burnt brick, however, belong essentially to the American period.

Monterey claims the honor of the first brick house, built in 1847 by Gallant Dickenson of bricks that were kilned there. In January, 1846, John Bidwell and L. W. Hastings were engaged to lay out the projected town of Sutterville, about four miles south of Sutter's Fort, near the Sacramento River. Within the next year or two the first real brick building of the Sacramento Valley, known as Zins's house, was constructed there. In its construction some of the 40,000 bricks that had been burned by G. Zins were used: he produced 100,000 bricks in 1848.

Sutterville, which at the beginning threatened to become a strong rival to Sacramento, did not succeed: within a few years it was scarcely more than a ghost town.

In *The Annals of San Francisco* we are told of the first brick building in that city, under date of September 6, 1847, by the entry:

> The first brick house was erected by Mellus & Howard, at the corner of Montgomery and Clay streets. This was the second brick building erected in Upper California, one having been previously constructed at Monterey.

But the account of William Heath Davis, in his valuable book *Sixty Years in California*, is at considerable variance with that in the *Annals*, and cannot be regarded as wholly accurate. Here is the way Davis remembered it:

> The first brick house in San Francisco was commenced in September, 1849, by the writer, at the northwest corner of Montgomery and California streets; forty feet on the first and eighty feet on the latter street, four stories high, with cellar. The bricks and cement, and other materials, were brought from Boston. The winter of 1849-50 was so rainy that the work on the structure was stopped early in November, and recommenced in April, 1850.

It was not until 1853 that the first brick house of Los Angeles was built, at the corner of Main and Third streets. In 1859-60 this house was occupied by Captain Winfield Hancock. But before that time brick had become common building material in various parts of California. So rapid was the increased use of bricks in San Francisco, following the series of disastrous fires, that by the end of 1854 the brick buildings in that city alone numbered 638, valued at more than $18,500,000.

Some interest attaches to the first use of granite in building. Bancroft has informed us that in San Francisco the "first granite-faced building was erected . . . by J. Parrott in 1852, completed in November, at a cost of $117,000." This was a three-story building, located at the northwest corner of Montgomery and California streets, and was first occupied by Adams and Co., and Page, Bacon, and Co.

PHYSICIANS AND SURGEONS

Dismissing from serious consideration the interesting Indian witch doctors, it may be said that with the exception of Monterey, provincial capital, and the surrounding region, Hispanic California, for most of the period, was virtually without skilled medical service. Exceptions to this statement, however, are both fascinating and significant.

Among those on board the little ship *San Carlos*, on the famous voyage to San Diego in 1769 was Don Pedro Prat, a surgeon of the Royal Navy, who thereby won the distinction of being the first trained doctor in California. The difficulties of that memorable voyage were incredibly great. All on board, including the doctor himself, were sick— the dreaded scurvy took a terrible toll. There were barely enough men with enough strength to man the ship, or to have custody of the camp, or care for the sick and dying. For the indefatigable pioneer doctor it was indeed a frightful introduction to California.

Don Pedro generously treated wounded Indians, who were freely received and cared for in a kindly manner. A little later came the second expedition, on the *San Antonio*, in search of Monterey. Those on board included Father Serra, Engineer Costansó, Captain Juan Pérez, and Surgeon Prat.

The doctor ministered to the sick under appalling conditions: many there were "to depart on their last long journey." It was not long till death took Pedro Prat himself: but he should be remembered as one of the founidng Spanish pioneers—the first surgeon of Alta California. The medical history, in the words of Dr. George Lyman, "goes back to the cradle of the new Spanish province; the sword, the cross, and the scalpel proceeded hand in hand."

As a general rule, the Arcadian Californians enjoyed excellent health. The conditions of life—balmy climate, outdoor living, congenial occupations—were conducive to health and simple happiness.

> "To live long without care," wrote Governor Borica in 1794, "come to Monterey. This is a great country; climate healthful, between cold and temperate; good bread, excellent meat, tolerable fish and *buen humor*, which is worth all the rest; . . . This is the most peaceful and quiet country in the world; one lives better here than in the most cultured court of Europe."

However, it would be inaccurate to imagine that there was complete absence of bodily ailments. Soldiers, mechanics, and especially sailors were often afflicted with scurvy, at times a devastating scourge; epidemics of small-pox were greatly dreaded—in a few instances they swept away great number of Indians with terrible swiftness.

And it is clear that those who say there was never a resident physician in California before the American conquest are equally mistaken. The activities of two Americans who entered California at very early dates must be mentioned here: each contributed a picturesque, weird chapter to our medical history, though neither was a licensed physician.

The first of these was James Ohio Pattie, whose *Personal Narrative*, even allowing for his propensity to exaggeration and prejudice, is one of the most amazing documents in all our annals. Under unprecedented conditions, he was thrown into prison by Governor Echeandía. But at that particular time the governor was entreated to devise some means to put a stop to the dread smallpox in the north, which threatened the country with destruction; and he had learned that Pattie had among his effects a small quantity of vaccine. In desperation he tried to induce his prisoner to vaccinate the people: more bad news from the north forced him to come to terms with the amateur "surgeon."

Pattie began to vaccinate on the 18th of January, 1829. Within a month all those at the *presidio* and the San Diego Mission Indians had been treated. Then Pattie proceeded from mission to mission, until—report says—a total of 22,000 persons had been treated by this amazing trapper —a record in American surgery!

The other American was John Marsh, a Harvard College graduate, who had reached California in 1836. Again, fact was stranger than fiction. Finding that there was no doctor in Los Angeles, and being in need of money, he announced himself as Doctor John Marsh, boldly presenting his bachelor's degree diploma—in Latin—as his credential. He had earlier intended to enter the medical profession.

Immediately there was great demand for his services. In less than a year he had received as fees an accumulation of horses, cattle, hides, and tallow—which he sold at a good price. In time he became the owner of a large ranch near the base of Mt. Diablo, continuing the practice of medicine as the only physician of the San Joaquin Valley, ultimately being reputed the "wealthiest cattle baron of California." With the fascinating details of his later years, and the tragic circumstances of his death we must not be concerned here. "Not only did he blaze a trail; he carried a torch."

One other name should be mentioned—none other than that of Platon Mariano Vallejo, son of the famous General M. G. Vallejo; for he earned the title of "The First Native-Born California Physician," a graduate of St. Mary's College in Baltimore, and later of the College of Physicians and Surgeons at Columbia University, ranking first in his class of seventy-two. Dr. Vallejo was born at Sonoma in 1841. He rendered acceptable service in the Union Army during the Civil War, and later practiced his profession in the city of Vallejo fifty-five years. He was a man of high professional and personal ideals, the epitome of whose life may be expressed in one word, Service. He died in May, 1925.

GREAT SEAL OF THE STATE

Almost a year before California was admitted into the American Union as the thirty-first state, "The Great Seal of the State of California" was approved by the Monterey Constitutional Convention of 1849.

Since the Great Seal dates back to the beginnings of the state, and is now in daily use in the office of the Secretary of State, in the Capitol at Sacramento, it is of interest to quote the official explanation accompanying the seal, as presented to the convention in September, 1849:

> Around the bend of the ring are represented thirty-one stars, being the number of States of which the Union will consist upon admission of California. The foreground figure represents the goddess Minerva having

sprung full grown from the brain of Jupiter. She is introduced as a type of the political birth of the State of California, without having gone through the probation of a territory. At her feet crouches a grizzly bear feeding upon the clusters from a grape vine, emblematic of the peculiar characteristics of the country. A miner is engaged with his rocker and bowl at his side, illustrating the golden wealth of the Sacramento, upon whose waters are seen shipping, typical of commercial greatness; and the snow-clad peaks of the Sierra Nevada make up the background, while above is the Greek motto "EUREKA" (I have found it), applying either to the principle involved in the admission of the State, or the success of the miner at work.

Thus appears, for the first time officially, in a single word from the classic Greek, the State Motto adopted well over a century ago—EUREKA. The real designer of the Great Seal was Major Robert S. Garnett, who "excelled in the use of his pencil." He was an army officer, sojourning temporarily in Monterey. It was presented to the Convention, however, by Caleb Lyon, one of the clerks of the convention. Discussion on the subject was participated in by the delegates, and several changes in the original design were proposed. Eventually Garnett's design, with minor changes, was approved; and on the 11th of October Lyon was authorized to superintend the engraving and to furnish the seal, to be delivered to the Secretary of State.

The singular appropriateness of the motto—and indeed of the design of the seal as a whole—has been well attested by each passing decade. The symbolism is remarkable. The strength of the young State is seen in the grizzly bear, most powerful of California animals; the miner at work with pick and shovel reveals the leading industry for years; the ships on the Sacramento River are a prophecy of commercial greatness; the galaxy of thirty-one stars represents a vital episode in the great American Epic—for California came into the Union as the sixteenth free state. Not least of all, the motto, "EUREKA," finds a new force and meaning with each new generation in this "Land of Heart's Delight."

Major Garnett, a native of Virginia, graduated at West Point Military Academy in the class of 1841. In 1843 he became an instructor of infantry tactics, later served as Aid-de-Camp to General John E. Wool, distinguishing himself in the battles of Palo Alto and Reseca de la Palma. He was Aid-de-Camp to General Taylor during the Mexican War. In 1851 he was promoted to a captaincy, then commissioned Major. During the Civil War he was promoted to a Brigadier-Generalship and assigned to the Department of West Virginia. He was killed in battle, July 15, 1861.

The use of Eureka as a geographical term probably originated in

California. By the year 1880 as many as forty different places had been so named. The common use of the term during the gold mining days is readily understood. There is a legend to the effect that when James T. Ryan landed at the beautiful port of Humboldt County in 1850, being fascinated by what he beheld, he exclaimed "Eureka!" The town that bears the proud name became the seat of county government in 1856.

AMERICAN PIONEER SOCIETY

A strong feeling of comradeship quickly and spontaneously arose among the men of '49, men whose deeds and character have been immortalized by Joaquin Miller, "Poet of the Sierras," men christened "Argonauts" by Francis Bret Harte. This feeling soon crystallized into a firm federation which, in the month of August, 1850, even before the admission of California into the Union, resulted in the organization, in San Francisco, of the Society of California Pioneers.

The declared object of this honored Society was "to cultivate the social virtues of its members, to collect and preserve information connected with the early settlement and conquest of the country, and to perpetuate the memory of those whose sagacity, enterprise, and love of independence induced them to settle in the wilderness, and become the germ of a new State." A quotation from the constitution sufficiently defines the character and qualifications for membership:

> The Society shall be composed of native Californians, foreigners residing in California previous to the conquest; and natives of other states and other countries, if citizens of the United States, resident here prior to January 1st, 1849, and their male descendants, who shall constitute the *first class*; and citizens of the old states of the Federal Government who shall have resided in California prior to January 1st, 1850, and their male descendants, who shall constitute the *second class*, and honorary members, who may be admitted in accordance with what may be prescribed in the by-laws.

The first officers of the Society included the following: President, William D. M. Howard; Vice-Presidents, Jacob R. Snyder, Sam Brannan, G. Frank Lemon; Corresponding Secretary, Edwin Bryant; Treasurer, Talbot H. Green. The Board of Directors consisted of eighteen members.

In the *Annals of San Francisco* is published a full list of members (including those deceased) as of 1854, with date of arrival and place of residence in California designated for each. The complete list numbers 354 members: among them appear many of the best-known names of founders of the commonwealth of California.

Through the generosity of James Lick, who paid high tribute to the Pioneer Society, a lot and building were acquired in 1874, on Montgomery Street. The present spacious home of the Society, Pioneer Hall is on McAllister Street. The large collection of paintings, photographs, documents, memorials and relics relating to early California is invaluable.

The chief publication of the organization is *The Quarterly of the Society of California Pioneers*, now a series of many volumes rich in source materials for the local historian.

On reading Bancroft's account in his *History of California* many members were deeply offended and incensed by certain parts of his treatment of the American pioneers, charging the historian with grave inaccuracies and total lack of sympathy. Drastic action was taken in 1894. A resolution was offered, "proposing that the name of Hubert Howe Bancroft be stricken from the roll of Honorary Membership." When put to a vote, "the Chair declared it *carried unanimously*, and that Hubert Howe Bancroft was no longer an Honorary Member." Signed by C. V. S. Gibbs, President; John I. Spear, Secretary. That some of the pioneers on reflection felt that the Society had erred in this action is of no special concern here.

The original pioneers have long since passed from the active scene: present members are chiefly descendants of the third and fourth generations. In July, 1933, Judge Charles A. Shurtleff (son of Dr. Benjamin Shurtleff), as President read to a meeting a summary of the activities and achievements of the Society, saying, in part:

> It is a great society which our Pioneer ancestry has transmitted to us and our descendants to protect, cherish, and preserve. . . . The formation of this Society in August, 1850 . . . the sole expression of the Pioneers, acting collectively, indicating that they felt that their early settlement and development of California should live in history. [He urged that] we, their descendants, should zealously observe that it was their wish that their courage, suffering, and forethought should survive in history, honored and revered through all time.

PEPPER TREE

Two species of trees that are not indigenous to California have become widespread and have won great popularity in the state. These are the eucalyptus, introduced from Australia, and the pepper tree, from Peru. Both are used principally for ornamental purposes, though the eucalyptus possesses also a fairly high degree of utility. Neither is able to withstand the coldest temperature experienced in certain parts of California.

A sailor is reported to have brought a twig of the graceful pepper tree in the year 1830. This was lovingly planted by Padre Antonio Peyri in the patio of Mission San Luis Rey, situated a few miles from Oceanside, in San Diego County.

The missionary fathers quickly formed a sentimental attachment for the beautiful tree, with its delicate fern-like branches and gracefully suspended boughs; they lost no time in planting cuttings at different mission establishments north and south. *Rancheros* also yielded to the attractions and beauty of these trees: they likewise gladly took cuttings and planted them about their ranch homes. Still later, rows of pepper trees were set out in avenues in a number of growing towns and cities. So popular did the new tree become that within a few short decades literally thousands were gracing the landscape, especially in Southern California. It seemed to vie with the tree of which James R. Russell wrote:

> The birch, most shy and lady-like of trees.

The late Senator R. F. del Valle told of the large pepper tree lending its beauty to the front lawn of the E. R. Forster ranch near the town of Puente. It had grown from a slip taken from the parent tree at San Luis Rey, having been planted in 1847; it became one of the most majestic trees of its species in the state.

John A. Berger, in his excellent history of the Franciscan Missions, makes special mention of another tree, at Purisima, perhaps the most widely publicized pepper tree in all California today, as he enthusiastically writes, "One old pepper tree has again burst into leaf as it was a century ago." It is not surprising that many uninformed persons are inclined mistakenly to link the pepper tree with the orange and olive as an original product brought to the old Missions by the early *padres*.

Today there is probably no finer display of pepper trees in the state—or anywhere else—than that to be seen in the entrancingly beautiful Euclid Avenue, with its gorgeous setting of well-kept green lawns, in the middle of the gently-sloping double highway connecting the prosperous towns of Ontario and Uplands, in Southern California. The pepper tree, first brought here from Peru, has enhanced the esthetic resources of countless communities in California.

The tree has one serious drawback: it provides a harbor for scale insects, which renders it quite susceptible to disease resulting from tree pests. On this account it has been found necessary in different localities to remove thousands of the otherwise attractive trees. To keep it beautiful and free from disease requires care and scientific treatment. The eucalyptus, on the other hand, has been found remarkably resistant to diseases that attack the pepper tree with such virulence.

EUCALYPTUS

The eucalyptus tree is not indigenous to California; but it has become the most numerous and most familiar of all trees introduced from abroad. Within a relatively short period after its introduction, to employ words attributed to Bishop William Taylor, it "dotted the whole country with great forests of evergreen, the most prominent landmarks of the Pacific Coast." It has been referred to as "the ubiquitous blue gum."

The name is derived from Greek words meaning "to cover with a lid." The buds have a "lid-like covering which falls off when the flowers open"—illustrating the appropriateness of the name. Its natural home is the subcontinent of Australia. Of the eucalyptus genus there are known to be approximately 300 species, the most common in California being the "Blue Gum" (*eucalyptus blobulus*).

When and by whom was the eucalyptus introduced into the Golden State? Credit has usually gone to the famous street preacher of San Francisco, William Taylor, later Methodist Missionary Bishop of Africa. George Wharton James, in one of his books, boldly states:

> It is an important historical fact that should not be forgotten that to William Taylor California owes its great eucalyptus forests and planta- tions. . . . He says: "There were no such trees on that coast when I went there in 1849. I sent the seed from Australia to my wife in California in 1863. Her seed-sowing made such a marvelous growth that a horticulturist neighbor of ours wrote me to send him a pound of the seed—. . ."

Harris Newmark, in his book *Sixty Years in Southern California* (3rd edition) tells us:

> When we bought the Santa Anita (1872), there were five eucalyptus or blue gum trees growing near the house. I understood at the time that these had been planted by Wm. Wolfskill from seed sent to him by a friend in Australia; and that they were the first eucalyptus trees cultivated in South- ern California. Sometime early in 1875 the Forest Grove Association started the first extensive tract of eucalyptus trees seen in Los Angeles, and in a decade or two the eucalyptus had become a familiar object; . . .

In the meantime the San Francisco Bay region and Santa Clara Valley had demonstrated the adaptability of the tree; and as early as 1865 a large plantation is reported to have been started near Santa Barbara.

But the question still remains—when and by whom was the eucalyptus first introduced into California? The belief that William Taylor should be given the credit has long persisted: and there can be scarcely a doubt that Taylor did much, if not most, in eucalyptizing California.

But it now seems quite clear that William C. Walker of San Francisco was one of the first — perhaps the very first — to introduce the eucalyptus and to list it in the catalogue of his Golden Gate Nursery (a copy of which is in the Bancroft Library). This was in 1856: the eucalyptus was listed at $5 each. In that year Mr. Walker planted seeds of fourteen varieties at the Nursery, located at Fourth and Folsom Streets, San Francisco. H. M. Butterfield, in an article on "The Introduction of the Eucalyptus into California," published in 1935, concluded that Walker "is the first definitely on record as having imported seeds of the eucalyptus into California." Mention is also made of Stephen Nolan, an Oakland nurseryman, as distributing the seed of the tree after 1861. The evidence is convincing that William Taylor was not actually first to introduce the eucalyptus into California. One of the oldest gum trees now standing in the state, a few miles from San José, is believed to have been planted by Joseph Aram, in 1858.

Early in the present century there was a craze for planting vast areas of land—much of it of inferior quality—to eucalyptus trees, to be used as hard wood for numerous purposes, especially for fine furniture, cabinet making, and the like. Easy fortunes were forecast. Sad to relate, this proved to be a bubble, as evidenced today by great acreages of straggling untended thickets of gum trees. But the eucalyptus remains in general firmly established—we begin to wonder how big some of the trees will be a century or two centuries later.

Vast as is the present acreage of eucalyptus in California, it is in its Australian home that it still maintains greatest importance. There for many years, where it attains enormous size and great height, it has been the most widely used commercial tree. There each year is harvested a total of a billion feet of lumber, valued at above a hundred million dollars. It is an article of export to Great Britain, South Africa, and New Zealand.

STATE FLOWER

It is true, as Nellie Van de Grift Sanchez has said, that "For countless seasons . . . the lupine and the poppy spread their glory of purple and gold on the hill slopes to the dull eye of the savage. . . ." Equally true is it that nature endowed these lovely plants with vigorous vitality, and a prodigal area, reaching from one end of California to the other—even overflowing to neighboring states both northward and eastward.

How fitting that the Golden Poppy should be chosen as California's

State Flower! It is found in abundance everywhere, its garish color reflects the glow of the Golden State, symbolic of perennial sunshine. An old Spanish legend tells of the time when an early Spanish leader —could it have been Junípero Serra?—exclaimed on first beholding the *copa de oro* in the splendor of noonday: "At last I have found the *Holy Grail!*" Then he reverently touched his lips to the beautiful golden petals. "Every poppy cup is a pot of gold at the base of a rainbow." And it was Frank Norris who likened them to "morsels of sunshine entrapped."

In accordance with a vote of the state legislature on "An Act to adopt the Golden Poppy as the State Flower of California," duly approved March 2, 1903, the *Eschscholtzia californica* (*Copa de Oro*), was officially adopted by the Golden State.

The first naturalist to picture and describe the California poppy was Louis de Chamisso, while on a scientific expedition with Johann F. Eschscholtz, a German surgeon, commanded by Otto von Kotzebue, under the patronage of Count Romanoff, in 1815. The flowers normally are "of a deep, rich orange, the four petals, with entire edges and each an inch and a half long." The color and size vary with the locality, due to environment: the flowers are smaller and usually a more clear yellow near the seashore and toward the end of the dry summer.

The selection of the state flower set a precedent. In 1931 the Valley Quail was similarly made the state bird; in 1937, a double choice was made for the state tree, generally known as the Redwood—*Sequoia sempervirens* and *Sequoia gigantea*. In this connection it may be permissible to mention two other items of symbolism: the grizzly bear, strongest of animals, which has long been extinct in California, was often used to typify the power of the state, appearing officially on its great seal; and the California Flag, an imperfect replica of the original Bear Flag of 1846, which now floats, along with the Stars and Stripes, over public schools and other state buildings.

The Golden Poppy has long since taken a conspicuous place as a subject in the literature of California. Prentiss Maslin's description has often been repeated:

> It possesses none of the modesty of the violet, the sweetness of the lily, nor the beauty of the rose; but standing alone and unique, it compels our admiration because of its wonderful coloring and sheen, which refuses to be transferred by the limner's art to board or canvas. It wins its place by its transcendent beauty, and lovers of nature, having once reveled therein, the memory of it lives a lifetime.

It is typical of the great Golden State, where nature disports her wondrous wardrobe and where the lowliest share her regal beauty with the mightiest of the mighty. Californians of every rank and station delight to join with their first Poet Laureate as she sings her immortal praises:

> Thy satin vesture richer is than looms
>   Of Orient weave for raiment of her kings;
>   Not dyes of olden Tyre, not precious things
> Regathered from the long-forgotten tombs
>   Of buried empires, not the Iris plumes
>   That wave upon the tropic's myriad wings,
>   Not all proud Sheeba's queenly offerings
> Could match the golden marvel of thy blooms.

PARK SYSTEM

It was in the final year of his life that President Lincoln affixed his signature to an act of Congress "whereby the world-famous Yosemite Valley and the Mariposa Grove of Giant Sequoias were acquired by California as the first state park in the nation." That was an act of historic significance to state and nation alike. It signalized the beginning of the auspicious movement for a far-flung system of national parks.

Nowhere else could there have been found so appropriate a spot for the inauguration of this movement as "The Incomparable Yosemite," so exquisitely described in the immortal prose of John Muir. Mark Daniels was well within the bounds of truth when he declared: "There is no equal area in the world which contains so many wonders of nature, magnificent scenes, glorious growth of flowers and forest trees."

Sharp criticism of the State's Commission's management of the Yosemite Valley aroused demands in Washington that an investigation be instigated into the delinquencies of administration. In the meantime, Congress in 1890 had created our first National Park of lands surrounding the state-owned area. The end result was a recession of the Yosemite Valley by the legislature in 1905 to the federal government. Thus it came about that the Yosemite National Park was rounded out—California's first state park, then our first National Park. An unapproachable precedent, indeed!

In the matter of both state parks and national parks California enjoys extraordinary distinction. Of the latter she proudly boasts Yosemite, Sequoia, Lassen Volcanic, and Kings Canyon Parks, with a grand total of approximately 1,700,000 acres. The list of state parks has now passed the one hundred mark, including such well-known spots as Big Basin Redwoods (Santa Cruz), Carlsbad Beach (San Diego), Castle Crags (Shasta), Frémont Peak (San Benito), and Point Lobos Reserve (Monterey). In addition to all these she has set apart more than a score of State Historic Monuments; eight National Monuments, which include Cabrillo (near San Diego), Death Valley (Mojave Desert), Joshua Trees (Riverside and San Bernardino), Lava Beds (Siskiyou, Modoc), and Muir Woods (Marin); and finally, eighteen national forests, located at intervals all the way from Shasta to San Diego.

No other state in the Union can approach such a record. The recrea-- tional facilities of California can be expressed only in terms of the superlative. As to their general value, these words from Secretary of the Interior Douglas McKay, with reference to national parks, are quite appropriate:

> Any national park is an economic, social, and spiritual asset of the Nation, and especially of the State or region in which it is situated. We can only estimate its economic value, and still less are we able to put a price on its cultural and spiritual values. We simply know that they exist, that they are tremendous; and that the opportunity to enjoy them is a necessity of this modern day.

SIERRA CLUB

The Sierra Club was born of a group of people dedicated to the cause "of protecting the irreplaceable values of the Sierra from ravages of the greed which unfortunately accompanies our civilization." More than to any other individual the credit for the organization belongs to John Muir, California mountaineer par excellence, the young Scotsman who first saw the Tuolumne Meadows in 1869. Noting the destructive effects of the sheep—"hoofed locusts"—on the forests and meadows, he resolved to do what he could to stop the devastation he was witnessing. He was urged "to get behind him a supporting organization on the Pacific Coast through which men of kindred aims could present a united front." Muir's active labors as master conservationist have long since become familiar history.

On Saturday, May 28th, 1892, in the San Francisco law office of Warren Olney, the club's name and purposes were formulated and agreed upon. The Articles of Incorporation were drawn up by Mr. Olney; a week later (June 4) the Articles and By-Laws of the Sierra Club were signed by the charter members, and officers were duly elected. No one was to be thought of for first president but John Muir, "unsurpassed," in the words of David Brower, "in the rôle of a prophet preaching the gospel of wildness and urging its preservation." He was continued in that office during the remainder of his life. Other officers included Warren Olney, vice-president; William D. Armes, secretary;

J. H. Senger, David Starr Jordan, Robert M. Price, Mark B. Kerr, Willard D. Johnson, and John C. Branner, directors. There were 182 charter members, including many prominent in public and in academic life.

As stated in the Articles of Incorporation, the original purposes of the Sierra Club were:

> to explore, enjoy, and render accessible the mountain regions of the Pacific Coast; to publish authentic information concerning them; to enlist the support and cooperation of the people and the Government in preserving the forests and other natural features of the Sierra Nevada.

So great have been the changes in respect to population and social conditions in the almost three-quarters of a century since the inception of the Club that some restatement of the original purposes long since became advisable. Strictly limited developments with reference to roads, hotels, ski lifts, and other features have been imperatively imposed to insure the best use of the great natural resources and their preservation for posterity. New encroachments constantly menace the glacial canyons, the towering sequoias, and the dashing mountain streams. What natural wilderness remains must be guarded and kept for the enjoyment of future generations.

The membership of the Club increased rapidly, until it reached into thousands of enthusiastic mountaineers and conservationists. The annual outings, including the Club's High Trip, have proved a source of recreational pleasure and cultural benefit to many from all walks in life —a unique experience in education in searching out the ways of Mother Nature at her best. Twenty-seven high country and wilderness area outings were scheduled by the Club for the summer of 1956 alone. These included five high trips, five base trips, six river trips, six knapsack trips, and still others.

In harmony with the purpose "to publish authentic information" the *Sierra Club Bulletin* appears monthly (except August), having now completed forty volumes. It has been ably edited by William Badè, Francis Farquhar, and others, and contains many articles and mountain experiences told by competent writers, as well as special reports, notes, and comments. Many of its illustrations are of exceptional beauty.

It was at a notable meeting of the Club in 1895 that Muir first gave public expression to his natural park idea, the "dream of his boyhood." And this was before the establishment of Yellowstone National Park. Indeed, it was not until 1916, with the creation of the National Park Service, after much vacillation, that Yosemite was placed on a thoroughly satisfactory basis.

One thing more—the Muir Trail. What more fitting monument could there be than the indescribable trail parallel to the crest of his loved Sierra Nevada, from marvelous Yosemite to the hundreds of peaks and pinnacles and ridges of the Kern River district. The beginnings of Muir Trail, as told by Theodore Solomons, deserve a place in the annals of the Sierra Club.

WILDLIFE CONSERVATION

Before the "gringo" came, California may well be thought of as a veritable hunter's and fisherman's paradise. The ocean, rivers, lakes, and mountain streams were filled with fish of many kinds. Feathered game, including ducks of many varieties, geese, swan, and sand-hill cranes, were to be found in unbelievable numbers—not to mention the great abundance of animal life in all directions. There were no game laws, and practically no hunters.

John Bidwell, eminent pioneer of 1841, reported that even the largest flocks of geese and ducks Californians of a later date ever saw were as nothing, *nothing!* compared to the incredible numbers of the very early period. Also, the vast feeding grounds attracted thousands of swan and sand-hill cranes—but scarcely a hunter in California to disturb them.

Another striking illustration may be drawn from W. H. Thomes' book, *On Land and Sea; California in the Years 1843-44-45.* The following is quoted from this fascinating book:

> Then I saw two or three thousand wild geese feeding near the pond, or lake, and making much noise with their complaints and honks. I thought it would be fun to dash into their midst, and see them take to flight. But, to my surprise, they did not seem to care for me, or the horse, being accustomed to seeing the latter in immense runs, feeding on the plains. When I was close upon them they parted to the right and left, and waddled out of the way, aided by their wings, and simply hissed at me for disturbing them in feeding, and would not move except for a rod or two. They could not have acted more stupid if they had been hatched in a barnyard, in Rhode Island, and waiting for their daily supply of corn.

Among game animals were great numbers of deer, antelope, and elk, as well as grizzly and other species of bear, the cougar (mountain lion), wolverine, and numerous others. The grizzly and the wolverine have long since become extinct; the antelope and elk, now carefully protected, are rare.

As an illustration as to how plentiful were once the elk, William Heath Davis wrote of seeing on Mare Island in the years 1840 to 1843, "as many as two or three thousand elk, it being their habit to cross and recross by swimming between the island and the main land." Richard Henry Dana told of the great numbers of deer that over-ran the islands of San Francisco Bay and surrounding hills. The herds of antelope in certain sections numbered into the thousands.

The story of the many kinds of fish in the state is similar, in most respects, to that of the animal and bird life.

All this was changed by the coming of the throngs of Americans. It was not long till steps were needed for the conservation of California wildlife. Pursuant to an act of the legislature dated April 2, 1870, the state established a Board of Fish Commissioners, a year before the U.S. Commission of Fish and Fisheries. Thus began the official wildlife conservation in California. Next came a recognition for the need of game conservation, which became an actuality following a recommendation of the Fish Commission in its Biennial Report for 1888-1890. Then step by step other milestones were set up in the development of wildlife conservation.

The people's ownership of fish and game was affirmed by the courts in 1894. In 1907 a hunting license law was adopted, and a fishing license law in 1913. In 1945 the legislature delegated to the Fish and Game Commission the authority to regulate the powers, fix the seasons and prescribe bag limits. In 1947 the Wildlife Conservation Board was formally established. At present California boasts the largest fish and game agency in the entire United States. The five-man Fish and Game Commission "formulates general policy matters and sets bag limits for hunting and sport fishing."

True conservation does not mean the total non-use of any resource, but rather the avoidance of waste, and the wise use that has careful regard for posterity as well as for the present generation. It applies to all our natural resources—water, minerals, forest, and land, as well as to wildlife. As described on another page, a good example of forest conservation is seen in scientific tree farming.

CHARTER OF THE UNITED NATIONS

In the San Francisco Conference in the spring of 1945 to draft and adopt the Charter for the United Nations is seen the fulfillment of many an early prophecy. Delegate R. M. Price, at the Monterey Convention of 1849, declared: "Our commercial capital, San Francisco, is, in my opinion, destined to be the center of the exchange of the world." It is now more than a century ago that William H. Seward said: "The Pacific Ocean, its shores, its islands and the vast regions beyond will become the chief theater of events in the world's great hereafter." That far-seeing

"Prince of California Pioneers," John Bidwell, in his Annual Address before the State Agricultural Society, in 1881, after referring to the early isolation of California, spoke these words:

> ... The bubble, isolation, has burst, and, lo, we stand face to face in competition with the world. We have discovered that we are no longer in a world by ourselves, but that we live on the same planet as other people, and that henceforth we must run the race of life in competition with all mankind. ...

It was a high tribute to California, and a keen recognition of the position and prospects of San Francisco that the City by the Golden Gate was chosen as the place where honored representatives of half a hundred nations of the world should assemble for the purpose of forming an organization whose noble object should be to assure the blessings of peace to all mankind.

Never had there been such a conference in the history of the state— this was the first. Among the distinguished delegates we find William L. MacKenzie King of Canada, T. V. Soong of the Republic of China, Henri Bonnet of France, Jan Christian Smuts of South Africa, V. M. Molotov of Soviet Russia, Anthony Eden of Great Britain, and Arthur H. Vanderberg of the United States.

Unfortunately, the prestige of the League of Nations, for which Woodrow Wilson had given his life, had failed. Its doom was sealed when World War II in all its fury lashed nations against nations. The need for an organization better adapted to deal with international tensions was urgent and admitted of no further delay. The stirring city of St. Francis was proud to be assigned the rôle of host to the memorable Conference; the history of the Empire State of the Pacific, not yet a century old, was enriched by the addition of an illustrious chapter.

Sessions continued from April 25 to June 26, 1945. On the 22nd of June Edward R. Stettinius, United States Secretary of State, submitted a preliminary draft of the United Nations Organization, providing for four principal organs: 1) a General Assembly, as the major policy-shaping forum; 2) a Security Council, to deal with military and political problems; 3) an Economic and Social Council, to grapple with questions involving economic and social conflict; and 4) an International Court of Justice, to adjudicate international disputes. The General Secretariat was to handle the administrative work, whose head officer was to be a Secretary-General.

The city of San Francisco and the state of California were duly impressed by the responsibility to the nation and the world to play well their part in a drama of supreme importance. In the matter of providing suitable accommodations for the many who planned to come for the Conference, in supplying needed information and affording library service for the delegates, and seeing to it that representatives from all over the world and the foreign press were given a fair and full picture of American life, including entertainment for the tired delegates— mention of these aspects is sufficient to suggest the numerous problems faced by hospitable San Francisco. The city's international status is illustrated by the fact that it ranks third in the nation—surpassed only by Washington and New York—in the size of its consular corps, which in 1956 represented fifty-six foreign nations.

The formation of the Charter for the United Nations was the culmination of an impressive series of steps, which included the Atlantic Charter Conference (August, 1941), the Declaration of the United Nations (January, 1942), the United Nations Food and Agriculture Conference (June, 1943), Bretton Woods Conference (July, 1944), and Dumbarton Oaks Conference (August to October, 1944). It was at the Yalta Meeting (February, 1945) that the decision was reached to hold the United Nations Conference in San Francisco.

For us, the question remains: was not the formation of the United Nations Charter a rich fulfillment of many early prophecies, also itself an inspiring prophecy of things yet to come? As it was California's first glorious event envisioning world peace, may it not prove to be the forerunner of others in future years?

Let our concluding words be those uttered almost a century ago by that peerless patriot-orator, Colonel Edward D. Baker:

> Our pride is for humanity; our joy is for the world; and amid all the wonders of past achievement and all the splendor of present success, we turn with swelling hearts to gaze into the boundless future, with the earnest conviction that it will develop a universal brotherhood of man.

INDEX

307